THINK BIG

THINK BIG

Adventures in Life and Democracy

PRESTON MANNING

M&S

National Library of Canada Cataloguing in Publication

Manning, Preston, 1942-
Think big : adventures in life and democracy / Preston Manning.

Includes index.
ISBN 0-7710-5675-3

1. Manning, Preston, 1942-   2. Reform Party of Canada – Biography.
3. Politicians – Canada – Biography.   4. Canada – Politics and government –
1993-   I. Title.

FC636.M36A3 2002   971.064'8'092   C2002-903212-1
F1034.3.M28A3 2002

We acknowledge the financial support of the Government of Canada through
the Book Publishing Industry Development Program for our publishing activities.
We further acknowledge the support of the Canada Council for the Arts and the
Ontario Arts Council for our publishing program.

Typeset in Goudy by M&S, Toronto
Printed and bound in Canada

This book is printed on acid-free paper that is 100% ancient forest friendly
(100% post-consumer recycled).

McClelland & Stewart Ltd.
The Canadian Publishers
481 University Avenue
Toronto, Ontario
M5G 2E9
www.mcclelland.com

1 2 3 4 5   06 05 04 03 02

CONTENTS

To Sandra . . .
and to Andrea and Howie, Avryll and John,
Mary Joy, Nathan, and David

THINK BIG

PREMIER'S KID

ERNEST CHARLES MANNING WAS A MEMBER OF THE ALBERTA legislature for thirty-three years, premier of Alberta for twenty-five years, and a senator of Canada for thirteen years. He was also my father, my mentor, and my hero.

As a boy, I would sometimes do my homework in a little anteroom off his office. I would leave the door ajar and listen as he talked with visitors. It was there that I got my first exposure to politics and government. My father told me that if I listened closely I would hear the sound most familiar to the ears of an elected politician – the sound of the grinding of an axe.

My father was first and foremost a Christian believer, and on Sunday he and my mother directed and participated in a Christian radio program. From the time I was twelve I took written notes of my dad's sermons and felt he was the best preacher I had ever heard. My father was also a farmer – we operated a dairy farm east of Edmonton – and on weekends we would farm together. After I graduated from university and he retired from politics, we went into business together again, this time operating a management consulting practice.

If we are a product of our roots and environment, mine included the Christian faith, Western politics and government, a tightly knit family, and a family farm and business. My dad the Premier was at the centre of it all, and, no doubt about it, I am a product of lessons learned as a "Premier's Kid."

■

My father and my mother, Muriel Preston, were drawn into politics in their mid-twenties, before they were married. It was the Great Depression, and misery, starvation, financial ruin, despair, and suicide were affecting thousands of lives. In response to the raw need of the people around them and their search for social justice, my parents' lives and home were infused with a panoramic sense of history and big ideas of economic and social reform, democratic processes, and populist politics. They looked for deliverance from the awful conditions that threatened to destroy their community. Mostly, they refused to accept the prevailing political notion of the traditional political establishment that there was nothing to be done but ride out the storm.

Their political mentor, William Aberhart, was also my parents' spiritual leader and intimate friend. Aberhart was my father's boss, first at the Prophetic Bible Institute, where he went to work after graduating from its bible college, and later in the provincial Social Credit government. Aberhart reminded young people that they had a moral obligation to care for both the spiritual and material needs of their neighbours, especially in desperate times. My mother, a legal secretary during the week, went from house to house across rural Alberta in her spare time with visitation teams, bringing spiritual and practical comfort to families who were without adequate food, clothing, or hope.

Meanwhile, my father became Aberhart's aide, chauffeur, and co-worker. The two criss-crossed the province for more than two years to promote the Social Credit philosophy, which in its early years was a mix of pre-Keynesian economics, social resentment, and untutored hope. Building a brand-new political party from scratch in the midst of the Depression was a seemingly impossible task, but

Aberhart was a skilled organizer as well as a powerful orator. He made maximum use of the tools available – public meetings, word of mouth, massive literature distribution, and a new technology the political potential of which was only beginning to be realized, radio.

Of course, the political and social establishment of the day decried Aberhart's economic and political ideas. The Economic Safety League, an interest group organized in Calgary by supporters of Conservative prime minister R. B. Bennett, described Aberhart and his Social Credit movement as "an omnium gatherum of political odds and ends: business failures, social misfits and imitating parrots," and he was mercilessly attacked and caricatured by the mainstream press. Aberhart considered himself an educator, and he was a reluctant politician. But the voters of Alberta trusted him more than they trusted the establishment of the day. Despite the fact that the Social Credit Party was a scant three years old, it was swept into government in 1935 with 54 per cent of the popular vote and fifty-six seats in a legislature of sixty-three members, including my father. It would remain in government for the next thirty-six years.

The election of 1935 altered the course of my father's life as well. He had come to Alberta from a Saskatchewan homestead to become a minister of the gospel, and at twenty-six years of age he found himself appointed to the Cabinet as provincial secretary. The next spring, following the completion of the new government's first legislative session, my parents were married. When I was born, on June 10, 1942, my father was the second most influential man in the Alberta Cabinet.

Aberhart served as premier of Alberta from 1935 to 1943. Courageous, bombastic, and stubborn, he was either loved or hated. He once told my father that in desperate times democratic politicians have one overriding responsibility – to give people hope. Aberhart was prepared to do and say whatever he felt would achieve that objective, and to run over anybody who got in his way.

He died prematurely after only one re-election and eight years in office, his health broken by the stresses and strains of presiding over a province that was technically bankrupt, the attacks of his opponents, and dissension within the Social Credit Party. While a historical canard has taken root that he was a discredited and even despicable failure, in fact, Aberhart gave new life and expression to an axiom of Western politics that inspires many Westerners to this very day: If you find the economic or political status quo unacceptable, Do Something! Initiate change – using the freedoms and tools that democracy provides.

When Aberhart died, my father was the natural choice of the Social Credit Party to succeed him. He became premier in 1943, one year after I was born, and his government was re-elected seven times. He retired undefeated in 1968 when I was twenty-six years old.

My father's philosophy combined fiscal conservatism with a compassion for people, born of his Christian faith and the suffering of the Depression. Whereas Aberhart was a crusader who could blast apart the status quo, my father was a builder and an administrator. He managed to reassemble Alberta's shattered finances after the Depression and navigate its economy through war and the post-war boom. He presided over the transformation of the province brought about by the discovery of oil in Leduc in 1947, his administration being one of the few in North America to remain in office throughout an oil boom without corrupting itself. He considered resource revenues to be money obtained from the sale of a depleting asset, which ought to be reinvested in other physical and social assets – roads, schools, hospitals, universities, libraries, and performing arts centres. The Depression taught him survival economics – that men cannot live without bread. The oil boom taught him development economics. But his Christian faith taught him that men do not live by bread or oil alone.

My father learned through hard experience to discipline and pace himself after facing a brush with death from tuberculosis, which he contracted during those first trying years in government. Perhaps his tenacious work habits were genetically transmitted, for his father was also driven to be constantly busy. I inherited, or learned to imitate, his work habits when I was very young and am given to long hours, a crowded schedule, and multiple responsibilities.

My father was not actively responsible for my political apprenticeship. Rather, my exposure to the affairs of public office came about by osmosis. As I began to ask questions about my father's work and the newspaper accounts I read of his meetings with the prime minister and the other premiers, he answered in a thorough and patient manner. When I expressed an interest in law-making, he told me that's what he did for a living and invited me to read the *Revised Statutes of Alberta*. Later he passed on to me Will and Ariel Durant's multi-volume *Story of Civilization* along with Winston Churchill's *History of the English-Speaking Peoples* and his five-volume memoir of the Second World War. Those books fuelled my passion for politics and the world of great ideas, and whetted my curiosity even more about what my father did for a living.

Ernest Manning led the Social Credit Party to re-election for a final time in 1967. Following that election, he assigned a group of talented and well-educated young men, including myself, to address the challenges of tempering small-c conservative principles with the social conscience of prairie populism. Referred to as "The Young Turks" by the newspapers, we were also called upon to organize the Social Credit leadership campaign to replace my father and the party's strategy for the 1971 provincial election.

Dr. Erick Schmidt, a sociologist serving as an assistant to the Cabinet, and I developed a *White Paper on Human Resources Development*. We did an end run around the senior civil service (rarely a wise thing to do) in drafting a plan for a new Human Resources Development Authority that would use a combination of education, health care, and social services to remedy inequities in needy communities. However, our first crack at proposing a big idea was not well received and died a quiet death several years later.

The second project in which I became involved at this time was more political. It was an investigation of the possibility of putting together the aging Social Credit Party of Alberta (which had then been in office for more than thirty years) with the up-and-coming Progressive Conservative Party of Alberta under its new leader, Peter Lougheed. There was never any wild enthusiasm for this study on the part of my father's ministers. Nor were the new and ambitious younger politicians who surrounded the Progressive Conservative leader very enthusiastic about it. But my father and Peter Lougheed gave the project a guarded go-ahead.

The government party (Social Credit) was represented in this study by Erick Schmidt and me. Mr. Lougheed's group was represented by Joe Clark, who was then one of Lougheed's executive assistants, and Merv Leitch, who would become attorney general and minister of Energy in the Lougheed administration.

Our "gang of four" convened on a number of occasions in quiet and confidential meetings, which Joe took great care in arranging. The main product of our efforts was a draft plan for merging the Alberta Social Credit movement and the Lougheed Conservatives into a new provincial party, the Social Conservative Party. The plan included a formal statement entitled "Basis of Union," a statement of principles to which the new party would commit itself, which Erick and I wrote and were most concerned about. It also included a section entitled "Procedures" – a detailed blueprint of how the two parties would actually be put together. This was the portion that Joe and Merv were especially interested in.

As a result of our different interests, our joint meetings gave us a false sense of progress. As Erick and I reviewed the section on principles, Joe and Merv would nod in agreement, mainly because they considered it largely academic and were in a hurry to get on to the political aspects. As we went through the section on procedures, Erick and I would nod in agreement, mainly because we considered it quite secondary. In a relatively short time, therefore, we were able to present my father, Peter Lougheed, and their respective advisers with a draft plan.

Needless to say, it was not greeted positively by either side. My father's ministers were not convinced that the Social Credit Party needed any infusion of new blood, especially if the donor was to be the upstart Lougheed group. And Lougheed's people were beginning to believe that they would form the next government of Alberta anyway. And so my first involvement in political synthesis at the practical (as distinct from the philosophical) level also came to naught.

After it was over, there was much concern among the leadership of both parties that "the draft plan" might be leaked to the media. Joe and I were detailed to dispose of the evidence. We decided that the best way was to haul the several boxes of drafts and background material out to our farm and burn it all in my parents' fireplace. Thus, my mother's only recollection of Joe Clark and me doing anything practical together during our political adolescence is the two of us sitting in her living room carefully feeding our rejected plan into the consuming flames.

Ernest Manning, however, had one more political project in mind before he retired, and once again I became intimately involved. With the downfall of the Diefenbaker administration in 1963, and the initiation of a process within the federal Progressive Conservative Party to replace John Diefenbaker with a new leader, some Conservative supporters saw a major opportunity to change the party from within. A number of Western and Ontario conservatives approached my father to see whether he was interested in entering federal politics. He told them that he was not, but that he did have some views on how federal politics might be realigned. These were set out in his book *Political Realignment: A Challenge to Thoughtful Canadians*,* for which I did all the research and the initial drafting. More than 30,000 copies of *Political Realignment* were sold (bulk orders were placed by Ontario and Alberta Conservatives for distribution prior to the Conservative leadership convention in September 1967).

The central thesis of the book was that Canadians deserved some real choices in federal politics, and that these were not offered by the current alignment of parties. My father then outlined a philosophical position, described as the "social conservative position," which was a synthesis of marketplace economics and some of the social concerns of prairie populists. He challenged the federal Conservatives to realign themselves along this axis, asserting that if they did so, the Progressive Conservative Party could prove to be an attractive home for supporters of the federal Social Credit Party and federal Liberals who were uneasy about the leftward drift of their party.

My father did not groom a successor – he thought such matters were best left to the people and the party. The leadership campaign that led to a convention in December 1968 became a battle between the party's old guard and the new generation, represented by a gentle, quiet-spoken farmer named Harry Strom. Strom won the

---

* Ernest C. Manning, *Political Realignment* (Toronto: McClelland & Stewart, 1967).

leadership in two ballots and governed for thirty-three months, creditably, but without ever gaining the profile and momentum necessary to re-elect the government. In August 1971, thirty-six years after Social Credit swept to power in Alberta, the electorate dismissed it. By then, I was already distancing myself from provincial politics and joining with my father to launch a new venture – this time in the private sector.

■

William Aberhart preached the Christian gospel from an evangelical perspective. Mankind was separated from God – this was the root of all evil and broken relationships. God had sent his Son, Jesus, to mediate between God and man through his teachings, death, and resurrection. To be reconciled to God, and to heal broken human relationships, one had to make a personal decision, based on faith, to accept Jesus as one's personal Saviour. My father, who had been raised in a nominally Christian home by good-living parents but had never made a personal faith commitment, did so after listening to Aberhart on the radio one Sunday afternoon.

He began to study the Christian Scriptures for himself, adopting as his guideline in life words from the Book of Proverbs: "Trust in the Lord with all your heart, and lean not unto your own understanding. In all your ways acknowledge Him, and He shall direct your paths." He felt called to study for the Christian ministry, and when Aberhart opened up a school for the training of Christian pastors at his Calgary Prophetic Bible Institute, my father left the farm (returning for spring planting and harvest) and enrolled as its first student.

Thus began a lifelong commitment to the life and teachings of Jesus Christ. It was through Aberhart's radio ministry that my father met my mother, who played the piano for Aberhart's services. My parents' home was founded on their Christian faith, and because both had been drawn to God and to each other through a Christian radio ministry, they had an ongoing interest in this method of spiritual outreach. When Aberhart died, my father, even though he was now premier of Alberta, continued his radio ministry under the name "Canada's National Back to the Bible Hour." The program (later shortened to half an hour) was broadcast weekly and featured an exposition of some Bible text by my father, with a variety of Christian music arranged and directed by my mother. Eventually it was carried by more than one hundred radio stations across Canada, becoming Canada's oldest continuously broadcast Christian radio program. My father and mother continued it until 1989, long after their retirement from politics.

As a child and a young man, I listened to more sermons and Christian meditations than I did political speeches and commentaries. The Christian faith, in particular the evangelical perspective my parents had adopted, was as much a part of my background and environment as Western populism and the Alberta government. One of the first times that both forms of faith – my faith in the West and in God's providence – were simultaneously tested occurred on the occasion of the 1954 Grey Cup game, when I was twelve years old.

The Edmonton Eskimos, representing the West, went into the game as underdogs. In those days, the winner of the Western Conference was decided by a best-of-three playoff, whereas the winner of the Eastern Conference was decided by a two-game total-point playoff. Obviously, this arrangement would not have withstood the test of regional fairness because it was heavily biased in favour of the East. To get to the Grey Cup, Western teams often had to play three playoff games, late in the fall on frozen fields, whereas the Eastern teams only had to play two playoff games in the milder November climate of the St. Lawrence basin. In 1954, the Eskimos had advanced to the Grey Cup after a brutal three-game playoff with the Winnipeg Blue Bombers, in which the Esks had suffered many injuries on the frozen turf. The Montreal Alouettes, on the other hand, had advanced after their two-game semifinal almost injury free. To make matters worse, the Alouettes outweighed the Eskimos by more than ten kilograms (twenty-five pounds) per man along the line. The oddsmakers favoured the Alouettes to win by two or more touchdowns, and some Eastern commentators hinted that it would be less embarrassing if the Eskimos simply didn't show up for the big game.

The situation was so desperate for committed Eskimo fans like me that extraordinary measures had to be considered to increase the Eskimos' chances of victory. I therefore inquired of my father, Christian layman and the premier of the province whose capital city the Eskimos represented, whether it was theologically permissible to pray for an Eskimos victory. After all, the Eskimos were the underdogs, and was not God always on the side of the underdogs? Even more important, the Eskimos were representing the West, and surely there was no question as to where God stood when it came to West versus East. My father advised that it was always a good idea to pray for God's will to be known and done in every situation. But he also said that I should be aware that in great contests there are often devout believers on both sides, so that God must take into account the prayers of both. Sometimes the prayers of neither can be answered fully (as Mr. Lincoln had observed in his Second Inaugural Address). No doubt there would be devoted fans in Montreal praying for an Alouette victory just as earnestly as I would be praying for an Eskimos victory, and when it came to the teams, it was quite likely that there would be Christian brothers on both sides.

In any event, I prayed fervently for an Eskimos victory, and when the day of the Grey Cup came, November 27, 1954, I was expecting not only a superhuman effort by the Eskimos but, if necessary, divine intervention on their behalf.

Throughout the first three quarters, the Eskimos played ferociously, and they were trailing by only five points early in the fourth quarter. But their injuries and the greater size and weight of the Montreal line were beginning to take their toll. With only three and a half minutes left in the game, the Alouettes were moving inexorably down the field to score the touchdown that would drive a stake through the Eskimos' heart. Then, suddenly, it happened!

Theologians and other students of the game are still divided over exactly what happened, and how it happened, but the authorized Edmonton version of the events is as follows. Montreal had marched to within one foot of the Eskimos' ten-yard line. In the Alouette huddle, Brother Etchevery, the Montreal quarterback, called for a sweep to the left, with Brother Hunsinger, the Montreal halfback, carrying the ball. In the defensive huddle on the other side of the line of scrimmage, desperate measures were being discussed, as the Eskimos' only hope was to stop the Montreal advance and somehow get the ball back. The referee whistled the ball into play and Etchevery handed it off to Hunsinger, who proceeded to run the halfback sweep to the left.

Now there are those who maintain that at precisely that moment Hunsinger heard a still, small voice whispering in his ear, "Lateral the ball, lateral the ball." There are others who maintain that Hunsinger heard no such thing. It is generally agreed, however, that for whatever reason, Hunsinger was not gripping the ball as tightly as he should have. As he moved to his left, Brother Tulley, an Eskimos linebacker, burst through the line hitting him low, just as Brother Prather, the Eskimos' defensive end, hit him high – and, wonder of wonders, the ball came loose. For Eskimos fans watching the spectacle, it was as if time stood still. That ball, propelled by Hunsinger's forward momentum, was destined by the law of gravity to hit the ground, but how would it hit the ground? If it hit the ground and rolled, there would be a free-for-all to regain possession. But if it hit the ground and *bounced*, a miracle was possible.

The football was now on its own. Slowly, oh so slowly – or so it seemed to Eskimos fans – it descended, hitting the ground. But instantly it bounced up and forward again, straight into the arms of Jack Dickerson "Spaghetti Legs" Parker. Brother Parker was the Eskimos' star offensive halfback, playing the same position on offence as Brother Hunsinger. (Oh, the symmetry of it all.) But as the Eskimos' defence tired late in the game, Parker had been called upon to play defensive halfback as well – and he needed no still, small voice to tell him what to do once he got his hands on the pigskin. He took off like a bat out of Hades for the Montreal goal line, which he crossed untouched by any Montreal tackler.

The game was now tied. (In the 1950s, a touchdown was worth only five points, not yet having been adjusted for inflation.) The contest of underdog versus favourite, West versus East, justice versus injustice, faith versus skepticism, now hung in the balance, the outcome depending on whether the Eskimos could kick the winning convert. Brother Bob Dean, the Eskimos' kicker, trotted out on the field, beads of sweat standing out on his brow. Normally the convert would have been a foregone conclusion, but Brother Eagle Keys – from Turkeyneck Bend, Kentucky, the Eskimos' all-star centre – had broken his leg earlier in the game and was unable to hobble onto the field. Brother Bill Briggs, the backup centre, was also hurt, so it was the third-string centre, Brother Don Barry, who would have to make the all-important snap for the convert. No time now for advice or instruction. The Eskimos were out over the ball. Straight as an arrow came the snap from Brother Barry to Brother Ray Wilsey, the Eskimo holder. In one deft motion, Wilsey pinned the ball, spinning it on its longitudinal axis so that the laces faced away from the kicker and towards the goalposts. "Thud" was the sound as Dean's toe connected with the ball – a "thud" that reverberated across the country, from the shores of Lake Ontario to the Rocky Mountains and back. High and clean flew the football, straight through the uprights. One more defensive stand, and the game was over. Final score: 26 to 25 for the Edmonton Eskimos!

Philosophers and theologians have argued for centuries as to whether there is definitive proof of divine intervention in the affairs of men. But for a small boy in Edmonton, Alberta, what further evidence was required than that provided by that miraculous bounce of the football on November 27, 1954?

By the time my high school years ended, I had developed solid spiritual foundations and had made a personal commitment of my own life to Jesus Christ. Not everyone growing up in my type of surroundings – a strong evangelical Christian home with parents who are actively preaching and ministering in their community – maintains a lifelong faith in God and trust in the gospel of Jesus Christ. In my case, however, I experienced little doubt of God's claim on my life or the efficacy of faith. What I did agonize over was not the truth of the gospel or the relevance of faith but how to apply that truth and faith in the real world – in personal and family relationships, in sports, in science, in business, and in politics – and how to share it effectively, and not offensively, with my community.*

■

While my father was a "public person" all his adult life, so was my mother. She was given a classical education, including music, at St. Mary's Convent in Calgary while her divorced mother spent the winters teaching school in small prairie towns. Although she made her living as a legal secretary before she married, music was her avocation. When I was growing up, she devoted much of her time outside the home to directing the music for the "Canada's National Back to the Bible Hour" radio ministry. She recruited a tenor soloist (and the comptroller of an Edmonton home-building company) named Gordon Beavis, then attending McDougall United Church in Edmonton, to sing on the program. His daughter Sandra is now my wife.

My mother frequently spoke at Social Credit meetings and conventions and was regarded in the party as both a leader and a role model for women. She was a wife and mother who cared for her family and supported her husband's career as a politician and lay preacher. My parents' common interests, sustained through sixty years of marriage, were their Christian faith and joint involvement in Alberta politics. It is also significant that, while everything my mother did in public life complemented my father's responsibilities, she attained leadership responsibilities, stature, and a reputation in her own right.

---

* Voters have every right to inquire of any candidate for public office, "What are your most deeply held values and beliefs, and how do these affect your personal and political behaviour?" In 1992, a year before the 1993 federal election, I wrote my own answer to this question in considerable detail and included it in Chapter 4 of *The New Canada* (Toronto: Macmillan Canada, 1992). It defines my spiritual creed and my views on how to manage the relationship between faith and politics. Over the last ten years, I have had the opportunity to work out that creed and relationship in the federal political arena. Readers will be able to judge from the following chapters whether I have been able to do so faithfully and credibly.

■

In spite of the obvious centrality of politics in my parents' lives, I grew up in a household in which that preoccupation ran a distant second in importance to relationships: our relationships with one another, with God, and with the spiritual and secular communities in which we fashioned our lives. My parents believed that life should be grounded on values and verities beyond politics, and that elective office is just one avenue that enlightened and caring people can take to serve their friends and neighbours in a free and open society.

My father therefore placed great importance on protecting his home life from the intrusions of politics. He rarely volunteered anything in the way of dinner-table conversation about his work. He rarely entertained political or government people in our home. He didn't permit the family to be used for political advertising purposes or to be drawn into campaigns. Inevitably, though, his responsibilities intruded in other ways – his telephone number was listed, so that people called him at home on constituency and political matters, and he was always at his desk writing speeches or sermons. I can recall him sitting at the kitchen table on various occasions using a mechanical adding machine to prepare budget speeches.

We were, on the whole, a well-contented family, and I was a happy child. My parents travelled a great deal, and I became accustomed at an early age to being left in the charge of other caregivers, most memorably Esther Galloway, who was our housekeeper for many years. Her husband, Ron, farmed near Fort Saskatchewan, Alberta, and later became foreman of my parents' dairy farm. They and their children became part of our extended family. One of my vivid memories is of the time my brother and I spent at the Galloways' farm when my parents went to London for Queen Elizabeth's coronation. They had no electric power, and we took turns participating in their family ritual of lighting the kerosene lamps at night. Ron introduced us to his massive Aberdeen Angus bull and allowed us to pitch rocks at it to see what it might do. The bull must have had a special reserve of patience for small boys because we survived the experience unscathed.

After renting several cramped apartments and homes in Edmonton during their first years of marriage, my parents purchased a tiny white bungalow not far from the University of Alberta after my brother, Keith, was born in 1939. They acquired a St. Bernard named Monty and developed a small garden on the postage-stamp lot. When I was six, we moved to a green, two-storey frame house in the heart of the well-treed Garneau district, across from the University Hospital and the University of Alberta campus. Our neighbours were mainly university people and professionals, and the mayor of the city, John W. Fry, lived next door. My father's office in the legislature was a short walk, or, in my case, bicycle ride, over the High Level Bridge.

Our unassuming residence, with a piano in the front parlour and small bedrooms up the stairs, was a short walk to Garneau Public School, an imposing two-storey brick edifice that loomed over me as I began my primary education. I was somewhat ahead of my class, having learned simple arithmetic and reading and writing at home. I also had a well-developed curiosity about history and a natural knack for science. If I escaped becoming a geek, in spite of my spectacles and bookishness, it was only because I enjoyed sports. In post-war Edmonton, young boys learned to throw a football, pedal a bicycle, hit a baseball, skate, and slap at a hockey puck almost before they learned to walk. My classmates and neighbours shared my fondness for being outdoors, playing games and exploring the river valley.

The greatest challenge of those early years was my relationship with my older brother, Keith, who had a difficult birth in which oxygen deprivation destroyed a part of his brain and left him developmentally arrested. If Keith's condition had been slightly worse, he would not have known or understood what he could not do; if his condition had been slightly better, he would have been able to cope with and overcome his limitations. But he was in a frustrating no man's land between those two conditions, and he often took those frustrations out on me. I resented that he could not keep up physically to the rest of us boys, and I was fearful, when our family went out together, that he would have one of his seizures in a public place.

I learned a great deal about unconditional love during that time. My grandmother (who taught him to read), mother, and father did everything in their power to search for a remedy for his condition. As they came to accept his situation, they searched for a medical regimen that would make his life more comfortable and found a place – a school in upstate New York – where he could get the best possible education. Keith's constant care cost my parents a great deal – emotionally as well as financially – a fact that I did not come to appreciate fully until much later in life.

My frustration and apprehension with Keith eventually turned to affection and friendship. As drug and educational therapy progressed, Keith functioned more normally. He lived at the Red Deer School Hospital for several years and eventually was able to return to Edmonton, where he lived in a group home and went every day to a special occupational workshop. He faithfully attended our home church – the Edmonton Fundamental Baptist Church – and had an affection for the Scriptures. His faith touched other lives.

Towards the end of his life, he took up residence in an extended-care home and married one of the residents, Marilyn Brownell. They were together for three years, which I believe to have been the best of his life. Keith died of a brain tumour in 1986 at the age of fifty-three.

∎

Through my formative years, Ernest Manning was a premier from Monday to Friday, a lay preacher on Sunday, and a dairy farmer on Saturday. My father had been raised on a farm and never lost his love of the land and farm machinery. In spite of their modest income, Keith's medical bills, and their determination to own a home, my parents made a down payment on a half-section of land on the banks of the North Saskatchewan River east of Edmonton. They called the place Westerlea. On weekends my father, along with Ron Galloway and a series of hired hands, slowly transformed Westerlea into a well-groomed, self-sustaining dairy farm with seventy head of milk cows, a loafing barn with a mechanized milking parlour, a home for Ron and his wife, Esther, a bunkhouse for our hired men, and a new, sprawling, ranch-style house to which we moved in the spring of 1954, just before I turned twelve.

The farm provided endless opportunities for a young boy's

appetite for the outdoors and for adventure. My best friends were dogs, a horse, and a calf – in that order. I once proposed to my father that dogs should be given the vote since they were often better judges of human character than people were. He said he would consider it, but cautioned that such a reform would probably alienate the cat-owner vote. At various times our farm dogs included a spaniel, St. Bernards, collies, litters of collie pups, a keeshond, a boxer, and a handful of mongrels. I played with them, chased cats, gophers, and birds with them, and suffered with them when they got into trouble.

And then there were the horses. North Yoachim, my friend on the neighbouring farm, and I each had a horse. His was a grey mare called Amigo and mine was a white, walleyed gelding that I had named Silver (though Ron called him Crowbait). North and I would ride for hours on the quarter north of our place and east of the Yoachims', along the banks of the river, where there was a large area of bush and gravel pits. Every so often, just around dusk, we would come across a parked car – some couple from town who had come out to the country to be alone together. We would cut boughs off poplar trees, wait until dark, and then come whooping out of the bush on horseback, beating the boughs on the roof and sides of the parked car. We were never really certain what was going on inside those cars, but we sure did flush out some confused and angry people that way.

Ron Galloway was a good mechanic, and the little I know about tools, engines, and farm machinery I learned from him. He was also an excellent herdsman, and under his direction our dairy grew and prospered. With Ron's supervision, I raised a shorthorn calf one year, named Touchdown, which won the 4-H championship for northern Alberta. I was going to name him Jackie Parker (after the great quarterback for the Eskimos) but my father said this wouldn't look good when eventually we had to take him to the packing plant.

From grade seven through grade twelve I attended a small country school named Horse Hill School. It was on a slight rise midway between old Fort Edmonton and Fort Saskatchewan, at a spot where the inhabitants of those forts used to graze horses. All my memories

of Horse Hill are happy ones. Mrs. Lepard helped me make the transition from the city to the country. Mrs. Cardiff, the social studies
teacher, encouraged me to read history. The principal, Mr. Kraychy,
nurtured my interest in science. And Dr. Kirchmeir challenged me
to "think."

But, like most teenagers, my fondest memories of those years have
to do with sports and friends. At Horse Hill, we would often choose
teams for football, hockey, or baseball by someone calling out "dairy
farmers against the pig farmers." This was basically a friendly rivalry,
but it did heat up at times. I was also part of a small gang called "the
Fearless Five." We often played on the same hockey and football
teams, and we looked after each other when there were scuffles.
Because I was small, membership in the Fearless Five was a great
benefit to me. The other members of the gang were North Yoachim,
Dave Carmichael (who had a good voice and was generally admired
for his imitation of Elvis Presley), and Laverne and Ed Wilkins.
Both of the Wilkins boys were excellent athletes, and Ed was my
best friend.

■

I entered the honours physics program at the University of Alberta
in the autumn of 1960 and for the next three years immersed myself
in my studies. For the first year, I lived at home on the farm and com-
muted the relatively short distance to Edmonton. After that, I found
an apartment in Edmonton with Ed Wilkins, who was also attending the U of A.

All my contacts with politics in those years came through my
association with legislators and practising politicians, not academics. I did not study political science at university. I had only a brief
and perfunctory experience with the university Model Parliament,
though it proved to be a seedbed for future Canadian politicians
including Joe Clark; Jim Coutts, principal secretary to prime ministers Lester Pearson and Pierre Trudeau; Grant Notley, Alberta NDP
leader until his tragic death in a plane crash; and Ray Speaker, a
long-serving Alberta MLA, Cabinet minister, MP, and colleague in
the Reform Party.

By the end of my third year at the university, my intellectual horizons had broadened and I was dissatisfied with the strict focus of my studies. Two events propelled me to switch to the arts faculty to study economics. The first was a "career counselling" session with Dr. Walter Johns, the university's president, who assured me that switching faculties was not the traumatic reversal I was making it out to be. The second was an unexpected encounter on the steps of the Alberta legislature early in 1962 with Sid Blair, the president of Canadian Bechtel, a subsidiary of the giant U.S. engineering, construction, and defence contractor headquartered in San Francisco.

Mr. Blair asked me what I was doing for the summer, and I replied that I would probably be working on the farm, as I had the previous two summers. He then inquired whether I would be interested in going to San Francisco and working for the summer with Bechtel's newly established research and development division. I jumped at the chance, and consequently spent from May to the end of August in San Francisco.

I rented a one-room apartment in a building on the corner of Bush and Powell, where the cable car came rattling through, ringing its bell at all hours of the day and night. Most of my time was spent on two projects – doing shielding calculations on a facility that Bechtel was building for W. R. Grace and Company to process spent fuel rods from nuclear reactors, and writing a speculative report on the possible commercial value of maser and laser devices. I also visited some of California's great scientific laboratories and institutes and saw first-hand the relationship among government, science, and business and the enormous task involved in managing and coordinating their joint interests and projects.

That fall, back in university, I took a full load of economics courses. At the end of the university year I knew I would have to make some decisions about whether to continue to postgraduate studies or move on to something else. One day, as I was sitting in a lecture room listening to a very knowledgeable professor who was a very poor communicator, I began to see my options in a new light. I could conceivably go on and get my M.A. or Ph.D., like this economist. Or I could find a business or government client who really needed this man's expertise and act as the link between the demand for specialized knowledge and the supply. Could I not "rent" the economist's brain for so much per day, hire him out at a higher rate, and use the difference to cover my cost and fee for service?

This, of course, is the essence of the consulting or knowledge business, and I found it an increasingly attractive option. It would give me exposure to all the knowledge and experience of specialized people while allowing me to remain a generalist.

But before getting into the consulting business, I undertook a three-year doctorate in practical experience. The first lesson began in 1964, when I went on a lengthy cross-Canada tour of churches and Christian youth groups to talk about the idea and the experience of spiritual reawakening. My interest was prompted by a challenge my father had made when he observed that, as Canada approached its 1967 Centennial year, the nation needed a renewal of faith. One of my closest friends, Ed Kennedy, joined me in this enterprise. Ed was the son of my father's friend Orvis Kennedy, who ran the political side of the Alberta Social Credit Movement and kept it connected to the national Social Credit Party, which held a significant block of seats in the federal Parliament. Ed and I shared a common Christian faith as well as the experience of having political fathers. Our journey across Canada was a memorable way to celebrate my graduation from university.

When I returned to Edmonton, I was recruited into my first campaign as a candidate for political office. In the 1965 federal election, the federal Social Credit Party, led by Red Deer MP Robert Thompson, needed a candidate in Edmonton East. The riding was the political preserve of Progressive Conservative MP Bill Skoreyko, who had a solid base of support in the Ukrainian and Eastern European community that dominated the constituency. The riding was a Tory stronghold, and I had a very slim chance of winning. But I thought the experience might be worthwhile, threw my hat into the ring, and finished a distant second.

After the election was out of the way, I began the work of launching my professional career as a consultant. David Wilson, executive director of the National Public Affairs Research Foundation, engaged me for the three projects already mentioned: the *White Paper on Human Resources Development* for the Alberta government, the plan for merging the Alberta Social Credit Party and the provincial Progressive Conservative Party, and the research leading to my father's book on "political realignment."

While this work was going on, the most important development of my entire life took place. In the spring of 1966, I asked Sandra Lilian Beavis, a student nurse and fellow member of the College and Career group at my church, out to dinner. Sandra was so taken aback at my call that she actually said she'd have to ask her father's permission – something she hadn't done with respect to any aspect of her social life for years. To my delight, she accepted and joined a foursome that included Ed Wilkins and his date.

Sandra came from a family where the level of activity around the household was in marked contrast to the Mannings. She and her three sisters lived in a household in constant motion with the comings and goings of a wide assortment of friends, family, and strays. In addition to her exuberant and outgoing ways, Sandra was also smart, serious, and a committed Christian. After completing high school, she attended Prairie Bible College in Three Hills, Alberta. It had a reputation for being straitlaced and prudish, and her friends thought it would be just a matter of time before she quit or was expelled. Instead, she graduated with a degree in Christian Education, a major in music, and a solid grasp of the basics of the Christian faith. Next she started nursing studies at the University of Alberta, with the intention of pursuing a career as a medical missionary.

Our differences were obvious, but we found that we had much in common, including a preference for each other's company. In October 1966 we became engaged, and we were married on March 23, 1967. Measured in terms of my future well-being, my family, and my business and political career, asking Sandra to marry me was the smartest decision I ever made. We've enjoyed life together for more than thirty-five years, sharing not only our faith, but also the satisfaction of raising five children, rich experiences in public life, the excitement of victory as well as the taste of defeat, and a commitment to the reconciliation of broken relationships and the advancement of big ideas. Sandra has sacrificed much more for me and my political career than I have for her, and that is a debt I shall never be able to repay. We are partners in life – a team in all we do.

On December 16, 1968, twelve days after Harry Strom assumed the leadership of the Social Credit Party and the Alberta government, my father and I incorporated M and M Systems Research Limited, later to be renamed Manning Consultants Limited, simply because that's what most people insisted on calling it. I was the president and general manager, responsible for building and running the firm. Ernest Manning would become a senator of Canada and a director on a number of corporate boards while continuing his radio broadcast work. But he was available and invaluable as an adviser and "rainmaker," helping me court and service our clients.

We did not want to take advantage of my father's former position, so we stayed away from provincial government work and the executive suites of the big oil companies. There was, however, no shortage of clients in other businesses who engaged us for a wide range of tasks and gave me an opportunity to learn the workings of a wide variety of enterprises, from scrap steel dealers to amateur hockey associations.*

Until he died, at the age of eighty-seven after a brief illness, faith, politics, and family remained my father's deepest commitments. His private life of faith and prayer and his life of public service were seamless. If he left a political legacy, thirty years after his departure from elective politics, it was that great politicians are builders, and that faith and family are key foundation stones on which to build. As the "Premier's Kid," this was the legacy that I took into federal politics in 1987, when once again the prairies burned with anger and discontent and I embarked upon the task of launching the Reform Party of Canada.

---

* More detail on my adventures as a management consultant is available in my book *The New Canada* (Toronto: Macmillan Canada, 1992), Chapter 3, Adventures in the Market Place, p. 53.

2

THE WEST WANTS IN

By THE TIME MY FATHER HAD RETIRED FROM PROVINCIAL
politics and we were launching our consulting practice, I had
reached several firm political conclusions. I was convinced that,
first, there was such a thing as a "democratic reform tradition" in
Western Canada, and it was a distinguishing and enduring characteristic of our political culture. It could be a powerful force for
change, and it usually expressed itself through the emergence of
third parties. In 1921, for example, the United Farmers of Alberta
swept to power with a populist government that led the fight with
the federal government to acquire provincial ownership of the
province's petroleum resources. In 1935, Social Credit came to power
in Alberta, and, nine years later, the Canadian Commonwealth
Federation (CCF) formed the government in Saskatchewan. The
two parties were diametrically opposed on economic fundamentals,
but both were committed to "grassroots democracy" and drew their
political strength from representing "the little guy."

Second, this tradition was part of an older and broader reform tradition that had expressed itself powerfully in various ways and at
various times throughout Canada as a whole. The rebellions of 1837
tapped into its currents. Baldwin and LaFontaine exemplified its

healing and unifying potential in the successful merging of Upper
and Lower Canada before Confederation. Joseph Howe of Nova
Scotia was a part of this tradition when he crusaded for responsible
government there. Elements of it played a crucial role in the formation of the Great Coalition that brought Confederation itself into
being. And the third-party tradition in Quebec that produced the
Bloc populaire, the Union Nationale, the Ralliement des crédi-
tistes, the Parti Québécois, and the Bloc Québécois was also
somehow tied in.

Third, I was sure that there was something in the cultural, demo-
graphic, economic, and political makeup of Western Canada that
caused this democratic reform tradition to break out in some new
form every twenty or thirty years. So, rather than participate politically at this time through either of the traditional parties, I would
wait, complete my political and economic education in the real
world, and become politically active again if and when the winds of
that Western reform tradition once more began to blow.

I consequently busied myself building our consulting practice and
with other things more important than politics – marrying Sandra,
setting up our first home, and raising a family of five active children.
These were "the waiting years," but they were wonderful years for us
as a couple and a family, filled with school, church, mortgage and tax
payments, good times with relatives and friends, synchronized swimming lessons, hockey, football, moving to an acreage, mowing lawns
and tinkering with water and sewer systems, playing with dogs,
summers at Lesser Slave Lake, and cheering on the Edmonton
Eskimos and the Edmonton Oilers.

I waited through the Trudeau years, which many Western
Canadians regard as the political equivalent of the Dark Ages. It was
as though Ottawa were a foreign country and Liberal ministers were
representatives of a foreign power. It wasn't just that the National
Energy Program transferred $100 billion worth of wealth from the
West to Ottawa and the consuming provinces; it was that even this
outrage was presented as being in our own best interests by federal
politicians and bureaucrats who claimed to understand those interests better than we did.

In 1972, when Joe Clark ran for the Progressive Conservatives in the federal riding of Rocky Mountain, he and his friends suggested I run for the party in Pembina, a rural constituency surrounding Edmonton. I declined – "I think I'll wait." Wait for what? At the time, I couldn't exactly say. On several occasions Joe and I had discussed the merits of working for change within the traditional party system versus challenging it from outside. Joe had been committed to working from within the Tory party since he was sixteen years old. He worked like a dog night and day and, to his credit, by 1979 he had clambered to the top of the greasy pole. Elected Tory leader and then prime minister, he would now have a chance to show what could be done "from within." But miscalculations and unpreparedness to govern cut that opportunity short, and less than a year later we were back to Trudeau and the Liberals.

Finally, the country had had enough of the Liberals, and in 1984 they gave the Tories and their new leader, Brian Mulroney, a massive majority in Parliament. The West had supported the federal Conservatives through all the dark days of the Trudeau administration and had great expectations of the new regime. In particular, the West expected spending to be controlled, the deficit to be dramatically reduced, tax relief, and a new sensitivity to Western aspirations and concerns. The West now waited impatiently – more impatiently than Mulroney and the Tories realized.

Spending controls and deficit reduction? Federal spending increased unabated, and the Tories ran even larger deficits than the Liberals. I heard the rumblings of disappointment in the boardrooms and on the streets as I made my consulting rounds.

Tax relief? The Tories kept increasing taxes, just as the Liberals had, to cover the ever-increasing spending. And in due course they would even introduce the hated GST, telling people it was "revenue neutral" when it was nothing of the kind. I attended some of the earliest of the anti-tax rallies that would eventually spring up all across the West. What began as whisperings of discontent would soon become a roar.

And sensitivity to Western concerns and aspirations? The Tories had sworn they would do away with the hated National Energy Program as soon as they took office. But they dragged their feet, collected hundreds of millions of dollars more through the Petroleum

Gas Revenue Tax, and did away with it only when the decline in oil prices made it expendable. When Quebec demanded recognition as a "distinct society," Mulroney made it his number-one constitutional priority, and, eventually, the centrepiece of his Meech Lake Accord. But the West's longstanding constitutional demand for an elected Senate was at first ignored, then watered down beyond recognition. As I listened in on business and political gatherings – farmers' meetings, chamber of commerce meetings, meetings of weekly newspaper editors and municipal politicians – I thought I heard a strange but somehow familiar sound. Cliff Breitkreuz, a municipal councillor from Onoway in Joe Clark's riding, came to see me in my office. "When are you going to stop studying and talking about a Western-based reform movement and start doing something about it?" he asked. It was the sound of the wind starting to blow through the prairie grass.

The grass was dry – very dry. One spark, and who knew what might happen? And then one day, the spark fell. It lit the grass around Winnipeg, but at night the glow in the eastern sky could be seen from as far west as Calgary and Vancouver.

In 1986, a tendering process involving seventy-five civil servants in three federal departments was established to select a contractor to maintain Canada's force of CF-18 jet fighters. If the contract had been awarded fairly it would have gone to Winnipeg-based Bristol Aerospace, which had submitted the low bid ($100.5 million) and received the highest score in an evaluation for technical competence. But the Prime Minister intervened, and the work was shifted to Montreal-based Canadair. Mulroney sent his Treasury Board president, Robert de Cotret, to Winnipeg to announce the decision, and ordered his Western ministers, including Jake Epp of Manitoba, to sell the decision as one "in the national interest."

Westerners had heard that line before, as the Liberal rationale for the National Energy Program. They hadn't accepted it then, and they certainly weren't about to accept it now. It was one thing to get out-of-control spending, chronic deficits, higher taxes, and anti-Western decisions made "in the national interest" from the Liberals. But now, to get the same thing from a Conservative administration that the West had worked hard to elect? It was simply too much to take. The hotheads talked about separation; cooler heads sought better alternatives, but all the conditions for a full-blown prairie fire were now present. The time of "waiting for something to happen" was over. Something was happening. It was time to act!

∎

On September 5, 1986, I dictated a short memorandum entitled "A Western Reform Movement: The Responsible Alternative to Western Separatism." I quoted Napoleon to the effect that there are times when it will be "bold actions, not further calculations, which will carry the day." There were plenty of ideas blowing around the West about the changes in federal policy required to address the West's concerns and aspirations. Missing were (1) the will to turn ideas, discussions, hopes, and fears into political actions; (2) strong and respected leadership; and (3) the funds necessary to do the job. To this memo I attached a copy of a column by *Alberta Report* editor Ted Byfield calling for a new Western-based Canadian political party. I then sent the memo to Byfield and two other champions of Western Canadian interests, Canadian Hunter Exploration vice-president James Gray, and political scientist Dr. David Elton, president of the Canada West Foundation. In my covering letter I proposed that we all get together for a meeting in Calgary to discuss "bold actions."

On October 17, Jim Gray hosted the meeting in his boardroom. David and I were present but Ted was ill. We were also joined by Bob Muir, who had been senior legal counsel for Dome Petroleum, and Doug Hilland, a corporate director and lawyer with strong oil patch connections. I presented the case for a new federal political movement dedicated to reforms that would make the West an equal partner in Confederation. There was as much reluctance in the room as there was enthusiasm. We did, however, agree that it was time to hold some kind of big, high-profile gathering somewhere in the West to air a reform agenda.

I was promoting this idea among my various political and business contacts when former Canada West Foundation president Stan Roberts came calling. He told me about a circle of which he was a part that had come to a similar conclusion. Stan was a good friend of Edmonton businessman and philanthropist Francis Winspear. Both were disaffected Liberals, Roberts having been a Manitoba MLA and provincial Liberal Party leader. The two had written off Mulroney as well, and Winspear had offered to put up $50,000 to draw together a group of Westerners interested in exploring political alternatives. He had asked Roberts to organize it. We agreed to work together and had Bob Muir draw up the papers for a legal entity called the Reform Association of Canada. Its first task would be to organize a Western Assembly on Canada's Economic and Political Future for the weekend of May 29–31 in Vancouver.

Six months later, on Sunday, May 31, 1987, at Vancouver's Hyatt Regency Hotel, a ballot was handed out to a colourful cross-section of disaffected Western Canadians listing four alternative courses of political action. It was a very Western and democratic way of doing things – have a big long discussion, argue vehemently for your preferred position, and then take a vote!

The "official delegates" who attended the conference included 58 from British Columbia, 100 from Alberta, and 38 from Saskatchewan and Manitoba. There were also 23 resource people and observers, 100 registered visitors, plus 350 delegates-at-large who joined us for the last day and the vote. Most were former members of the major traditional parties.

I had been heavily involved in "recruiting" these delegates, mainly through personal contacts, but the majority were attracted through advertisements in Western publications, in particular, Ted Byfield's *Alberta Report*. A banner behind the podium proclaimed the objective that had brought everyone together – "The West Wants In." The phrase had first appeared in *Alberta Report* in a guest editorial by economist Ralph Hedlin, and through his magazine Byfield had elevated it to the status of a battle cry.

The official delegates sat through almost two days of presentations and discussions. Besides delegate recruitment, my other major task had been to organize guest speakers and small task forces to make these presentations. The aim had been to produce suggestions for a Western Agenda for Change to be debated in plenary sessions and workshops and eventually voted on by the delegates. By Sunday morning the agenda had been approved and included such staples as free trade, Senate reform, balanced budgets, and regional fairness in national decision making.

But the truly political task of the assembly still lay before it, and that was to decide by what means this Western Agenda for Change was to be advanced. Four options were placed on the table: (1) to work within a traditional political party (and if so, which one?); (2) to create and support a new broadly based pressure group; (3) to create and support a new broadly based federal political party; or (4) "other" – which might range all the way from doing nothing to secession.

Not everyone was happy with these choices or this process. I had written to Mulroney and the other federal party leaders inviting them to send a senior spokesperson to argue for option (1). But Mulroney had responded by forbidding his MPs to attend. Since the theme of the assembly was "the West wants in" – not out – we had deliberately kept Western secession off the ballot and discouraged known advocates of separation from attending. Jack Ramsay, then leader of the secessionist Western Canada Concept, came anyway and was quite irate with me for denying him delegate status. (Several years later, Jack, after much personal agonizing, decided that "reforming the federation" enjoyed far more support among grassroots Westerners than leaving it. He joined the Reform Party and ran for us in the huge Crowfoot constituency, becoming one of our most conscientious MPs and one of my most solid supporters.)

I addressed the assembly only once, to make the case for option (3) – the new party. I argued that the new party should have a positive orientation and vision (it should be more than a protest party); that it should be ideologically balanced, moving beyond the old categories of left and right; that it should have higher performance and ethical standards than the traditional parties (it should aim "to do politics differently"); that we should avoid the extremes, eccentricities, and single-issue preoccupations that had marred some of the West's earlier attempts at political innovation; and that our aim should be to create not a regional party but a truly national one.

After the ballots were distributed, marked, and counted, Stan Roberts announced the results – 75 per cent in favour of creating a new, broadly based federal political party with its roots in the West. There was a roar of approval from the more than five hundred people in the room. It was just the beginning, but we were on our way!

■

Before leaving Vancouver, the delegates to the Western Assembly established a steering committee to organize a Founding Assembly for the proposed new party. When the Founding Assembly convened at the Winnipeg Convention Centre on October 30, 1987, a total of 305 voting delegates were in attendance: 140 from Alberta, 90 from British Columbia, 65 from Manitoba, and 10 from Saskatchewan.

On its first day, the assembly voted unanimously to create a new federal party, formally cementing commitments made in Vancouver. We then chose the name "Reform Party of Canada" from among thirty alternatives. Next, the assembly adopted a common-sense constitution, the draft of which had been prepared by Bob Muir and myself. It embodied our most important principles, including commitments to fiscal responsibility, equality of citizens and provinces, and democratic accountability. If we wanted the operations of the federal government and Canadian constitutional relationships to reflect such principles, we had to be consistent in applying them to ourselves. We were to be an open, transparent organization in which every member was treated equally and fairly. We agreed to accept leadership from an elected leader and council, which in turn would be accountable and responsive to the membership.

The assembly then turned to the task of policy making. Some of the issues we wrestled with – the CF-18 affair, the Meech Lake Accord, deficit elimination, and free trade – have since been settled or have otherwise taken their place in history. Others – economic justice for the West, constitutional equality, social service reform, tax relief, direct democracy, Senate reform – have yet to be resolved.

The Founding Assembly's last and toughest decision was to pick an executive council and a leader. There were two leadership candidates, Stan Roberts and myself.

I had been running a very low-key, low-cost campaign through the summer while putting most of my effort into organizing the assembly. Stan Roberts declared his candidacy less than a month before the Winnipeg assembly and ran a more traditional campaign of posters, press releases, and an assembly hospitality suite. However, Stan had entered the leadership campaign late in the day and had not made the same effort I had to establish personal contact with the delegates prior to the assembly. He quickly sensed that he did not have enough support to win the leadership, and he soured on the process. He attempted unsuccessfully to get one hundred new delegates registered after the deadline. Then he turned on the interim executive, charging that they had lost control of the process. A tense meeting was held in a basement room of the Convention Centre involving Stan and Francis Winspear, Bob Muir and myself, and the convention chairman, Jo Anne Hillier. Stan tried to convince Jo Anne that the leadership vote should be deferred and that he and I should be co-leaders in the interim. Bob and I insisted that the leadership vote should proceed as scheduled since picking a leader had been one of the declared purposes of the assembly from the outset. Jo Anne tried to find a procedural compromise that would satisfy Stan, but in the end he walked out, charging that there were irregularities in delegate registration and handling of funds.

In the awkward moments that followed, I was acclaimed the new leader of the Reform Party. It was hardly a spectacular coronation. My daughter Mary Joy later gave me a small plaque that sat on my desk until I left Parliament fifteen years later. It quoted words spoken by Jesus of Nazareth to his ambitious disciples when they were quarrelling among themselves as to which one should be chief: "He who would be chief among you, let him be the servant of all."

Stan Roberts later sought but failed to win the Reform Party nomination in 1988 for the B.C. riding of Saanich–Gulf Islands. But he stayed with the party. When he died of a brain tumour in August 1990, many of his friends and associates concluded that his "out of character" behaviour during the Reform leadership contest was the result of the personality changes that are an early symptom of that illness. It certainly wasn't the Stan we knew and respected. He was a thoughtful, big-picture man who believed in our vision of Western Canada as an equal partner in a strong and democratic Confederation and worked hard to achieve it.

■

On January 1, 1988, I put Manning Consultants Limited into mothballs and converted my Edmonton office into the headquarters of the Reform Party of Canada. The Mulroney government had been elected in 1984 and so, given that our governments are elected for a five-year term but usually seek a new mandate after four, 1988 was almost certain to be a federal election year.

The Winnipeg assembly had decided that initially we should run candidates only in Western Canada. But the task of fielding a credible slate of Reform candidates, and organizing an election campaign from scratch, was a daunting one. When I first met with Neil Weir, our campaign director, to explain the magnitude of the task before us and the very limited resources we had to achieve it, he recommended the "Fort Edmonton strategy." According to Neil (though I questioned his historical accuracy), several times in the early days of the nineteenth century Fort Edmonton was undersupplied and undermanned. To create the impression to hostile outsiders that it was much stronger and better fortified than it actually was, its few inhabitants would run around frantically inside, yelling very loudly, and firing out of as many gunports as possible. Frantic activity by the few, he said, would be the key to a credible campaign.

Consequently I decided to hit the campaign trail immediately. Our executive councillors and key volunteers guided the creation of Reform constituency associations in more than eighty federal ridings. We had plenty of financial and organizational limitations, but we were hoping for sixty to seventy candidates. As things turned out, we managed to field seventy-two Reform candidates: thirty in British Columbia, twenty-six in Alberta, four in Saskatchewan, and twelve in Manitoba.

We had only one major crisis as we prepared for the election. Controversial Vancouver columnist (for the *North Shore News*) Doug Collins, who was regarded by many, including Reform Party members, as an extremist on racial issues, tried to capture our nomination for Capilano–Howe Sound. I told Collins that if he were nominated, I would sign his nomination papers only if he would endorse a resolution passed by the constituency association that neither the association nor its candidate support any public policy that discriminated against people on the basis of race. Collins refused and attempted to pack the nominating meeting with his supporters. His "nomination" by the hijacked meeting was voided and an orderly meeting attended by Reform members only was later held to pick an official Reform Party candidate.

After consultations among our executive council, campaign team, and the local constituency association, it was decided that the best place for me to run would be in the magnificent Yellowhead riding, stretching west from Edmonton to Jasper, where none other than Joe Clark would be my opponent. If we wanted to contrast traditional party representation with the accountable, effective, democratic regional representation that Reform hoped to offer Westerners, Joe would be the perfect foil.

I challenged Joe to a series of one-on-one debates. He declined this invitation but did agree to participate in a series of all-candidate forums. The first of these was held in the resource town of Whitecourt. The debate itself and my contribution to it appeared to go over quite well with the crowd, but it was during the question period that the fun really started. A colourful fellow from Fox Creek zeroed in on the one question that Joe could not readily answer: "Mr. Clark, could you tell us why we should vote for you when you won't vote for us?" And before Joe could stop him, he started down the list: Meech Lake, Senate reform, the CF-18 contract, language legislation, federal spending, capital punishment – all the items on which Joe's positions were miles away from those of a majority of the people in that room. As he ploughed through the list, the crowd cheered each item. That Whitecourt forum gave us a theme and a slogan that we would use again and again across the West and throughout the campaign. The theme was real representation and the slogan was, "Why should we vote for you, when you won't vote for us?" This was more effective than anything an advertising professional could have thought up.

Back in Yellowhead, we set out to knock on as many doors as we could. One of my chief door-knockers was a retired druggist from Edson named Randy Murray. Door-knocking with Randy and his wife, Donna, was an adventure in itself. On one of our first calls early in the campaign, Randy and I knocked on the door and introduced ourselves to the lady who opened it. Before we could say anything more, she asked, "What is your position on the ozone layer?" As I contemplated a scientifically correct answer, Randy blurted out, "We're in favour of it, at least the Western portion."

Trailer courts, of which there are many in resource service towns, presented quite a challenge. There seemed to be about as many dogs as people, and because of my love of dogs, I often got sidetracked. My most traumatic door-knocking experience occurred in the town of Swan Hills. It was getting late, the sky was threatening rain, and we were tired. As I leaped up the porch steps to greet a man at his door, his puppy ran across the step, and I stepped on its paw. The poor thing started to howl. The owner, glowering at me, swept up the dog and disappeared into the house, to be replaced by his bewildered wife. Here is the great test of a political door-knocker. In a town where dogs are more highly valued than politicians, what do you say under these circumstances? I said: "Good evening, my name is Joe Clark and I'm running for Parliament."

It would take a volume all on its own to recount the stories that collectively tell the tale of Reform's constituency-based grassroots election campaign of 1988. Finally, however, voting day, November 21, was upon us, and Sandra, the children, and I drove out to Edson to watch the results with our Yellowhead warriors. I finished second, with 11,136 votes to Joe Clark's 17,847. Our troops quickly decided this was worth celebrating and proceeded to do so until the wee hours of the morning. A year-old party, running against a senior minister and former prime minister, had picked up 29 per cent of the vote and reduced the incumbent's percentage of the total vote from 74 per cent to 45 per cent.

My campaign manager, Ginny Assmus, who had done a superb job in pulling together an organization from scratch across the huge Yellowhead constituency, couldn't resist pointing out to me one significant item among the poll-by-poll results. In the town of

Neerlandia, where I had not spoken during the campaign but Sandra had, the results were 197 votes for me and 23 for Joe.

On the national scene, the Mulroney government was returned to power with a reduced majority, and free trade with the United States – which we, of course, supported – was assured. No Reformers were elected to Parliament in the 1988 election, but across the West we garnered 275,000 votes. In Alberta we collected 15.4 per cent of the popular vote, in British Columbia 5 per cent, and in Saskatchewan and Manitoba less than 1 per cent.

We had run a $1.6-million campaign and finished in the black. As a bonus, our membership grew by almost three thousand during the campaign. The Reform Party of Canada, as the marketers say, successfully "branded" itself as a legitimate political party. We had not achieved any miraculous breakthroughs, but we had received enough support to encourage us to persevere. And little did we know that our first "electoral success" was just around the corner.

■

Five days after the 1988 federal election, Progressive Conservative MP-elect for the northeastern Alberta riding of Beaver River, John Dahmer, died of cancer. On January 21, 1989, the Prime Minister called a by-election for March 13. The Reform Party was ready. We had nominated our candidate, a teacher named Deborah Grey, twelve days previously. She had run fourth in the November general election, having been nominated just five and a half weeks before election day. During the general election campaign, she proved herself a superb communicator, got the attention of the community and local media, and gathered a determined organization around her. Now she was ready to run again.

Deborah Grey was born on Canada Day – July 1, 1952 – in Vancouver. She received her education in Vancouver schools, then at Trinity Western College in Langley, B.C., and she graduated with Bachelor of Arts and Bachelor of Education degrees from the University of Alberta. She loved the outdoors and fell in love with northeastern Alberta, taking teaching positions first on the Frog Lake Indian Reserve and later in the town of Dewberry, where she was employed at the time of the general election and subsequent by-election. She had a general interest in Canadian politics but no strong party affiliation. In September 1988 a local nurse, Liz White, introduced her to the Reform Party and to Pat Chern, soon to be president of the Reform Constituency Association in Beaver River. On a quick trip to Vancouver, she found herself sitting in the airport beside executive councillor Gordon Shaw, who immediately sensed her potential as a Reform candidate and encouraged her to pursue the opportunity. People who had met Deb sometimes described her as a cross between singer Anne Murray (of "Snowbird" fame) and Margaret Thatcher, the Iron Lady of British conservatism. Some wit labelled her "the Iron Snowbird" and the nickname stuck.

Deborah is a practising Christian whose faith is real, personal, and practical, and she is generally conservative in her political philosophy. She has that interest in and fondness for people – all sorts of people – that makes her a natural representative of their interests. But she is also a principled person who stands up for what she believes. By temperament and conviction she is ideally suited to establishing and maintaining that dynamic tension between representative and constituents that is at the heart of "principled democracy."

There was some thought that I, as the party leader, should contest the Beaver River by-election myself. But after meeting Deb, I was convinced not only that she should be our candidate but that if she were to become the first Reformer to get to Ottawa I could not have hand-picked a better initial representative of our cause.

Three words describe Deb's second Beaver River campaign – she smoked 'em. With 11,154 votes in total, 4,242 more than the PC runner-up, the Iron Snowbird was on her way to Ottawa. What she has accomplished there in the thirteen years since her first election victory is a book in its own right.

Five days after her by-election victory, a dinner was held in Deborah's honour in Calgary. As a special guest, I had invited ninety-three-year-old Douglas Campbell from Winnipeg, still sharp as a tack and, to my knowledge, one of the last living Progressives in the West. Mr. Campbell was elected to the Manitoba legislature in 1922, one year after the 1921 federal election that sent sixty-five Progressives to the House of Commons, including Canada's first female member of Parliament, Agnes Campbell McPhail. Mr. Campbell, who went on to become premier of his province in 1948, knew all of the old Progressive leaders and MPs and had been a personal friend of McPhail. I wanted him to meet our Deborah Grey – the first Reform member of Parliament – and when he did so he turned to me and said, "It's remarkable!" "What's remarkable?" I asked. "She's a lot like Agnes Campbell McPhail. She really is."

Just inside the east door that leads from the hall outside the House of Commons Chamber to the Opposition lobbies, there is a small marble bust of Agnes Campbell McPhail on a pedestal. To this day, whenever Deb passes it, she says good day to Agnes and gives her a pat. Both of them have made Canadian political history.

■

The master of ceremonies at that send-off dinner for Deborah was another remarkable Canadian, and he too would soon be making Canadian political history. His name was Stan Waters – General Waters – a prominent Calgarian, war hero, and business executive. Sixty-nine-year-old Stan Waters had served in the military for thirty-four years, fought with distinction in the Second World War, risen to the rank of lieutenant general, and commanded the Canadian Armed Forces from 1973 to 1975. After his retirement from the military, Calgary's Mannix family appointed him president of the Loram Group, a heavy-construction conglomerate. He plunged into community life with organizations such as the Chamber of Commerce, the United Way, and the YMCA, and was an active Progressive Conservative as well as a member of the National Citizens' Coalition and the Fraser Institute. He was one of the thousands of disillusioned Conservatives who joined the Reform Party during the Mulroney era, saying, "I didn't leave my party. My party left me."

That year, 1989, was destined to mark the first-ever "senatorial election" in Canada, and Stan would be the Reform Party's candidate. How such an election ever happened is an interesting story in itself. After all, for 122 years Canadian prime ministers had appointed senators rather than having them directly elected by the people.

For more than a decade, prominent Western Canadians from various political backgrounds, my father among them, had tirelessly promoted the concept of a Canadian Senate that would be elected, with equal numbers of representatives from each province and powers to make them effective representatives of regional interests. It became known as the Triple-E Senate concept (for Equal, Elected, and Effective). Bert Brown and the Canadian Committee for a Triple-E Senate lobbied leaders and members of all federal political parties to endorse it, and it became a key plank in the Reform Party platform. To compel the direct election of senators in Canada would require a constitutional amendment, but there was nothing to stop a province from conducting an election to select its preferred nominee and then challenging the prime minister to appoint the people's choice.

In 1988, an Alberta seat in the Senate had been made vacant by the death of Senator Donald Cameron. Alberta premier Don Getty, with a provincial election looming, wanted something to bolster his position as a defender of Alberta's interests on the national stage. What better way than to promise Albertans the opportunity to elect their Senate nominee directly? In March 1989, the provincial Conservatives were re-elected with a reduced majority and, after some hesitation, passed the Alberta Senatorial Selection Act. The act provided for the election of Alberta's first Senate nominee to be held in conjunction with the province-wide municipal elections scheduled for October 16, 1989.

On August 28, the Reform Party nominated its candidate – Stan Waters. Stan and I then took off on a non-stop, seven-week, province-wide campaign. Stan was a great campaigner. The Mulroney government had just introduced the hated Goods and Services Tax. The GST and the out-of-control spending that fuelled the federal government's appetite for tax revenue therefore became hot topics of discussion at Senate election meetings. Stan had one line that he delivered so forcefully in every speech – as only a former commando and commander of the Canadian army could do – that it would make the hair stand up on the back of your neck: "If . . . I . . . could . . . CARVE . . . two . . . words . . . into . . . the . . . HEART . . . of . . . every . . . politician . . ." (pause for effect) ". . . they . . . would . . . be . . ." (Stan would glare for a moment at the audience as if they were candidates for the opera-tion) ". . . CUT SPENDING!"

On October 16, 620,000 Albertans – 40 per cent of the eligible voters – cast ballots for their "Senate nominee." The turnout was slightly larger than the average turnout for Alberta municipal elec-tions. Stan Waters received 257,523 votes, or about 42 per cent of the total votes cast, and 120,000 ahead of his nearest rival, Liberal candidate Bill Code.

Because of the size of his constituency – the entire province of Alberta – Waters personally received more votes in support of his bid to go to Ottawa than any other candidate for federal office had ever received in any Canadian election. Notwithstanding this massive support, it was necessary for Premier Don Getty to lobby long and hard to get Prime Minister Mulroney to acknowledge the result and appoint Waters to the Upper Chamber. Only when Getty threatened to withdraw his support for the Meech Lake Accord did the Prime Minister accede to the democratic will of the people of Alberta. On June 11, 1990, 238 days after the Alberta senatorial elections, Stanley Charles Waters became Canada's first directly elected senator. It was another first for Alberta and Reform.

■

The Reform Party of Canada continued to grow. On October 17, 1989, an overflow crowd of delegates from across the West poured into Edmonton's Convention Centre. We had plenty of reasons to celebrate. We were a party of 26,000 members with a million-dollar-a-year budget and a hefty bank balance. We had a new MP and senator-elect. Our principles and policies had been tested and strengthened in the crucible of electoral politics.

At the Edmonton assembly, Reformers declined to divert their resources and energies into provincial politics. When the debate turned to the question of whether to organize nationally – east of the Manitoba border – delegates also expressed concerns about resources and timing. But "the West wants in" was still our aim, and as Stephen Harper reminded the delegates, "the West will never get

in by keeping others out." The Edmonton assembly defeated a resolution calling for the party to remain Western only and reaffirmed
our commitment to create a national party. This left us with the task
of defining how the Reform Party should push into Ontario and the
provinces farther east.

Between the Founding Assembly in Winnipeg and the Edmonton
assembly, the two biggest issues on the federal stage were free trade
and the Meech Lake Accord of April 30, 1987. Reform was strongly
in favour of trade liberalization and had expressed this clearly in the
1988 election campaign. Reform was just as strongly opposed to the
Meech Lake Accord, as much for the top-down, closed-door manner
in which it was developed as for its contents.

In April 1991, in Saskatoon, the Reform Party held the largest
and most important assembly since its inception. This one –
attended by 1,400 people including media and observers – had mon-
umental implications for the future. We now had 62,000 members
and representation in virtually every federal riding in the West. But
we had also been receiving expressions of interest and invitations to
expand from people living in ridings east of the Manitoba-Ontario
border. The key decision for the members was whether – and how –
we would become a truly national party.

In preparing my speech to the delegates, I thought of another
meeting long ago at which the pioneers of the West were faced with
a similar choice. It took place seven days before Christmas on a bitterly cold night in the little prairie town of Indian Head in southeastern Saskatchewan. The year was 1901, and on the stage in the
soft glow of the kerosene lamps were two of the leading political
men of the old West. Premier Rodmond Roblin of Manitoba (grandfather of my father's friend Senator Duff Roblin) would try to persuade the crowd of more than a thousand that they should support
the expansion of the boundaries of his province to include a portion
of what was then the Northwest Territory. But F. W. G. Haultain,
premier of that territory, would argue that the future of the West
would be best served by the creation of one big province to negotiate from strength with the federal government and to counter-
balance the weight of Ontario and Quebec within the federation.
Those who wanted to carve the great Northwest into smaller

With my father, Ernest Manning, in 1965.

Reform Party fonds, University of Calgary Archives

Sorting through the results
of an internal Reform Party
survey concerning the 1992
Charlottetown Accord.

Interviewer with Rick Anderson and
Cliff Fryers (right) analyzing results
on election 1993 night.

Reform Party fonds, University of Calgary Archives

With Reform Party candidate Bill McArthur in the Vancouver Quadra riding
during the 1993 campaign in Vancouver.

Election victory cheer with Youth Bus workers.

With Sandra, election 1993, the night of the fifty-two-seat win.

Moving Avryll and John's "Old House to the New Foundation," 1997.

Election bus 1997.

"To Whom Does This Desk Belong?"
speech, election campaign 1997.

In the middle of a media scrum on the night of election 1997.

Kim and Wayne Hicks' family, participants in the Reform Party's tax-relief experiment, in the official opposition leader's office, December 1997.

Reform Party fonds, University of Calgary Archives

Media and campaign 1997 team.

The whole family with Cliff Fryers and Ian Todd (far right)
celebrating the election 1997 result.

The family gathers round in the official opposition leader's office, Thanksgiving 1997.

Fishing trip on Kitchener Lake, 1996.

Many stories to tell my grandsons and Nathan, spring 2002.

Christmas family fun in Turks and Caicos, 1999.

provincial fragments were "Little Westerners," he said. Those who saw beyond parochial interests and narrow provincial boundaries were "Big Westerners," and he had come to encourage that crowd to think big.

For three days at our Saskatoon assembly we tested the breadth and depth of Reform's vision. There was a contingent of delegates who were reluctant to expand eastward and recommended that the party "stay regional." These members felt our primary aim should be to establish a solid beachhead in Parliament and use the leverage of that position, just as the NDP had done for years, to influence the policies of the government and the other parties.

On the morning of April 6, delegates heard the report of our Expansion Committee, headed by Gordon Shaw and Reg Gosse. Reg reported that Reform already had 6,000 members in Ontario and fifty interim constituency associations ready to go if the Reform membership authorized expansion. "Ontario wants in," he declared to loud cheers from the audience.

Gordon Shaw completed his report by placing before the assembly a resolution in support of expansion, seconded by Stephen Harper. Delegates then had the chance to debate the issue. Eric Kipping from New Brunswick came to the mike to say Atlantic Canada wanted in, and the assembly cheered. There were calls for the question to be put. There had been enough talk. Cliff Fryers, chairing the meeting, called for a vote and a field of green "Yes" cards waved in the air, authorizing the leadership to conduct a party-wide referendum on the question of expansion. The delegates sensed they had done something out of the ordinary, perhaps historic. They stood up, congratulating each other.

Then it started. Someone on the far side of the room started singing "O Canada." It spread across the room until everyone was standing, turning towards the Canadian flag behind Cliff's podium. They sang, not with that awkward restraint with which the national anthem is so often sung at formal functions in Canada, but as if they meant it. The media were caught by surprise, and so were the assembly officials and those of us at the front. We were witnessing that rarest of events, a spontaneous expression of genuine Canadian patriotism at a federal political meeting.

That night I spoke to the entire assembly on "The Road to a New Canada." For forty minutes I elaborated on Reform's definition of the New Canada as a balanced, democratic federation of provinces, distinguished by the conservation of its magnificent environment, the viability of its economy, the acceptance of its social responsibilities, and the recognition of the equality and uniqueness of all its provinces and citizens. Our vision was not a parochial or regional one. It was a national vision – rooted in the perspective of Big Westerners prepared to reach out to their counterparts in other parts of Canada – and the delegates roared their approval.

Two months later, on June 3, 1991, my executive assistant, Ken Warenko, handed me a single sheet of paper from the party's auditors. It contained the results of the special party referendum on expansion. A total of 24,942 party members – 42.4 per cent of those eligible to vote – had participated in the mail-in balloting. Of those responding, 92 per cent had voted in favour of the resolution to expand eastward! Haultain would have been proud; I certainly was.

3

KNOW MORE!

———————————— ■ ————————————

IN AUGUST 1992, IN CHARLOTTETOWN, P.E.I., PRIME MINISTER
Brian Mulroney presided over a nine-day meeting of Canada's first
ministers, territorial leaders, and aboriginal leaders. Their purpose
was to strengthen national unity through amendments to the
Constitution of Canada. At its conclusion on August 28, Mulroney
announced their unanimous support of a twenty-page document
entitled "The Consensus Report on the Constitution." It became
known as the Charlottetown Accord.*

I was at the Reform Party's national office in Calgary when the
Charlottetown Accord was announced. In the previous year, travel-
ling across the country promoting Reform's vision of the New
Canada to anyone who would listen, I had felt first-hand the sense

---

* The Charlottetown Accord was divided into six sections. The first included a Canada
Clause that endeavoured to define Canada's fundamental values. It included an affirmation of "the role of the legislature and Government of Quebec to preserve and
promote the distinct society of Quebec" and a description of Canada's social and economic union. The second section proposed changes to federal institutions such as the
Senate, House of Commons, and Supreme Court. The third section proposed changes
in the roles and responsibilities of the federal and provincial governments, in particular a strengthening of provincial jurisdiction in such areas as labour markets, training,

of "constitutional fatigue" that afflicted increasing numbers of Canadians. Canadians wanted genuine constitutional peace, or at least a holiday from constitutional wrangling. But Charlottetown would offer them neither.

We were like kids piled into the back of the family car with Dad at the wheel. We're trying to get to our destination – a place called National Unity – before nightfall. Dad keeps saying it's just over the next hill, but we never seem to get there.

For a while, we let Pierre Elliott Trudeau drive the car. He says he knows exactly how to get to National Unity. It's on Repatriation Drive, just over New Constitution Hill. Trudeau drives fast, with one hand on the wheel and the other out the window giving the finger to passersby. But when we get to New Constitution Hill, National Unity is nowhere to be found. And by then René Lévesque is jumping up and down in the back seat yelling that he's going to be sick if we don't let him out.

Next we let Joe Clark drive the car, briefly. Joe says that National Unity is at a place called Community of Communities. But he misplaces the map and forgets to check the gas tank, and before we know it, Joe has been replaced by Trudeau again, and then by Brian Mulroney.

Meanwhile, Mom (the voice of common sense) is sitting patiently beside Dad saying, "Why don't we stop and ask directions? Why don't we ask the people whether they have any idea where National Unity is? After all, it's their country." But Dad will hear none of it. Father knows best! Brian is determined to succeed where Trudeau failed. He says he is absolutely certain that National Unity will be found in Meech Lake, just outside of Ottawa.

So we start to drive there, but then Clyde Wells and Elijah

forestry, mining, tourism, housing, recreation, and municipal and urban affairs. The fourth section provided a new addition to Canadian constitutional law, namely, recognition of the inherent right of aboriginal people to self-government within Canada. The fifth section proposed changes to the formula for amending the Constitution, giving each province and the federal government a veto over future changes to the Senate, House of Commons, and Supreme Court. The final section itemized other constitutional issues, from property rights to the implementation of international treaties, which were discussed by first ministers but not resolved.

Harper, with the support of a lot of other people, block the road. So the Meech Lake trip is abandoned.

Now Brian is telling us that National Unity can be found by returning to Charlottetown, where it all started in 1867. But first, as a partial concession to Mom, we have to visit all our relatives along the way, and seek their advice.

So we go to Quebec, where Mr. Bourassa insists that the key to National Unity is "distinct society," and Mr. Allaire says it's decentralization, and Mr. Belanger and Mr. Campeau say, whatever it is, Quebec wants a new constitutional offer by October 26 or it will hold a referendum on sovereignty.

And then Mom says we'd better check with the other relatives too, so we participate in an eight-month citizen consultation of some 400,000 Canadians conducted by Keith Spicer, as well as public consultations conducted by two joint committees of the Senate and House of Commons.

And then we go to a big meeting with the other premiers at the Pearson Building in Ottawa, under the chairmanship of Joe Clark, who is now the Constitutional Affairs minister. There we are told that the keys to National Unity include the Triple-E Senate for the West, self-government for the aboriginal people, and a "social contract" to satisfy the NDP provincial governments.

By now Brian thinks that all this visiting and consulting with the relatives is getting out of hand. And meanwhile most of us kids in the back of the car need to go to the washroom and are just hoping that Dad will stop the car so we can get out.

So Dad does stop the car . . . and then he drives on to Charlottetown *by himself.* There he has another closed-door session with the premiers, aboriginal leaders, and territorial leaders where, after a lot of talking and drinking, the Triple-E Senate proposal is watered down, Spicer is largely forgotten, and polls warning that Canadians are sick and tired of this kind of constitution making are completely ignored.

Brian and the other first ministers emerge from the meeting declaring that it is the Charlottetown Accord that will take us to National Unity.

But Mom, and the rest of us kids, we don't think so.

■

The one big difference between the handling of the Meech Lake and Charlottetown accords was that the latter was to be subjected to the approval or rejection of the Canadian people through a nation-wide referendum. Curiously, the government's House leader, Harvie André, did not represent the referendum as a significant step towards the democratization of constitution. making in Canada when he introduced the legislation authorizing it. Instead, he described it as "simply a matter of management prudence."* The reality was that the government had reluctantly acceded to pressure for democratic ratification originating with the provinces, in partic- ular Quebec, Alberta, and British Columbia, and with political forces outside Parliament, in particular, the Reform Party.

Quebec governments, whether Liberal or sovereigntist, had accepted the principle that major changes in constitutional arrange- ments should be ratified by democratic referendums. The Reform Party, already a force to be reckoned with in both Alberta and British Columbia, had adopted this position as part of its federal platform. In British Columbia, the Vander Zalm government had passed the Referendum Act in 1990. It required constitutional amendments passed by the legislature to be ratified by referendum before they could become law. In Alberta, the Progressive Conservative govern- ment of Don Getty, many of whose members were also federal Reformers, passed similar legislation in the spring of 1992.

Thus, by the time the provisions of the Charlottetown Accord were being formulated, the laws of Quebec, Alberta, and British Columbia ensured that their people (45 per cent of Canadian voters) would vote directly by referendum on any package of pro- posals that changed the Constitution. Significantly, this democratic impulse came from the two parts of the country with the greatest predisposition to innovate politically, the West and Quebec. The federal government had little choice but to provide a national refer- endum for ratifying constitutional changes.

On September 10, the House of Commons approved a resolution

---

* *Hansard*, May 19, 1992.

accepting the Charlottetown Accord by a vote of 233 in favour to
12 against. The only MPs to vote against the Accord were the 9 Bloc
members, 2 independents (Alex Kindy and Pat Nowlan), and the
Reform Party's Deborah Grey. Of the 159 government members who
approved the Accord that day, only one, Jean Charest, would be
returned to the House after the next federal election.

Of the 48 Progressive Conservative MPs representing Western
ridings in the thirty-fourth Parliament, not one chose to represent
by his or her vote the reservations of hundreds of thousands of
Westerners. Within fourteen months, the Progressive Conservative
government would lose every single one of those ridings, the majority of them to Reformers.

And so the stage was set for the Charlottetown Accord to be
ratified or rejected not by acts of the federal Parliament and the
provincial legislatures (all of which had approved it) but by the
people of Canada voting in a national referendum. The referendum
was scheduled to be held on October 26, 1992, under Quebec legislation in that province, and under federal law in the rest of Canada.
The question to be voted on was, "Do you agree that the
Constitution of Canada should be renewed on the basis of the
Agreement of August 28, 1992?"

■

Immediately after the Charlottetown Accord was announced on
August 28, I met with some of my key advisers at the Reform Party's
national office in Calgary. Tom Flanagan and Stephen Harper, in
particular, wanted me to announce Reform's total opposition to the
Accord and launch our "No" campaign immediately. I resisted this
for several reasons.

First, although it was obvious to most Reformers that the agreement was seriously flawed, these flaws were by no means obvious to
everyone. I felt that it was important to announce our opposition
after some reflection, and not precipitately.

Second, the Reform Party of Canada had been created as a "democratic populist party." As its leader, I had an obligation to consult
our grassroots members before announcing our position. A volunteer

army fights best when it has been asked rather than told to join the fray. During the week beginning September 2, I sent out a three-page memo to our key people seeking advice on how to handle the Charlottetown Accord. I invited responses from all nominated Reform Party candidates and authorized a survey to go out in our regular monthly mailing to all members. In the Reform Party archives in Calgary are responses from constituency executives, organizers, and grassroots members, and from candidates who eventually won election to the House of Commons under the Reform banner. I believe that each of them fought harder and more effectively in the referendum and subsequent federal election campaigns because they were directly involved, from the beginning, in key strategic decisions affecting those campaigns.

Third, I wanted to consult our members and constituency people on the practical matter of whether we could muster the resources required to fight *two* national campaigns within a year – a national referendum campaign in 1992, *and* the expected federal election campaign in 1993. I was much better acquainted with the state of the Reform Party's finances than were my policy advisers. If we were going to fight an effective referendum campaign, it would be much better for us to fight a shorter (six-week) campaign than a longer one, where we would run the risk of "fading in the stretch." I therefore took almost two weeks, from August 28 to September 10, to consult and to consolidate our position, and to prepare to launch our campaign. Eventually we would receive almost 30,000 replies to our internal survey, only 2 per cent advising Reform to support Charlottetown, 69 per cent advising opposition, and 29 per cent urging us to present the public with a balanced assessment of the package and then "let the people decide."

In the end, this consultative approach stood us in good stead. Unfortunately it also created tensions with two of my key policy advisers, Tom Flanagan and Stephen Harper. Tom and Stephen interpreted "the delay" in attacking the Charlottetown Accord as a personal reluctance on my part to oppose it. This was not the case, but it would not be the first time that Tom and Stephen and I would differ on the extent to which we should involve the grassroots of the party in strategic decision making. At this point, I did not fully appreciate that while Stephen was a strong Reformer with respect to our economic, fiscal, and constitutional positions, he had serious reservations about Reform's and my belief in the value of grassroots consultation and participation in key decisions and my conviction that the adjective to distinguish our particular brand of conservatism should be "democratic."* Over the next ten years I would be challenged again and again – particularly by academic conservatives – as to why I went to such lengths to consider the opinions of rank-and-file Canadians on everything from the Constitution to tax reform. My answer was simple: "It's their constitution and it's their money!"

When these internal disagreements were eventually leaked to the media – as such disagreements invariably are – they gave our opponents fresh ammunition with which to attack me and Reform. "Friendly fire" invariably attracts "enemy fire," a consequence Reformers were to experience repeatedly in the years ahead.

■

Thomas Jefferson once wrote: "I know of no safe depository of the ultimate powers of society but the people themselves, and if we think them not enlightened enough to exercise their control with a wholesome discretion, the remedy is not to take it from them, but to inform their discretion."** The aim of our participation in the campaign would be to "inform the discretion" of Canadians concerning the constitutional proposals put before them and to trust their judgment to make a wise decision.

On September 10, Sandra and I made our way to the auditorium of the Western Canada High School in Calgary. There, to an enthusiastic group of supporters, I announced that the Reform Party of Canada, after due deliberation and consultation with its members,

---

* Both Stephen's and Tom's dislike and mistrust of the "populist" dimension of Reform is reflected in their essay, "Conservative Politics in Canada," in *After Liberalism*, ed. William G. Gardner (Toronto: Stoddart, 1998), pp. 178–82.

** Thomas Jefferson, letter to William C. Jarvis, 1820, quoted in *The Writings of Thomas Jefferson: Memorial Edition*, eds. Andrew A. Lipscomb and Albert Ellery Berg (Washington, D.C., 1903–04), 15:278.

would form a committee to promote a "No" vote in the upcoming referendum campaign.

Behind me was a large white-and-green banner. "KNOW MORE" it proclaimed – a phrase suggested by one of our own grassroots members. Its double meaning fitted our situation perfectly. If Canadians made an effort to "Know More" about the Charlottetown Accord, we were convinced they would vote "No." And if Canadians, weary of top-down, behind-closed-doors constitution making, voted "No" to Charlottetown, there would be "NO MORE" constitution making of that variety for many years to come

I urged my audience, as I would urge dozens of audiences across the country, to read and study the Accord for themselves. If you do, I told them, this is what you will find: it weakens rather than strengthens the economic union at a time when jobs and tax relief should be the priority; the partially reformed Senate proposed by Charlottetown can simply be overridden by the Commons and is not the Triple-E Senate Westerners have been demanding; the Accord will not satisfy the legitimate aspirations of Quebecers and is not the required anti-dote to separatism; the Accord makes the constitutional standing of many Canadians (francophones, aboriginals, women) dependent on their race, culture, language, and gender and is therefore at variance with the principle that all Canadians should be treated equally under the law; and the provision of a constitutional veto to each senior government will cast the Constitution in concrete and is therefore a vote of non-confidence in future generations.

And finally, I explained, the Charlottetown Accord was not really an "agreement" but a framework for future constitutional negotiations in more than two dozen specified areas. Its adoption would bring not constitutional peace but more years of constitutional wrangling.

I concluded by saying that unless we said "NO MORE" by voting "No," the fabled dream of a constitutional lawyer would come true and become a nightmare for Canadians. This lawyer spent his entire adult life working in the Canadian constitutional industry. But one night he dreamed that he had died and gone to Heaven, where he asked St. Peter whether he could get an answer to a troubling question.

"Certainly," said St. Peter. "What is your question?"

"Will the Canadian constitutional dilemma ever be resolved?"

St. Peter disappeared for a while, but then returned to report the following: "I have presented your question to the Almighty, and this is His answer: '*Yes*, the Canadian constitutional dilemma will be resolved . . . *but not in my lifetime.*'"

■

In Alberta, the federal government had enlisted a powerful coalition of business and community leaders to bring out the "Yes" vote in the West. The coalition, consisting of more than three hundred individuals and groups with impeccable connections to the Alberta business and political establishment, was named the "Together for Canada Committee," with former Alberta premier Peter Lougheed as its honorary chairman.

Our referendum campaign team was drawn from a group of talented Reformers, very few of whom would be considered "people of influence" by the media. But they were able, dedicated to the cause of democratic constitution making, and determined to organize a campaign that would appeal to rank-and-file Canadians. Many of these people would go on to play major roles in the Reform Party and federal politics, but the Charlottetown referendum campaign was the first time we would work together on a national campaign effort.

The "Yes" committee and their governmental and business allies across the country basically ran an "executive campaign" – endorsements of the Accord by prominent persons, expensive literature, high-priced print and TV ads, and heavy reliance on the argument that since "everyone important" is supporting the Accord, you should too.

Reform's "No" committee ran a very different style of campaign. Our principal communication tool was a four-page broadsheet – a large, fold-out information brochure printed on cheap newsprint – which we intended to deliver door to door by mobilizing our 200 constituency organizations and grassroots army of 130,000 members. When I released copies of our *Know More* broadsheet at a press conference, it was greeted with scorn by our opponents and most of the mainstream media. It was more than 13,000 words long and included an analysis of the Accord, the principal reasons for voting "No," and a complete copy of the Charlottetown document with the weakest and most suspect sections circled in green.

The idea that you could persuade busy, working Canadians to read, let alone carefully consider, a lengthy constitutional document written in legalese was ludicrous, our opponents maintained. Canadians should learn about the Accord from their political elites and the media, and act on their advice. But Reformers believed that "the people themselves" were capable of understanding and dealing with "the ultimate (constitutional) powers of society" and that our role was to "inform their discretion." Our Reform constituency organizations and field workers ordered and paid for 1.5 *million* copies of that broadsheet and personally delivered them door to door in every federal riding where we had some local organization.

"Why are they afraid to show you the entire Charlottetown Accord document?" our canvassers asked. "Here, take our broadsheet, containing the entire Accord, and our 'No' arguments. Study the 'Yes' arguments also, and make up your own mind!" And Canadians did – by the hundreds of thousands.

We also carried out a limited advertising campaign. Our modest television budget permitted us to do very little by comparison to the mammoth television blitz of the "Yes" committee. But we learned a lesson that was to stand us in good stead in later campaigns. If you can design a low-budget ad that strikes a responsive chord with your target voters while incensing your opponents and at least a portion of the media establishment, you can get a lot of bang for your buck.

One of our ads portrayed the Charlottetown Accord as the "Mulroney Deal," describing it as "a bad deal now, and a bad deal forever" and "a vote of non-confidence in the next generation of Canadians." The characterization was accurate. Mulroney had initiated the process that led to Charlottetown and he was its most prominent spokesperson. Predictably, the "Mulroney Deal" ad incensed the government and some of the media. But the more they discussed it and decried it, the more the "Mulroney Deal" penetrated the public consciousness, with the desired effect, from our standpoint.

The most effective "No" commercial was produced by Bob

Johnson, a one-man video production company in Millarville, Alberta, in the heart of Reform country. Bob's commercial focused on a battered Volvo in a used car lot owned by "Brian and the Boys." The car was labelled "Constitution," and the voice-over consisted of a fast-talking salesman trying to persuade a wary couple to buy the obviously flawed vehicle. As Hugh Winsor of the *Globe and Mail* observed: "When this type of do-it-yourself message is combined with the hard-hitting and well-produced advertising sponsored by the Reform Party of Canada, the result overwhelms the more slickly produced campaign of the YES Committee, at a fraction of the cost."*

■

The other component of Reform's "Know More" campaign was an election-style speaking and media tour. It took Ian Todd, Ron Wood, and me to more than seventy news conferences, talk shows, and one-on-one media interviews, and more than thirty campaign meetings and rallies in various parts of the country, from September 10 to October 24. I also took part in two major debates, one at the University of Guelph between myself and Audrey McLaughlin, the leader of the federal NDP, and the other in Calgary with Conservative MP Bobbie Sparrow, whom I would run against in the federal election the following year.

If there is one aspect of democratic political action that I love better than all the rest, it is the public political meeting, with an audience of real people (not a "stacked" audience) and a big idea to be presented and debated or a big issue to be decided. Over the past fourteen years, I have actively participated in up to two hundred such events per year – all of them involving organization, personal preparation, a public speech, a question period, and follow-up.

You have a big issue – the constitutional future of Canada, for example – that is important to people's lives. You have a principled position on that issue that you believe is worth fighting for. And in a free country, with the help of friends and supporters who believe as you do, you can find or create a public venue – a forum, a luncheon,

---

* *Globe and Mail*, October 22, 1992.

a dinner, a classroom, a high school assembly, a public meeting or rally – from which to "inform the discretion" of others, hear their questions and concerns, and try to persuade them to decide in favour of the position in which you believe.

During the Charlottetown campaign, Ian would be on the phone weeks or days in advance, securing the venue and making sure it was set up to our satisfaction. Ron Wood was likewise engaged in making the media arrangements. Ninety per cent of my preparation time was spent on getting the message right, reworking a text that I had usually written myself, but with useful input from others. I am a receiver-oriented communicator. I assess in advance the audience, and the context in which I will address them, and continue to do so even while I am sitting on stage or waiting at the back of the hall to be introduced. I have a communications plan in mind, and a particular response I am trying to evoke from members of the audience. I have an objective I wish to achieve – in this case, it was to persuade the members of that audience to mark an X beside "No" on the Charlottetown referendum ballot on October 26.

What do I know about that man or woman or young person who is sitting in the third row? Who are they? What are they thinking, feeling, expecting? What words, images, emotions projected into the mind and heart of that person in this town, on this day, in this hall, in competition with a thousand other messages – drink Coke, your Visa payment is overdue, Vote "Yes" on Charlottetown, boy it's hot in here, my foot's itchy – will have that effect?

I wait impatiently for the introductions to be over. When Sandra is with me, she squeezes my hand three times: I love you. It's our code.

Then it's my turn. I start with thank-yous. They are more than formalities; I really mean them. This opportunity wouldn't exist if the people hadn't made an effort to come, and if a lot of unseen people hadn't done their jobs.

I turn to the subject at hand. As usual, it takes me a while to get "cranked." The first time I give a particular talk, I feel tied to the text. After a while, however, and as I get more comfortable with my subject, I gain freedom and confidence. After giving a talk half a dozen times, I begin to feel what resonates and what doesn't. I present my arguments. I illustrate them, humorously if possible. I retell our recent constitutional history in terms of Dad at the wheel and us kids in the back; everyone can identify with that.

Sometimes there is applause. Political speeches are supposed to have "applause lines" every few sentences, but I'm uncomfortable with that technique. (My media people are rolling their eyes.) Applause can break your line of thought; more seriously, it can break the audience's line of thought. I know how to cut off applause – by launching into my next sentence before any applause can start. (My media people are saying, "Please don't do that!") Maybe I'm not a good politician.

I conclude with an appeal for action. I am not giving this speech to hear myself talk, and surely you didn't come just to listen. Democracy is not a spectator sport. If you choose not to involve yourself in the politics of your country, you are destined to be governed by those who do. If my words are carrying your judgment, I want you to *do* something. (I hold up the "KNOW MORE" broadsheet.) Take it! Read it! Make up your own mind! The Constitution of your country belongs to *you*, not to them. Vote on October 26! Thank you! Applause (there they go again).

Ian gives me the hand-held mike. We're going to have a question period. But unlike the Question Period in the House of Commons, here answers will be given. You can also use this time to give us advice. The question time is for me the most invigorating part of a genuinely democratic political gathering. If organized interest groups are present, you can see them manoeuvring to capture the floor mikes. But soon enough, you get to spontaneous questions from real people. Once in a while, the questioner is as nutty as a fruitcake. Relax – it's a free country. Sometimes the questioner is angry and antagonistic – you'd better get used to the reality of democratic dialogue, it's not always refined and restrained. Most of the time, however, the questioners are polite and sensible.

Rule number one for the question period: *Answer the question.* Rule number two: *Answer the question.* Rule number three: *Answer the question.* Rule number four: If you don't know the answer, *say so.* People appreciate it.

By now the chairperson is closing the meeting. It's time to go. But I want to stay awhile. I don't like to be like Bongo the Bear in the

story we used to read to the kids – the circus bear who did his thing
in the ring and then was immediately hustled off to his cage until
the next time. Sandra and I like to meet people and listen to what
they have to say. If you listen carefully, often they will feed back to
you the message you tried to impart to them, but often they'll say it
better than you did, in language and with emotion that will resonate
better with future audiences if you incorporate their words and feelings into your next presentation. Where do you think I got the story
about Dad in the driver's seat, and the rest of us feeling like kids in
the back of the car?

■

The Charlottetown referendum campaign was, by and large, a
positive and encouraging experience. But there were also some
low points.

A prime minister, because of his position and the attention
given to his words by the media, can do more than any other participant to "set the tone" of a campaign. At the very outset of the
Charlottetown campaign, both Mulroney and former prime minister Clark drew the battle lines between "pro-Canada" and "anti-
Canada" forces. The opponents of Charlottetown were "enemies of
Canada." When these statements themselves were criticized as
extreme, Mulroney briefly backed off. But as the polls began to indicate that support for Charlottetown was slipping, and that the "No"
side was picking up steam, he and other prominent spokespersons
for the "Yes" side returned to the attack with a vengeance.

Mulroney told an audience of Atlantic Canada business people
that a "No" vote would throw large numbers of people out of work in
their region. In a fiery speech in Sherbrooke, Mulroney identified all
the gains that Quebec had made through Confederation, and then
"ripped up the list" to indicate what would happen if Quebec voted
"No" to Charlottetown. In late September, he and Premier Bourassa
both declared that a "No" vote would plunge the economy into crisis.
This theme was reinforced by a Royal Bank report declaring that a
"No" vote would be disastrous for the economy, and on September 29
the Canadian dollar plunged to its lowest point in four years

(80.15 cents U.S.) amid massive selling. From then on, dire predictions concerning the economic and political chaos that would follow a "No" vote became the central theme of the "Yes" campaign.

On October 5, I responded with my own predictions. Let the reader judge whose proved more accurate.

> If Quebec votes No, as now seems likely, federalists in Quebec will need to begin in earnest to define a better federalism than that offered by Robert Bourassa, Brian Mulroney, and Jean Chrétien. If they cannot, a sovereignist government will likely come to power in the next Quebec provincial election.
>
> A strong No vote, outside as well as within Quebec, would also signal the end of the Mulroney administration and its replacement by a new federal government with a profoundly different agenda.
>
> If the Reform Party has anything to do with shaping that agenda, it would include the following:
>
> • A re-focusing of the energies of the federal government and the first ministers on the economy.
> • A moratorium for a time on first ministers' constitutional conferences of the type that produced this agreement.
> • A challenge to Quebec sovereignists to choose once and for all between independence and Canada, making clear that sovereignty-association as they define it is not an option.
> • An open invitation to all federalists, including Quebec federalists, to help define a better federalism than we have thus far known.

On October 7, I spoke to a group of about eighty students at Concordia University in Montreal. My theme was "Reform's search for a better federalism." I dealt head-on with the "Yes" side's claims that Reform was anti-Quebec and anti-Canada – false accusations that nevertheless would dog us for years to come. If opposition to Charlottetown was opposition to Quebec, why were Jean Allaire and Pierre Trudeau both advocating a "No" vote? It was obviously possible to be anti-Charlottetown and pro-Quebec. With respect to the charge of being an enemy of Canada for "siding with the separatists," I simply quoted Trudeau's reply to the same accusation by a journalist after his famous Maison Egg Roll speech of a few days before: "They say 'No' because they want a weaker Canada. I say 'No' because I want a stronger Canada. So don't go saying it's for the same reasons."

The Concordia meeting itself went fine, but while it was going on a gang of demonstrators, many of them from off campus, lined the hall outside with protesters and pickets denouncing Reform and myself as anti-French and anti-Quebec. Ian and Ron made a quick assessment and determined that the only way we could get out was to go right through the middle of them with all the national media in tow. As we ran the gauntlet of yelling demonstrators, signs were swung at both us and the media, and a full-blown donnybrook would have broken out had not the campus security people helped us to a secure area. We waited for almost an hour until the Montreal police arrived to escort us out of the building.

In the end, no one was hurt, but the message conveyed by the visuals on the evening news was bad for Reform, the university, and the "No" campaign. It appeared to confirm that rejection of the Accord meant "trouble" in Quebec.

■

Months before the date of the Charlottetown referendum had been set, the Reform Party had scheduled its 1992 National Assembly to be held in Winnipeg on October 21–24, the weekend before the vote. Five years before, almost to the day, we had held our founding convention in Winnipeg, with 150 delegates representing 3,000 members, and minimal media attention. This time there would be 1,700 delegates representing 130,000 members and national media coverage. In 1987 we'd had no real organization and no nominated candidates, even though a federal election was expected in 1988. In 1992, we had constituency organizations in about 200 federal ridings, and we already had more than 100 candidates in the field.

The Charlottetown Accord campaign contributed mightily to our preparedness for the next election. In order to make the door-to-door delivery of our 1.5 million Charlottetown broadsheets, we needed foot soldiers in every poll. These people became the foundation of

our poll organization in scores of federal ridings. In order to participate in the referendum campaign, our riding organizations had to
become skilled at organizing and managing public meetings and
forums, hosting the events of the leader's tour, organizing media
events, and distributing material to local media. And to finance all
this activity, they had to develop their fundraising and budgeting
capabilities. All this they had done on a scale and with an enthusiasm beyond my wildest dreams.

Our financial people estimated that we would spend about
$350,000 on our Charlottetown "No" campaign, but that revenues
from the campaign's fundraising activities would bring in about
$520,000. These estimates proved to be accurate, and the
Charlottetown campaign strengthened our federal election campaign war chest by about $170,000.

And for our nominated candidates and party spokespersons across
the country, the referendum provided a perfect dry run for the
federal election. They had to familiarize themselves with a major
policy position and present that position clearly in various forums –
often facing experienced and formidable opponents as well as skeptical media and audiences. Those of our people who participated in
these activities found their confidence increased rather than shaken
by the experience. They found that our background research and
arguments on the Charlottetown Accord were every bit as good as,
and often better than, those of the "Yes" side. They found that public
audiences are often willing to side with a sincere and well-prepared
underdog, particularly when the opponent is arrogant and contemptuous of the challenger. And they learned that government ministers
and MPs – whom they had previously seen only on TV and who often
presented themselves as the "great of the earth" in their communities, were often "not so great" when measured close up. Our candidates, more often than not, came away from their debates and public
forums believing, "I could beat this person in an election contest!"

This, then, was the atmosphere that permeated the halls and the
sessions of Reform's 1992 Winnipeg assembly, as convention chair
J. D. Lees called the delegates to order.

Of course there were still problems and obstacles to overcome at
the assembly itself. I had warned our campaign team that we had not

heard the last of stories on "internal dissent." And sure enough, several *Globe and Mail* writers who "covered" the Reform Party accumulated all their material on this subject and published it again in the midst of our convention under such headlines as "Reform Party a house divided" and "Manning under attack at Reform convention." But when the time came for a vote on my leadership, as required at every Reform assembly by the party constitution, I received a positive endorsement from 96 per cent of the voting delegates.

October 24, 1992, was a great day for me and for the Reform Party, and a great conclusion to our "No" campaign. Out in the field, our members were mobilizing for one final push to "get out the vote" on October 26. And at the convention our delegates spent most of the day debating, amending, and passing policy resolutions. This they did with care and enthusiasm, knowing that the resolutions they adopted would become the key planks in our election platform the following year – a living, breathing demonstration of democratic platform building in action.

That evening it was my turn to address the assembly and the country at large by means of a nationally televised keynote address. Once again, for the benefit of the television audience, I went over the basic reasons for voting "No" to Charlottetown and outlined the national agenda that Reformers believed should be pursued after its defeat. I concluded by appealing to Canadians to regard the next federal election as a great opportunity to change their country for the better, and by asking Reformers to make the effort and the sacrifices necessary to communicate our vision of a New Canada to all who would receive it. If we did so, we would be able to say – paraphrasing the words of the self-sacrificing hero of Charles Dickens's *A Tale of Two Cities* – "It is a far, far better thing that we do than we have ever done before."

Sandra and I returned to Calgary on Sunday, weary but satisfied that we had done our best in the Charlottetown campaign, and exhilarated by the enthusiasm of the Winnipeg assembly. We arose fairly late on Monday morning, referendum day, walked to a school near our Calgary home, and cast our ballots. All across the country, millions of Canadians were doing the same thing. This was only the third national referendum in Canada's history (the other two dealt with Prohibition and Conscription). There is no danger of Canada overdosing on direct democracy.

That evening, our family, friends, and most of the campaign team assembled at the Palliser Hotel, where the national media had set up their cameras and local anchor desks to report and comment on the results.

Two months previously, when the Charlottetown Accord was initially unveiled and all that Canadians knew about it was that most of their political leadership said it was the greatest thing since sliced bread, it had enjoyed close to 65 per cent support nationally, according to the polls. But tonight, after two months of exposure and debate, the only poll that counted was telling a very different story.

In British Columbia, the Accord was defeated, 68 per cent "No" to 32 per cent "Yes." In Yukon Territory, it was 56 per cent "No" to 44 per cent "Yes." In Alberta, 60 per cent "No" to 40 per cent "Yes." In Saskatchewan, 55 per cent "No" to 45 per cent "Yes." In Manitoba, 62 per cent "No" to 38 per cent "Yes." And in Quebec, 57 per cent "No" to 43 per cent "Yes." The West and Quebec, for very different reasons, had solidly defeated the Charlottetown Accord. In Ontario and Nova Scotia, there had been an almost even split, with Ontario voting 50.1 per cent "Yes" and 49.9 per cent "No," and Nova Scotia voting 51.2 per cent "No" and 48.8 per cent "Yes." Significantly, aboriginals (who will play an increasingly important role in future constitutional negotiations), voting on reserve, voted 62 per cent "No" to 38 per cent "Yes."

Only in New Brunswick (52 per cent "Yes"), P.E.I. (74 per cent "Yes"), Newfoundland (63 per cent "Yes"), and the Northwest Territories (61 per cent "Yes") did the Charlottetown Accord enjoy solid support.

The Accord had been rejected by Canadians outside Quebec by 54 per cent "No" to 46 per cent "Yes," and in Quebec by 57 per cent "No" to 43 per cent "Yes."

As the results rolled in, an enthusiastic crowd of Reformers gathered at the Palliser and at our national office. My brief remarks to them were the same ones I had offered to the media: The people of Canada have made their decision. They, not we, are the "winners." It is time for a moratorium on constitutional negotiations. It is time to get on with other priorities, like the economy and reform of Parliament.

The results of the vote on the Charlottetown Accord graphically demonstrated that the Canadian people wanted to teach their political elites a lesson – the lesson that the Canadian Constitution ultimately belongs to the people, not to first ministers and their friends, and that henceforth the Canadian people would have the first word and the last word as to whether and how the Constitution was to be amended. And if constitution making in Canada was to be done democratically, it would be the obligation of our political parties and leaders to propose and adopt measures whereby this may be accomplished. As Neil Nevitte has observed,* the Charlottetown Accord provided a vivid illustration of the growing independence of Canadians, their growing impatience with the authoritarianism of hierarchical structures, their growing preference for "bottom-up" political formations, and the "decline of deference" among Canadian voters.

The last word on this subject? The same as the first word: "I know of no safe depository of the ultimate powers of society but the people themselves, and if we think them not enlightened enough to exercise their control with a wholesome discretion [first ministers, academics, media people, politicians, multinational executives – take note], the remedy is not to take it from them, but to inform their discretion."

---

* Neil Nevitte, *The Decline of Deference* (Peterborough, Ontario: Broadview Press, 1996).

4

REVOLUTION, EH?

SUPPOSE CANADIANS DECIDED TO HAVE A REAL POLITICAL revolution. What would it be like?

It wouldn't be like the French Revolution; storming the Bastille and chopping off heads just isn't our style. It couldn't be an American-style revolution with Boston Tea Parties and such; Environment Canada would never give us a permit for dumping tea in a Canadian harbour. And it wouldn't be like the Russian Revolution; most of our Marxists are in ivory towers at universities and don't like marching in the snow.

No, if Canadians decided to have a real political revolution it would probably be like the 1993 federal election – unpredictable (no one guessed that the governing Conservatives would go from 169 seats in 1988 to two seats in 1993), contradictory (what other country would elect a separatist Opposition to its federal parliament?), and organized from the bottom up (both the Bloc and Reform ran "populist style" campaigns).

Any revolution, to be truly Canadian, would also have to be "extremely moderate." In 1993, Canadians might have wanted a fiscal revolution to reduce the deficit and taxes, but at the end of the day, they chose to put Liberals, who hate balancing budgets, in charge of the process, just to be sure that the fiscal revolution wasn't carried to excess. Go figure!

But I am getting ahead of myself. In a bottom-up revolution, it is the local commanders and workers *in the field* who are most important, and it is the role of the leader and his team to help recruit them, supply them, support them, and, above all, inspire them. So let me share with you a few recollections of my role as Reform leader in the 1993 federal election, starting with my efforts to inspire candidates to pick up our banner.

■

It's the summer of 1993. Nominations and other preparations for the federal election expected in the fall are in full swing.

You are a fiscal conservative – you want the federal budget balanced, and you're tired of waiting for the federal Tories to do it. You are a discontented federalist – you want to make the government more responsive to the needs of your part of the country. You are a social conservative – you want a stronger commitment from your government to the well-being of the family and the preservation of law and order. You are a small-d democrat – you want to make federal politicians more accountable to electors. You are a reformer at heart – you want to "change the system." And you are thinking that maybe it's time for you to do more than merely talk about the need for change. Maybe it's time for you to get directly involved in the politics of your country.

Somehow your name has got onto my list as a "prospective candidate." I ask Virgil Anderson, our Coordinator of Election Readiness, to call you up and invite you to a two-day meeting in Ottawa. You come, we meet. I invite you, and several other prospective candidates, to come with me. I want to show you what it is that Reformers want to change in Ottawa.

We walk from our hotel to the Centre Block on Parliament Hill. It's summer. Parliament isn't sitting. There are lots of tourists, but we're not tourists. We're here on business – political business. We enter the Centre Block through the east door, walk up the stairs, and there it is – the Senate of Canada. See the nice Red Chamber?

It sleeps 108. Its priorities are Alcohol, Protocol, and Geritol. It's unelected, ineffective, inequitable, and unaccountable.* Reformers want to come to Ottawa to change that. Will you join us?

From the Senate chamber we walk down the hall to the main rotunda of the Centre Block. We turn right and go into Room 253D – the Railway Committee Room – where the Commons Finance Committee meets. See the sombre picture, on the north wall, of the monument at Vimy Ridge – a monument to self-sacrifice, to the loss of Canadian lives in the First World War. What does our generation of voters and politicians know about self-sacrifice? See the famous painting on the south wall. It's a composite of the meetings of the Fathers of Confederation at Quebec City and Charlottetown. That's John A. Macdonald standing. And that's Alexander Galt, sitting a few seats to the left of Macdonald and across from George Brown. Galt's job was less glamorous than Macdonald's but just as essential. As the first Finance minister after Confederation, he would have to figure out how to pay for the new country and its new government.

It is in this room – between the monument to self-sacrifice and the portrait of the Fathers – that the honourable members of the present Parliament meet to scrutinize the federal budget and its spending provisions. Under Liberal scrutiny, the cumulative effect of chronic overspending – the federal debt – grew to $170 billion. Under Conservative scrutiny, it has grown to almost $500 billion, with annual deficits of more than $30 billion. Maybe if we're nice the guard will show us where the committee keeps its rubber stamp.

Parliaments were invented to constrain the spending powers of kings and their successors. But despite all the Finance Committee meetings, hearings, reports, budget reviews, and scrutiny of spending, that's the one function that this Parliament and its committees have utterly failed to do. Reformers want to come to Ottawa to change that. Will you join us?

---

* In reality, this description of the Senate is a little too crude and one-sided. There are a few conscientious people in the Senate, although their presence tends to blur rather than clarify the need for reform. For a more balanced and detailed assessment of the state of the Canadian Senate, see my speech on this subject to the House of Commons, *Hansard*, April 20, 1998.

But let's hurry on. Back to the main rotunda, and turn right. Here we are at the House of Commons. The high temple of Canadian democracy. Right? The chamber where democratic representation and freedom of speech are held sacred. Right? Wrong! Years and years of excessive party discipline have made this House of the People into the House of the Parties. This House has become a place where voting is anything but free; a place where members are punished by the prime minister and the whips for voting in accordance with their constituents' wishes (on the GST, for example) and rewarded for voting against those wishes; a place where you can't propose alternative multicultural or immigration policies without being called a racist; a place where you can't question the wisdom of affirmative action programs without being called anti-women or anti-minority; a place where a "smart" remark in Question Period gets a national headline and a spot on the evening news, but where the continuous, daily violation of the great principles of freedom of voting and freedom of speech goes unnoticed, unreported, unchallenged, and uncorrected. Reformers want to come to Ottawa to change that. Will you join us?

Oh, I see that you were going to stop and get a drink from the water fountain. But I wouldn't do that if I were you. Many of the people who drink the water in here – members of Parliament in particular – end up with that Ottawa fever. Maybe your MP has some of the symptoms. First, the memory starts to go. Sufferers forget all those commitments that were made during the election. Then it's the hearing . . . it gets harder and harder to hear the voices of the folks back home. After a little while the head starts to swell, and that can be fatal. Reformers have a prescription for Ottawa fever – it's called recall, a process that would let constituents get rid of faulty MPs. Maybe you can help us get it included under Medicare.

It's time to go. But, oh yes, there are two fellow Reformers I'd like you to meet before we leave. Over here – just east of the Centre Block with their backs to the river, keeping a watchful eye over the Parliament – are the statues of Robert Baldwin and Louis LaFontaine, leaders of the old Reform parties of Upper and Lower Canada, the men who gave Canada responsible government. "Good morning, Bob. *Bonjour*, Louis." Whenever I come to Ottawa I always come here, to pay my respects, and to chase away the pigeons.

(These pigeons – they must be Liberal or Tory pigeons – are always crapping on Bob and Louis.)

In their day, these old Reformers were the underdogs. It was the colonial elites who had all the money and the power, who practised partisan patronage on a scale that would make Brian Mulroney and Jean Chrétien green with envy, who resisted every modest proposal to change the system and denounced Reformers as dangerous extremists and radicals. But time and history were on the side of reform, not the status quo. Responsible and representative governments prevailed over colonial government and the Family Compacts. Reformers like Baldwin and LaFontaine laid the foundations for a New Canada, the Canadian Confederation that replaced the old colonial order.

We want to rekindle the Reform flame on Parliament Hill. How about it? Will you join us?

■

With the Liberals there are two routes to getting a nomination – the bottom-up democratic route, in which you have to convince party members to vote for you at a constituency nominating meeting, and the top-down anti-democratic route, in which the leader simply appoints you as candidate, regardless of what the people in your constituency want. With Reform there is only one route – the bottom-up democratic route. But as leader of the party I am still vitally concerned about how candidate recruitment and nominations are handled. The quality and integrity of this activity will have a direct bearing not only on our electoral success but also on the quality and success of our performance in Parliament.

All Reform candidates are asked to complete a forty-page candidate questionnaire. Its purpose is to gain information on the background and abilities of the individuals seeking our nomination, and to encourage prospective candidates and their families to think through exactly what they are getting themselves into. It has always amazed me how some people are absolutely convinced that they want to be an MP when they have no idea about the nature of the job, the requisite knowledge and skills, the time and travel requirements, the need in many cases for two residences, and the strains on family, health, and finances that will be imposed upon them. In the early days of Reform, we found that some candidates, invariably men, would make the decision to seek a nomination without consulting their spouse, let alone other family members. We finally altered our candidate questionnaire to require the signature of the spouse on the completed form, in an attempt to ensure that the decision to run for public office was a family one, not an individual one.

We particularly reminded prospective candidates of the sad but oft-proven truth that if you are suffering from a financial problem, a marital problem, or a substance abuse problem, it will only get worse, not better, if you become a member of Parliament.

Many fine individuals are reluctant to enter the public arena because they are unwilling to subject themselves and their families to media and partisan abuse; or they don't believe that their participation can "make a difference"; or they are unwilling (this is particularly true of business executives, professionals, and entrepreneurs) to take a lower income or to put business assets in a blind trust.

Many of the women candidates we attempted to recruit were repelled by the intense partisanship that characterizes election campaigns, Question Period, and political discourse through the media, and the destruction this wreaks on interpersonal relations. "Until someone changes the system," they told us, "we don't want to be a part of it."

Candidate recruitment and nomination is a fundamental building block of any system of democratic governance. It is an area that I fervently believe all Canadian political parties must constantly seek to improve if we are to raise the quality of democracy and government in this country. In 1993, our Reform constituency associations for the most part did a credible job in encouraging competent people to seek our nominations. They sincerely tried to "do it better" than the traditional parties. Unfortunately, in the end it was a breakdown of the nomination process in *just one constituency* that cost Reform a breakthrough in Ontario in the election and the position of Official Opposition.

■

So there's this bottom-up revolution brewing in Canada, eh? Strange brew indeed. In November 1992, Canadians rejected the advice of their elites in the Charlottetown Accord referendum. Throughout 1992 and early 1993 they joined Reform (and the Bloc) in record numbers. Meanwhile public support for the governing Conservatives plummeted. In April 1993, with the PCs at 18 per cent in the polls, Prime Minister Mulroney announced that he would depart.

On March 25, 1993, in Vancouver, Kim Campbell, the Defence (and former Justice) minister in Brian Mulroney's cabinet, launched her campaign for the leadership of the federal Tory party. Kim's campaign theme was "the politics of inclusion."* Her chief opponent was Jean Charest, the Environment minister. The leadership vote was scheduled to take place at a national delegate convention in Ottawa on June 13.

In announcing her candidacy, Kim Campbell emphasized her "vision of democracy and politics." She seemed to be one of the few Conservative ministers who understood the defeat of Charlottetown, describing it as a public reaction to what Canadians perceived as "an elite process designed to make fundamental changes to their government." If Kim had persevered in expanding this theme, she might well have seriously eaten into our growing appeal with the electorate, particularly in Western Canada. Democratic reform, after all, had been one of our key themes from the inception of the Reform Party. We had long held the position that real, lasting reform could be achieved only if the federal political and parliamentary system was made more democratically accountable to Canadians.

But at this point Kim was competing more with Jean Charest than with Reformers. And the media failed to believe that her commitment to democratic reform was more than a passing campaign fancy. As she herself ruefully observed, "It seemed strange to me that issues that had generated the rise of the Reform Party, namely those relating to the credibility of the political process, seemed unimportant to the press covering the [leadership] campaign."

---

* Kim Campbell, *Time and Chance: The Political Memoirs of Canada's First Woman Prime Minister* (Toronto: Doubleday Canada, 1996).

From that point on, the Conservative leadership contest became more and more a contest of personalities. Wasn't Jean Charest the charismatic leader that federalists were looking for – the perfect answer to Lucien Bouchard? Wasn't Kim Campbell modern, bright, and *a woman*? Wouldn't it be marvellously progressive if the Conservative Party, not the Liberals, were to give Canada its first woman prime minister?

And so, in a country where federal spending, deficits, and debt were clearly out of control – and the governing "conservative" party was having a full-blown leadership contest – none of the candidates, including the front-runner, felt compelled to come to grips with the fiscal issues in a forceful and substantive way. What a golden opportunity for the Reform Party.

On March 29, 1993, in Toronto, I unveiled our "Zero in Three" plan. I began with the bad news. This year, the federal Conservatives would run a deficit of about $36 billion, their eighth in a row. Accumulated federal deficits had created a "debt hole" $460 billion deep. If you wanted to get out of a hole, the first thing to do was to Stop Digging!

Then the good news: Zero in Three, our plan to stop the digging and eliminate the deficit in three years. Assuming that federal revenues increased modestly over the next three years, we proposed the following: we would keep federal funding at current levels for health care, education, child benefits, guaranteed income supplements, and veterans' pensions. Then we proposed to place contributory programs like the Canada Pension Plan and Unemployment Insurance on a self-sustaining basis, and to refocus non-contributory programs such as Old Age Security on those Canadians whose incomes were below the national average. Finally, we wanted to reduce federal transfers to individuals and provinces, reduce subsidies to business and special interests, identify waste, and reduce spending on federal administration and other programs. Total annual savings: $19 billion.

For the next two weeks, our candidates and I spoke "with one voice" on Zero in Three. We put out a letter to our 130,000 members that described the plan and asked them to share it with their neighbours. We invited Reformers to order bulk copies of a cheap version to distribute door to door in almost two hundred federal ridings. Of course, much of the initial reaction, from sources close to the government, was negative. That's always the reaction of the Canadian political establishment to any proposal or idea "not forged in their own furnace and hammered on their own anvil." But the public response, and that of some media, was positive. Reformers had always been labelled as "policy wonks" – strong on substance, short on style – so this was encouraging. We persevered!

Federal Finance minister Don Mazankowski presented the last budget of the Mulroney administration on April 26. We watched closely. The federal Tories, in preparation for the upcoming election, might actually have brought in a genuine deficit-cutting budget. But five minutes into the 1993 Budget Speech we knew it wasn't going to happen. In contrast to our plan for Zero Deficit in Three Years, the federal PCs planned to increase the federal deficit to $35.5 – $1 billion more than their projection in December of the previous year, $8 billion more than they had projected one year previously, and $15.5 billion more than they had projected five years previously. I felt sorry for Mazankowski. He never received the recognition he deserved for doing much of the "heavy lifting" for the Mulroney regime.

Just as our Zero in Three campaign was winding down, the Tory leadership convention was held in Ottawa. Ian Todd and I attended as observers. Friday, June 11, focused on policy forums, but these were of little substance, set up to showcase the leadership contestants, not to firm up the policy foundation on which the PCs would fight the next election. Friday night was devoted to a final tribute to the Mulroneys. It was overdone, just as much of the criticism of Mulroney was overdone. It will take time to cool the passions on both sides and arrive at a fair assessment of Brian Mulroney's place in our history. Saturday featured the big speeches from each of the candidates. Jean Charest delivered a campaign-style speech, assuring the delegates that "the Bloc is a crock," and Kim Campbell read a "prime ministerial" speech.

Finally, it was decision-making time. After two rounds, Kim Campbell had 1,817 votes to Jean Charest's 1,630. The new prime minister, and the leader that I would be competing most directly against in the federal election, was a Western-based Conservative, Kim Campbell.

Both of us had conducted national campaigns during the preceding three months. The personality-driven campaign to choose a prime minister had captured most of the national headlines, while our "issue campaign" was given little attention by the media. In fact, coverage of Reform's activities – particularly in the national and urban media – had slowed to a trickle since the Charlottetown days. Pundits began to predict Reform's demise. *Sun* columnist Sean Durkin wrote about our "struggle to recapture days of former glory" and the "desperation and worry" that had set into our camp. This was a source of frustration for our new candidates, who felt that Reform's Zero in Three plan was resonating well with the public. Perhaps the media was missing a big story? Time would tell which campaign – Reform's Zero in Three program or the Conservative leadership campaign – ultimately had more relevance for the future.

■

On July 9 and 10, 1993, all our key people from across the country came to an election planning meeting that took place in the boardroom of Cliff Fryers's Calgary law office, while the Calgary Stampede festivities were in full swing on the street below. An entire day was spent on campaign strategy – assessing the strengths and weaknesses of our opponents as well as our own, planning the organization of the War Room and Leader's Tour, reviewing candidate recruitment and preparation, and analyzing polling data.

Our immediate objective was to "break through" and win a substantial number of seats in Parliament. No matter how down-and-dirty our opponents became, we would stick to the high road. We would run a campaign rooted in principles and policies, not personalities. Our aim would be to polarize the electorate. It would be "Reform and the people versus the political elites and traditional parties" – "us versus them."

Our main themes would be the economy (Zero in Three), criminal justice ("re-balancing priorities"), and political reform ("change the system"). Our campaign would roll through three phases: "Let the People Speak," "Let the People Compare (the options)," and "Let the People Choose" (choose Reform). We anticipated that we'd run into problems with credibility, visibility, morale, and money (these were all tied together); with the predicaments that inexperienced candidates might find themselves in; and possibly with questions about the role Reform would play if the election produced a minority government.

My job was to inspire and motivate our own troops, and to gain public support through the communications opportunities presented by the Leader's Tour. Execution of the plan would need to be a team effort. Virgil Anderson had organized an "election pool," and we each made our best guess as to how many seats Reform might win. Tom Flanagan, as I recall, was pessimistic, saying we might win seven. Virgil was wildly optimistic, hoping for eighty or more. My guess was fifty.

Only one small, dark cloud hung over the planning session. Its origins lay in whether we should "think big" or "think small." Tom Flanagan was conscious of our low standing in the polls. Both he and Stephen Harper wanted us to focus most of our campaign revenues and activity in the West. The rest of us felt it was imperative that we run a bigger, more national campaign, in particular, one that included Ontario. This was what our members had asked for when they voted for eastward expansion.

In the end, we decided to run a national campaign, which meant we needed a campaign director with national experience. Rick Anderson was the natural choice. Most of the people who had run national campaigns for the federal Liberals and Conservatives wouldn't touch us in 1993. Rick, however, was different. He had gained his national campaign experience with the federal Liberals but had been with us since 1991. (We had all belonged to other parties before joining Reform.) Rick and his wife, Michelle, believed in our cause and had helped found the Reform Constituency Association in the eastern Ontario riding where they lived.

During the Charlottetown referendum, Rick had been identified with the "Yes" side. At the time, he was employed by Hill and Knowlton, the consulting and government relations firm. Almost all of his major corporate clients were on the "Yes" side, and it would have put Rick in a serious conflict if he had publicly taken an opposite position. Of course, this caused some consternation among our people. But Rick had accepted the public's judgment on Charlottetown and was prepared to move on. And far from having reservations about our strategy for the 1993 election, Rick was enthusiastic about making our democracy-based campaign succeed.

Stephen and Tom had never forgiven Rick for being on the "wrong side" of Charlottetown. But the problem with getting Stephen to accept Rick and the challenges of a national campaign went deeper. Stephen had difficulty accepting that there might be a few other people (not many, perhaps, but a few) who were as smart as he was with respect to policy and strategy. And Stephen, at this point, was not really prepared to be a team player or team builder.

In any event, in the summer of 1993 Stephen was adamant that Rick Anderson not be our campaign director, and he was prepared to air his objections in the media. We discussed the situation with our candidate representatives across the country. They unanimously endorsed the national campaign organization as proposed, with Rick Anderson as director. They suggested that a group of Alberta candidates appeal to Stephen to reconcile his differences with Rick. In due course, a group including Jim Silye, Bob Mills, Ian McClelland, Diane Ablonczy, and Ray Speaker met with Stephen. Their message was, "We want Rick on the team. We want you on the team." But Stephen refused to budge. He withdrew from the national campaign effort to work almost exclusively on his personal campaign for election in Calgary West. This was a blow to our overall campaign effort, and it put more of a burden on those who had to fill the gap left by his withdrawal.

■

On Monday, September 8, 1993, Kim Campbell announced October 25 as the date for the general election. The campaign had officially begun.

We started out with an exceptional campaign team – democracy is a team sport – and these are some of the members who made it work.

Ian Todd, my personal assistant, is quiet, reliable, tireless, faithful, and infallibly attentive to every detail. He could have been making far more money with far less frustration doing something else (his family owns and operates an oil and gas company), but Ian is 100 per cent dedicated to the Reform cause and to me, and we could not have gotten along without him.

Cliff Fryers, a stern-looking man and one of the best tax lawyers in Calgary, is better at chairing a meeting than anyone I've met. He has been chairman of everything for Reform, and now was acting as chairman of our election campaign team. He can be tough as nails, intimidating to those who don't know him, but he has a heart of gold. The friendship of Cliff and his wife, Leslie, an equally talented lawyer and a lovely person, is priceless to Sandra and me.

Rick Anderson, a friendly man with a blond beard, is one of the best political strategists in the country. He has excellent communication skills, knows the national media, and was the only member of our team with national campaign experience. He lived just outside of Ottawa with his down-to-earth wife, Michelle, and their family. They joined us at a time when most of the political brains in Ottawa wouldn't touch us with a ten-foot poll. Sandra and I have profound respect for Rick and Michelle and a deep appreciation for their friendship.

And then there were the Three Musketeers. They managed virtually every big convention, media event, and meeting I was involved in, and they coordinated the Leader's Tour in this campaign. Daphne Pirie organized "luncheons for the curious" in Calgary when we first started out. Mary-Jane Shaw did anything that needed to be done, from raising money to keeping membership lists to operating a free "bed and breakfast" for itinerant Reformers in her home in Vancouver. Finally, the third Musketeer was Ellen Todd, also known as Napoleon because she organized events as if they were military operations. She is Ian Todd's mother; the whole family supported Reform from its inception. Daphne, Mary-Jane, and Ellen were committed, able, tireless friends and volunteers whose contribution to Reform and support for Sandra and me were valuable beyond measure.

There were many other important members of the team in that election. Gordon Shaw, husband of Mary-Jane, a retired Imperial

Oil executive and founding member of the party, had recruited Deborah Grey as a Reform candidate. Fraser Smith, a businessman from the West Coast, moved to Calgary for the entire campaign to run our War Room. Daphne Pirie's husband, Jack (of Sabre Energy), was a strong supporter in every way from day one. Jennifer Grover, Bob van Wegen, Dimitri Pantazopoulos, Al McGirr, Ron Wood, and Bryan Thomas helped to find the right themes, facts, words, and images by which to communicate the Reform message to the public. There were all the support staff at the national office – Glenn McMurray in charge of the books, Diana Rodwell organizing the volunteers, Virgil Anderson, Neil Weir, and Ken Suitor supporting the candidate recruitment and nomination activities of the constituencies. And then there was Harry Robinson, my personal campaign manager in Calgary Southwest, who had to run a campaign with an absentee candidate.

So many people contributed to the national campaign – working with and organizing the volunteers, opening and processing piles of mail, packaging and shipping candidate materials all over the country, and fielding endless numbers of phone calls from the public. And they, in turn, represented only a fraction of the thousands of other volunteers across the country who donated their time and energy to the Reform cause.

I didn't fully realize it at the time – and I don't suppose that they knew it either – but when all the campaigning and politicking and reforming was over, it wouldn't be the speeches or the headlines or the crowds that we would remember. It would be each other – the team, the family, the friendships that were forged and strengthened in the furnace of democratic politics – that we would treasure.

■

This was the first Reform campaign in which representatives of the national media were actually assigned to cover us. At first, only nine media people signed up to ride on our less-than-fancy campaign bus. The big news was supposedly over there with Kim's team, and Reform still ranked fourth in the editorial lineup. Personality, not substance, was still the main draw in this campaign.

A few, like CBC soundman Dwayne Williams and CBC cameraman Herb Tyler, stuck with us for the whole forty-seven days. Herb became an unofficial wagon-master, suggesting where scrums should be held to get the best visuals, and warning us (on a long stop-and-go ride down the Malahat Highway on Vancouver Island) that the brakes on the bus were going to go if the driver didn't start making more use of the gear shift.

One reporter – the CBC's Kevin Tibbles, at that time quite junior in rank – was among the first to sense that Reform just might be "the little engine that could." He presented a piece on the dedication of our volunteers, showing our bus stopping on a highway in B.C. where volunteers were waiting to give us box lunches. The CBC brass must have felt he was going soft on us, because he disappeared from our campaign and was replaced by Paul Adams. But Kevin's instincts were right, and by the end of the campaign twenty-seven media people had joined our campaign tour.

Our transportation arrangements for the media were not the fanciest. By the midpoint of the campaign we had replaced the bus on one swing through the West with two small planes rented from Ken Borek Air. One night, after a rally in Moose Jaw, the media plane somehow got off the runway and became stuck in the gumbo. The media people on hand, who had been imbibing a little and were in a jolly mood, all piled out and endeavoured to push the stranded aircraft out of the mud. All to no avail. Finally a Reform volunteer with a pickup truck pulled the plane back on the runway, but word got around that the Reform campaign tour was "different."

Fortunately, some of the media became intrigued by our "let the people speak" meetings, not because they had suddenly become enamoured with Reform or grassroots democracy, but because covering such meetings was like covering a game of Russian roulette. Nobody, including ourselves, had any idea what people might actually say once we opened up the mikes to the crowds.

We were at the first of our "Let the People Speak" rallies at St. Joseph High School in Edmonton. I had just a stool and a hand-held mike. I wanted to get the audience to tell me what they thought this election should be about. Not surprisingly, the majority of the comments were not about policy issues but about politicians. "Politicians never listen to anybody." "They think too much in the short range rather than the long term." "Everybody talks a really good game when they want to get elected." "They promise anything we want to hear, but I don't believe them."

Similar sentiments were expressed in meetings across the country – sometimes in the form of jokes. From B.C.: "What's the difference between a dead skunk and a dead politician on the Coquihalla Highway? There are skid marks in front of the skunk." From Ottawa: "What do you call ten politicians at the bottom of the Rideau Canal? A start!" And from Saskatchewan: "How many politicians does it take to grease a combine? Fourteen, if you put them through very, very slowly."

In this election, we had 207 candidates and their support networks, a national team approaching 100 people, and 60 student groups at campuses across the country. Add to that the 130,000-plus members of Reform who took to the streets to change their country and you start to understand the meaning of "grassroots."

Each volunteer supported the campaign in his or her own way. Retired pensioners handed out lawn signs from the backs of their trucks. Young people delivered flyers, business people worked the phones, and grandmothers waved signs at the side of the highway. Families joined together for Trans-Canada convoys and cavalcades. Young parents held coffee parties for their neighbourhoods. People who had never been involved in politics before, but were "mad at Ottawa," helped to raise the $5 million we need to campaign, $10 at a time. And students plastered posters around campuses, participated in feisty debates, and cheerfully devoured pizza at midnight while preparing to do it all again the next day.

Nothing seemed to dampen their resolve. Not the attacks of our opponents, not the long days of campaigning, not the sacrifice of family time for the cause. I felt quite sure that all this enthusiasm would serve me well as one big support system when the going got tough. The "grassroots" nature of this campaign exceeded my wildest hopes. But this is what democracy ought to be about – a bottom-up revolution that involves the direct participation of the people whose futures are at stake.

■

About halfway through the second week of the campaign, it was time to change tactics. We called our second phase "Let the People Compare." This was where we would contrast our positions on three major issues with those of our opponents. We picked the three biggest concerns expressed by Canadians over the past few years, and again during the "Let the People Speak" phase of the campaign: jobs, crime, political accountability.

First we compared the Reform approach to tax relief from our Zero in Three plan to the Conservative and Liberal platforms. We wanted to "put money back into the working man's pocket," the Liberals wanted to take it out of your pocket, and the Conservatives talked like us but acted like the Liberals.

Then we compared our proposals for safer streets, homes, and schools through criminal justice reforms, under the theme of "Restoring the Balance," to those of the Conservatives and the Liberals. We wanted to fix the Young Offenders Act and the parole and sentencing systems and place more emphasis on victims of crime. The Conservatives had had their chance to reform the criminal justice system but had failed to do so. For the Liberals, it was not really a priority.

And finally, we were committed to making politicians more accountable through tangible parliamentary and democratic reforms like recall, more free votes, and a reformed Senate. To get attention, we used the theme: "So you don't trust politicians? Neither do we." This one really hit home when we applied it to the PCs and Liberals, each with an appalling record in the areas of accountability and integrity.

These three themes were presented to Canadians in public meetings and debates, and in our grassroots campaign literature and TV ads. On the ground, it was the Reform candidates who did the comparing, and they got a pretty good reception.

The national leader's campaign continued to focus on the federal deficit and presented our Zero in Three plan as the solution. But we didn't have the horsepower to impose our agenda on a federal election campaign dominated by the traditional parties; we had to play off their initiatives and mistakes. This is where Rick Anderson's experience and abilities were particularly helpful.

With unemployment at around 11 per cent in Canada, the economy and jobs topped the list of people's concerns. Not surprisingly then, on the very first day of the campaign, Kim Campbell was asked a question about unemployment. In her reply, she dwelt on the difficulties, not the possibilities, of reducing Canada's unemployment rate. The Liberals immediately spun these remarks to mean that the Conservatives did not believe unemployment could be reduced until the year 2000. Reformers might have been playing Russian roulette with our "Let the People Speak" approach, but the Conservatives were the first to shoot themselves in the foot. A few weeks later they would shoot themselves in the knee by mishandling the deficit issue. By the end of the campaign, they would be shooting themselves in vital organs.

If "jobs, jobs, jobs" was the problem, as Chrétien maintained, what was the solution? According to the Liberal Red Book, unveiled on September 15, the federal government would need to take the lead in "creating jobs" by spending taxpayers' money – in particular, $2 billion on an infrastructure development program to which the provinces and municipalities were expected to contribute equal amounts. It was amazing to me that commentators who accused Reform of offering "simplistic solutions to complex problems" could swallow the grossly inadequate proposal that structural and cyclical unemployment in Canada could be solved by a $2-billion federal investment in infrastructure.

My response was to say that if a $700-billion economy can be stimulated in this way, you could also jump-start a 747 aircraft with a flashlight battery. And if government spending was the key to job creation, everyone in Canada should have had two jobs already. In an economy like Canada's, where the vast majority of wealth-creating jobs are in the non-governmental sector, then surely removing the barriers to private-sector job creation (like high taxes fuelled by out-of-control spending) would be a more effective way of dealing with unemployment.

This is the "conservative" approach to job creation. Logically, then, the new prime minister and leader of Canada's traditional conservative party should have come down hard on the federal spending and deficit issues during the election campaign. But no such thing happened. During her leadership campaign, Kim Campbell had made a pledge to balance the budget in five years. Now, she came under pressure to supply details concerning how this would be done. On September 20, Campbell announced that she would release some of these details, including a consideration of social spending. But only three days later she refused to discuss the substance of the issue: "You can't have a debate on such a key issue as the modernization of social programs in forty-seven days. . . . [An election campaign] is the worst possible time to have that discussion . . . because it takes more than forty-seven days to settle anything that serious."*

On September 27, Campbell attempted to put some deficit numbers on the table. But her figures didn't add up, and it was evident that her grasp of this issue was shaky. One would have thought that the leader of a conservative party and government would have had a grasp of this issue superior to that of any other political leader and party. But, as Campbell herself acknowledged in her autobiography, neither she nor the government was "up to speed" on this issue at all. And their efforts to become so, during the heat of an election campaign, proved to be too little too late.

Over the next three weeks, we made the federal deficit and our plans for eliminating it the centrepiece of the Leader's Tour and our advertising. An editorial in the *Globe and Mail* helped our cause – it was the best review Reform had received to date. It summarized Zero in Three in considerable detail, described it as "the only deficit plan we've seen," and challenged the other parties to match it. Our candidate network had already latched on to it, and by the weekend after it was published tens of thousands of copies were being handed out at doors across the country.

But not all the feedback was positive. The traditional parties accused us of wanting to "slash and burn" social programs, which was untrue. And it was difficult to explain quickly and simply to voters how getting spending and debt levels under control would lead to better job opportunities – that lasting jobs with good salaries are created by the private sector, and that process is dampened by

---

* "PM won't touch key issue," *Globe and Mail*, September 24, 1993.

high taxes and debts. The Liberals' simplistic "create jobs through public spending" was far easier to communicate.

In interpreting political campaigns "after the fact," it is very easy to be strategically wise. "We saw this opportunity," (e.g., Kim Campbell's vacating the deficit field), "and we seized it. Weren't we clever?!" In reality, such opportunities are never so evident as they might be made to appear in retrospect. A real campaign is a blur of activity, a cacophony of noise and confusing signals that no one fully controls. The campaign headquarters is a command post under siege. The candidate campaigns are a flurry of non-stop activity. A Leader's Tour has been described as "a moving bubble." Carefully constructed feedback loops are helpful, but their signals are also subject to a variety of interpretations.

Planning, strategy, logic are all important to the success or failure of a campaign – but so are intuition, experience, unexpected opportunities, hard work, and blind luck. That is why it is always possible to say to the strategic thinker (and I consider myself to be one), "If your strategic insights were so clear and accurate in Campaign A, which you won, what happened to them in Campaign B, which you lost?" A good question, to keep us humble.

■

Most people pay very little attention to federal politics, even during the initial stages of a federal election campaign. But about three weeks before the election, public interest begins to quicken, sparked by the leaders' debates and the considerable media attention they attract.

After long and arduous negotiations (handled for us by Cliff Fryers), we were invited to participate in the English-language debate scheduled for Monday, October 4, in Ottawa. On Friday, October 1, we travelled to Ottawa for three days of preparation, and on Saturday morning we met to plan our approach. We needed to work on my opening and closing remarks and to anticipate key questions from the media panel, as well as the tactics and responses of the other leaders. Our team was fairly confident in my ability to handle the issues. They wanted to focus on improving my style and presentation skills. This was an area where I needed all the help I could get. In addressing public audiences, I tended to start slow and finish strong. For the leaders' debates I needed to be strong from the outset. I also had a tendency to be "too polite" and would hold back instead of vigorously interjecting myself into the discussion. This hesitancy can be fatal in a five-person debate where everyone is clamouring for attention.

We spent some time discussing the "defining moment" possibilities. The primary interest of the media, in covering leaders' debates, is to identify a "defining moment" in which a leader makes a serious gaffe, or another leader scores a "knockout blow." Our strategy was for me to look and sound credible, stick to our issues, correct some of the misconceptions about Reform, and generally stake out the high ground. Media expectations of me were fairly low, which was good. Maybe we could surprise them. It was Kim Campbell who was under pressure; the best a prime minister can hope for in these debates is a draw.

On Sunday we held two practice sessions. Allan McGirr, our communications director, set up a mock studio – five podiums, complete with lights and video cameras to "televise" our practice session. Our team members played the parts of Kim, Jean, Lucien, and Audrey. There was a lot of horsing around and the mood was upbeat. In the last election we'd been excluded from the leaders' debates; we were happy just to be there.

I found these sessions uncomfortable, mainly because I am not a very good actor. I felt self-conscious "pretending" to debate when I knew it wasn't the real thing. And I felt the mounting pressure. My colleagues, friends, and supporters across the country wanted so desperately for me – for us – to do well. Nevertheless, the experience was helpful in forcing me to focus on style and presentation as well as content, and in anticipating the arguments and tactics of our opponents.

On Monday evening, after a "light" day in which I rested up, it was finally time to walk the short distance from the hotel to the Ottawa Conference Centre.

■

Sandra and I hold hands, Sandra cheerful and encouraging as always. Rick and Cliff spot a white rabbit – is it a good or bad omen? Ian is clutching our "game ball" – a football we picked up to relieve the tension. It will soon assume legendary status in our party as a good-luck charm.

Earlier in the day, Ian participated in the "draws" that decided the speaking order and where we would stand on stage. I will be positioned in the middle, flanked by Jean Chrétien and Kim Campbell to my right and Lucien Bouchard and Audrey McLaughlin to my left. I will speak first in the opening round for one minute, and have one minute again for concluding remarks.

We enter the Conference Centre. Ian, as always, has "advanced the venue" and knows the way. After my session in makeup, there is time to kill. Rick gives his parting advice and leaves to join the rest of our group. Cliff stays with Sandra and me in the dressing room.

Rick, Ian, and Al start to flip the football around. While they are thus harmlessly engaged, the Prime Minister and her team of very important persons swirl by en route to her dressing room. "You boys shouldn't be playing in here," she says.

I enter the studio feeling ready, but also feeling the pressure of high expectations, knowing that Reformers are glued to their television sets. I don't want to let them down. Anne Medina, the host, invites me to deliver my opening comments. I do, noting that this is the first time in decades that the leaders of the old-line parties have been challenged on the national stage by political newcomers. The reason for this, I say, is that many Canadians are not happy with what the old parties are offering and want a fresh alternative. I invite viewers to watch the debates carefully and decide which leaders deal with the problems only by addressing the symptoms, and which one gets to root causes and offers common-sense solutions.

The debate proceeds, back and forth. There are questions from the audience. I am beginning to relax.

The worst moment for Kim Campbell comes when Lucien Bouchard demands to know the federal deficit for the last fiscal year, and Campbell is unable to answer. For fiscal conservatives, the inability of the leader of a conservative government to handle the deficit issue is the unpardonable sin that is driving many of them into our camp. The irony is that Lucien knows – and cares – less about the federal deficit than Campbell does.

I conclude my remarks by presenting the notion that if there is to be a defining moment in this election, it should be based on what is real and relevant, and not on political posturing. "Let the defining moment in this election be the moment when you go into the polling booth alone, without television, without radio, without a newspaper, and vote with the courage of conviction for what is right for yourself, your children, and your country." These are truly words from the heart, and I say them with conviction.

At last it's over. We shake hands with everyone. The Prime Minister knows it has not gone well for her. Our own assessment is that I made no serious mistakes, but could have been more aggressive. The general assessment of the debate by the media is that no one really won . . . or lost, and that none of the five party leaders has given an exceptional performance. A bronze medal for everyone. How Canadian!

■

After the debates, as we continued along the campaign trail, we felt the tide turning. A wave of support was building across the country. The standing ovations were becoming more frequent and lasting longer. Momentum was building, and the media were intrigued – not just the local and rural media, but the networks and the national papers. Now they wanted to join us on the bus. Our tour organizers back home scrambled to accommodate the additional journalists, reporters, and crews. Things were going our way. But in an election campaign, you never know what might happen next.

According to a compilation of polls conducted throughout the election by Angus Reid, Gallup, Environics, Ekos, and ComQuest/ Globe, and published after the election, Reform reached its point of highest support – 19 per cent nationally and more than 20 per cent in Ontario – around October 8. Reform's support had doubled since the election was called. The Reform Party also recorded its lowest level of support – 14 per cent – towards the end of the week of October 13. In other words, with little more than two weeks to election day, Reform had the support and momentum to win at least fifty seats in the West, break through in Ontario, and form the Official Opposition. But something happened on or around October 13 to break that momentum. That "something" is remembered in Reform circles as "the Beck affair," and I am reminded of it to this day every time I am in Toronto and see an orange-and-green Beck taxi.

On Wednesday, October 13, I met with Joe Peschisolido, our candidate for Etobicoke North. We did a talk show at CHIN radio and then made our way to the Osgoode Hall Law School at York University, Joe's old alma mater, for a noon meeting with students and faculty. We met the dean in her office and proceeded to the lecture hall. I was introduced and began to speak, but I was interrupted by students. They read excerpts from an interview in their student newspaper with Reform candidate John Beck, candidate in York Centre. The statements attributed to Mr. Beck – on immigration, same-sex couples, youth crime, and the environment – ranged from the extreme to the bizarre, and if left unchallenged would have confirmed every negative stereotype of Reform painted by our opponents.

I had never met Mr. Beck, but the statements attributed to him by the students bore no resemblance whatsoever to Reform Party principles or policies. I told the meeting I would investigate and take action, but the damage was done and the media smelled blood. We holed up in the dean's office, where Rick and Ian got on the phones to Cliff and Virgil in Calgary. This candidate had to go. We would find out later how he got through our safeguards. We emerged from the dean's office into a huge scrum. I confirmed that the students' allegations concerning Beck's remarks were substantially accurate and that he had resigned as our candidate in York Centre.

The party's subsequent investigation of the Beck affair revealed that, in a last-minute effort to make sure Reform had more than two hundred nominated candidates including a candidate in every riding in Ontario, the party's elaborate safeguards to protect us against undesirable candidates had been bypassed in a few of the weakest Toronto ridings. The constituency association that nominated Mr. Beck had only a handful of members. There had been no real candidate search. Mr. Beck had volunteered to let his name stand. His candidate questionnaire had not been properly scrutinized by our campaign people. The constituency association had found out about his bizarre views only after his nomination papers had been filed. Mr. Beck's candidacy had slipped through the cracks.

One serious breakdown in our candidate nomination process, coming to light as it did at the most critical time in the federal election campaign, did enormous damage. That most precious of commodities in the latter stages of a campaign – momentum – had been lost. Not only did the Beck affair do damage to the momentum of our national campaign, but it also impacted negatively on the closely fought local campaigns of dozens of our best Ontario candidates.

Reform candidates in Ontario who had been on their way to winning their seats by 500 to 1,000 votes ended up losing those seats by similar margins. In our post-election analysis of what went wrong in Ontario, "the Beck affair" was the most frequently mentioned cause. I can only repeat that the integrity of a democratic political party's nomination process is critical to maintaining the integrity of its principles, image, and campaign efforts, and later, its parliamentary performance. Reformers learned this lesson the hard way in 1993.

■

Despite the setback, we had no time to cry over spilt milk. We were operating on coffee and adrenaline, and there was little opportunity to reflect on our mistakes. We were into the last ten days of the campaign, our "Make Your Vote Count" phase, and it involved a series of big election rallies from Halifax to Victoria. For this last phase of the campaign we chartered an Air Nova plane nicknamed "Winds of Change" by one of our stalwart national office volunteers, Gordon Burroughs.

At the Halifax rally on October 18, my theme was "Back to the Liberals or Forward with Reform?" In Ottawa, Toronto, and London my stump speech was built around the question "How Will Ontario Decide?" Old federalism or new federalism? Fiscal irresponsibility or fiscal responsibility? A separatist Official Opposition or a federalist

Official Opposition? Succumbing to the politics of fear, or embracing the politics of hope?

In returning to Toronto, we returned to the scene of the Beck debacle. But on the positive side (for us), the wheels were falling off the Conservative campaign. On October 15, the PCs aired a TV ad targeted at Chrétien that appeared to ridicule his facial features and was met with universal censure. On October 17, Cabinet minister Bernard Valcourt proposed firing the entire Conservative campaign team and replacing it with a team of Cabinet ministers for the final week. And on October 19, Isabel Bassett, one of the PCs' star Toronto candidates, wrote an open letter cutting her local campaign free of the national PC campaign.

Our Toronto rally, held in the Metro East Trade Centre, was our largest of the campaign to date, as 4,500 people jammed into this vast hall – missing the Toronto Blue Jays' World Series game – to consider new options for their country. Everyone in attendance at this rally believed we would win seats in Ontario.

On October 20, after another rally in London, we made a brief stop in Brandon, Manitoba, before flying on to Calgary. In Calgary, I was once again on home turf, but disturbed by reports from the ridings, where the handwriting was on the wall for Conservative incumbents, that the campaign had turned vicious. In my riding of Calgary Southwest, for example, Tory workers were going to the nursing homes and seniors' residences, taking old and sick pensioners by the hand, and telling them that if Reform was elected we would take away their pensions and their health care.

The national media and political establishment were outraged at the Conservatives' attack ad on Chrétien. But why was it that even more vicious tactics aimed at Reform evoked no similar outrage? Why the silence when Sheila Copps compared me with David Duke of the Ku Klux Klan, or when old-line party hacks intimidated sick and elderly voters with the most despicable lies? Why the double standard? In the end, the attacks backfired in the West, where Reform was best known. But in Ontario and other parts of the country many of those accusations were damaging.

The campaign was winding down. We were sprinting to the finish line: an address to the Calgary Chamber of Commerce, a series of meetings in B.C., and a great boisterous rally at the Butter Dome on the University of Alberta campus in Edmonton – our largest of the campaign. Voters were coming out by the thousands to see us.

If only we had had the advantage of daily rolling polls (we couldn't afford them) in our Alberta ridings, we would have known that we were within a hair's breadth of taking three more Edmonton ridings. I could have spent one more day campaigning in Edmonton, but as it was, we went on to Red Deer for a great central Alberta rally – an area where we already had all the seats sewn up. Had we taken those three Edmonton seats, Reform, not the Bloc, would have formed the Opposition in the thirty-fifth Parliament.

Finally it was back to Calgary on Sunday, October 24, for the last official Reform rally of the 1993 federal election campaign. We arrived at the Stampede Corral where a crowd of several thousand was waiting. Workers, candidates, supporters, and ordinary citizens were gathered there, chanting, singing, and waving flags. Lights were dimmed and the music turned up. Sandra and I stepped onto the stage with our candidates. The crowd roared. We were having fun.

I was on my last reserves, but I felt energized by the sheer enthusiasm of the crowd. I offered my thanks to everyone for their work: to our campaign team, our candidates, our constituency workers, our volunteers, our staff. I delivered the rallying cry: "If you want to teach the old-line parties – the one that has failed you and the other one that has betrayed you – a lesson they will never forget, in the only language they will ever understand, then elect Reformers to Parliament. In this election, make your vote count."

■

On the evening of Monday, October 25, we assemble at a suite in the Four Seasons Hotel in downtown Calgary. Sandra, our children, and Cliff and Leslie, Rick and Michelle, Ian, Ellen, Virgil, Woody, Gordon, and Mary-Jane – the core of our campaign and national office teams – are with us. Rick and Cliff have been on the phones. The Tories are gone – a complete rout. The Liberals are in. The Bloc is doing very well in Quebec. And in Ontario, lots of votes for Reform, but we lead in only two seats, and both are very tentative.

Before the night is over, 982,691 Ontarians will have voted for Reform, we will finish second in fifty-seven ridings, and Ed Harper from Simcoe Centre will become our first Ontario MP. We had hoped we would win more seats in Ontario; we must settle for one. Everything now hinges on the Western results.

The polls close in Manitoba and Saskatchewan – five seats for Reform! Now it's Alberta. Good old Alberta – ever willing to take a chance on something new. The Eastern commentators, who have been explaining Reform as a "rural protest movement," check their notes as all six seats in Calgary, Canada's most dynamic and forward-looking city (I'm prejudiced), go to Reform. I am elected in Calgary Southwest, thanks to the efforts of Harry Robinson's team and almost 1,000 volunteers.

A huge roar goes up from the assembled crowd at MacLeod Hall in the Calgary Convention Centre as the Calgary results are posted and a sea of Reform green sweeps across the television map. And then the B.C. results start to come in. More great news. Before the night is out, twenty-four of B.C.'s thirty-two seats will have gone Reform.

It is clear that the Liberals will form the government, but who will form the Opposition? The Bloc has fifty-four seats and we have fifty-two; but three seats in Edmonton are bouncing back and forth. If we win all three, we beat the Bloc; if we win two, we're tied (and we will argue that the tie goes to the federalists). At the Calgary Saddledome, where an NHL game is in progress, they are posting the results on the scoreboard, and there are whoops when we briefly appear to be tied with the Bloc, and groans when we drop behind.

In the end, we lose all three seats in Edmonton by a total (after recounts) of 329 votes. Don't ever let me hear anyone say that their vote doesn't count. In this case, the votes of a few hundred people would have made the difference between a federalist and separatist Official Opposition in the Canadian Parliament.

Finally, it becomes clear that we have secured fifty-two seats in the House of Commons, Ottawa, Canada. A breakthrough!

It's getting late and the media desks are starting to close down. We'd better hurry if we want any national coverage of our victory celebrations.

Ian hands me the phone, saying that it is the Prime Minister on the line. I almost commit a terrible faux pas; I am already thinking it is Prime Minister Jean Chrétien and almost say, "*Felicitations*, Jean." But actually it is Kim Campbell on the line, Prime Minister for at least a few more days. I thank her for her congratulations, but don't know what else I can say. She is more the inheritor than the author of tonight's devastating defeat. Thank you, Kim, and good night.

Sandra and I make our way to MacLeod Hall, where a great crowd of Calgarians has assembled. Jorge Avilés sings "O Canada" the way it ought to be sung. We're escorted through the crowd by our team and RCMP officers Phil Northrup, Bill Neary, and Carmen McKnight, with whom we have developed a lasting friendship. The cameras and lights move in to form a tight, moving circle. We want to embrace our workers, grasp the hands of our supporters, and savour these moments among so many friends. The new MPs are introduced. I say a few words of thanks and a few words to the media: "Reformers, we are on our way! This is what our dream has done."

When the last Parliament was dissolved, the standings were PCs 152, Liberals 79, NDP 43, Bloc 8, Reform 1, Independents 2, Vacancies 10. Tonight when the smoke finally clears from the ballot boxes, the standings in the new Parliament will be PCs 2, Liberals 177, Bloc 54, Reform 52, NDP 9, Independent 1.

There's only one way to describe what's happened. Revolution, eh?

5

MR. MANNING
GOES TO OTTAWA

THERE WE WERE IN OTTAWA AT LAST – FIFTY-TWO REFORMERS, all of us champing at the bit. But only one of us (Deborah Grey) had ever occupied a seat in Parliament, and Ray Speaker was the only one with experience in a provincial legislature. We had lots to learn. We were inexperienced in everything from parliamentary procedure to dealing with the Ottawa press gallery, but nevertheless empowered to challenge the Ottawa political establishment, including the Liberal government, on behalf of the folks back home.

The political events and issues that would shape the thirty-fifth Parliament and federal politics from 1993 to 1997 included the Liberals' promises of "ethical government" in their first Throne Speech; separatists as the Official Opposition; the matter of a new prayer for the House of Commons; the appointment of a new Governor General; the missed opportunities of the Paul Martin budgets; damaging federal cuts to health care funding, and even more damaging resistance to health care reform of any kind; the broken GST promise; the expulsion of John Nunziata from the Liberal caucus; Canadian peacekeeping efforts in Rwanda and the former Yugoslavia; controversial legislation on gay rights and gun control; constitutional amendments affecting Newfoundland and

Quebec schools; the Krever Inquiry into tainted blood; the Somalia Inquiry into alleged military misconduct; the turbot war starring Brian Tobin as Captain Canada; Cabinet shuffles and patronage appointments to the Senate; the Mulroney Airbus suit; Bill Clinton's visit to Ottawa; the throttling of a protester by the Prime Minister on Flag Day; the impact of Mike Harris's election and the Common Sense Revolution in Ontario; Lucien Bouchard's near-fatal illness, recovery, and later departure to become premier of Quebec; and the disasters of the Saguenay and Red River floods.

But the most significant political event during this period was the Quebec referendum on sovereignty in October 1995. It was the looming shadow of this potential disaster that provoked the sharpest clashes between myself and the Prime Minister, and the subject deserves a special chapter of its own (Chapter 6).

Apart from the great issues of the period, this was a time when my colleagues and I had a number of "first time" experiences.

■

As the leader of the third-largest party, I took over Audrey McLaughlin's former offices on the fifth floor of the Centre Block. We decided that we wanted to use Audrey's large corner office for strategy and Question Period planning sessions, so my assistant Jean Marie Clemenger and I crammed ourselves into the two small offices formerly occupied by Audrey's assistants, and this became our work-place for the next four years. By keeping my own office demands modest, I hoped to minimize turf wars among my own MPs for "the best" offices.

Like most members of Parliament, I had to find a place to live while in Ottawa. Sandra and I had decided to keep our principal place of residence in Calgary. While Parliament was in session, I would commute home, once a week if possible, for Friday and the weekends. While some Reform MPs rented apartments in Ottawa, and a few bought condos, Ian and I bunked in at the Travelodge Hotel on Queen Street. The hotel had named each floor after a province and I was given, appropriately, Room 1111 on the Alberta floor on a semi-permanent basis. Room 1111 consisted of a bedroom, bathroom, sitting room, and kitchenette, and was made available at the very reasonable rate of $35 per night, provided Ian and I spent a certain number of nights a year at that hotel. Ian was usually located on the same floor.

"The House is not a Home," former Tory House leader Erik Nielsen ruefully observed in his book by that same title. But it is the workplace of members of Parliament, many of whom worked very hard to get there, and I was no exception.

Our first House leader, Elwin Hermanson, and our first whip, Diane Ablonczy (actually we called her the "caucus coordinator" because we didn't like the authoritarian connotations of the term "whip"), had met with House officials to draw up a seating plan for Reform members in the thirty-fifth Parliament. As party leader I was entitled to a seat in the front row of the Opposition benches. But Reformers wanted to break down some of the traditional distinctions between the front- and backbenchers, so initially I chose to sit in the second row. Naturally this attempt to "do things differently" earned us nothing but scorn from the other parties and the media, evoking no serious consideration whatsoever of the point we were trying to make, and by the second session I had moved to the first row.

The first time I formally sat in the House of Commons was on Monday, January 17, for the election of the Speaker. But the "initial sitting" that actually stirred my emotions and has stuck in my memory was late one night during that first month, after the House had closed for the day, when I came down to the Chamber and asked the guards to let me in to retrieve some papers from my desk.

The Chamber was only partially lit, empty, and completely silent. As I sat for a moment alone in my seat, I found I could much more easily envision what that House should be like and might still become than I could when it was filled with partisans and political noise. For some peculiar reason, I seem to sense the Spirit of God more readily in a church when it is empty and silent than when it is full of people and noise. And that night, with the House empty and silent, my experience was similar.

For me, the House of Commons is "the temple of democracy," where the spirit of democracy ought to reside and be expressed in its purest and most potent form. But most of the time, the actual operations of the House are in direct contradiction to this ideal. Voting is neither free nor representative; freedom of speech is circumscribed, not encouraged; the will of the prime minister, the will of the parties, the interests of the media – not the will of the people – are the driving forces.

But sitting there that night, I could dream a little. What if the prime minister's seat were occupied by a democrat rather than an autocrat? What if the Speaker's chair were occupied by a strong reformer genuinely committed to democratization of the institution? What if the government House leader were a genuine servant of the legislative majority instead of a flunky for the Cabinet? What if the majority of the seats were occupied by members who truly believed in their hearts that those seats did not belong to their party, or to themselves, but first and foremost to the people back home? These were the sentiments that came to me in a flood on that late-night visit to the House in January 1994.

■

Among the many tasks we faced in the first days and weeks were the hiring of the leader's office staff and parliamentary assistants. With the help of Gordon Shaw, Stephen Greene (my first chief of staff), and Darrel Reid (our first policy director), we gradually assembled our team. These folks, who became our first co-workers in Ottawa, will always occupy a special place in our minds and hearts.

Besides our own staff, there were also all the House of Commons custodial staff and security people, including the "green shirts" who service and maintain the place and whom we were also meeting for the first time. They had heard all sorts of wild stories about these Reformers from the West – that we wanted to fire everybody to save money, that we were anti-French, that we rode horses and would probably try to stable them in the Centre Block rotunda. But they soon found out that we were down-to-earth MPs representing ordinary folk, and they did everything possible to show us the ropes and make us feel at home.

Several years later, just before Christmas 1996, we hosted a "thank you" breakfast in the elegant Confederation Room in the

West Block for House of Commons staff. We were surprised at how
many came and were shocked to learn that this, too, was something
of a first. One older woman, dressed in her finest outfit, seemed close
to tears, and I asked her if something was wrong. She told me, hesi-
tantly, that she had been in that room many, many times before –
but always on her knees, scrubbing the floor. This was the first time
in twenty years that she had actually been invited to a function in
that room as a guest, and the first time that she had been officially
thanked for her services.

■

When Mr. Smith went to Washington in the old Jimmy Stewart film
he saw a number of things that needed changing, but he was told
that it couldn't be done. When the Reformers came to Ottawa this
was our experience as well – not just with the big things, like balancing the budget and democratizing the House, but even with the
most minuscule matters.

For example, we were given a committee room in the West Block
as our "caucus room," where our fifty-two members would meet
together each Wednesday morning. We wanted it set up with tables
arranged in a square, not with chairs arranged theatre style as had
been the custom. But we were told it would not be possible to fit that
many tables into the room and arrange them that way. Yes, it is possible, we said, because we have actually measured it. But, we were
told, it would not be possible to provide simultaneous translation for
every table arranged in that way. No problem, we said, because our
caucus is largely unilingual and doesn't really need simultaneous
translation. But, but, but . . . it simply can't be done! But yes, yes, yes
. . . we still want it done.

And then there was the momentous issue of trying to change the
pictures on the walls. This was not exactly big-league stuff, but if
we were going to get things done differently we had to start somewhere. The pictures on the walls of our caucus room were black-
and-white photos of former parliamentarians, most of them Liberals
and most of them dead. Pictures of Liberals, dead or alive, make
some of our members uncomfortable. We wanted our walls adorned

with pictures of reformers from the past – Baldwin, LaFontaine, Howe, and Brown, or preferably Western reformers like Riel, Haultain, Crerar, McClung, Wisewood, Woodsworth, Aberhart, and Douglas. But, but, but . . .

So then we tried again with the pitchers of ice water. Every caucus and committee meeting in Ottawa since time immemorial has been provided with pitchers of ice water placed on the meeting tables. This is a very commendable practice given the dryness of much of the discussion at such meetings. But there is one small, technical flaw in how this is done – without fail the pitchers are two-thirds full of ice and only one-third full of water. And so when honourable members, or more often their guests, try to pour the water into a glass, there is never enough. And invariably, in the attempt to extract the very last drop of water from the pitcher, the ice ends up spilling all over the table. This wastes ice, embarrasses the pourer (who might be a distinguished person), and disrupts the meeting. Moreover, these ice-spilling incidents are legion. They occur numerous times every day, in dozens of meetings, year after year after year. If all the ice spilled in Ottawa through this practice were collected in one place it would constitute a small glacier.

To be fair, I should say that the one place where this problem has been resolved is in the House of Commons itself, where pages deliver glasses of water drawn from coolers in the lobbies. If this brilliant reform had not been instituted, and ice-water pitchers of the standard variety were provided on members' desks, a Zamboni would be required to smooth the ice-strewn aisles after every Question Period. Obviously, there is a clear and urgent need to reform the ratio of ice to water in those committee and caucus room pitchers. Everyone knows it, but nothing is done about it. It just can't be done because "that's the way pitchers have always been filled around here."

What does it take to change the seating arrangements in a caucus room, the pictures on the wall, the ratio of ice to water in a pitcher in Ottawa? A demonstration? A hunger strike? A royal commission? An Order-in-Council? An act of Parliament? An act of God? How can we hope to change the procedures of the House or the budget or the laws of the land if we can't get a caucus room, a photo, or a pitcher changed?

In the end, some Reform MPs and their staff changed the caucus room tables and replaced the old pictures with new ones of reformers, thus proving to a skeptical establishment that it could be done. But the ice-water pitchers? We're still working on that.

One further attempt to do things differently sticks in my mind, although it wasn't so trivial or so funny. Reformers have long been in the habit of opening any public meeting in which we participate with the singing of "O Canada." It surprised us therefore to learn that the national anthem was rarely, if ever, sung or played in the House of Commons. So on April 20, 1994, during national Citizenship Week, in a fit of patriotism, the irrepressible Deborah Grey moved "that Standing Order 30 be amended by adding the following words: 'and (the Speaker) shall cause Canada's National Anthem to be played or sung in the House every Wednesday immediately preceding oral questions.'"

Because this was an Opposition motion and not on the Order Paper it required unanimous consent to be put to the House. Much to our surprise, when the Speaker asked whether there was such consent, it was the Liberals, not the Bloc, who denied it. They seemed to think that the motion was deliberately provocative; it might offend the separatists. Don Boudria, the deputy government whip, raised procedural objections and ended up insisting that the proposal be sent to a committee for further study.

Send it to a committee? What kind of national government needs a committee to tell it whether it is appropriate to sing or play the national anthem in the national parliament? And what kind of a national parliament is it where even as simple and patriotic a procedural reform as that is obstructed and sidelined?

■

Every morning that the Parliament of Canada is in session, a small army of Opposition researchers and communications people get up with the birds. They scour the media and research files to prepare provocative questions to be put to ministers of the government in the daily Question Period.

An even larger army of government researchers and communications people also get up with the birds. They scour the media and research files to *anticipate* the questions that will be put to ministers in the daily Question Period, and to provide those ministers with "briefing notes" to aid them in responding to or evading the anticipated questions with provocative rebuttals.

Every day that the Parliament of Canada is in session, at 11:00 a.m. on Fridays, but at 2:00 p.m. on other days, refined and abbreviated versions of these preambles, questions, responses, nonresponses, and rebuttals are then hurled across the House of Commons by Opposition members and government ministers in the hope of getting a ten-second hit on the evening television news or a headline in the next day's newspaper. This in essence is Question Period – a distinguishing feature of the Parliament of Canada, and indeed all parliaments modelled after the Mother of Parliaments at Westminster. If witnessed frequently enough by earnest members of the public, it can destroy their faith in Parliament, politicians, and democracy more rapidly than any other political experience.

This need not be so. Question Period has the potential for bringing to light facts that the public has a right to know, for calling ministers and governments to account for their words and actions, and for providing substantive answers to substantive issues of public policy. It can also serve to test and display the character and ability of both Opposition critics and government ministers. And, on occasion, it serves all of these purposes.

On Wednesday, January 19, 1994, I rose in my seat in the House of Commons to put my first question to the Prime Minister. Predictably, my question was on deficits, debt, and taxes.

Mr. Preston Manning (Calgary Southwest): Mr. Speaker, my question is for the Prime Minister.

At the same time that we are facing record debt and taxation levels to which the hon. member has just referred, we are also facing record levels of unemployment. Many economists and business people feel there is a direct connection between the two, that high debt and taxes kill private sector job creation.

Would the Prime Minister give the House the government's view on the connection between high record levels of debt and high record levels of unemployment and tell us whether the government believes that deficit cutting is essential to private sector job creation.

Right Hon. Jean Chrétien (Prime Minister): Mr. Speaker, we understand that we have a huge debt in Canada. Yesterday apparently we surpassed the fantastic figure of $500 billion. It is a big burden that the Conservative Party left as a legacy with which we must start our work today. It is a reality and it is a big problem for the nation.

There are two ways we can solve this problem and it will take some time. We have to cut expenditures but the main thing we can do to reduce the debt is to make sure that there are jobs in Canada for Canadians so that they can work and produce growth and produce taxes. That is the way we want to approach the problem.

My first question was too long and convoluted. A better version would have been simply, "Does the Prime Minister believe that high taxes kill jobs?" Because the Prime Minister rarely responds directly and substantively to any question, the more words there are in the question, the more tangents he can take to avoid the real issue. A question that mentions "record debt," "record tax levels," "record unemployment," and "private-sector job creation" gives him at least four different tangents to pursue. And if any politician is addicted to tangents it is Jean Chrétien.

This was the first of hundreds of questions that I would ask the Prime Minister and various ministers over the next seven years. And although I did my duty, I resented the time spent on Question Period. The public benefits were just not worth the effort. I am not an actor, and I feel dishonest when called upon to "manufacture" sentiments that I do not really feel. Early on I got into the habit of half reading questions rather than putting them spontaneously, which further reduced my effectiveness. In my nine years in Parliament I cannot remember a single answer from the Prime Minister that struck me as either insightful, inspiring, or statesmanlike. Frankly, on most days I would have preferred to have been answering questions rather than asking them. Why is it that a question-and-answer session at a public meeting can be one of the most informative, stimulating, and gratifying exercises in democracy imaginable, but Question Period in the House of Commons falls so far short of the mark?

■

For many Canadians, reading a government budget is an even better cure for insomnia than sleeping pills. But our interest is usually rudely awakened when we feel the fingers of the taxman in our pockets – the place from which every one of those billions of dollars in a federal budget is extracted. Reformers had campaigned long and hard on the need to stop the waste and overspending of taxpayers' dollars by the federal government. It was, therefore, with great anticipation that I hurried on February 22, 1994, to the "lock-up" in a well-guarded room of the Centre Block for an advance peek at the first budget of the new Liberal administration.

By the time I got there, members of our Finance team were already huddled around a table of budget documents like wolves around a moose carcass. But they were shaking their heads. This Liberal budget fell far, far short of what was required to "get the federal fiscal house in order." No attempt had been made by the Chrétien government to make budget balancing and tax relief the keys to job creation. The Finance minister proposed to reduce the federal deficit by only $6 billion, mainly through cuts to the defence budget. He devoted two-thirds of his first budget speech to announcing increased "creative engagement" by the government in the economy, including eighteen new spending programs.

We quickly developed our talking points: "First the Liberals gave Canadians the Red Book. Now they've given us the Red Ink Book." And while Paul Martin was delivering his maiden budget speech in the Chamber, Reform's Finance team was already working the media assembled in the foyer just outside. Stephen Harper addressed the French media as well as the financial papers. Dr. Herb Grubel, the best-trained economic mind in the House, gave his analysis. Jim Silye critiqued the budget from a businessman's perspective, while Ray Speaker dissected it from the standpoint of the provinces. Many of our MPs would soon be calling home to their local media and relating our position to their local situations.

This was really the first time since we had arrived in early January that I felt we were all doing something together – something important and something every one of us believed in. The main bone of contention between Reformers and the Liberal government on fiscal matters was speed. We would keep up the pressure to ensure that the federal budget was balanced as soon as possible. There would be other lock-ups and budget days, but this first budget pulled us together and gave us a mission for the next three years.

■

As the MP for Calgary Southwest, the establishment of a solid working relationship with my constituents was a high priority for me. This involved setting up an efficient constituency office to deal with their day-to-day problems, answering correspondence and telephone inquiries promptly, communicating through my regular "householder,"* and holding regular town hall meetings to discuss the issues of the day and answer questions. But one of my most interesting and instructive interactions with my constituents came about in April 1994 over the issue of physician-assisted suicide.

The issue had become a major topic of discussion as a result of the tragic case of Sue Rodriguez, a B.C. woman suffering from a degenerative nerve disease. Sue had taken her own life in February 1994 with the aid of an unidentified doctor, after her attempts to gain court permission for a legally sanctioned physician-assisted suicide had been denied. Later that month a special Senate committee had been appointed to examine the issue, in particular, to determine whether the Criminal Code prohibition against assisted suicide should be lifted or modified.

In representing constituents on moral and ethical issues, Reform advocated a process whereby the MP would make his or her own position on the issue known but would also engage in a consultative process – the more democratic the better – to ascertain the will of the constituents on the matter. If a clear consensus among

---

* The "householder" is a mailing piece sent by MPs to their constituents on a regular basis at public expense.

constituents existed, Reform MPs were committed to represent that view by their vote in the House, even if they personally disagreed with it.

In order to consult with my constituents and ascertain their thinking on this issue, I undertook a rather elaborate democratic experiment. First of all, I prepared a householder for distribution to every home in the riding. It provided background information on the issue, four arguments in favour of legalizing physician-assisted suicide prepared by supporters, four arguments against prepared by opponents, a statement of my own personal position (against) and the reasons behind it, and a questionnaire on the issue that constituents were encouraged to complete and return. Second, I advertised and held the first-ever electronic town hall meeting in Calgary Southwest. It was televised live over a local cable channel and constituents were invited to respond to an onscreen question by touch-tone telephone. The electronic town hall featured a panel chaired by myself representing various views, and interaction with a studio audience (randomly selected citizens). Third, I held a regular town hall meeting, attended by about three hundred people, at which another questionnaire was distributed after a lively discussion. Finally, I commissioned a scientific public opinion survey of my constituents' views on the issue.

This then allowed me to compare the data from four different sources – the mail-in ballot, the electronic town hall meeting, the regular public meeting, and the scientific survey. Interestingly enough, all four sources (from 82 per cent on the scientific survey to 60 per cent from the electronic town hall TV survey) showed strong support for allowing physician-assisted suicide "subject to certain conditions." The list of conditions was quite extensive, including everything from consent requirements to living wills to consent of more than one physician to specifications like terminal illness, unbearable physical pain, and severe psychological distress. Behind the numbers, my extensive discussions with constituents on this matter showed that, for many people, "fear of death" had been superseded by "fear of dying." And while they appeared willing to relax the straightforward Criminal Code prohibition against physician-assisted suicide, what they wanted in its place were a set of protective restrictions against abuse. With respect to what these protective restrictions should be, there was a wide range of opinions and much less consensus.

Because of my willingness to represent my constituents' position even if I disagreed with it, I got a respectful hearing and expanded opportunities to argue my position that the government's role should be to encourage and facilitate the protection of human life rather than to permit or facilitate its destruction. In the end, the Senate committee recommended that the Criminal Code prohibition be left in place, and the issue never came to a vote in the House. But the experience of using various democratic devices to consult my constituents and to ascertain their views on a weighty moral issue was one of the most instructive of my political life. Had I not been party leader, and had more time to focus solely on my own constituency, I would have engaged in many more such democratic exercises. Reform later held two national electronic town hall meetings, one called "You Be the Finance Minister" and the other on national unity. These experiences convinced me more than ever that if one engages in this sort of democratic consultation often enough and thoroughly enough, it is possible for an experienced and innovative elected official to determine whether a consensus among constituents truly exists, and how to reinforce it or to challenge it depending on the circumstances and principles involved.

■

If part of the maturing process is learning through mistakes, the Reform Party and I certainly had ample opportunities to mature during our first term in Ottawa.

Some of the earliest difficulties we got into involved the "pension and perks" issue. We were calling for the elimination of wasteful government expenditures and reduction of spending generally. This required "leadership by example" from all MPs, including ourselves. And so when, as the leader of the third party, I was offered an official car (valued at $30,000) and a driver (to be salaried at $30,000-plus per year), I turned the offer down. But, we reasoned, it did no good to turn this "perk" down if nobody knew we had done so, so we turned it down "with a flourish," by holding a news conference in which I gave the keys back to a startled Public Works official. The media considered it a "stunt," which it was, and four years later, when I actually needed a car and driver as leader of the Opposition, the whole thing came back to haunt us.

It was the same line of reasoning and style of communication that eventually got us into the "Stornoway problem." The federal government was $508 billion in debt. If it had been a public company its bankers would have demanded that it sell assets. We had a list of federal government assets that included everything from public lands and shares in Crown corporations to embassies and official residences. Stornoway, a historic house in Rockcliffe and the official residence of the leader of the Opposition, was one of these. Lucien Bouchard had declined to move into it, preferring (also for symbolic reasons) to live on the Quebec side of the Ottawa River. And so I had said on several occasions that the federal government should either sell Stornoway or turn it into a bingo hall and apply the proceeds to reduce the deficit and debt. The remark amused public audiences at the time, but again it would come back to haunt me four years later.

The MPs' pension plan was a more serious matter. The pension plan for senators and members of Parliament, as modified by the previous government, was the most generous pension plan in the country. The Liberal Red Book had proposed to reform it, and in February 1995 the government introduced legislation to do so. While the Liberal plan adopted some of the features proposed by Reform – such as raising the age of eligibility to fifty-five years and ending "double-dipping" – it still provided MPs with pension benefits more than twice as generous as private-sector plans. The Liberal scheme also established a two-tier system whereby eighty-nine MPs who already had more than six years' service would receive the benefits available under the old pension plan and begin collecting the instant they left Parliament, no matter how young they were. Thus, assuming they left Parliament in 1997 and lived until age seventy-five, Brian Tobin would receive $3.9 million in total pension benefits, Svend Robinson $3.5 million, David Dingwall $3.6 million, and Sheila Copps $2.5 million.

When the Reform caucus first got to Ottawa we established our own Pay, Pension, and Perks Committee. It was never our intention that MPs go from a gold-plated plan to no pension at all; instead we recommended a reformed plan more comparable to the pension plans available to other Canadians in their places of employment. But once again, all this got lost in the shuffle. And in our zeal to "lead by example" on the issue of fiscal responsibility, our MPs ended up, years later, in the untenable situation of having to choose between the Liberal pension plan and no pension security at all for themselves and their families. This is something I should never have allowed to happen.

■

In the spring of 1996, Reform was having considerable success pounding the Liberal government over its broken GST tax promise. Chrétien had insulted an "ordinary Canadian" at a televised town hall meeting for insisting that he honour his promises. The broken GST promise had brought about the expulsion of John Nunziata from caucus and the resignation of deputy prime minister Sheila Copps – the Liberals were on shaky ground. In the midst of all this – and not by coincidence or accident – the government introduced Bill C-33, making sexual orientation grounds for prohibiting discrimination under the Human Rights Act, an issue that Reform was far less prepared and able to handle than tax issues. This was ground on which Reform was vulnerable, and it did not take long for that vulnerability to manifest itself, for the media to amplify it, and for the Liberals to exploit it as a welcome diversion from their own troubles.

The Reform Party was committed to the principle of the equal treatment of all Canadians in law, regardless of their personal characteristics, and we opposed discrimination against homosexuals. But we also felt that basing entitlement to protection from discrimination on personal characteristics like sexual orientation was unwise and itself discriminatory, and we opposed the bill. At the same time, the Reform Party was committed to upholding the freedom of its members and all Canadians to express their beliefs, and that included beliefs (religiously based or otherwise) about homosexuality. How to maintain and communicate these positions in a balanced way was a challenge, and at this point in our political experience we were ill prepared to meet it. Reform was being dragged on to ground littered with land mines, and it did not take long for one of our troops to step on one.

Bob Ringma, MP for Nanaimo-Cowichan, was a solid citizen who had served his country faithfully and well as a member of the Canadian Armed Forces, where he had risen to the rank of major general. Back in November 1994, Bob had given an interview to a Vancouver Island newspaper in which the interviewer had focused on discrimination against homosexuals in the workplace. Bob was uncomfortable with the direction of the questioning. Nevertheless, he continued the interview, and at one point, when pressed to say what he would do in the hypothetical situation in which customers objected to service from a gay employee, he was reported to have defended the right of the employer to dismiss such an employee or move them "to the back of the shop." Someone sent a copy of the article to Peter O'Neil of the *Vancouver Sun,* and when Bill C-33 became a subject of public discussion in the spring of 1996, Peter followed it up, making Ringma's remarks the subject of a feature article.

I was away from Ottawa at the time the story broke and my caucus officers had to deal with the initial allegations of prejudice and gay-bashing. Did Bob's words reflect our party's position? No. Would Bob be apologizing for or distancing himself from his earlier remarks? At first the answer was "No," then "Maybe," then sometime later "Yes." Would Bob then be disciplined, and if so how? The caucus officers announced that Bob would be stepping down as whip and might be suspended from caucus. What about Dave Chatters, the member from Athabasca, who had defended Bob's remarks? And what about Jan Brown and several other MPs who were denouncing "rednecks" in the caucus and demanding their expulsion? The controversy was spiralling out of control.

Something had to be done. I investigated the matter and issued a statement saying that comments attributed to Bob Ringma and Dave Chatters were completely unacceptable and did not represent the positions of the Reform Party. I suspended both from the Reform caucus until the July caucus meeting, at which time their status would be re-evaluated. And I was about to suspend Jan Brown as well for her unhelpful contribution to the situation, when she decided to resign from caucus on her own.

None of these initiatives was well received, and in the end I was criticized by all concerned. Bob and Dave and their supporters felt that they had been treated unfairly and that their freedom of speech and belief had been constrained. The gay community, of course, demanded stronger action (expulsion). And those who opposed the extension of homosexual rights on moral or other grounds accused us of weakening that position. The caucus and the party felt that I had taken much too long to act, allowing what should have been a two- or three-day affair at worst to spin into a much longer ordeal.

This painful incident alerted us to the fact that we had much work to do to handle such issues better in the future. Increased dialogue with members of the gay community, sparked by this incident, at least led to a better understanding of respective positions. A "rapid response team" of key caucus officers and staff was established to handle future crises more effectively. It was significant that the blow-up over gay rights had not been triggered by some intemperate remark from a member of our "family caucus" – headed by Sharon Hayes and labelled the "God squad" by our opponents – but by members who had no direct responsibilities for Bill C-33. A few years later, under the leadership of Eric Lowther, we developed a more solid and defensible position on how to reconcile freedom of belief and expression with equality rights and the right to freedom from discrimination. But all of this came long after what turned out to be one of our worst weeks in Parliament.

When our members got into trouble, as in the case of Bob and Dave, they certainly got my attention. But I also made the mistake as leader during those early years of not paying enough attention to members and co-workers when they did well, or when they were discouraged, or when they needed help in defending themselves from unfair attacks by others. I was intensely proud of how far each of my MPs had come, through all kinds of adversity and opposition, in order to sit together as Reformers in the Parliament of Canada, but I rarely communicated this to them in any meaningful way. If someone was doing a good job I tended to leave him or her alone, while spending too much time on a few "high-maintenance" members. And when my colleagues were the subject of personal attacks from our political opponents, I tended to treat such attacks with the same icy indifference with which I treated attacks on myself.

This all came home to me one day in the House when Defence minister Doug Young insulted Deborah Grey in a particularly demeaning way. During an exchange in the House over the MP pension plan, he referred to her as "more than a slab of bacon." He was later forced to withdraw his remarks.

If one of our members had directed a personal slur of this kind towards a female member of the government, the House would have been up in arms demanding apologies or expulsion, and every women's rights group in the country would have come to that member's defence. But that didn't happen when our female members – Deborah Grey, Diane Ablonczy, Daphne Jennings, Sharon Hayes, Margaret Bridgman, Val Meredith, Jan Brown – were the targets.

On this particular day, I happened to be sitting right beside Deborah when Young aired his insult. My instinctive reaction was to ignore it completely: "Don't pay any attention to him, Deb. He's just a Liberal jackass." But that was *not* what Deborah needed to hear from me at that particular time. She, despite her tough exterior, had been deeply and personally hurt by Young's remark. What she wanted was for me to feel her pain as she felt it, and to rise to her defence with passion and ferocity. She is one of my dearest friends and my most stalwart ally, but I let her down.

■

Prior to and during the federal election campaign, the Chrétien Liberals had accused the Mulroney administration of lacking integrity and high ethical standards. Prime Minister Chrétien consequently committed himself to a new era of "ethical government," including the appointment of an ethics counsellor reporting to himself. If his statements on this subject were taken at face value, Canadians had reason to believe that their new prime minister was committed to avoiding conflict of interest, abstaining from partisan patronage in government appointments and contracts, accepting responsibility for the actions of his ministers, dealing openly, fairly, and expeditiously with any charges of government impropriety, honouring his election promises, and "telling the truth" even when it hurt.

As Opposition members in the thirty-fifth Parliament, it was our responsibility to hold the government accountable to these ethical standards. It was in the discharge of this responsibility that we had our first encounters with "Liberal ethics" in practice.

The Dupuy Affair
In the fall of 1994, the Chrétien government had a golden opportunity to demonstrate how its ethical standards applied to conflict-of-interest situations. The minister for Canadian Heritage, Michel Dupuy, who was responsible for the Canadian Radio-Television and Telecommunications Commission (CRTC), had written a letter to the CRTC supporting an application for a radio station licence by one of his constituents. Instead of frankly acknowledging the minister's conflict of interest, requiring him to resign, and clarifying the guidelines governing ministerial relations with quasi-judicial regulators, the Prime Minister denied there was a problem, sought to excuse the minister's conduct, and maintained that no guidelines had been violated. The Prime Minister's ethics counsellor took no action to investigate the matter until hounded to do so by the Opposition and media pressure, and ended up merely whitewashing the Prime Minister's handling of the affair.

Eventually, under intense pressure from the Opposition, Dupuy was obliged to resign. But the affair revealed several things about "Liberal ethics." It revealed the hypocrisy of the government's commitment to dealing with conflict of interest. It was obvious that neither the Prime Minister nor the ethics counsellor could be counted upon to hold ministers to a high standard in that area. It also became apparent that "Liberal ethics" involved a double standard. At the same time that Chrétien was turning a blind eye towards Dupuy's conflict of interest, his government was preparing to pursue an investigation of former prime minister Brian Mulroney over an alleged conflict of interest in the Airbus affair. The Chrétien government was apparently very much concerned about conflict of interest when it might discredit members of the previous administration, but indifferent to conflict of interest when it involved its own ministers.

The Broken GST Promise

It is important to distinguish between honest mistakes and deliberate efforts to deceive. There are occasions when public people make commitments in good faith, and later discover they are unable to keep them. In such cases, the ethical course of action is to acknowledge the mistake frankly and fully, and to be more cautious in future.

But often promises are made for political gain – such as winning an election – and the maker of that promise knows full well that it is being misunderstood, or that it cannot possibly be kept, but continues to make it anyway. In the judgment of many Canadians, including some members of his own administration, this was the principal ethical violation of Jean Chrétien in the 1993 federal election. He allowed and encouraged Liberal candidates, including Cabinet ministers, to promise that the Liberals would scrap, kill, and abolish the GST if elected. "If the GST is not abolished under a Liberal government, I will resign," declared Sheila Copps at a CBC town hall on October 18, 1993. And after the election, the Prime Minister himself was quoted by the *Ottawa Citizen* on May 2, 1994, still maintaining that "We hate it [the GST] and we will kill it." But, of course, the GST *was not* abolished by the new Liberal administration.

Chrétien, as a former Finance minister, must have known, even as Liberal candidates were campaigning on the GST promise, that he could not possibly abolish it without making massive spending cuts and/or other tax hikes to finance it. (The GST at the time was bringing in $10 billion per year.) But Chrétien and Martin had no intention or plan for doing either. Not only did the Prime Minister fail to scrap, kill, and abolish the GST once in office, but he began to deny that the Liberals had ever implied that they would. Rather than come clean and apologize, he blamed the Opposition and the media for misinterpreting him, and blamed Canadians for misunderstanding the situation, thereby revealing yet another dimension of Liberal ethics – when caught acting unethically, deny, deny, deny, and blame anybody and everything but yourself.

Some members of the Prime Minister's circle appeared to see the GST broken promise for what it was. John Nunziata voted against the Liberal budget because it failed to keep that promise, and was expelled from the Liberal caucus for his stand. Sheila Copps eventually resigned her seat (and won it back again in a by-election) because she acknowledged that she had deceived her own electors on the GST issue. Even Finance minister Paul Martin eventually conceded that in the case of the GST a promise had been made that could not be kept. But the Prime Minister steadfastly refused to acknowledge the GST deception for what it was.

Suppressing the Krever Inquiry

Historian Jack Granatstein has observed that "Conservatives falsify the past, socialists falsify the future, and Liberals falsify the present . . ."*

During Chrétien's first term, two major public inquiries were commissioned to "get at the truth" concerning two tragic events. The first was the inquiry of Justice Horace Krever into how the Canadian blood supply became tainted with infections (in particular those associated with HIV/AIDS and Hepatitis C) that ultimately killed or damaged the health of thousands of Canadians. The second was the Somalia Inquiry charged with determining the facts behind the March 1993 deaths of three unarmed Somalis, including the alleged death by torture of sixteen-year-old Shidane Arone, at the hands of members of the Canadian Airborne Regiment. The extent to which the government was prepared to co-operate with and facilitate these investigations, or to obstruct and frustrate them, revealed a great deal about the nature and depth of its commitment to "ethical government."

In the case of the Krever Inquiry, the Chrétien government was anxious to "get at the truth" so long as the blame for the tainted-blood scandal could be attached to the previous Conservative administration and the Red Cross. But as soon as evidence started to surface that there had been warnings concerning problems with the Canadian blood supply as early as 1982–84, when the Liberals were

---

* J. L. Granatstein, *Who Killed Canadian History?* (Toronto: Harper Collins, 1998), p. 3.

still in power, and that Krever intended to name names and assign responsibility, the Chrétien government's enthusiasm for truth seeking suddenly vanished.

The government even went to court to try to restrict Krever's investigations, and when it came to compensating victims of tainted blood, the Chrétien government drew an arbitrary line at 1986. It reluctantly agreed to compensate victims of Hepatitis C who had received tainted blood during and after that year, but not before, arguing that no tests existed prior to that time that would have revealed the contamination of the supply. This contention was disputed at the inquiry, and Justice Krever concluded that "compensating some needy sufferers and not others cannot, in my opinion, be justified." As Premier Harris wrote to the Prime Minister on June 14, 1999: "It would be unfortunate if the federal government continues to treat those infected between 1986 and 1990 differently than those infected outside this window. As you know, the findings of the Krever Royal Commission do not support restricting assistance to only the 1986–1990 victims. Indeed, the Royal Commission identified federal government failures to protect the integrity of the blood system dating back as far as 1981 and even 1978."

The consistent efforts of the Chrétien government to frustrate the Krever Inquiry was an ongoing issue throughout much of 1995–1997. But my most memorable personal impression of the intersection of Liberal ethics and the Krever Inquiry, and its impact on those affected, occurred in the House of Commons on the night of April 28, 1998. A vote was in progress on a Reform motion calling for the government to accept its responsibility to compensate *all* victims of Hepatitis C who had contracted the disease through tainted blood. The Liberal government forced its backbenchers, many of whom agreed with the motion, to vote against what compassion and their own personal ethics told them was right. The motion was defeated by a vote of 154 against (all Liberals) to 137 in favour. But my eyes were on two individuals in the Chamber who symbolized in a most dramatic way the impact of Liberal ethics on those personally affected.

As the Liberal members, many of them looking very uncomfortable, stood up one after the other, on orders from the Prime

Minister, the House leader, and the whip, to vote down the motion, my eyes focused on the Liberals' back row immediately across the House from my seat. I watched as Dr. Carolyn Bennett, a Toronto MP and medical doctor whose patients had included victims of tainted blood and who had been an active supporter of Hepatitis C sufferers, stood to cast her vote against the motion, and then slumped sobbing back into her chair. She wasn't the only Liberal backbencher with tears in her eyes, and there were tears in the eyes of people in the galleries as well.

To my left, in the gallery just above the government benches, sat a teenager with his father. I had been introduced to him by Dr. Grant Hill. His name was Joey Haché. Joey was a victim of Hepatitis C who had contracted the disease from tainted blood after 1986. He himself would be eligible for compensation under the government's policy, but he had become a spokesperson for *all* the victims. When the vote was over, he stood and slowly started to clap his hands together. At first I wasn't sure what he was doing, but then it became clear that he was applauding those who had supported the motion. The security personnel in the gallery knew who he was and had come to admire his advocacy of the victims' cause, but it was their duty to remove him from the Chamber, since demonstrations in the galleries are not permitted. As they gently led him out, members on the Opposition side of the House looked up, and then slowly – first Reform, then the Bloc, and then the NDP and PCs – rose to their feet applauding Joey for having the courage of his convictions.

As I walked from the Chamber that night, I found myself asking again, "What's wrong with this place?" Almost every one of those Liberals opposite, if they had been free to vote as a mother or a father or a caregiver, would have stood with Joey Haché and not with their party on this issue. And almost every one of them, as decent human beings, if allowed to cast their ballot on the basis of their own morals and judgment, would have chosen to support the motion. But in our Parliament of the Parties, once they came under the discipline of the Prime Minister, the House leader, and the government whip, even the Hippocratic oath of a medical doctor to "do no harm" was subjugated to the Liberal ethic of "Do no harm to the party, no matter who else gets hurt."

Suppressing the Somalia Inquiry

The Somalia Inquiry began in the spring of 1995. As it endeavoured to get to the root causes of the tragedy in Somalia, its focus shifted from events that occurred in 1993 when the Conservatives were in power to allegations of cover-up and the shredding of documents at the Department of National Defence from 1993 to 1995 under the Liberals. Investigative reports by CBC reporter Michael McAuliffe and charges by Information Commissioner John Grace that the military was altering documents that had been requested under the Access to Information Act eventually led to the resignation of Chief of Defence Staff General Jean Boyle. General Boyle had testified before the inquiry but accepted no responsibility for wrongdoing at Defence headquarters, preferring to shift responsibility to subordinates. The Prime Minister and Defence minister David Collenette took the same tack. To get Collenette out of the kitchen without accepting any blame for the fire, the Prime Minister accepted his resignation in October 1996, ostensibly because the minister had found himself in conflict of interest over a letter written to the Immigration and Refugee Board on behalf of a constituent. (This was the same type of offence on which the Prime Minister had vigorously defended Dupuy a year earlier.)

■

By now parallels were being drawn between government obstruction in the Krever and Somalia inquiries. In each case, an inquiry had been set up to get to the bottom of a tragedy, and to determine who was to blame. But when "getting to the bottom" meant investigating "those at the top" – Liberals as well as Conservatives – the government had begun to obstruct its own inquiries. Finally, with the possibility of an election in 1997 and the Prime Minister anxious to "clear the decks," the new Defence minister ordered the Somalia Inquiry to complete its hearings by March and report by June. The inquiry eventually wound up its proceedings, shedding some light on the events it had been established to investigate but never really getting to the truth buried by the upper echelons of the Defence department and the government.

What had we learned about Liberal leadership on the ethical front as a result of our first encounters with Liberal conflict of interest, patronage in appointments and contracting, broken promises, and the obstruction of public inquiries? Perhaps Bob Evans summed it up best in an opinion piece that appeared in the *Globe and Mail*, May 11, 1996, under the headline "Where Have All the Leaders Gone?"

Over the past one and a half years we have watched three major inquiries unfold in Canada – on the tainted blood scandal, the carnage at the Westray coal mine in Nova Scotia, and the vicious excess in Somalia of the now-disbanded Canadian Airborne Regiment. The genesis of the reviews is our need to learn about the human error or malfeasance that resulted in loss of human life.

What we are finding is a truly chilling commonality among those being investigated – an unwillingness or inability of leaders to accept responsibility for what happened.

We gave these people lots of money and plush offices and pretty uniforms and deference and sometimes adulation, and in return we wanted their best efforts and their principled, honourable behaviour. We expected them to be leaders.

But when the coal dust hit the methane, when the bullet hit the Somali, when the HIV hit the hemophiliac's bloodstream – when it was time to pay the price of leadership – they all filed for moral bankruptcy, hired lawyers, and began behaving like the least among us rather than the best. . . .

Stripped of all its trappings, leadership is the exercise of moral courage. This is what we have forgotten.

■

There is one particular day towards the very end of our first term – February 5, 1997 – that stands out most dramatically in my mind whenever I hear the words "Liberal ethics." Within the course of a few hours, I had occasion to confront Speaker of the House Gilbert Parent, the Prime Minister's ethics counsellor, Howard Wilson, and the Prime Minister himself on that very subject.

The day before, there had been an altercation in the House during a speech by Darrel Stinson, the Reform member of Parliament from Okanagan-Shuswap.* A Liberal backbencher, John Cannis, the member for Scarborough Centre, yelled "racist" at Stinson. Stinson, a straight-talking former prospector with a colourful vocabulary, denounced Cannis in unparliamentary language, calling him a liar, among other things, and threatening to punch him out then and there. No physical altercation actually occurred, but the incident generated charges, counter-charges, and various points of order.

To put Stinson's reaction in context, ever since Reformers had arrived in Parliament, we had been subject to repeated personal insults from Liberal members, including Cabinet ministers, often involving such slanders as "racists," "extremists," and "traitors to Canada." Usually these words were said just loudly enough to be heard by our members (who sat at the end of the chamber farthest from the Speaker), but not loudly enough to catch the attention of the Speaker or to be recorded in *Hansard*. For Darrel Stinson, Cannis's insult was the last straw.

The next day I went to see the Speaker about the affair. He stated the obvious: that the initial insult by Cannis was unparliamentary and that Stinson's response was unparliamentary. Both were out of order, and both would be asked to withdraw their remarks or face expulsion from the Chamber.

But my purpose in visiting the Speaker was not to discuss a point of order. It was to raise a point of principle. When that Liberal backbencher called Stinson a racist, he was not simply uttering a personal insult, he was uttering a lie. I know Darrel Stinson far better than Cannis ever will, and he is no racist. My bigger concern, I told the Speaker, was that, in the Canadian House of Commons, a member, a Cabinet minister, even a prime minister, can lie to the House, and as long as it is done in "parliamentary language," that lie violates no rule, practice, or protocol of the House. If, however, another member identifies that lie for what it is – in the language that 99 per cent of Canadians would use if they were lied to – the use of the word "lie" is deemed unparliamentary, and the use of that

---

* *Hansard*, February 4, 1997.

word *is* a violation of the rules and protocols of the House, for which the member uttering it can be disciplined.

The Speaker simply acknowledged, somewhat ruefully, that it is not the business of the officers of the House to sort out truth from falsehood, only to determine whether the words used were parliamentary or unparliamentary. To lie to the House is permissible, provided it is done in parliamentary language. So that was that. While the House is officially offended by the word "lie," it is not necessarily offended by the lie itself.

I left the Speaker's Chamber and headed to Question Period to ask the Prime Minister some pointed questions on the same subject – the ethics of the government, or, more correctly, its apparent lack of them. The Prime Minister had presented himself as the ultimate guardian of the ethics of the government and had made reference to the "ethical guidelines" to which he and his ministers were subject. I decided to test him, raising four specific incidents in which various ministers, including the Prime Minister himself, had been embroiled, all of which had serious ethical dimensions involving right and wrong or truth and falsehood, not merely differences of policy or political opinion.

These incidents included: the alleged murder of a Somali civilian by Canadian peacekeepers, and the alleged cover-up of the circumstances surrounding that murder by high-level officials in the Defence Department; the deaths of hundreds of Canadians from tainted blood, and the allegation that high-ranking officials of the Liberal administration from 1982 to 1984 ignored early warnings of the problem because they did not want it to become an issue in the 1984 federal election; allegations that the Justice minister had allowed the Justice department to go on a political witch hunt to discredit former prime minister Mulroney over suspected conflict of interest and kickbacks connected with the Airbus purchases; and the Prime Minister's repeated denial that the Liberals had ever promised to "kill, scrap, or abolish" the Goods and Service Tax, despite overwhelming evidence to the contrary.

On February 5, I asked the Prime Minister: "Do any of these activities violate the Prime Minister's ethical standards, or by his standards are all these activities ethically acceptable?"* He responded by saying, "In political debate we may have differences," and then proceeded to attack me and the Reform Party. In other words, the Prime Minister refused to acknowledge any ethical dimension in the incidents, only "political differences."

After Question Period, I went to a meeting of a Special Joint Committee of the House and Senate on a Code of Conduct for Members of Parliament. I wanted to put the same questions to the Prime Minister's ethics counsellor, Howard Wilson, who just happened to be appearing before the committee that day. I asked the ethics counsellor whether *he* saw an ethical dilemma – an integrity issue, an issue where right and wrong was at stake – in any of these incidents. The ethics counsellor's reply was not only weak and evasive, but it captured in a paragraph the moral relativism that characterized the attitude of the government. He said to me: "I think you are speaking about policy questions, questions in which there is a difference between opposition parties and that of the Government. It's the essence of our democratic system. I don't believe I can go and take your question any further than that."**

In other words, political interference and cover-up in the investigation of a murder, stonewalling an inquiry into tainted blood from which some Canadians died, alleged misuse of the powers of the Justice department, denying you broke a key campaign promise – in keeping with the ethics of the Prime Minister and his ethics counsellor, these are simply "policy questions" on which "differences" exist between political players.

What is this, this utter ambivalence to moral standards of any kind that I encountered that day in three of the most important offices of the national government? It is *moral relativism*, at the highest levels of the government. It is a moral relativism that not only blinds our parliamentarians and senior bureaucrats to ethical issues but also robs the government of any real moral authority on any subject.

---

* *Hansard*, February 5, 1997.

** Transcript of the February 5, 1997, meeting of the Joint Committee on Code of Conduct, Ottawa, p. 6.

I am reminded of a study of integrity conducted by the historian D. C. Somervell. He focused his investigation on two nineteenth-century British statesmen: William Gladstone, the moralist – who, if he didn't see right and wrong in an issue, was uninterested – and Benjamin Disraeli, the pragmatist – who rarely saw right or wrong in any issue, only differences of opinion. And what was Somervell's conclusion? That while it is an error to discover moral issues where none are in fact at stake, *it is a greater error to be blind to them when moral issues really arise.**

It would of course be a mistake for a member of Parliament – including a practising Christian like myself – to see moral issues in every matter before the House. But from time to time, moral issues of real significance do arise. To go to war or not – a moral as well as a political question for every generation in every century. To abolish or retain slavery. To use the Bomb or not. To provide or not provide legal protection for the unborn. To support the good and restrain the potential evil of the genetic revolution. To help the poor or not. To address the AIDS epidemic in Africa or walk by on the other side of the road. To declare war on terrorism or not, and to follow through or renege on that declaration. If indifference or moral relativism blinds us to the necessity of moral standards on which to base these choices, we are in danger of making fundamental mistakes. And if a government refuses to recognize ethical standards and practise ethical behaviour in the regular day-to-day conduct of public affairs, where will it get the skill or the authority to deal with the big moral issues when they are thrust upon it?

---

* D. C. Somervell, *Gladstone and Disraeli* (Garden City: Garden City Publishing Co., 1928), p. 66.

6

OUI OU NON

THE MOST SERIOUS POLITICAL EVENT TO OCCUR DURING MY
first term in Parliament was the Quebec referendum on sovereignty
in October 1995. The nearly disastrous mishandling of Canada's
interests in that referendum gave Jean Chrétien the dubious distinction of coming closer than any other Canadian prime minister
to presiding over the breakup of the country. Not only did he grossly
underestimate the demand for fundamental change in Quebec, he
also completely misunderstood how Western Canadians like myself
express love of country.

When someone asks me how I express my love for and commitment to Canada, I say, "By doing something." I'm better at expressing my feelings through actions than with words. And it's in my
nature, as a Westerner with roots in the newer part of Canada, to
express my passion for my country by building something new and
better for our future. That is what I'd set out to do when I became
involved in federal politics, and it is the motivating force behind my
approach to national unity.

Sandra and I believe, based on our personal experience and
Christian faith, that love is the key to the strongest and most enduring relationships. Love of God, love of family, love of neighbour,

love of country ought to bind Canada together more strongly than any ribbon of steel or constitutional covenant. And yet how far we seem from that ideal.

At the practical level, any family counsellor will tell you that strong relationships depend on a few key things – honest and open communication, mutual respect, reflection and growth, humility, sacrifice, and sharing in both failures and successes. The strength of a relationship also lies in anticipating the dangers and pitfalls that life brings, and finding ways of avoiding or alleviating them before it's too late. A game plan that organizes your life helps too – one that addresses the concerns and aspirations of each family member.

Everyone should realize that you can't take the unity of a country as large and diverse as Canada for granted – just as you can't take a marriage, or any relationship, for granted. Our unity is dependent on healthy relationships among Canadians of all stripes, in all communities and regions. These relationships require constant work and attention, regular reality checks, continual upgrading of support systems, and the work of keeping dreams alive for the future. This is why strained relations among the diverse regions and peoples of Canada, or between Quebec and the rest of Canada, should never be taken for granted or come to be accepted as unpleasant but unavoidable characteristics of the status quo.

By the time I arrived in Ottawa in 1993, I had long considered ways to cope with the threat of secession. The first were preventative measures, "changes to federalism" that would deal with strains in our federation and the underlying causes of secessionist sentiment. The second were tough-love measures, "consequences of secession" that would communicate the negative realities of secession to those thinking of leaving and guide a contingency plan to protect our country in the undesirable event of an attempted breakup.

Unnoticed by the Ottawa political and media establishment, I had already had some modest but relevant experience in dealing with separatist sentiment first-hand. In the early and mid-1980s, reaction to the Liberals' National Energy Program and early disillusionment with the Mulroney regime had produced the ingredients for a full-blown secessionist movement in the West. The founding of the Reform Party in 1987 – with its emphasis on "reforming federalism," not leaving it – channelled much of this dangerous Western discontent into more constructive political action, while Ottawa slept blissfully on.

During the first half of 1994, when Reformers were doing so many things for the first time in Ottawa, I kept an eye on the national unity front. I was looking for any sign at all that Chrétien had a vision for dealing with the separatist threat, and wondering whether he was prepared to pursue the reform of federalism as a way to win back the hearts of separatists in Quebec and elsewhere. I was also looking for any indication that Chrétien was willing to communicate the "hard realities" of what separation would mean to those who seemed to believe that it could occur painlessly and at little cost to themselves. These realities would include not only economic and social costs, but the possible partitioning of Quebec and the potential for violence.

■

Ottawa is the second-coldest national capital in the world, next to Ulan Bator in Mongolia. If the separation of Quebec from Canada could change its climate, the separatists might just have a winning argument. On a bitterly cold day in January 1994 I had my first meeting with Jean Chrétien since my election to Parliament and his election as prime minister. This was to be the first of a dozen such meetings over the next eight years, and they always followed the same pattern.

Ian and I would go to the Prime Minister's parliamentary office, Room 309-S on the third floor of the Centre Block. We might have an informal word or two with Jean Pelletier, his chief of staff, or Bruce Halliday, his executive assistant, before I was ushered into the office. There, after greeting me, Chrétien would seat himself in a chair at the end of a low coffee table, and I would sit on a sofa to his left.

On this first occasion he was obviously tired, but he was friendly, and anecdotal, which is his style. When I asked about his family, he spoke warmly of his wife, Aline, and her helpfulness to him. He also referred to his children and grandchildren, inquired about Sandra, and asked me to convey his respects to my father.

As was usually the case in my meetings with Chrétien, I was the one with the agenda. I asked him if there were any aspects of his legislative program for which he was seeking all-party support. He mentioned "parliamentary reform," though he was vague on the details, and Canadian involvement in peacekeeping operations in Bosnia. It was left to me to ask, "And what about Quebec?"

In the ensuing discussion it became obvious that Chrétien was deeply hurt by charges that he had "betrayed" Quebec's interests in the past, and by the low level of support Quebecers had given him in the recent election. It was also obvious that he considered the sovereigntist challenge to be essentially a Quebec issue that only Quebec politicians could properly address, and the perspectives of the rest of Canada on this issue, in particular those of unilingual reformers from the West, were at best irrelevant and at worst misguided and dangerous.

When I raised the idea of "reforming federalism" to give Quebecers a compelling reason to stay with Canada, he reverted to a familiar mantra. To him reform meant "constitutional change" – unnecessary and unwise in light of the failures of Meech and Charlottetown. When I suggested that there were all kinds of ways of reforming federalism without changing the Constitution, he did not disagree, but he said that the way to do it was to make incremental changes and to address practical problems administratively through routine federal-provincial negotiations. When I expressed concern that such an approach would not provide an attractive-enough vision of a better federalism to compete with the separatist dream of an independent Quebec, he simply shrugged.

I left this meeting – which had lasted eighty minutes instead of the scheduled twenty – on cordial terms with Chrétien, but with the sinking feeling that he really had no forward-thinking strategy for combating separatism and advancing federalism that would compete favourably with Bouchard's vision in Quebec or attract positive support from the rest of Canadians.

Have you ever been at a neighbourhood barbecue when a family feud breaks out and no one quite knows what to do? You are standing there in line to get your burger and drink, just minding your own business, when all of a sudden the Bouchards and the Chrétiens from down the street (they're related, you know) start going at it. Someone in the family wants a divorce, and every member of the family is getting in on the act about whose fault it is and who did what to whom, including what Uncle Pierre did to Aunt Renée in 1982. The voices are getting louder and louder so nobody else can hear or say anything, and the chairman of the barbecue committee keeps saying "Order, order," but nobody's listening. In your heart you'd like to help, but you're not sure how, and they don't want anyone to "interfere," so about all you can do is look busy fixing your burger and try to stay out of it, at least for the time being.

Well, this is what happened on several occasions in the House of Commons during the first few months of the thirty-fifth Parliament when the "family feud" broke out between the Bloc and the Quebec Liberals, including the Prime Minister, and any naive hopes Canadians had that the debate over the future of Quebec in Confederation might be fought on the high ground of competing visions or costs versus benefits were dashed.

The feud would be ignited by provocative questions from the Bloc to the Prime Minister or a Cabinet minister over some Quebec grievance, real or imagined – the announced closure of the military college in Saint-Jean, the failure to consummate a Canada-Quebec manpower agreement, the reopening of the drug patent law. The Liberals would respond in kind, with a few gratuitous insults thrown in. The House would then erupt into a series of back-and-forth exchanges between Quebec MPs, mostly in French and rarely recorded in *Hansard*, that would leave the Speaker struggling for order.

On such occasions, a family counsellor in the gallery would have noticed several things. She would have noticed, for example, that the Prime Minister could never remain statesmanlike and "above the fray"; he was part of the problem, not part of the solution. And that counsellor would have noticed especially the peculiar body language of the rest of the House. While the Quebec Liberals and Bloc members would be leaning forward – half rising from their seats, yelling at each other, and even shaking their fists – the majority of other MPs would be literally leaning back in their seats, as if to distance themselves from the fracas. On such occasions even the most talkative non-Quebec MPs were strangely silent and bewildered: "What the heck is this?"

Those were my feelings as well. The difficulty for me, as the leader of the third party, was that I often had to resume the questioning, usually on some other subject, when the Speaker had finally restored order, but the House and the press gallery were still abuzz with the preceding outburst.

A quote that seemed most fitting was one of Edmund Burke's from his *Reflections on the French Revolution*: "Because half a dozen grasshoppers under a fern make the field ring with their importunate chink, whilst thousands of great cattle, reposed beneath [the trees], chew the cud, and are silent, pray do not imagine that those who make the noise are the only inhabitants of the field . . ."*

■

My unease grew with the apparent lack of leadership and preparedness on the part of the Chrétien government to deal with the separatist threat in a substantive way that would also take into account the concerns of the rest of Canada. Of course it was conceivable that the Prime Minister and the government were doing more thinking and planning on this subject than they were willing to share with us. But if that was in fact the case, the results were certainly not evident to the House, the media, or the public.

Within our own caucus I had assigned Stephen Harper, our best mind when it came to strategy and policy, to the unity file. He was also one of the four bilingual members of our caucus. Stephen and I were ably assisted in dealing with the unity issue by Scott Reid of our research department. Scott had authored several relevant books and

---

* Edmund Burke, *Reflections on the French Revolution*, Harvard Classics, Vol. XXIV, Part 3 (New York: P. F. Collier & Son, 1909–14), para. 143.

articles, including *Lament for a Notion* (1993) and *Canada Remapped: How the Partition of Quebec Will Reshape the Nation* (1992).

I also expanded my own schedule of discussions with other key players who could help to deepen my understanding of the Quebec situation, or even assist in prodding the Prime Minister.

In March, I met with several Mohawk chiefs from Quebec who made clear in no uncertain terms their view (a view shared by the northern Cree) that if Canada was divisible so was Quebec, and that they were quite prepared to "fight" any attempt to make them part of an independent Quebec.

I met with Tom d'Aquino, the president of the Business Council on National Issues, whose membership included the CEOs of many of the biggest companies in the country. BCNI's view was that the country was headed for financial disaster if the government didn't move more quickly to control spending and the deficit. Tom was working on a plan (called the Renaissance Plan) that included a scenario for action if the country "hit the wall." I was in wholehearted agreement concerning the seriousness of the financial situation but expressed caution about the timing of any pronouncements on the subject, so as not to feed the separatists' argument that the near-disastrous fiscal state of the federation was yet another reason for Quebec to leave.

My most interesting consultation occurred on April 25, 1994. That morning Ian and I boarded a flight for Montreal. Upon arrival we took a cab to 1250 Boulevard René Lévesque, and the elevator to the twenty-fifth floor, where we introduced ourselves to the receptionist in the law offices of Heenan Blaikie. I was then taken up one more flight of stairs to a small office with a cluttered desk at one end and a couch and chair at the other. The sole occupant of the office was Pierre Elliott Trudeau.

Mr. Trudeau was very cordial. He appeared smaller, older, and frailer than I had pictured him in my mind, and I was reminded of how much time had flown by since he had been prime minister.

After some initial pleasantries, I got directly to the point. What vision of federalism needed to be communicated to Quebecers in order to defeat the sovereigntists? Did federalism need a new face – a change in personality and principles – to succeed?

Mr. Trudeau offered the opinion that Mulroney had tried to put a new face on federalism, but his approach had been misguided, based on the "two nations" theory and wholesale decentralization and too dependent on a dangerous alliance with separatists. Trudeau appeared to be saying that federalism did not so much need to be reformed as reaffirmed (my words, not his). He conceded that federalism did not appear to have a strong champion in Quebec and offered no comment on Chrétien one way or the other.

Trudeau said it was important to make clear to the world that we weren't going to have a referendum on sovereignty every few years. The question needed to be settled once and for all. I then asked him to what extent he thought questions about the consequences of separation should be raised in the public arena in advance of the Quebec election and referendum. He did not hesitate at all in saying, yes, such questions should be raised, and publicly. We needed honest dialogue on the complexity and costs of separation to show that, rather than "resolving" anything, separation would lead to years of complex, counterproductive negotiations that would benefit no one at the end of the day.

Towards the end of our discussion he offered the opinion that, on the constitutional principle of the equality of citizens under the law, his views and mine were not that dissimilar. But when it came to language policy, he felt that Reform's emphasis on territorial bilingualism was misguided.* The unattractiveness of our language policy would prevent Quebecers from hearing what we were really saying on any other issue.

I couldn't help but smile and replied that I understood well what he was saying. When he was prime minister, Western Canadians like myself never really heard what he was saying about equality or appreciated that he was actually opposed to "special status" for Quebec, because his language policy of official bilingualism got in the way. To us it appeared to favour one group over another. How

---

* By territorial bilingualism, we meant that French should be the official language of Quebec, English the official language outside of Quebec, and that official bilingualism would apply only in jurisdictions where the number of French and English speakers warranted it.

ironic – for all concerned – that "language policy," which was supposed to improve communication and understanding among
Canadians, should become one of the greatest obstacles to better
communication and understanding.

■

On our way back to Ottawa that night I did a quick calculation. If
the Quebec provincial election were to be held in the fall, and the
PQ won, it would still take them six to nine months to get their
canards in a row before holding a referendum. That meant there was
still over a year for the federalists to produce a fresh and exciting
winning strategy. But only if we got down to work *now*!

With no leadership or urgency emanating from our federal government, it was time to do something on the unity front ourselves.
On May 2, the Reform members of Parliament held a special meeting
to develop our "Quebec Strategy." We spent a lot of time discussing
how to get the right balance between promoting our vision of a
better federalism and discussing the harsh realities of secession,
when the media is so much more prepared to amplify the negative
than the positive.

In late May, with national unity occupying centre stage in the
House, I asked the Prime Minister what vision of federalism he
proposed to fill the growing national unity vacuum. He launched
into his Pavlovian response that this meant constitutional change,
to which he was opposed. So I reminded him that we could do it
through non-constitutional reforms. Now the Prime Minister said
the key to better federalism lay in "non-duplication of services"
and he was opposed to "so-called new things" and "the big scheme
à la Reform." Did this mean federalists were going to campaign
under *his* "grand scheme," the glorious banner of "non-duplication
of services"? Was this how we were going to vanquish the separatist dream? I then switched tracks and asked him to assure
Canadians that his government would develop a principled federalist response to the key issues that Quebec separatism raised. But
he went off on another tangent, saying that good government was
the answer to everything.

Tuesday, June 7, was our Opposition supply day in the House, the day we could propose our own motion for all-day debate and hold a vote at the end of the day. We decided to put to the House a motion that defined a vision of a new and better federalism. Government members would have the opportunity to put forward their alternatives. But despite the seriousness of the issue, and the fact that there had been no real debate on the unity issue in Parliament since the election, the House was virtually empty (so often the case on Opposition supply days). There were a handful of Liberals, but for most of the debate no senior ministers; Bouchard and a handful of Bloc MPs; and the Reformers.

Our motion read:

> That this House strongly affirm and support the desire of Canadians to remain federally united as one People, committed to strengthening our economy, balancing the budgets of our governments, sustaining our social services, conserving our environment, preserving our cultural heritage and diversity, protecting our lives and property, further democratizing our institutions and decision-making processes, affirming the equality and uniqueness of all our citizens and provinces, and building peaceful and productive relations with other peoples of the world.*

We were excited. This was not just a piece of paper or an Opposition stunt – it was a vision for our country and people, a dream around which Canadians could rally. The first phrase paraphrased the opening paragraph of the BNA Act, a pretty good place to start. The remainder defined what Canadians had told us should be the distinguishing characteristics of our federal union as we moved into the twenty-first century. The motion was positive and inspirational. It did not criticize the government, and it provided an opportunity for members of the House to fill the vacuum on the national unity issue.

I also took the opportunity to announce three other Reform initiatives that we genuinely felt would contribute to filling the vacuum.

---

* The debate detailed in the following pages can be seen in its entirety in *Hansard*, June 7, 1994.

We would put together a New Canada Task Force and work together to describe this vision of a New Canada in greater detail, involving Canadians from sea to sea. We would form a Contingency Planning Group to prepare a reasoned, principled federalist response to all those inevitable and troubling questions that the threat of Quebec secession raises for Canada. Finally, we would put the results of these two initiatives together into a vision statement and plan for the revitalization of federalism for all Canadians and Quebecers to consider.

Throughout the day, various Reform MPs fleshed out this framework with solid contributions, drawing on their own experience and critic responsibilities. Jim Silye reached out to the Bloc members, Diane Ablonczy related our vision to social services, Randy White to fiscal responsibility, Deborah Grey to democracy, Val Meredith to justice, Jim Abbott to ecology, Stephen Harper to the principle of equality, and Elwin Hermanson to culture.

The response from the Bloc and the government was predictable. The first government speaker, Fernand Robichaud, the secretary of state for Parliamentary Affairs, accused the Bloc and Reform of wanting to divide Canada, and moved an amendment. You'd have expected him to substitute a Liberal vision for ours. Instead, he stripped our original motion of any visionary content and simply affirmed the desire of Canadians "to live together in a federation." What a pathetically inadequate response. Imagine a home threatened with breakup and all the head of the house can propose is a resolution that "we all live together in this house." Bouchard jumped on the opportunity. Since the government was obviously offering nothing more than the status quo, there was no other option: Quebec would be better off on its own. "Canada has no power when it comes to changing anything," he noted, and he went on to say that any federalism based on the principle of equality of provinces would be utterly unacceptable to Quebec.

Liberal MP Jane Stewart admitted that she was "confused by the motion" and said, "My God, what is wrong with the Canada that has grown and developed over the past 127 years?" This expression of complacency and utter indifference to the constitutional concerns of others was typical of the mentality of Ontario's Liberal MPs. It was enough to drive everyone else up the wall.

Then came Sheila Copps, deputy prime minister and the most senior government minister to participate in the debate. She went on a rant against the Reform Party. She professed an emotional commitment to Canada but was incapable of translating that emotion into a vision, plan, or strategy to keep the country together.

I have been criticized for having grand ideas and plans but failing to find the words to express them in an emotional way. But to me, having mere words without any plan or actions to back them up is a far greater shortcoming.

Later in the day, the motion as amended by the Liberals was passed, 179 members in favour and 49 members (all Bloc) against. This Reform motion, gutted by the Liberals, was the only legislative action taken by the Parliament of Canada on the "unity issue" in all the months preceding the Quebec referendum on sovereignty. If this was the best that the governing party of Canada could do to seize the high ground before the referendum campaign, our country was in deep trouble.

Early the next morning Ian Todd hand-delivered a letter from me to the Prime Minister's Office.* It was the most important appeal I ever made to the Prime Minister. It repeated my view that it was the responsibility of federalists to advance a positive and unifying vision of Canada, and to honestly and openly consider the real consequences of separation, so as to dispel the myth being propagated by the separatists that secession would involve little pain, cost, or disruption for Quebecers.

I attached a list of twenty hard questions on which Canadians and the federal government would have to take a firm position if Quebecers did in fact vote "Yes" to sovereignty – questions on such matters as how the federal government would protect the rights and interests of Canada in such a situation, involve the provinces and the rest of Canada in any negotiations, deal with partition requests and boundary disputes, deal with requests from Quebec aboriginal groups to remain in Canada, handle demands for joint citizenship and use of the Canadian dollar, secure the federal debt and compensation for Canadian assets, react to recognition of Quebec claims by foreign

---

* This letter is reproduced in its entirety in the Appendix.

governments, manage trade and treaty issues, ensure a transportation and utility corridor to Atlantic Canada, deal with military and security issues including threats to public order, ensure the integrity of ecosystems shared by Canada and Quebec, and respond to requests from an independent Quebec for "special association" with Canada.

The sovereigntists were out there telling Quebecers that these issues could be resolved with little discomfort or disruption after a "Yes" vote. Was it not the duty of the federal government to spell out in black and white what Quebec secession would really mean, both for Canada and Quebec, and to do so *before* any Quebec referendum vote?

I followed up my letter by going to see Chrétien in his parliamentary office on June 14. After some discussion of other topics, I mentioned my letter of June 8 concerning the danger of a vacuum on the national unity front that the separatists would fill, the need for a positive federalist vision, the need to answer the hard "what if" questions.

Chrétien responded by saying that he had tried to persuade Quebec premier Daniel Johnson to hold a referendum in conjunction with the upcoming provincial elections in Quebec but had not been successful. He made no mention of my twenty questions other than to say that he had people "studying" these types of issues. He did muse about whether a referendum on separation should require more than a 50 per cent plus one majority, but said nothing about how Quebecers might react to what they would perceive as a change in the rules since the last referendum.

I asked repeatedly about *strategy*. Chrétien responded by talking about *tactics* that had been employed fourteen years ago in 1980. He recalled, with obvious relish, how in 1980 the federal health department had tied up most of the best billboard sites in Quebec prior to the referendum. This denied these advertising sites to the PQ, and they were later made available to the federalist campaign. (Was this, I wondered despairingly, the way we were going to win the referendum fight?)

When I again stressed the idea of promoting a "better federalism" to combat the sovereigntist dream, Chrétien once again made it quite clear that there was nothing wrong with the status quo. He reverted to his usual response, that Canada was the best country in the world. (If only I could count how many times I heard that line over the years.) If an honest question were to be asked, he said, federalism "as it is" would win. (I wanted to say, "But if the sovereigntists frame the question, it will not be 'honest.'") In case I wasn't getting the point, he then put it in the negative. He *did not want* to offer Quebec the option of "status quo plus," because Quebecers on these constitutional matters were "like children" (his words). If you even hinted that there might be a "plus" they would go for more, as would the other provinces. They wouldn't believe you had a bottom line, and this would hurt the cause of federalism.

Our discussion was over. I returned to my office and reflected on what I had just heard from the Prime Minister of Canada. The gnawing fear in the pit of my stomach grew rather than subsided each time I met with Chrétien. The Canadian ship of state was headed into stormy weather but our captain saw no need to change course.

■

On September 12, 1994, as expected, the sovereigntist Parti Québécois under Jacques Parizeau was returned to power in the Quebec provincial elections, ending nine years of Liberal rule in that province. The Chrétien government was now faced with a separatist Opposition in the federal Parliament and a separatist government in Quebec City.

At the Reform Party's National Assembly in Ottawa from October 14 to 16, I devoted most of my keynote address to outlining the three approaches of the three main parties in the House of Commons with respect to Canada's future. "Leave Home" was the separatist option; "Don't Worry, Be Happy" was the position of the status quo federalists; and "Rebuild Our National Home" was the Reform option. I then detailed the changes to federalism that we considered essential to provide Quebecers, and indeed all Canadians, with that "third option" – *une troisième voie* beyond the separation of the Bloc and the status quo federalism of the Chrétien Liberals.

By late 1994, the stark contrast between the "do nothing" approach in Ottawa and the flurry of activity in the Quebec National

Assembly was becoming painfully obvious. On December 6, the PQ government introduced A Bill Respecting the Sovereignty of Quebec, declaring Quebec to be sovereign. The bill provided the Quebec government's "answers" to the hypothetical questions that Ottawa refused to address, including how they would negotiate debt and asset division, the integrity of Quebec territory, dual citizenship, use of the Canadian currency, and so on. The bill also provided for an extensive public consultation process, designed to further demonstrate that the sovereignty initiative was being pursued democratically.

By now it was clear even to the most obtuse federalists that the sovereigntists were gaining ground. This finally prompted some action. Daniel Johnson announced that the provincial Liberals would boycott the PQ's consultation process, and he became the official head of the "No" forces in Quebec. The federal Liberals recruited former provincial Cabinet minister Lucienne Robillard to coordinate strategy with the provincial "No" forces. Jean Charest, leader of the federal Progressive Conservatives, joined the "No" team. And the 1995 federal budget was modified to ensure that there would be no significant drop in transfers to Quebec in the immediate future.

In November 1994, Lucien Bouchard, the sovereigntists' most eloquent spokesperson, was diagnosed with a life-threatening bacterial infection requiring amputation of his leg. Bouchard did not return to the Commons until February 22, 1995, and his absence reduced the effectiveness of the Bloc in promoting their cause in the House. We felt genuinely sorry for Bouchard and his family, and this somewhat muted the tone, if not the substance, of attacks on the Bloc's positions. In the end, Bouchard's courageous battle for his life enhanced his political stature. "*Que l'on continue. Merci,*" he had said to his doctors, and many Quebecers saw spiritual and political significance in his recovery. Perhaps destiny had spared his life because there were greater things in store for him.

At the spring convention of the Bloc Québécois, Lucien Bouchard outlined his "*virage*" – a proposal to combine a vote for sovereignty with a proposal for a new "economic and political partnership" with Canada to be negotiated on a nation-to-nation basis. This proposal was designed to bolster support for a "Yes" vote from soft nationalists in Quebec, and to take advantage of the weakness in the federal government's position and its unwillingness to address any questions concerning what might happen after a successful "Yes" vote.

The new initiative was formalized on June 12, 1995, by Parizeau, Bouchard, and Mario Dumont, the leader of the Action démocratique du Québec (ADQ). An August poll then showed the "Yes" side and the "No" side virtually tied at 45 per cent. The same poll showed that a large majority of Quebecers would be willing to consider a reformed federalism as opposed to Chrétien's status quo federalism (what a surprise). Still no response from Ottawa.

When the National Assembly was recalled in September, Parizeau introduced Bill 1, An Act Respecting the Future of Quebec, which contained an appeal to every segment of the Quebec electorate, from aboriginals to minorities to public servants. The bill offered so-called "answers" – slanted to place sovereignty in the most favourable light – to all the questions about the consequences of a "Yes" vote, questions that Chrétien continued to dismiss as "hypothetical."

On September 11, Premier Parizeau announced that the referendum would take place on October 30, 1995. Quebecers would be asked: "Do you agree that Quebec should become sovereign, after having made a formal offer to Canada for a new Economic and Political partnership, within the scope of the bill respecting the future of Quebec and of the agreement signed on June 12, 1995? Yes or No?"

The campaign to determine Quebec's future role in our Canadian home, and its relationship with the rest of the country, had begun in earnest.

■

During the 1995 referendum campaign, Reform's activities within Quebec were confined to speeches and interviews by our intergovernmental affairs critic, Stephen Harper, and some of our Quebec Reformers. We also supported the "No" campaign with advertisements and brochures, including our "Third Option for Quebec" material.

During this period I travelled to nine of the ten provinces of Canada. I participated in seventy-one public meetings outside Quebec, attended by more than ten thousand people, at which Canadians from the neglected and uneasy rest of Canada expressed their interpretation of the referendum question and their understanding of what a "Yes" or "No" vote would mean. These travels and meetings received little or no coverage in the national media, whose eyes were focused on the battle within Quebec itself. But it was these meetings that gave me a better grasp than any other federal leader on the growing frustration in the rest of Canada. It was not just the future of Quebec that was being decided by the Quebec referendum but the future of all of Canada, and Canadians in the rest of Canada wanted a say.

During the first part of the referendum campaign the federalist side remained confident of success – too confident. This complacency was reinforced by the sovereigntists' early difficulties. Economic studies, released by the Quebec government and purporting to show the benefits of sovereignty, were met with considerable skepticism and little public interest. Aboriginal leaders, who were strongly opposed to separation, decided to boycott the Quebec referendum altogether and conduct their own. And Parizeau's "hard edge" turned off undecided voters. Chrétien continued confidently to predict that Quebecers would reject sovereignty and declined an invitation to join Johnson, Bouchard, and Parizeau in a pre-referendum debate.

When Parliament reconvened on September 18, the campaign was already well underway. Chrétien and Bouchard jousted over which one was more committed to respecting the democratic will of the Quebec people. In my view neither one was a principled democrat. Bouchard was willing to accept a majority "Yes" vote, but said that if the vote was "No," the sovereigntists would simply keep having more referendums until they got the desired result. Chrétien was willing to accept a "No" vote, but was unwilling to acknowledge the legitimacy of a simple majority "Yes" vote, or to say what threshold a "Yes" vote would have to achieve to be "legitimate."

I felt strongly that the growing ambiguity concerning the meaning of "Yes" and the meaning of "No," and the dividing line between them, was dangerous, especially to the federalist side. As a democrat, I believed that issues should be decided, if at all possible, by a simple majority vote – 50 per cent plus one. Our experience within the Reform Party was that if you required super-majorities or double majorities to settle some issues but not others you ended up arguing endlessly about the justification of these exceptions and the legitimacy of the final results. Since the federal Liberals, including Trudeau and Chrétien himself, had accepted 50 per cent plus one as the dividing line in the first Quebec referendum on sovereignty in 1980, I felt it was dangerous for the federal government to argue now for some higher majority. It would look as though the federalists wanted to "change the rules" late in the day simply because they were afraid of losing.

I also felt that raising the percentage to 60 per cent or higher, as some Liberals mused, would play into the hands of the separatists in another way. It would allow more Quebecers to think that they could vote for separation – thereby strengthening the hand of their provincial government in its dealings with Ottawa and the rest of Canada – without actually separating. It would encourage "strategic voting," something Quebecers are intuitively more adept at than any other electorate in Canada, a "we can have our cake and eat it too" position.

Of course the critics jumped all over me, charging that supporting 50 per cent plus one as the dividing line in the referendum played into the sovereigntists' hands. I argued that federalists could and should turn 50 per cent plus one into a two-edged sword that would give everyone incentive to pull back from the precipice. If Canada could be divided by a 50 per cent plus one vote in Quebec, then Quebec itself could also be divided by a 50 per cent plus one vote through partition referendums. If a municipality in Quebec, or the northern Cree or the Mohawks, voted 50 per cent plus one to stay in Canada, then those votes too should be respected. What was good for the goose was good for the gander. Or, more correctly, what was bad for the goose was bad for the gander.

To Chrétien's simplistic argument that he couldn't allow "one vote to destroy Canada," I pointed out that if he actually believed the bar should be set at some higher level, *say so*, and introduce legislation immediately to enforce such a threshold. What was most dangerous to our cause was the ambiguity of his position on the consequences of a "Yes" vote and the voting threshold at which those consequences would become real. To those Liberal backbenchers and media people who questioned my "loyalty" because my questions made the Prime Minister's position look weak and confused, my response was simple. The Prime Minister's position *was* weak and confused.

Towards the end of September, the results of a large poll conducted by SOM and Environics confirmed our worst fears. All the "hypothetical questions" that the Chrétien government refused to entertain were being asked by voters and answered by the sovereigntists. The poll showed that large numbers of Quebecers were swallowing Bouchard's "partnership" line, that Quebecers could separate but still enjoy most of the benefits of Canadian citizenship. It found that 62 per cent of Quebecers believed they could use the Canadian dollar after separation; 45 per cent expected to retain their Canadian passports; 69 per cent anticipated an economic union with Canada; and almost 60 per cent believed there would be an economic and political partnership with Canada after a "Yes" result. It was becoming apparent that Bouchard the "partnership negotiator," not Parizeau the hard-line separatist, could win the referendum for the "Yes" side. Not surprisingly, on October 7 Bouchard was appointed chief negotiator for the proposed partnership between Canada and a sovereign Quebec, and leader of the "Yes" campaign.

Although Reform's influence in Quebec was marginal, we resolved to do what we could. Stephen Harper and Scott Reid had fleshed out our proposed changes to federalism, our New Confederation proposals. These we released on October 15 through a televised address by myself over TVA in Quebec, followed up by speeches and media interviews by Stephen and myself in Montreal the next day and newspaper ads in selected Quebec newspapers during the final days of the campaign. At a minimum, we hoped to show that there was support for "changing federalism" in the part of the country we truly represented – the West – and to invite Quebecers to vote "No."

Our basic message dealt with the negative meaning of a "Yes" vote to the rest of Canada and the positive potential of a "No" vote. If Quebec voted "Yes" it would be seen as a decision to get out of Canada, period, not a decision to enter into a new and better union. But if Quebec voted "No," the rest of Canada would see it as a "No" to both separation and the status quo, paving the way for the reform of federalism.

On October 20 an Angus Reid poll showed the "Yes" side ahead for the first time. It was now apparent even to Chrétien that his strategy was not working. Ideas that he had steadfastly rejected now had to be tried, even though it was extremely late in the day and any new promises made would be met with tremendous cynicism.

There was no time left. No time to bring forward, explain, and promote forward-looking changes to federalism that would inspire both Quebecers and the rest of Canadians. All that could be done by the "No" campaign at this point was to trot out some of the old, failed bromides from the past. Johnson renewed his call for constitutional change – the old Liberal hobby horse "distinct society," a veto for Quebec over future constitutional change, and decentralization of powers. At a federalist rally in Verdun on October 24, and in a televised address to the whole country the next day, Chrétien promised them all – a complete and abject reversal of his position. It was a pathetic, weak response from the leader of the "best country in the world" as it faced its most serious crisis in recent history.

For most of the referendum campaign Chrétien had left the rest of Canada out of the picture, but during that last week the Canadian public finally got fed up and took action that may very well have tipped the balance in favour of "No." Unity rallies were held across the country, culminating in a great national gathering of more than 100,000 people at Place du Canada in Montreal. Sheila Copps made it clear that Reformers would not be welcome and that Stephen Harper, our chief bilingual spokesman on the referendum, would not be allowed to speak. But many Reform MPs went anyway, as did many of our staff and family members, my own included.

What happened in Montreal was not a traditional political event. The people who came to Place du Canada stole that moment from the politicians and made it their own. They took a "No" campaign whose leadership was floundering and bereft of ideas and they filled it up with energy and friendship and a contagious desire to preserve a united Canada from sea to sea to sea. The energy and patriotism were there – they'd been there all along – to reach out to Quebecers, to draw a responsible line in the sand, to reform federalism, and to unite the country. What was missing was the leadership to rally behind.

My son Nathan, my daughter Avryll, and her husband John made the trek to Montreal, and what impressed them? Not the presentations by the "leaders," but the people, the obvious passion of those who rallied behind the flag, and their conversations with Quebecers. They went to get some lunch at a shopping centre food court, and Nathan, the most bilingual of the three, fell into conversation with some janitors. Nate explained why they were there, and the janitors explained their skepticism. But they were talking about Canada and Quebec and what was important, and if only those personal relationships could be multiplied a hundredfold, a thousandfold . . .

The public rallies that started in different parts of the country that last week and culminated in Montreal ought to tell us something again about relationships being at the heart of national unity. The rallies were not about legal or administrative or political relations between Quebec and Ottawa or Quebec and the rest of Canada. They were about relationships among people – Canadians wanting to get together with each other to declare their commitment to Canada, Canadians wanting to reach out to the people of Quebec. The rally in Montreal was not about terms of separation or proposals for renewing federalism. It was a cry from the heart that Canada be preserved. But for cries from the heart to translate into meaningful, permanent, productive relationships – for a date or a romance to become a life-enduring marriage and family – the impulses of the heart need to be captured and woven into enduring relationships for the future. This was the responsibility of Canada's federal political leadership, a responsibility it had dismally failed to discharge.

■

The day of the Quebec referendum and the weekend before it were the three most miserable days of my political life. The Prime Minister had not only ignored Reform's well-intended advice and efforts to help, he had resented them. On many occasions, the government had exhibited more hostility towards Reform than it had towards the Bloc. Just as we'd feared, the federalist campaign had been a disaster, and here we were just hours before the vote with the outcome entirely up in the air. If the vote on Monday, October 30, went the wrong way, by Tuesday we would be in the greatest political crisis this country had ever experienced – and it would have been entirely preventable. The political leadership of Canada should never, ever have let the country get to this point.

On the night of October 30, our Reform team met on the fifth floor of the Centre Block to watch the results. As the initial returns came in, our hearts sank; the result was going to be razor close. By the end of the night, we breathed a collective sigh of relief with Canadians all across the country when it appeared confirmed that the "No" side had won, albeit by the narrowest of margins. The final tally (confirmed days later):

- Number of Quebecers voting "No"   2,362,648 (50.6%)
- Number of Quebecers voting "Yes"   2,308,360 (49.4%)
- Margin of "victory"   54,288 (1.2%)

If fewer than 28,000 Quebecers, out of the 4.67 million who voted, had voted differently, the sun would have risen Tuesday morning on a politically divided Canada and a bitterly divided Quebec.

I could barely bring myself to watch a shaken Jean Chrétien on television saying that he had heard Quebec's cry for change and would respond to it over the next few months.

We had done what little we could to lead from behind, but until the very last week of the campaign Chrétien had refused to offer any change at all. He had rejected the idea of asking the courts to rule on the legality of secession. He had rejected the possibility of giving legislated expression to the wording of an honest question on the sovereignty issue, or attempting to define what constituted an acceptable majority. He had rejected the task of addressing the "hypothetical" questions that might have made clear the consequences of secession to all concerned. And he had done nothing to involve the rest of Canada and their political representatives in the federalist strategy. Every effort by the Reform Party and others urging him to take such steps had been not only rejected but characterized as unhelpful, politically motivated, and even treasonous. And yet, over the following months and years, the government would reluctantly adopt virtually every one of these measures in some form. Within days it would introduce a motion on "distinct society" and a Quebec veto. Then it would pursue a Supreme Court reference on the legality of unilateral secession. It would eventually introduce the Clarity Bill to address the issue of what constituted a clear question and a clear majority on the issue of secession. And it would reluctantly accept a proposal from Canada's premiers to reform federalism, called the Calgary Declaration.

If only Chrétien had gone down this road earlier and with enthusiasm. The result, I am convinced, would have been a decisive federalist victory in the Quebec referendum, a clear mandate to reform federalism, and the creation of a more solid constitutional foundation for *all* Canadians for the twenty-first century.

7

FRESH START

As early as the spring of 1996 — fifteen months before
the federal election of June 1997 — we had decided that offering
Canadians a "Fresh Start" would be our election theme. But at our
National Assembly in Vancouver in June of 1996 I applied this
theme not only to the country but to Reform itself. In their first
three years in office, the Liberals had shown a lack of integrity. But
what about the integrity of the Reform Party? How committed were
we to sticking to the big issues of priority to the vast majority of
Canadians and not allowing ourselves to get sidetracked on secondary agendas? Were we prepared to face the fact that some voters perceived Reform as narrow and extreme, and to root out the factors
that perpetuated those misconceptions? Were we prepared to strive
for a new level of competence, so that Canadians would have
confidence in our ability to deliver on what we promised? In other
words, were we prepared to make the effort and exercise the self-
discipline needed to make the transition from an opposition party to
a governing party?

In mid-October 1996, Ed Harper, our lone Ontario MP, and I
conducted a "Fresh Start" pre-election tour in Ontario. This culminated with the unveiling of our complete Fresh Start platform

on October 17. The platform unveiling took place before a large crowd at the London Convention Centre, with simultaneous Fresh Start events being held by Reformers in 160 federal ridings across the country.

The main themes of the Fresh Start platform were a fresh start for the economy via tax relief, a fresh start for families through family-friendly tax and social policies, a fresh start for social fairness through targeting federal social spending on health, education, and pensions, a fresh start for justice through criminal justice reforms, and a fresh start for national unity through the principle of equality and re-balancing the powers. The final item of our platform package was our "fresh start guarantee." This was Reform's pledge to put in the hands of voters the democratic tools required to hold their elected representatives, including Reformers, accountable after the next election. These tools included referendums, citizens' initiatives (referendums initiated by the public), free votes in the House of Commons, and a "recall" mechanism that would allow voters to fire an elected MP for cause.

Over the next two months, when I was not in the House, Ian and I were on the road, sometimes accompanied by various MPs, to pre-sell the Fresh Start platform in as many communities as possible. In Calgary, it was the main subject of my annual Leader's Dinner as well as a Calgary Southwest town hall. Then it was on to B.C., hitting Vernon, Kelowna, Penticton, Princeton, Hope, Chilliwack, Maple Ridge, New Westminster, Ladner, and Vancouver. The next month, it was Halifax, Fredericton, Ottawa, Winnipeg, Saskatoon, Fort McMurray, and major Leader's Dinners in Edmonton and Toronto. In Parliament, I used the pre-budget debate on December 11 to outline our Fresh Start platform in the House. Then, after the Christmas break, it was another round of Fresh Start rallies in Ontario.

While we were doing everything possible to get our Fresh Start message out to the electorate, the discouraging thing for the party membership and our MPs was that we were showing no upward momentum at all in the polls. And despite numerous gaffes by the government, including a poor performance on "integrity issues" – the Somalia and Krever cover-ups, the broken GST promise, the $50-million out-of-court settlement with Mulroney over Airbus –

public confidence in Chrétien and the Liberals, according to the opinion polls, appeared to be as high as ever.

Stephen Harper gloomily concluded that we were going nowhere and would likely lose badly in the next election. Rather than pitching in to help turn things around, Stephen again chose to withdraw. This was now the third time that Stephen had vacated the field prior to a big battle – the first time being when he retreated from our Charlottetown Accord campaign, and the second time when he withdrew from the 1993 national election campaign to concentrate solely on his own riding. In the fall of 1996, Stephen announced that he would resign his seat before the election, which he did. The media predictably interpreted this as yet another sign that Reform was in decline, which made it even more difficult to energize the pre-election campaign.

Notwithstanding this setback and the seeming lack of progress in the polls, Reform soldiered on under my leadership and that of my core team, the caucus officers, committed national council executives, key staff in Ottawa and Calgary, and dedicated constituency executives. Hundreds of thousands of copies of our Fresh Start platform were delivered door to door by our grassroots army in scores of federal ridings. Small Fresh Start meetings were held in Quebec to push our *troisième voie* concept. Fresh Start speeches were given in connection with every nominating meeting. I got a great boost to my own morale when Reform received its largest-ever campaign contribution, $1 million from the estate of Calgary businessman Art Child. The concept of a Fresh Start through tax relief also received a boost from Paul Martin's February 18 budget, which contained the opposite – a major hike in payroll taxes (CPP premiums). And the release of the Conservative platform in March 1997 by leader Jean Charest enabled us to compare our platform favourably with the Conservatives' prior to the election.

■

Throughout much of my life, I have found myself "preparing" for something that lies ahead, something my personal intuition anticipates. For example, I became convinced many years ago that the

West would generate another new federal political party, and thus began to prepare for that eventuality. I also became convinced that coping with secession threats to national unity would be the greatest challenge facing federal politicians in Canada in the latter part of the twentieth century, and I became a lifelong student of that subject. I have had similar presentiments concerning the possible consequences of the emergence of Asia as a super-region to the future of the western world and concerning the nature of the issue agenda of the twenty-first century. These presentiments always inspire me with the "urge to prepare." I should hasten to add that when I follow through on these presentiments, I invariably find other people who have had the same anticipations, often earlier and with more insight than I. But for me this constitutes a confirmation that I am on the right track, and it further stimulates my desire to prepare and to encourage others to prepare.

Throughout 1996 and the first part of 1997, yet another of these presentiments began to occupy my mind and lead me to consider what preparation was appropriate. I was conscious, as a result of my first few years in Parliament, that the Chrétien government was embroiled in a number of issues having a distinctly moral and ethical dimension. When elected in 1993, Chrétien had promised a new era of ethical government, but in practice the government's record on morality and ethics in public office was deplorable. What if "integrity" became an issue during the next election, and the public actually demanded some serious answers from federal political leaders on how to provide moral and ethical leadership in a pluralistic society? Or what if the country or the Parliament faced some future development – a war, or a challenge like the one posed by the genetic revolution – that demanded moral and ethical leadership? How would I, how would Reform, respond to such challenges and questions, particularly in an election context? And what should one do to prepare?

My own approach to morality and ethics is rooted in my Christian faith. But how could one explain that, and comment on moral and ethical issues from a Christian perspective, in a country that has virtually banished faith from the public square and embraced moral relativism as the floating standard for judging behaviour, including the behaviour of governments?

Early in 1993, the Angus Reid Group conducted "The Religion Poll," a comprehensive public opinion survey of the religious attitudes and beliefs of Canadians, and the results were published in the April 12 edition of *Maclean's* magazine. The survey of more than 4,500 adults found that eight out of ten Canadians affirmed their belief in God, and that two-thirds of all adults subscribed to the basic tenet of Christianity, the death and resurrection of Jesus. Almost one-third of the adult population claimed to pray daily and more than half to read the Bible or other religious literature at least occasionally.*

Any discussion of the moral and ethical dimensions of public policy in Canada – by politicians, academics, and the media – would need to "connect" in some way with the values and world view of the Canadian people, which, according to this survey, were very much "Christian." But as the *Maclean's* article pointed out, these Christian beliefs held by a significant portion of the Canadian electorate were *not* shared by Canada's political and media elites. And, the article continued, "what the poll does not answer is why, given what it reveals about an overwhelmingly Christian populace, there is a near total absence of religious discourse in Canadian politics, the media, and advertising. 'Christianity,' notes Angus Reid vice-president Andrew Grenville, 'is flourishing outside the elites, and without attention from elites.'" In other words, there was a huge "disconnect" between the substantial role of faith and Christian beliefs in the lives of the average Canadian, and the very limited role that faith and those beliefs played in the lives of our political leadership.

Moral leadership in a pluralistic society requires one to respect those moral and ethical values that are not faith-based. Canada has gone a long way in that direction, so far that Antonio Lamer, when he was chief justice of the Supreme Court, declared Canada to be a

---

* A similar poll conducted by Ipsos-Reid for CTV and the *Globe and Mail* in April 2000 found that 67 per cent of Canadians said their religious faith is "very important" to their day-to-day lives, and that seven in ten Canadians (69 per cent) agree that through the life, death, and resurrection of Jesus, God provided a way for the forgiveness of their sins.

"secular society." But faith communities, in particular Christian faith communities, also constitute a significant portion of our pluralistic society, as "The Religion Poll" demonstrated, and they have played the dominant role historically in shaping our moral and spiritual heritage. Moral leadership in our society therefore must of necessity involve bridging the current "disconnect" between political leadership and people of faith. As a practising Christian active in politics, I felt a particular responsibility to do something about this disconnect.

At the same time, I was well aware of the dangers of moving in this direction. Despite the professions of our Charter of Rights and Freedoms that all Canadians are to enjoy freedom of religion and expression, there is an open hostility on the part of many of our political and media elites to any attempt to connect faith to public policy or faith perspectives to the morality of public policy. The American constitutional doctrine of the separation of Church and State has been unofficially adopted in Canada, and has ironically been interpreted not only as keeping the institutions of Church and State separate from each other (with which I strongly agree), but as grounds for banishing faith perspectives from the public arena altogether. Anyone who tries to relate their personal religious faith to public policy or political action in Canada can expect to be grossly misrepresented and misunderstood. They will be accused of committing what has come to be regarded as the unpardonable sin – that of "mixing religion and politics."

I was even more acutely aware of the dangers, to both religion and politics, of regarding the faith community, in particular the Christian community, as an "interest group" to be targeted and mobilized for political purposes. I have sometimes been asked by people aware of my evangelical background and connections why I don't "go after the Christian vote" – especially the evangelical and conservative Catholic vote – which the pollsters have identified as substantial and which I would know how to mobilize. This question was raised again in preparation for the 1997 election, when it was pointed out that Reform, despite allegations to the contrary, hadn't won even a "fair share" of the so-called Christian vote in the 1993 election.

I had steadfastly resisted the temptation to mobilize the Christian vote for Reform, and continued to do so – rarely speaking in churches on political themes, never encouraging the sale of party memberships at church gatherings, never targeting Reform literature or campaign appeals directly to the Christian community or its leaders, and never, directly or indirectly, asking Christians to vote for me or my party "because I share your faith." If voters who were committed Christians wanted to support Reform, they were free to do so for exactly the same reasons that other Canadians would support Reform. And if they wanted to do something "special" for those of us among the Reform leadership who shared their Christian commitment, let them pray that we would conduct ourselves with wisdom and discretion so as to be a credit, not a discredit, to our faith and to our country.

My reasons for taking this position were twofold. First, appealing for votes on the basis of religious faith is ultimately bad politics and bad public policy, conducive to creating permanent and divisive cleavages among the electorate that can destroy the unity of a party and even a country. But second, and more important, mobilizing votes on the basis of religious commitment can be particularly destructive to the religious community itself and its testimony to the rest of the public. If a self-professed Christian politician, who relies openly and heavily on the Christian community for support and resources, makes errors in judgment, or takes foolish positions on matters of public policy, or, worse yet, is caught lying or cheating, he can not only damage his party and the country, but also damage the reputation and influence of the faith of which he is supposedly an example. Moreover, if a self-professed Christian leader takes political advantage of the trust of the Christian community, making promises and commitments to them which in the end he is unable to honour, he plants seeds of disillusionment and mistrust, not just among the public at large but in churches and faith organizations, which will yield acrimony and division for years to come. Destroying the faith of anyone in the political process is bad enough; destroying the trust of a faith community that is trusting by nature is even worse.

I am well aware that there are Christians, and those of other faith communities, who actually *want* to be recognized and treated by politicians and the political parties as interest groups. They *want* to be treated as politically significant. They *want* to offer their votes in return for political support of their views. But my response is to ask, "Do you really know what you are asking for, and the potential damage you may suffer if your wishes are granted? Do you know what most modern politicians, in their heart of hearts, consider an interest group to be? It is a group of people who put their own interest ahead of everybody else's. Is that really how the Christian community wants to be viewed?"

If a political interest group is influential enough to become a significant voting bloc, it will attract attention all right, but what type of attention? Become "politically significant" and you will attract the attention of pollsters and strategists. Your members will be polled, your demographics documented and dissected, your preferences and dislikes profiled, and your language and modes of expression studied. The psychographic pollsters will want to know what your members "feel" as distinct from what they "think," and what words and images are most likely to trigger those feelings. Then "messages" embodied in literature, speeches, statements by leaders and candidates, sound bites, and radio and television advertisements will be fashioned from this body of knowledge. You will feel your "hot buttons" being pressed and massaged, and it will be a pleasant sensation. You will hear and see messages designed to tell you "exactly what you want to hear in the language you want to hear it" from politicians who need your votes. Do you long to be assured that the politician is "a Christian just like you," "born again," or "called of God"? That can be arranged – easily, if the politician himself has a Christian background and commitment. And if he doesn't? A good communications persons can teach most politicians all the religious buzz words they need to "speak the language" within a week (witness Bill Clinton's discourses on "repentance and forgiveness" after the Monica Lewinsky affair). Does the politician want to shield himself from criticism? Then he will tell you that his critics are tools in the hands of the forces of evil, and appeal for your help in thwarting their diabolical attacks.

And for what purpose is all this done? To advance *your* values and *your* cause and the relevance of the Christian faith to contemporary society? Perhaps. But more likely the principal objective is *to get your vote.*

The relationship of the politician to the interest group – particularly of the faith-motivated politician to faith-based interest groups and voting blocs – is complex. It will most likely be a mixture of genuineness and falsity, of truth and error. There are genuine "born again" politicians. There is such a thing as being under attack by evil (what is terrorism all about?). But the challenge for the Christian, particularly once faith groups get established as "significant political interest groups," is how to tell the genuine from the false when deception is a big part of the political game, and self-deception is the most dangerous deception of all. My advice to people of faith: do not pray for recognition as a powerful interest group and the attention of politicians such status will command. Seek rather, as Christ told his followers when he first sent them forth to do "public work," to be "wise as serpents and harmless as doves."

The fact that there was no apparent public appetite for addressing the morality of governmental behaviour, despite the obvious ethical shortcomings of the Chrétien government, was to me a symptom of a deeper problem – the low level of spirituality and sensitivity to the "good and evil" dimensions of public policy among North Americans generally. For years I had studied the phenomenon of "spiritual renewal" or "spiritual revival" throughout the history of Christendom – the ebb and flow of Christian conscience and spiritual vitality, from the days of Augustine and the decline of the Roman Empire, to the days of Martin Luther and the Reformation, through the Counter-Reformation, to the Methodist revival in England under John and Charles Wesley, to the American "awakenings" commencing with Jonathan Edwards, right down to the twentieth-century lives of Christians as diverse as Albert Schweitzer, Billy Graham, and Mother Teresa.

The essence of Christian teaching on spiritual revival is that it begins with "you" not "the other guy." This point is extremely important. If I were to suggest publicly that there is an issue of "right and wrong" in connection with the behaviour of the Chrétien government on some matter such as the war on terrorism, it would then be necessary to state by what *standard* I judge that policy or action to be right or wrong. And as soon as I define that standard, thinking people – including my opponents – will apply it to me and my behaviour and policies as well. And since none of us can claim moral perfection with respect to ourselves, our actions, and our policies, none of us will fare very well in the rigorous application of objective moral standards in the public arena. Which is why the choice is either to avoid such considerations altogether (as we have been doing in Canada) or to start them, not by seeking to point out the ethical shortcomings of other people's policies and actions, but by dealing first with our own moral and ethical shortcomings. "First cast the plank out of your own eye," said Jesus. "Then you will see clearly to take the splinter out of your brother's eye." With these thoughts in mind, I composed a short prayer for "spiritual revival" in Canada, starting with me, and resolved to pray it privately in every community I visited during the election.

All of the above constituted my "personal preparations" to deal with the issue of moral integrity and leadership in a pluralistic society, should it arise during the 1997 election campaign. I would not try to make morality an issue, but I would be prepared if it came up. Surprisingly to me, despite the dismal record of the Chrétien government from 1993 to 1997 on matters of ethics, the issue was never raised with me in any significant way by any religious leader, interest group, or member of the public during the entire campaign. Perhaps Canadians really didn't care about such things, or perhaps the time for caring still lay in the future.

■

I also gave some attention to my "image" in the period running up to the 1997 election. In the beginning I was loath to give this subject much of my time. Why couldn't the media and the public just focus on what I had to say, instead of obsessing about my voice, hair, spectacles, smile, and clothes? Of course I knew intellectually that if you are going to communicate effectively with people in this age of television, you simply can't divorce substance from image. I just didn't want to deal with the challenge on a personal level. Finally, my communications people convinced me by saying that if my personal appearance, bearing, and idiosyncrasies actually *distracted* people and kept them from hearing or seeing what I was trying to communicate, it would be wise to do something at least to minimize the distractions.

Diane Craig, an Ottawa consultant who has since become a good friend of Sandra's and mine, was invited to advise on clothes and manners, and with additional help from various specialists we got to work on "the image." As a Christmas present in 1996, paid for out of her hard-earned real estate fees, Sandra sent me to Dr. Howard Gimbel, the Calgary eye specialist, to get laser surgery on my eyes. That did away with the spectacles, which, according to my critics, made me look nerdish and professorial. Dr. Carl Boyko, a state-of-the-art Calgary dentist recommended by Diane Ablonczy, capped my teeth, thus giving me a better smile. We then went to several hairstylists in Ottawa and Calgary before asking Kari Lydiard of Style Council in Calgary to care for my hair on a regular basis. And it was Sandra, Diane Craig, and Ian Todd who undertook to get me a more leader-like wardrobe and make sure "the look" was appropriate for whatever the occasion.

Then there was the "problem" of my voice. I was accused of pronouncing certain words – like Refooooorm, Mulroooney, and veeee-sion – in a peculiar way, and of having a high, squeaky voice that was irritating to listen to. I was probably doing more public speaking at that time than any of the other federal leaders – several hundred speeches a year – and the pitch of my voice tended to rise the more tired I became. I was aware of the importance of speaking from the diaphragm, not the throat, to keep my voice relaxed and properly modulated. I just didn't practise that technique rigorously enough.

I enrolled with a voice coach for two sessions. Ron Wood then leaked the fact that I was "studying voice" to a couple of journalists. They listened the next time I gave a speech, and by golly if they didn't perceive a marked improvement. A couple of stories were written to this effect, and soon there were no more stories about my voice. Personally I don't think there was any change at all, but the media seemed to think there was an improvement and that was all that mattered. If only everything else could have been fixed so simply.

Since the media had an inordinate interest in this whole subject, I gave a full report on my image-repair experience to the 1997 Press

Gallery Dinner in Ottawa. I told the assembled scribes that I had first gone to the eye doctor to see about new spectacles, having strained my eyes trying to read the French on corn flakes boxes. But when I told him there was something wrong with my "veeeesion" he not only performed laser eye surgery, he sent me to a speech therapist. As soon as I got my eyes fixed, I looked in the mirror for the first time with my 20/20 "veeeesion," and it was then that I saw the hair. I never knew it looked like that. The last time I saw it that clearly "a little dab would do ya." Something had to be done, and someone suggested that perhaps I should imitate Jean Charest's hairstyle, which was full and frizzy. I was sure that Jean was wearing a wig, so we consulted with several used-hair salesmen on this matter, including one in Sherbrooke. They told us that Charest's hair was for real, but for me to maintain a similar style I would have to stick my finger in a light socket at least three times a day. So we dropped that idea and went to a conventional hairstylist, who gave me a new cut. As I was admiring it in the mirror, I smiled because it looked so cool. But then I saw the teeth. I never really realized they were that colour and that crooked, so we had them all capped. Finally I said to my people, "Is there anything else you are not telling me?" They responded with a list of thirty-one items, including the need to better coordinate my shirts, ties, and suits.

To tackle this problem we started with the ties, enlisting the help of a "tie consultant" in Calgary who had a truly unique service. He would come to your house or office with his laptop computer and a program for designing custom-made ties. Then he would feed all sorts of relevant information into this computer – like your hair colour, eye colour, skin colour, diameter of your Adam's apple, the distance from your navel to your chin, your astrology chart, the *Farmers' Almanac*, and your appointment schedule – and it would design a tie exactly right for every circumstance.

There was the "power tie," which radiated executive authority; the "come-hither tie," which was warm and friendly; the "back-off tie," which established psychological distance – not to mention the "look at me" tie and the "don't look at me, I'm just part of the woodwork" tie. We bought them all, but the problem was that I couldn't remember which tie did what. Sandra tried attaching little yellow stickum notes to each tie, but they came off in my suitcase, and worse, they reattached themselves to the wrong ties. I lived in mortal fear of going to a meeting with Gilles Duceppe or Buzz Hargrove supposedly wearing my "back-off" tie, only to find out that I had on my "come-hither" tie.

Finally I gave up, and simply submitted to Ian Todd's critical once-over every morning before setting off for our appointments. If I had on the wrong combination of shirt, tie, and suit, I would try to excuse myself by reciting Carl Sandburg's commentary on Lincoln (from the first volume of his biography), that "his clothes said, 'He was thinking of something else when he put us on this morning.'" Ian was not amused, but slowly my image improved.

■

By the spring of 1997, Reform was in full campaign mode. On one weekend in mid-April we field-tested our grassroots army by having it deliver 900,000 copies of our Fresh Start platform door to door in more than 150 federal ridings. We had been holding nomination meetings steadily and were well on our way to fielding more than 230 candidates. I was nevertheless conscious that at the grassroots level of the party, and among the electorate generally, there was not the same energy level as there had been prior to the 1993 election, when disillusionment with the federal Conservatives and antipathy to Brian Mulroney were at their peak. But in terms of candidates, platform, and campaign expertise we were much better equipped in 1997 than in 1993. Whereas our success in 1993 had been primarily due to the strong and vigorous activity of our grassroots army, our success in 1997 would depend more on the effectiveness of the national campaign and the national Leader's Tour.

Our campaign strategists, in particular Rick Anderson, had correctly anticipated that the election would be called early, most likely for April 27, 1997. We scheduled a Reform conference in Toronto for April 24–26.

As we had anticipated, Chrétien went to see the Governor General the Sunday after our conference and the federal election was called for June 2. Our big campaign bus, with Fraser Smith as wagon-master and "Fresh Start" emblazoned all over it, was ready and waiting at our Toronto hotel. We were off and running before the Prime Minister had finished his press conference, proclaiming that Reform offered Canadians a Fresh Start, that the Liberals offered them a False Start, that the NDP needed a Jump Start, and that the Tories might not get started at all.

That first day of campaigning involved stops at three Toronto constituency campaign offices, including that of Janice Lim in Mississauga Centre. This was not strong territory for Reform, and unfortunately Janice had got herself into immediate difficulty by raising the Ringma affair. My emphasis on "issues" – like taxes, families, crime, unity, and accountability – consequently got lost in stories about Janice's remarks.

There was actually something quite bizarre and contradictory about the way the Toronto and national media pounced on poor Janice that first day. Here was a slight, female Reform candidate of Asian descent – herself a complete contradiction of the Reform stereotype – surrounded largely by middle-aged, white, male Anglo-Saxon reporters, physically crowding her and accusing her of harbouring hidden prejudices. If an impartial observer had taken a video shot of that scene, the visuals and voice-over would themselves have provided a very powerful statement on prejudice and discrimination.

The next morning, I engaged in a session with commuters at Toronto's Union Station, the most frequent response being, "Election? What election?" Then we were off to the CBC studios for the first of what were to be daily five-minute appearances by various party spokespersons on the national network, followed by question-and-answer sessions with reporters.

That day the whole team piled onto the campaign bus, media in tow, for a campaign lunch in Brantford, followed by an evening rally in London North Centre, where another of our dynamic young Ontario candidates, Tara Bingham, was campaigning. From there it was on to St. John's, Newfoundland, and then to a rousing rally in Fredericton with most of our New Brunswick candidates. The crowd gave a warm reception to my speech, "A Fresh Start for the Atlantic Economy." I contrasted the Liberals' discredited "contribution" to the economy of that region – handouts and subsidies to the few –

with Reform's free-enterprise, free-market approach of tax relief for the many and expanded North-South trade with "the Boston States." The crowd responded enthusiastically, and we felt for the first time that we might have a chance of capturing our first seat in Atlantic Canada.

By the afternoon of Tuesday, April 29 – the third day of the campaign – we were headed to Quebec City, where I was scheduled to meet Gilles St-Laurent and eight other Quebec candidates. We wanted to communicate our Fresh Start for Quebec via "*la troisième voie*" – not the separation of the Bloc, not the status quo federalism of Jean Chrétien and Jean Charest, but reform of the federation through equality and a re-balancing of powers. Gilles, a law professor at Laval, and his wife, Mychelyne, a prominent criminal lawyer and TV personality – both warm and sincere people – were credible spokespersons for this position. But there was minimal media interest in this event since our campaign efforts in Quebec had already been dismissed as mere tokenism by both the national and regional media and we were given no chance of winning any seats. The CBC-TV representative in Quebec City was particularly contemptuous of our efforts and made it clear that he had no intention of covering our visit.

What that correspondent didn't know was that earlier in the week Cliff Fryers had received a most interesting fax at our campaign war room in Calgary. It appeared to be a copy of the new Liberal Red Book, which was to be released by the Prime Minister with great fanfare later in the week. Cliff immediately asked our source to send the original to Reform's parliamentary research office in Ottawa so that we could verify that it was the real thing. He also faxed a copy to the Leader's Tour care of Ian Todd so that we could take a look. This fax – more than a hundred pages long – started arriving at a machine at the reception desk of our hotel in St. John's, precisely when Ian was checking us in with two dozen media people right behind. The desk clerk went out of his way to tell Ian that he had a big, long, important fax for him, causing Norm Ovenden of the *Edmonton Journal*, who was within earshot, to inquire what all that was about. Fortunately the media crew and half of our own gang had been imbibing fairly heavily on the flight over to the Rock, and in the hazy atmosphere that prevailed as everyone piled into the hotel Ian was able to escape to his room with the fax without any further questions. Once there, he and Rick and Larry Welsh examined it carefully – they couldn't believe their eyes. Larry became so excited that he began to jump up and down on the bed. Then, in consultation with the war room in Calgary, they hatched the plan to have me release the Liberal Red Book on behalf of Mr. Chrétien in Quebec City.

The next day, Paul Wilson and our policy people in Ottawa completed their analysis of the Red Book's contents. To no one's surprise, they found that the Liberals had no intention of increasing efforts to control costs and eliminate the deficit in order to deliver tax relief quickly. Instead, they intended to unveil promises to spend taxpayers' money in more than a dozen areas. At this point it was our Ottawa office that had the actual copy of the Red Book, so Frank Hall, our Atlantic campaign liaison person in Ottawa, was dispatched to deliver the precious document to me. He caught up to us in Fredericton just as we were leaving for Quebec City.

And so it was that, late on Tuesday afternoon, we invited the national and local media in Quebec City to an unscheduled news conference on a balcony at the Château Frontenac Hotel, overlooking the mighty St. Lawrence. Less than a mile away were the Plains of Abraham, where the French forces under General Montcalm and the British forces under General Wolfe had fired many musket volleys into each other more than two centuries ago. We now had an opportunity to fire a volley of a different sort into the Liberal campaign. "Goodbye Red Book, Hello Cheque Book" was my announcement, as I "unveiled" the Liberal election platform. (The phrase had been suggested by Jim Armour, our deputy communications director.) We then handed out copies of the Liberal Red Book to all media present. The media on our tour were of course ecstatic at the opportunity to "scoop" their brethren on the more prestigious Prime Minister's tour. We also made sure that as many as possible of our candidates got their copy of the Liberal Red Book before the local Liberal candidates got theirs. Thus in many communities we were able to scoop the Liberals at the local level as well as the national level. This was just the boost we needed to energize our grassroots troops at the outset of the campaign. The only people who were unhappy about this campaign coup were our opponents, the Liberals in particular, and the CBC's Quebec City man, who had to buy his copy of the Red Book second-hand from one of the other networks.

Meanwhile, in Manitoba, the Red River was overflowing its banks, flooding thousands of acres and endangering major parts of Winnipeg and many smaller communities. Chrétien had sought to take political advantage of the situation by having himself photographed heaving a sandbag into place. Manitobans were less than impressed, and a controversy broke out as to how the federal election could be properly carried out in southern Manitoba under such disastrous conditions. I called upon the Cabinet to exercise a little-known section of the Elections Act (section 13), which empowered it to withdraw the election writ in ridings affected by the flood, and to reschedule the election in those ridings within three months. Such action first required certification by the chief electoral officer that (by reason of the floods) it was "impracticable" to hold the election in the affected ridings. I publicly urged the chief electoral officer to provide such a certification, and the Liberals were forced to take a position for or against these proposals. It did not escape the commentators, particularly in Manitoba, that Reform appeared to know the Elections Act better than the Prime Minister. While the government dithered, homemade signs appeared around southern Manitoba urging voters to "Sandbag the Liberals." (Jean-Pierre Kingsley, the chief electoral officer, subsequently announced that in his judgment it was "not impracticable" to conduct the federal election in the flooded ridings. Southern Manitoba would vote on June 2 along with the rest of the country.)

One of the keys to successful campaigning is that when you have something going for you – like "Goodbye Red Book, Hello Cheque Book" – you stick with it as long as you can. This we continued to do as our Leader's Tour rolled on to Saskatoon, Vancouver, Surrey, and Edmonton. In Edmonton I was met at the municipal airport by Deborah Grey, who gave me a fast ride around the tarmac on her motorcycle before we jointly addressed a Reform rally in a nearby hangar. Deborah demonstrated her skill at "Red Book tossing," and

I explained that, just as the Edmonton Oilers were Canada's best hope in the NHL playoffs (then in progress), so was Reform Canada's best hope in the election playoffs. All in all, great optics and great fun, apart from the fact that the local constabulary threatened to arrest us for riding a motorcycle without helmets and driving an unauthorized vehicle on a runway.

The only sour note in the first week of the campaign came, predictably, not from our opponents but from within. Miro Cernetig of the *Globe and Mail*'s Vancouver bureau, a self-professed authority on Reform, ran a long article gloomily predicting that the party had made a mistake in seeking to be more than a regional party, that we were most likely on our way to ignominious defeat, that I was clearly a liability to the party, and that the June 2 election would be my "last hurrah." His sources for this insightful intelligence? Not the Liberal or Tory backroom boys, but Ken Whyte, Ted Byfield, Tom Flanagan, and Stephen Harper. Why people who professed to be supportive of the principles of Reform would provide comments disparaging its election efforts, at the very time when scores of Reform candidates and thousands of grassroots Reformers were working their hearts out to make the campaign launch a success, was beyond me. It has something to do with what someone has called "the conservative sickness," an affliction (similar to that found in some inbred species of mink) that causes a certain breed of conservative to devour its own.

■

The big difference for me personally between the 1993 and 1997 federal election campaigns was that this time Sandra was with me. We knew what we were doing, and we enjoyed doing it – together. While the days would begin very early, because of the media deadlines they would sometimes end before nine in the evening and we would have time for a stroll – on the waterfront in Halifax, in a park in Toronto or Regina, on the boardwalk in Quebec City, or on the seawall in Vancouver. In addition to offering sound advice, Sandra brought fun and laughter to the campaign bus and the whole Leader's Tour. While I would be working on the next day's speech,

Sandra would sometimes join the media crew – singing karaoke in Owen Sound with Sean Durkin of the Ottawa *Sun* and missing the campaign bus in Toronto with CTV's LeeEllen Carroll.

As we arrived at each new campaign stop, Sandra would make it a game to see if she could guess the identity of the plainclothes RCMP or OPP people who were usually awaiting us. On more than one occasion, she walked up to somebody who appeared to be trying to make themselves inconspicuous and said, just for fun, "I know who you are." Usually she was right, but not always, which led to some interesting encounters with baffled strangers, whom she would disarm by saying, "I know who you are. You're a voter, and we're looking for your support."

On one occasion, Sandra and I went on a walk along the Rideau Canal in Ottawa prior to a campaign event, with the intention of getting a bite of supper by ourselves at a restaurant. As usual, we were accompanied at a distance by two plainclothes RCMP officers. When we entered the restaurant, one of them took a table not far from us. The other then entered a few minutes later, ostensibly "looking for his friend" and in the process walking around the restaurant, "casing the joint" so to speak. This was their standard modus operandi in such situations, and Sandra was quite familiar with it. But for some reason on this occasion, as soon as Sandra saw the second officer, she stood up, waved at him, and said, "Over here, Officer. Over here. Your friend is over here," pointing to his colleague, who by then was rolling his eyes heavenward. I'm sure that Ian got an earful that night about "Momma Bird" blowing the RCMP's cover. But I'm also sure that every one of the RCMP assigned to us would have gone to the wall to keep both Sandra and me from the slightest harm.

Sandra is very outgoing in crowds, particularly if they include young people or parents with babies. This would sometimes lead to our getting separated going in or out of venues, and I would hear the nearest RCMP officer whispering into the microphone in his sleeve, "Momma Bird is out of the nest. Momma Bird is out of the nest, again!" To this day, if I want to tease Sandra about her spontaneous departures from a pre-established plan, I whisper into my sleeve, "Momma Bird is out of the nest."

Our campaign efforts were also energized by the initiative of some of our younger Reformers, headed up by Kory Teneycke, who took it upon themselves to help "win Ontario." They raised enough money on their own to finance a month-long bus tour, complete with accommodations at what they described as "the worst hotels that Ontario has to offer." Dubbing themselves "The Reform SWAT Team" – with Andrew Stec as wagon-master, Andrew Jones as advance man, and Rob Taylor as volunteer coordinator – young people from university campus associations and high schools soon filled up the bus and set out to meet their target of visiting thirty ridings in thirty days.

Motivated by morning music videos and fuelled by pizza and doughnuts, the team campaigned vigorously, helping out in every way possible, from dropping literature to chanting and waving banners at Leader's events to mounting counter-demonstrations to quell the occasional group of protesters. For a little variety and stimulation (this was an energetic bunch), the SWAT Team would also drop into the campaign offices of opposition candidates to see what they could stir up.

More than two hundred young people came and went from the Reform SWAT Team bus. For many, it was their first experience of political campaigning, and it made for many "first time memories." As well as lasting friendships, it created a lasting interest in politics – Kory, Andrew, Rob, and others, like Jenni Byrne, Shuv Majumdar, and Ben Perrin, all went on to work in some capacity for Reform after the election.

■

In the months leading up to the federal election, the national unity issue, while not on the front pages, was always simmering somewhere in the background. After the Quebec referendum of 1995 it was obvious that some plan – Plan A, as it came to be called – was required to offer some form of renewed federalism to Quebecers and other concerned Canadians. Our idea of Plan A was a complete rebalancing of the powers between the federal and provincial governments and affirmation of the principle of the constitutional equality of citizens and provinces. The Liberals' idea of Plan A, however, was simply to affirm that Quebec was a "distinct society" and to give everybody (but particularly Quebec) a veto over future constitutional change. It was typical of Chrétien's negative approach: Don't empower anybody to "do something" – that would be too radical and extreme. They might actually change something. Instead, empower everybody to stop anybody else from doing anything by giving everyone a veto. Chrétien liberalism at its dynamic best.

During the first two weeks of the federal campaign, any attempt to discuss proposals for improving federalism drew nothing but yawns from the media and the voters. But on May 7 a startling revelation came out of Quebec that once again thrust the national unity issue onto the national stage in a negative rather than a positive way.

The first week of the campaign had been a disaster for the Bloc Québécois. Its new leader, Gilles Duceppe, had been photographed at a cheese factory wearing a protective cap that made him look like an alien from outer space. His campaign bus had also got lost on several occasions, and the Quebec Federation of Labour – one of the sovereigntist movement's staunchest supporters – declined to endorse the BQ. Then on May 7 the Quebec newspaper *Le Soleil* published an excerpt from a soon-to-be-published book by former premier Jacques Parizeau in which Parizeau made clear that if a majority of Quebecers had voted "Yes" in the 1995 referendum, the Quebec government would have moved immediately to declare independence unilaterally without waiting to "negotiate a new partnership with Canada" as promised in the question on the referendum ballot. Suddenly, all those issues that we said needed to be addressed by a Plan B – a contingency plan for dealing with an actual secession attempt – could no longer be dismissed as "hypothetical" or extreme, and all the federal leaders were called upon for a response.

Even before the Quebec referendum, Reform had been asking Chrétien and the Liberal government to clarify their position on what they would do to protect Canada's interests in the event that Quebec attempted, democratically or undemocratically, to secede. It seemed obvious to us that unilateral secession was illegal, and that the government should say so. But the government had refused to take a position.

When Quebec City lawyer Guy Bertrand wrote Chrétien (prior to the referendum) urging him to refer the question of the legality of a unilateral secession attempt to the Supreme Court, Chrétien again refused, saying the question was political, not judicial. Bertrand then initiated an action as a private citizen, which in August 1996 resulted in a judgment by Justice Pidgeon of the Quebec Superior Court rejecting arguments that the courts had no jurisdiction over the secession issue and posing four questions on its legality that he said merited judicial determination. Then, in September 1996, the Chrétien government did a complete about-face, took over the whole process without any credit to Bertrand, and referred the question of the legality of secession to the Supreme Court of Canada.

While we were supportive of this long-delayed and modest display of backbone, Jean Charest, leader of the Conservatives and the Prime Minister's ally in the referendum campaign, was not. In March 1997, just weeks before the federal election, both Jean Charest and Joe Clark strongly denounced the government's support of the Supreme Court reference case and declared that there was no need whatsoever for a Plan B. The newly released Conservative platform put all the Conservative eggs in the Plan A basket, the principal egg being yet another affirmation of the tired old "distinct society" concept.

Reform's Fresh Start election platform contained a two-page section on national unity, evenly balanced between our Plan A proposals to reform federalism and our Plan B contingency proposals to deal with secession if the sovereigntists forced it upon the country. No federal political party had publicly raised Plan B issues more consistently than Reform or publicly outlined its contingency thinking.

And suddenly, national reporters like Susan Delacourt were writing that "the Plan B national-unity strategy is starting to look like a very good idea." Unhampered by any compunction about sticking to the facts, Chrétien and Stephane Dion immediately began to claim that they had been Plan B enthusiasts all along, pointing to their belated support of the Supreme Court reference case and their belated interest in clarification of separation terms as "proof" of their enthusiasm. What Chrétien and Dion still steadfastly refused to say, however, was what the Liberals actually proposed to do if Quebec at some future time attempted a unilateral secession. Jean Charest, on the other hand, still insisted that no Plan B was necessary and that he would even abandon the Supreme Court reference case if given the chance to do so.

Parizeau's revelation, rather than any statement of mine, made the Plan B aspect of national unity a federal election issue. But it was now quite appropriate for me to address the subject, and to address it pointedly, which I did. My speeches – starting in Victoria on the night of May 8 to a crowd of 1,000 people, including one of B.C.'s foremost constitutional experts, Mel Smith – contained a blunt challenge to the other federalist leaders, in particular Chrétien and Charest: "Do you finally agree with us that it is time to have a real contingency plan to deal with an attempted secession? If you do, show the public your plan, we'll show them ours, and let the voters decide who is best prepared to protect Canada's interests and deal with that contingency."

■

The leaders' debates were to be held in Ottawa in the second week of May. The networks had given us seven possible topics, from which they intended to choose five. We prepared content, key messages, and rebuttals on Jobs, Economy, Social Programs, Vision of the Twenty-first Century, Unity, Justice, and Role of Government, as well as opening and closing remarks. With so much instruction and advice on content and style, I felt a little like the man who was advised to keep his eye on the ball, his ear to the ground, his nose to the grindstone, and his shoulder to the wheel. The big challenge would be to do all those things simultaneously and actually get the job done.

Much of our preparation work had to be done on Sunday for Monday's debate, so there was no opportunity to go to church. In any case, my presence at a church service during an election, while perhaps conducive to politicking, would not have been conducive to worship. This Sunday, however, we received numerous calls of support and encouragement from our children, assuring us of their love and prayers. Avryll, who always used to give her teammates inspirational quotations and Bible verses before swim meets, had one for me. From the Apostle Paul's letter to Timothy: "I remind you to fan into flame the gift of God, which is in you. . . . For God did not give us a spirit of timidity, but a spirit of power, of love and of self-discipline" (II Tim. 1:6-7, NIV). Who could ask for better support or encouragement than this?

On Monday, May 12, after a short nap in the late afternoon and a light dinner, I was escorted without incident by my team and a group of Reform supporters through the crowd of partisans who surrounded the National Conference Centre to my dressing room. After makeup and the obligatory group photo, the debate began.

The theme of my opening and closing remarks was a challenge to the voters to make a choice. Did they want more of the same from the traditional parties – big government, high taxes, and special status for some – or did they want a Fresh Start with Reform – smaller government, lower taxes, and equality for all?

We all went after Chrétien on the issue of jobs. I asked him to describe how a job was created, because Canada needed several million of them. Chrétien responded with a non-answer, citing the government's "record," while Charest and I both argued that deficit reduction and tax relief were the stimuli needed.

As soon as Charest presented himself as a deficit fighter and tax cutter, I raised the credibility issue that had driven so many Conservatives into the Reform camp. The Mulroney government, of which Charest had been a member, had been given nine years to reduce the deficit and had instead pushed it up to record levels. The Mulroney government, of which Charest was a member, had been given nine years to lower taxes and had instead repeatedly raised them and introduced the hated GST. With such a record, how could Canadians possibly have any faith in Tory promises to reduce the deficit or taxes now? Charest's rebuttal – to the effect that "that was then and this is now" – was weak.

On health care, I went after the government's priorities. If health care was such a priority, why was the Prime Minister pouring money into Bombardier (already a profitable company), a canoe museum in his riding, and a hundred other lower-priority projects, instead of putting that money into health care? But in the helter-skelter back and forth among five political leaders about what was wrong with Medicare and what should be done about it, I was not able to clearly establish a critical point: if you are going to cut health care transfers to the provinces – which the Liberals had done – you simply *must* open up the Canada Health Act to enable the provinces to get the money from different sources.

Nothing significant happened until the discussion on national unity. While the camera was on the others, I could see Charest practising – actually mouthing the words and gesturing – his prepackaged statement. This he then proceeded to give when the camera turned on him: "If there's one commitment I've made to my children, it's that I'm going to pass on to them the country I received from my parents." This received applause from the assembled audience, the only applause of the evening, and I immediately sensed that most of the media would consider this a "defining moment," regardless of how artificial and staged it might have been. My response to the unity issue was, as usual, long and sound on substance but lacking the emotional appeal of Charest's response. It was only after the debate (how often we politicians think of our best lines *after* the meeting, debate, or interview is over) that it occurred to me that my immediate comeback should have been, "If there's one commitment I've made to *my* children, it's that I'm going to pass on to them a *better* country than I received from my parents. *That is the difference between the traditional parties and Reform.*"

There is always an awkward moment immediately after such debates when the leader returns to his team for the post-mortem. On the one hand, his people want to assure him that he has done well, in order to sustain morale for the rest of the campaign. On the other hand, they want to be realistic, because if mistakes have been made or someone else has scored a telling point, there are countermeasures to be taken. My gang's assessment was that Alexa McDonough and Duceppe could be ignored, that Chrétien had not done well and some Liberal votes had been shaken loose, that I had scored high on substance, but that Charest had scored high on emotion. What remained unsaid, because we all knew it, was that at least in the short run, emotion counts for more than substance. I felt disappointed that I had let our troops down.

Thus my old nemesis returned to haunt me. I had learned love of country long before entering federal politics, from people who had given their entire lives to public service or to writing passionately about the country's history. But the only way I seemed capable of personally demonstrating my emotions about Canada was to meticulously study the dangers and opportunities that lay ahead, to devote endless hours to coming up with potential safeguards, solutions, and policies that would advance the national interest, and to work like a dog to persuade my fellow citizens to support those safeguards, solutions, and policies. But studying, thinking, planning, and working hard count for little if you can't also express your concerns and commitments in ways that connect with people emotionally. I had a great deal of difficulty doing that, even on a personal level, let alone publicly.

The French debate was held the next night. Because of my limited facility in French, only my opening and closing remarks were *en français*, and I replied to questions in English. I did get one mixed compliment on my French from a Quebec commentator. He declared that my accent was not too bad, but had I really intended to declare war on Chile?

■

In the days immediately following the leaders' debates we continued to follow our "issue-based" campaign strategy. "Chrétien has no plan for jobs or unity," I told the regular CBC morning news conference, "but we do – let me tell you about it." On to North Bay, hometown of Mike Harris, where our candidate, Laurie Kidd, and I urged voters to bring the deficit-cutting and tax-relief dimensions of the Common Sense Revolution to Ottawa. Then to Montreal for one of those "staged" CBC town hall meetings, this one on national unity. Charest and McDonough were supposed to attend, but both bailed out. A waste of time. Then on to St. Catharines for an emotional law-and-order rally attended by several families of victims, including the family of Kristen French, one of the victims of Paul Bernardo

and Karla Homolka. I appealed to the audience to put the Liberal
justice system on trial during this election. Let the Liberals defend
it if they could. I reiterated the charge that the Liberal justice
system frequently put the rights of criminals and persons accused of
crimes ahead of those of law-abiding citizens and victims. I then
asked the audience – the jury – to tell Canadians whether they
found the defendant innocent or guilty. "Guilty!" they roared back.

We had now completed the first three weeks of a five-week campaign. The next two would be the ones that really counted. It was
therefore time to take stock, and make any mid-course adjustments
required to position us properly for the last big push. While
Chrétien was not doing well, Charest and the Conservatives were
rising in the polls, mainly on the strength of the boost he had gained
through the leaders' debates. We, on the other hand, had started
well, but our support was not growing as it should have. A *Globe and
Mail*/Environics poll released on May 17 showed the Liberals down
in support among committed voters from 47 to 40 per cent, the
Conservatives up to 25 per cent from 16 in March, and Reform up
to 18 per cent from 12. There was still lots of room for voters to shift,
49 per cent of respondents saying that they might change their vote
before election day. But the *Globe* emphasized the "soaring appreciation" for Charest in Quebec and projected that the Tories would
form the Opposition with fifty seats if the current trends held.

In our judgment, both Chrétien and Charest were vulnerable on
the national unity front. Both constantly expressed their commitment to Canada and Quebec in emotional terms, but neither had
any substance to back that commitment up. It was time for us to
attack these weaknesses and put forward our own alternatives, and
we had the ammunition to do so. It would also be up to me to try to
raise the emotional content of our national unity positions to
match the substantive content, and this would prove to be my
greatest challenge.

On Monday and Tuesday I was back in Atlantic Canada for a
rousing breakfast rally in Halifax with my former chief of staff,
Stephen Greene. Then it was on to Yarmouth, Saint John, a big rally
in Hampton, New Brunswick, and then a stop at a Fredericton
Burger King, home of the Big Whopper. I had wanted to get onto

the "integrity" theme somewhere along the campaign trail, and that's what this stop proved to be about, although not on the profound philosophical level that I had envisioned. Many voters in Atlantic Canada were simply mad at the Liberals for lying – for telling "whoppers." To help make this point, our communications people persuaded the Burger King staff to present me with a specially made plate of the Liberals' Biggest Whoppers. There was the Job Whopper ("We will create jobs in Atlantic Canada"), the GST Whopper ("We will kill, scrap, and abolish the GST"), the Health Care Whopper ("We will sustain and improve Medicare"), the Gold-Plated MP Pension Whopper, and so on. I was invited to comment on each Whopper, which I did, and the media loved it.

As the election progressed, the NDP and some of their more militant union supporters became increasingly frustrated that their own campaign was simply not getting off the ground, while Reform's campaign was picking up speed and even support among traditional NDP voters. In Ontario and B.C., Reform was doing very well among blue-collar workers by hammering away on "increase your take-home pay by demanding tax relief," our commitment to families, and our tough positions on crime. And the NDP was not well positioned at all to take advantage of the growing focus on national unity, particularly the popularity of Plan B. Since most PQ and BQ supporters considered themselves social democrats, the NDP couldn't attack separatism without attacking their own.

Upon our arrival in Guelph, Ontario, in the early afternoon of May 21, we were supposed to address a small outdoor rally organized by the local candidate, Lyle McNair, near the university. But the local NDP and union organizers had assembled a crowd of students and rent-a-mob types to surround the venue chanting accusations of racism, homophobia, sexism, etc. We had not had enough advance warning of this reception, so as soon as our campaign bus pulled up, it was surrounded by this mob. Our only options then were to simply pull out and appear to have been "chased out of town," or attempt to go ahead and exercise our democratic right to hold a political meeting, knowing that the visuals would not be pretty. The RCMP and OPP dutifully provided a "wall" through the mob of yelling, sign-swinging demonstrators, who had also added spitting to their repertoire. Sandra and I slowly made our way to the stage, where Lyle was waiting. There was actually another crowd present, consisting mainly of our own supporters and regular voters, some of them with children, but they too were being jostled and insulted by the protesters.

Lyle and I endeavoured to say a few words, which were completely drowned out by the yells of the protesters. After a few more attempts we made our way back to the bus and departed. The whole affair, of course, provided the media with all kinds of action and colour, particularly focusing on one of the front-row demonstrators, who had green hair and teeth that appeared to have been filed to sharp points. Rick Anderson's oldest daughter Jaimie was with us that day and became separated from Rick and the bus during the melee, causing some anxious moments. We soon found her, however, and the bus was on its way. Rick's only comment to the media on the whole affair was, "We might have lost the green hair vote." Avi Lewis and friends tried to organize a similar reception in Toronto when I made a short appearance at a MuchMusic venue, but that time we were better prepared, and a large group of our own young people from the Reform Youth Bus were present to out-yell and out-perform the protesters.

Peaceful demonstrations that do not infringe on the political rights of others are a legitimate form of political expression in Canada, but in my view much could be done to improve the media coverage of such events in order to give the public a more truthful picture of what exactly is going on. For example, when the cameras are behind or among the mob – on the side of the demonstrators, facing the police and the targets of the demonstration – the viewing public gets the demonstrator's perspective. But when the cameras are positioned facing the mob – showing the scene from the perspective of the police and the people who are the targets – the viewing public gets an equally important perspective of the event. *Both perspectives* are needed for balance.

If the aim of the media is to show demonstrations as they really are, not simply as they are staged to appear, the cameras should also probe the crowd to show the faces and actions of the organizers and directors of the scene, not just the front-line extras. In most "political demonstrations" such as the minor one in Guelph, if you look back past the first three or four rows of demonstrators you may well spot the local CUPE organizer, the NDP (or some other party) campaign manager, the rent-a-mob guys from Toronto, or whoever is actually in charge of the affair, giving instructions on what to yell, when to yell it, and where to move to get into the camera shot. These people should not be allowed to remain anonymous. They are players in the political game, even though they are using others, and they should be responsible for their actions. If someone gets hurt, or if someone's rights are infringed, they should be just as accountable as the police and the front-line activists.

On May 23, I visited the town of Napanee, Ontario, accompanied by our Reform candidate Sean McAdam and his fiancée, Lisa Samson. This is the town where Sir John A. Macdonald, exhausted and deathly ill, gave his last public address in 1891. And the Town Square where I was scheduled to speak was the place where Sir John A. had also given his first speech – on the National Policy and federal-provincial relations – in the 1882 federal election campaign. It was a very special occasion for Sandra and me on two counts. First, because I could identify with the history of the place and would be speaking on the very theme that challenged and tormented Macdonald for most of his political life. And second, because we were with two very special people. Lisa had joined Reform as a high school student in Calgary. Sean joined us when we first began organizing in Ontario, running for us as a candidate in 1993. Both of them had come to work for Reform in Ottawa after the 1993 election, and now they were going to be married. They were one of several dozen bright and active young couples – she from the West, he from Ontario – "brought together" by Reform and for whom Sandra and I had a special place in our hearts. If only we could bring the country together in the same way.

In my address, I delineated the inherent inequality of the "two nations" concept, special status, "distinct society," and a host of subsidiary federal policies at the heart of the traditional parties' conception of federalism. This I contrasted with Reform's principle of the equality of all citizens and provinces under law and the constitutional measures and federal policies that flowed from it. Why did busy and practical Canadian voters need to be interested in any of this? Because when the unity of your country is continually under threat, the capacity of your national government to address the day-to-day issues of concern to you – jobs, taxes, crime, health care – is drastically reduced. And why did Ontario voters need to pay attention to these competing visions of unity? Because the traditional one was being championed by federal politicians from Quebec (Chrétien and Charest), the equality vision was coming to them mainly from the West, and Ontario, as the elder sister of Confederation, was in a position to tip the balance one way or the other.

The media, particularly in the context of a national election campaign, dislike these heavy-duty speeches full of reasoned argument because they are irreducible to the short, colourful clips desired by the television networks, and they never mesh neatly with the preconceived ideas of editors as to what is relevant and newsworthy. To be fair, however, our media gang gave it their best shot, using some of the visuals of the Town Square and asking me in the scrum to illustrate how citizens and provinces were treated "unequally" under current constitutional arrangements.

I did not answer that question on the spot as well as I should have. But over the next few days we rolled out the more comprehensive answer. The provinces were not treated equally in the Senate, nor was there the equality of genuine representation by population in the House. The federal spending power was not exercised equally; the subsidization of clothing factories in Quebec killed clothing factories in Ontario; federal taxation of energy enterprises favoured publicly owned energy companies over private ones; federal tax policies discriminated against families that chose to raise their children at home; federal purchasing policies, distorted by patronage, were exercised unequally (witness the CF-18 maintenance contract); federally tolerated internal barriers to trade fostered inequality; the Indian Act and the reserve system perpetuated inequality; and the list went on and on.

The following week, the *Globe and Mail* – founded by reformer George Brown – came out in favour of Charest as its preferred choice for leader of the Official Opposition. But Sean McAdam called me to say that all was not lost. The Napanee *Beaver* had come out solidly for Reform.

◼

Several months before the federal election, we had prepared and tested eleven television ads for possible use in our national advertising campaign. At the front end, our caucus, executive council, and I all had input and looked at some of the rough cuts. But it was up to our campaign team to refine and produce the final ads.

A couple of them contrasted the national unity positions of the other federal leaders with my own. The first, which ran in the early part of the campaign, was relatively innocuous. The second was stronger. It began with stark black-and-white images of Chrétien and Charest filling the screen, accompanied by a voice-over: "Last time these men almost lost our country, and they will do it again . . ." (the visual then switched to the Quebec referendum result – YES 51%, NO 49% – and "DISTINCT SOCIETY" in big bold letters) ". . . when these men" (the picture switched to stark black-and-white images of Duceppe and Bouchard) "hold their next referendum. Preston Manning and the Reform Party believe there is a better way to keep our country together." (The picture switched briefly to me and then to an outline of our Fresh Start platform on unity.) "Equality of all provinces. A real plan to deal with any future votes on separation. And a voice for all Canadians, not just Quebec politicians." (The picture switched back to Chrétien, Charest, Parizeau, and Bouchard.) "Reform! Now you have a Real Alternative."

The purpose of this ad was to draw attention in a compelling way to the unity issue; to contrast the separatist challenge (represented by Bouchard and Duceppe) with the ineffectual nature of the traditional federalist responses (represented by Chrétien and Charest) as demonstrated by the near-loss of the 1995 referendum; to call for a better plan to bring clarity and resolution to the national unity issue; and to insist that the voices of all Canadians, not just politicians from Quebec, be heard and respected in the formulation of such a plan.

In my mind, the origins of the theme of this ad – particularly the part about needing "a voice for all Canadians, not just Quebec politicians" – went back to the 1995 Quebec referendum campaign. Remember? I was the only federal leader during that period to tour the rest of Canada holding open question-and-answer sessions. I was the one who heard first-hand the concern felt by large numbers of Canadians, often edged with bitterness and resentment, that the future of their country and their children's country was being decided by the politicians and voters of one province, and that the national government was doing nothing to give them a voice in that decision, let alone a vote. I was the one who was told on numerous occasions, in different ways: "Canada and its Constitution belong to *all* of us. Quebec politicians and voters should *not* have a monopoly on determining our constitutional future." Nor did it escape me that this sentiment was most strongly expressed in British Columbia, the province where polarization over issues is a distinguishing feature of the political culture, and the province that had voted most strongly against the Charlottetown Accord. The messages of our 1997 national unity ads were not, therefore, some spur-of-the-moment creation; they had deep roots in widely shared and long-standing public sentiments and were strategically sound.

After the leaders' debates, and the temporary boost to Charest's support, it was important that I vigorously reaffirm Reform's position on national unity and contrast it starkly with those of Chrétien and Charest. There was general agreement among myself, Rick, and the Calgary war room not only that it was time to run the second national unity ad but that it had to be "torqued up" to make its message even more compelling. The actual "torquing" was left to Bryan Thomas, subject to Cliff's approval in Calgary. After some debate, it involved superimposing a large red circle with a slash through it – the universal symbol for NO – across the onscreen faces of Chrétien, Charest, Duceppe, and Bouchard. Our point was that Chrétien's and Charest's status quo federalism, plus "distinct society" and their reluctance to embrace a Plan B, were as much a threat to national unity as Duceppe's and Bouchard's advocacy of sovereignty association. We urged Canadians to say no to all of them, and to affirm that *all* Canadians, not just Quebecers and

Quebec-based politicians, must have a say in the constitutional future of the country.

Rick Anderson ended up taking a lot of the heat for this ad after it became controversial. But in fact, by the time Rick actually saw the torqued-up version it was a *fait accompli* and on its way to be aired. Rick's wife, Michelle, never did like it, nor did a number of other women involved in our campaign, and if I had known that, I would probably have had second thoughts myself. The bottom line, however, was that I had told Calgary to "torque it up," they had done so, and now we would have to live with the consequences, good and bad.

The ad ran for the first time on Thursday, May 22, and provoked the expected storm. On the positive side, its message accurately expressed the feelings of a large cross-section of Canadians whose views had been ignored by the traditional parties. It also enraged our opponents and those media and members of the public who had never accepted our positions on national unity. The madder they got, the more they talked and commented on "the Quebec ad." The TV networks showed the ad as a news or commentary feature dozens and dozens of times, giving it much more air time than we could ever have hoped to pay for.

On the negative side, the ad was repeatedly misrepresented as anti-Quebec and anti-French. Frequently the television commentators would show our ad – the visuals – *with their own voice-over*. What the ad was saying – that all Canadians, not just Quebec politicians, should have a say in Canada's constitutional future – was replaced with someone else's misinterpretation. We were unable to counteract this effectively, particularly in Quebec, and so the commentaries on the ad reinforced the misconceptions of those who wanted to believe the worst about Reform.

Abraham Lincoln once said that an effective political strategist is "able to raise a cause which shall produce an effect, and then fight the effect."[*] In our case, the Quebec ad provoked an "over the top" reaction from both Chrétien and Charest that Reform was

---

[*] Carl Sandburg, *Abraham Lincoln: The Prairie Years II* (New York: Charles Scribner's Sons, 1948), p. 115.

able to campaign against for the remainder of the election. Speaking in Hamilton, Ontario, Chrétien accused me of running "the most divisive campaign in Canadian history" and of appealing "to the worst instincts in society." Not to be outdone, Sheila Copps, that gentle angel of tolerance and moderation, accused me of "taking us down the path to war." Charest also joined the chorus, repeatedly calling me a "bigot" who was appealing to "the worst in human nature" and thereby implying that the more than two million Canadians who voted Reform in the last election were bigots too. In Western Canada, all of this was like waving a flag in front of a bull, but it was the Liberals and Tories that the bull wanted to stomp on, not Reform.

The rolling polls conducted during the campaign, and published afterwards as part of a study called *The 1997 Canadian Federal Election*,* showed that our support increased 5 per cent nationally after the ads aired – the biggest gain of the campaign. Caution must be exercised in attributing any shift in voter support to single causes, but it was after the airing of the Quebec ad and Charest's and Chrétien's reactions to it that PC support dropped from 22 to 18 per cent in Ontario and Liberal support dropped from 41 to 29 per cent in B.C. and from 58 to 50 per cent in Ontario.

■

The growth in support for Charest and the Conservatives in Ontario and the West peaked and went steadily downward, particularly after his bigotry accusations. The support for Chrétien and the Liberals in Alberta and B.C. collapsed, ensuring that both provinces would remain solidly in the Reform camp. In Ontario, the national unity dimensions of the campaign mainly generated "uncertainty," so that significant numbers of undecided voters became fair game for anyone who could relieve their anxieties. By the last week of the election, the polls were predicting a Liberal minority government with Reform solidly in second place.

---

* Neil Nevitte, Andre Blais, Elisabeth Gidengil, and Richard Nadeau, *Unsteady State: The 1997 Canadian Federal Election* (Toronto: Oxford University Press, 2000).

The week of May 19, the second-last week of the campaign, was one of the most exhilarating weeks of political campaigning I had ever experienced. National unity, about which I felt strongly and which I was well equipped to discuss, had emerged as a defining issue. And for once we had the "air cover" through our television ads to reinforce the Leader's Tour speeches and the work of our people on the ground.

By the end of the week, the Leader's Tour was back in Calgary facing three critical questions. How could I introduce more emotion and passion – my genuine feelings – into my presentations on the future of the country? Should we continue running the second Quebec ad through the last week of the campaign? And how should we handle the possibility of a minority government? Answers to those questions could very well determine the outcome of the election.

On Saturday, May 24, Sandra and I went over to Cliff and Leslie Fryers' house. Sandra, Cliff, and Rick had been talking among themselves. I could tell they had something important and probably painful to say to me, and it was Cliff – who is brutally honest – who got to the heart of the matter. My team felt that I was coming across to too many voters as well versed on the issues but lacking in heart, emotion, inclusiveness, and the desire to lead. They felt this was particularly evident when I got onto the national unity issue. I offered intellectually defensible solutions to the problems that were dividing the country, but where was the passion and emotion that would prove I really cared?

Over the next few days I searched for those analogies that would better enable me to express my real feelings for Canada and Canadians. Not openly expressing your love for your country when you really do love your country . . . is like, what? It's like . . . yes, it's like me not telling Sandra that I love her even though I do. And moving Canada on to a better constitutional foundation for the next century . . . is like, what? It's like . . . why, it's like what Avryll and her husband, John, are doing this very month. They are taking an old house which they like very much, and prefer to a new house, and they are lifting it off its crumbling foundation and putting it on a new one to make a better home for themselves and their family. Isn't that in a nutshell what Canada has to do?

And so in Kelowna on May 27, and later in the day in Abbotsford at a rally of more than 1,500 people, and throughout the week in Edmonton, Saskatoon, Toronto, Windsor, Owen Sound, Peterborough, London, and Calgary, this was my new focus when it came to presenting the defining issue of the election:

National unity is not just a legal issue or constitutional issue. It's about saving the country we love for ourselves and our children. It demands a response from the heart as well as the head.

Sandra and I have been married for 30 years. Like many couples we sometimes have this conversation: Do you still love me? Of course I still love you! Then why don't you say so? – say the words! And so I say the words. And then I also remember the words to the old song, "Don't just tell me, SHOW me!"

This is the kind of conversation we must have about our country. We must find ways of saying more clearly and openly that we love our country (Quebecers are good at expressing this). And we need to find more concrete ways of demonstrating that love through plans, actions, deeds that unite, that strengthen the relationship of Canadians – ALL Canadians – to each other.

At the outset of that last week of the election campaign we also had to decide whether to continue to run the infamous Quebec ad. Our original plan had been to run it only for week four, and then to switch to what I thought was our best ad for the last week. This last ad featured an actual desk from the House of Commons and me asking voters to whom it belonged. Did it belong to the MP who sat in it? Some traditional MPs certainly seemed to think so, always referring to "my seat." Did it belong to the parties? The traditional party leaders and whips sure seemed to think so when they would tell the occupant of that seat what to say and how to vote. But didn't this seat belong to the voter? And wasn't June 2, election day, the day the voter should take it back by voting for Reform and democratic reforms such as referendums, free votes in Parliament, and recall?

I loved that theme, and the ad and the speech we had built

around it. I had actually used this prop several times over the past year, but the media never picked up on it until the last week of the election. Ian had arranged for the desk to be brought to every venue. I would open up the top and pull out a whisky bottle, a Geritol bottle, and an oxygen mask: "Maybe this desk actually came from the Senate." Or I would pull out a copy of Stevie Cameron's book on Mulroney, called *On the Take*, open the fly-leaf, and read the inscription, "To Jean from Dad." "Maybe this was Jean Charest's desk," I'd quip, reminding the audience that Jean Charest had said he thought of Brian Mulroney as his political father.

In the end we decided to go with the original game plan. We dropped the Quebec ad and ran the Seat ad. In retrospect, this was probably a mistake. Ads that test high with focus groups during the pre-election period, when voters are not really engaged and the election battle is not yet joined, might not be as effective when the circumstances change. André Turcotte, our pollster, had warned us of this and had pleaded for funds to re-test our ads during the writ period and to do a tracking study. It was in the pre-election plan, but it was chopped two days before the writ was dropped.

■

By the last week of the campaign, the Liberals knew they were in serious danger of losing their majority, losing votes to the NDP and the PCs in Atlantic Canada, to Reform in the West, and perhaps to both Reform and the PCs in Ontario. We too were aware, as much by intuition and reports from the ridings as by any concrete polling data, that a minority government was increasingly likely.

In the West, minority government was not seen as a problem to be concerned about but a result to be welcomed. If the Liberals formed a minority government with Reform as Official Opposition, Reform could drive the fiscal, constitutional, criminal justice, and parliamentary reform agendas even more effectively than it had as third party. And if a Conservative rump, mainly Red Tories, joined the Liberals to prop them up, so much the better. That's where Red Tories belonged anyway.

But in more cautious and conservative Ontario, minority govern-ment was not viewed with favour. Minority government meant uncertainty and risk, and Ontario hates uncertainty and risk. While we did little to address Ontario's fears about minority government (I'm not sure what we could have done), Chrétien and the Liberals took full advantage of them. All during that last week, Chrétien hammered away on the simple theme that the last thing Canada needed was a minority government because it would not be strong enough to stand up to the separatists of Quebec. A vote for the Liberals was a "safe vote" – safe for the voter and safe for the country – and enough Ontario voters bought that argument to once again deny Reform the Ontario breakthrough we so much wanted and needed. One can only wonder what might have happened had we stuck with the Quebec ad to the end and dealt with the minority government issue head on in that last week. But then elections are always full of "wonders," especially after they are over.

Our election rallies during the last week were some of the largest of the campaign. Ezra Levant came along to "warm up the crowds" and to provide me with a rousing introduction. And I was at last both intellectually and emotionally engaged with my main speaking themes. In Edmonton, at the Butter Dome on the campus of the University of Alberta, my old alma mater, the Reform rally drew more than 4,000 people, while Chrétien and Martin drew about 600 people to their event across town. The arena was awash with signs and Canadian flags, and the rally began – as did all Reform meetings – with a rousing rendition of "O Canada." The Edmonton-area can-didates, led by Deborah Grey, were introduced to great applause. Then it was time for Ezra to introduce Sandra and me. With strobe lights darting all over the arena and Van Halen's "Right Here, Right Now" blaring from the loudspeakers, Sandra and I made our way from the back of the arena to the front, shaking scores of hands along the way. With our faithful RCMP guard, plus Ian, Woody, Rick, and the television cameras, we slowly pressed our way through the crowd until at last we were on the stage where "the seat from the House of Commons" awaited its moment. Sandra would thank the crowd for their presence and their support, and then it was my turn.

"This seat belongs to you! Who will occupy it on your behalf after June 2? What will be said in your name and on your behalf from this seat on jobs, on taxes, on crime, on unity, on parliamentary reform? Let me tell you what will be said if you entrust this seat to your Reform candidates . . . And what will be said on national unity? Is it not time to move the Canada we love off the crumbling foundations of 'two nations,' special status, and 'distinct society' and lovingly and gently place it on the new foundation of equality of citizens and provinces?" Avryll and John were in the crowd that night, and they knew it was their house that had inspired this analogy. More pounding music and flashing lights as a group of flag-waving young people escort us off the stage and through the crowds to the exit.

The next day saw a similar rally in Saskatoon with most of our Saskatchewan candidates. The day after began with a breakfast rally with the Chamber of Commerce in Waterloo. Charest was again charging me with bigotry, and a Tory organizer tried to disrupt the meeting. The crowd hissed him down. Then it was on to Toronto for a major televised speech to the Empire Club. I used the seat from Parliament again. This was downtown Toronto, not downtown Calgary, but there was a standing ovation at the end. A Tory organizer told Ian as we left the hotel that if all Ontario could see and hear this presentation, Reform could win Ontario. But alas, all that Ontario voters would see or hear of this presentation was the tiny snippet that made its way through the media filter. We simply didn't have the funds to finance an Ontario-wide telecast.

But no time to think of that. It was on to Windsor, in an aircraft of dubious vintage and capacity that had our media crew asking nervously about insurance. The following morning a big breakfast rally in Owen Sound. Another rally in Collingwood, and Peterborough, and then a standing-room-only crowd of 2,000 in London. Our campaign team was on its last legs as we pulled into Forest, Ontario, for our last Ontario event of the campaign. At last we were on our way home. One final noisy rally at the Stampede Corral in Calgary with three to four thousand supporters, all the bells and whistles, and all the Calgary-area candidates. The 1997 federal election campaign was finally over.

My prediction, written in my personal journal: sixty seats in the West, and if we could break through elsewhere, up to fifteen in Ontario and two in the Maritimes.

■

On the night of Sunday, June 1, Sandra and I sneak back to the Calgary airport to pick up our daughter Mary Joy, who has come in from New York to be with us on election day. Avryll and John have come down from Grande Prairie. The boys have both been working on my campaign in Calgary Southwest and seem confident that the riding is safe. Our daughter Andrea and her husband, Howie, are with us too – the whole gang rallying around as they always do when any of us are in a "big competition."

It's June 2, 1997, election day. Sandra and I vote at the Dunston Poll in Grant Hill's Macleod riding, where an overly zealous deputy returning officer resists letting the media get their traditional picture of the leader casting his ballot. I am too tired to care. We have dinner with the family at the Westin Hotel downtown, where we have a room and will watch the results. One great thing about politics and elections – you can always tell the score at the end of the day.

It doesn't take long for the news to come in after the polls have closed. The initial results are disappointing again. Atlantic Canada has rejected the Liberals (good news), but the protest vote has gone to the NDP and the Tories, not to us. In Quebec, the Bloc loses seats, which is good, but it is the Liberals and not the PCs who gain. We hold our breath as the Ontario results come in. Alas, no break-through for Reform. For some reason (we will look into the causes later) the vote turnout itself is lower than in 1993. We lose our one seat in Simcoe Centre, and Paul Shaw comes within 500 votes of winning in Simcoe-Grey. But it's the same old story as in 1993 – thirty-eight second-place finishes, and twenty-eight seats where the combined Reform/Conservative vote is more than the Liberals', but no seats. For the Ontario candidates who came in a close second, the results are deeply disappointing.

The gloom in our room is palpable, but it begins to lift somewhat as the Western results roll in. Three seats for Reform in Manitoba, up from one. Eight seats in Saskatchewan, up from four. Twenty-four seats in Alberta, including all the Calgary ridings and my own constituency of Calgary Southwest. Once again, Harry Robinson and crew have run a winning campaign with an absentee candidate. And most satisfying of all, twenty-five seats in British Columbia, all the seats we had held before plus Gurmant Grewal in Surrey Central, the first opposition member of Sikh origin to be elected to the Canadian Parliament.

And so, we won 60 seats in total for Reform, up from 52 in 1993. This compares to 44 for the Bloc, 21 for the NDP, 20 for the PCs, and 155 (a bare majority) for the Liberals. We did not "go down," as our critics so confidently predicted. We increased our seat totals to become the Official Opposition, and this time it was the national campaign that pulled the fat out of the fire.

The record would show 2,513,070 votes for Reform, 19.1 per cent of the total vote, compared to 2,446,705 for the Tories, or 18.6 per cent of the total vote. Quite an accomplishment, all things considered. Over two and a half million Canadians were persuaded to vote for a political option that didn't even exist ten years before. Outside of Quebec, Reform polled 27 per cent of the total vote, compared to 18 per cent for the Tories. In Ontario, Reform polled 886,787 votes compared to 982,691 in 1993, a drop attributed mainly to the lower voter turnout in Ontario and the fear of minority government. In Alberta, Reform polled 577,551 votes in total in the 1997 federal election, compared to 483,914 for the Klein Conservatives in the 1997 provincial election. When it comes to "who speaks for Alberta" on constitutional issues, Reform is in good shape.

Jason Moscovitz of the CBC would be the one who summed it up best: Charest won the leaders' debate, Chrétien won (just barely) the election, but Reform won the campaign.

Later that night I speak to our supporters at the Convention Centre in downtown Calgary. From nothing to Official Opposition in ten years is quite an accomplishment, I say, and unprecedented in Canadian history. *What* we built – a legitimate, influential national force that will replace one of Canada's biggest and oldest traditional parties as the number-two party – is admirable in itself. But *how* we built it – through the development and deployment of the instruments of democracy – is what I am most proud of. How can I ever thank our campaign team, our executive councillors, our caucus members, our candidates, our staff, our grassroots army of political foot soldiers, and the voters enough? Somehow I would find a way.

8

LEADER OF
THE OPPOSITION

THE FIRST THING VISITORS SAW WHEN THEY WALKED INTO THE office of the Leader of the Opposition during my tenure there was a large oak desk with a high-backed green chair and two large Canadian flags behind it. On the underside of the desk were two buttons. One rang a buzzer in my secretary Jean Marie's office next door; the other was an alarm to summon security in case I found myself alone with a "problem person." I never pushed the alarm button so I'm not sure what would have happened if I did. When Rick Mercer, of "This Hour Has 22 Minutes," came to visit he pleaded with me to push the button just for the heck of it. (Rick could be a problem person sometimes.) He wanted to get a camera shot of the RCMP SWAT team bursting through the door.

I sat at the big desk only for formal meetings and to sign letters and documents. Most of the time, I worked at a table by the window on the right (as you came in the door), the one piled with papers and books. For those most comfortable with a clean desk, I had the big desk; for those who like a messy desk, there was the table. We aimed to please.

Straight across from the desk was a fireplace that looked func-tional but didn't work, like a lot of things in Ottawa. On the walls were two pictures that reminded me of where I came from: one was of an old John Deere tractor and the other of four cowboys given to me by the Pirie family in Calgary. Around the room were pictures of family that Sandra arranged, a sketch of Sir John A. Macdonald given to me by the Pope family, and a "Reform cane" carved out of cherry wood by a supporter of William Lyon Mackenzie after the Reform Rebellion of 1837.

Among the unique and beautiful features of that office were the walls and ceiling. When the Parliament building was rebuilt after the fire of 1916, the architects, J. A. Pearson and J. O. Marchand, gave their personal attention to the decoration of this room. The style is English Renaissance Revival, typical of the mid-seventeenth century, with exquisite oak woodwork, framed panelled walls, and a decorative plaster ceiling displaying the flowers, fruit, and foliage of Canada. The coats of arms of the provinces as they were in 1920 (Newfoundland is missing and those of Quebec and Nova Scotia have since been revised) are also incorporated into the ceiling – all combined with elegant frescoes.*

For the murals around the walls above the panelling, J. A. Pearson opted for scenes from the age of chivalry. If you studied them you would see in turn depictions of the following "virtues" of the medieval world: "Struggle" represented by knights in combat (which reminded me of Question Period); "Justice" represented by an empress-like figure seated on a throne; "Fidelity" represented by a knight holding the banner of his lord in his right hand; and so on through "Conciliation," "Watchfulness," "Fearlessness," and "Wisdom." Of all these murals, however, the most instructive is that depicting "Vision," a knight astride a black charger receiving his direction from an angel. The archivists tell us that Mackenzie King developed a particular interest in the decoration of this office when he became Leader of the Opposition. That this was so is demonstrated by the fact that the face of the angel in the mural is none other than that of Mackenzie King's mother – the daughter of William Lyon Mackenzie, and the person whom King revered in life and continued to consult through seances after she died. In addition to persuading the architect to have the

---

* I am indebted for much of this information to a paper by Audrey Dube, Office of the Curator, House of Commons, 1997.

artist put his mother's face on the angel, King also had a secret passage installed just under the "Vision" picture. In my time, when I gave the panel a gentle push, it became a door leading through the passage to Jean Marie's office. But in King's day the passage extended all the way to the outside hallway, enabling him to leave the office undetected and to avoid unwanted visitors in the outer office. Thus, as I never tired of telling visitors, we had in the mural and passage a perfect representation of modern Liberalism: above, the glorious vision of some noble purpose being imparted to mankind by an angel of Liberal persuasion; and below, a secret passage through which the Liberal in office could escape the burden of the Vision.

■

As Leader of the Opposition from June 1997 to March 2000, I had three priorities: to hold the government accountable for its actions or inaction; to develop and present constructive alternatives on those issues where we considered the government misguided; and to create a principled political alternative to the government itself.

My efforts to achieve the latter – to create a united alternative to the federal Liberals – are described in a later chapter. And rather than provide a complete catalogue of the activities undertaken from 1997 to 2000 concerning accountability and policy alternatives, I have selected half a dozen items that will give the reader at least a sample of the varied preoccupations of the Opposition during this period. These include pushing for tax relief and Senate reform, our positions on the Clarity Bill and the Calgary Declaration, key debates and votes in the House, and (Chapter 9) holding the government's feet to the fire for its unethical behaviour with respect to the APEC inquiry, the fiscal mismanagement of the Human Resources department, and the "Shawinigate" affair.

By the time Reform became the Official Opposition in mid-1997, the Liberals had made a 180-degree turn from the 1993 election and were fully committed to eliminating the federal deficit and balancing the budget. We still disagreed on the timetable (Reform wanted to go faster) and the means (Reform wanted to do it by cutting spending, whereas the Liberals were doing it by raising taxes).

Nevertheless, the deficit was shrinking, and it was time for us to "move the goalposts." Our next objective was to make tax relief for Canadians and reduction of the federal debt national priorities.

In our minds, balancing the budget was a means to an end, not an end in itself. We wanted to get federal spending under control in order to make it possible to offer Canadians genuine tax relief, which would leave more dollars in the pockets of consumers to spend and businesses to invest, thus increasing personal incomes and creating more jobs in the private sector. We also wanted to apply a major portion of future government surpluses to reducing the massive federal debt, the annual interest payments on which were consuming almost one out of three tax dollars ($45 billion per year). Imagine what might be accomplished if even half of that amount were available to spend on health care or national defence or the justice system.

The aspect of the tax relief issue to which I was most committed was its "democratization." This is essentially moving an idea beyond academic discussion and the relatively narrow circle of the interest groups into the hearts and minds of millions of voters, in such a way and on such a scale that politicians seeking election (no matter what their political stripe) simply cannot afford to ignore it. Not surprisingly to anyone who has faith in "the common sense of the common people," we received much assistance and support in achieving this objective from ordinary Canadians.

In February 1997 a letter was delivered to my parliamentary office that had been sent to me by a woman named Kim Hicks. It caught the attention of everyone who read it – my correspondence staff, my personal assistant, and me – and soon found its way, with Kim's permission, into my presentations on tax relief both inside and outside the House.

Kim Hicks lived in Wood Point, New Brunswick, and was the married mother of four children ages two to eight years. Her husband, Wayne, was employed as a mechanic at a local garage. Even with Wayne working a lot of overtime, their family income was around $30,000 per year. Her concern was that they simply couldn't make ends meet, and that taxes – the heavy taxes that Canada levies on the "working poor" – were the straw that was breaking their backs.

Our kids won't be going to the dentist this year, but the child down the road, whose mom is on welfare, will. We have refinanced and refinanced and we just can't do it anymore. We live on credit because we don't have enough clear money to use money. Pay the needed payment and then borrow it over. We are sick of it. People with 4 kids who make $30,000 a year are poor too, but our kids don't count. By the time we pay our taxes our $29,000-30,000 is a joke! We are afraid that we are going down and there is nothing we can do. Promises and empty talk – we are sick of it. We are trying to be a family in a time when family means squat! Also now with this new HST we will pay more for our kids' clothing, heat, power, telephone. We don't buy big ticket items. We pray our washer will wash one more load, and that it will be nice out so we can put our clothes on the line to save on electricity and so that the squeaky drier will be there when we need it. We, again, are going to lose and so will our kids.

I'm sorry for this long letter. I really don't know what I expect. I wrote to Mr. Axworthy when he was Human Resources Minister. I got an I'm sorry and an I understand and a lot of statistics that I don't care about. It won't help us feed or clothe our kids.

Please *don't* send me one of those short form letters saying that you're sorry. Also please don't tell me to contact my MLA or Premier – they don't care.

I wrote Kim back saying that she was not alone. There were other families all over Canada in the same predicament, and many who would identify with her feelings and concerns. I also pointed out to her that if the tax relief proposals contained in Reform's Fresh Start platform could actually be implemented, families like hers would receive about $3,000 per year in tax relief and would in effect be removed from the federal income tax rolls altogether.

Of course, since the Liberals and not Reform won the 1997 election, taxes were continuing to increase, not decrease. Nevertheless, on July 1, after the federal election, I wrote Kim Hicks again, this time asking her and her family to participate in an experiment. Let's pretend, I suggested, that Reform won the election, and that our tax relief plan was now being implemented. She and her husband would have $3,000 more in disposable income this year than they had last year. What I wanted to know were the answers to several questions. First, what would she and her husband actually do with that $3,000? Would they save it, spend it? *How* would they spend it? We wanted to know because there were welfare state economists in the government, and Liberal, NDP, and even Red Tory members in the House, who would argue that that $3,000 could be better spent by the government on assistance programs to "help" families like Kim's than it could by those families themselves. And second, how would the receipt of such tax relief make Kim and her family feel? Her original letter to me had expressed despair and desperation and helplessness. Could $3,000 in tax relief have any positive impact on those feelings at all?

My letter to Kim was accompanied by a cheque for $4,000 (from Reform Party funds, not my parliamentary budget), which the family was to pretend was their "tax relief" from Revenue Canada. The cheque, of course, had to be for $4,000 in order to give Kim and her husband $3,000 net, because – you guessed it – the $4,000 was subject to about $700 in income taxes and would trigger reductions in the family's eligibility for the Child Tax Benefit and GST credit.

Since Kim and her family didn't know me from Adam and had an understandable suspicion of politicians, I had my letter delivered to Kim personally by an old and trusted friend, Innis McCready. Innis was a long-time resident of New Brunswick, a long-standing member of the Reform Party's Executive Council, a gentle and warm-hearted Christian gentleman, and a good friend. If Kim and her husband had any questions about me, Reform, or the sincerity of the offer, Innis was the right person to answer them.

Innis went to see Kim and Wayne. They agreed to participate in our experiment, and less than a month later I got two letters back from Kim. They were well worth sharing with the caucus, the Parliament, and the public. We invited Kim, Wayne, and their four boys – Matthew, Brandon, Nathan, and Luke – to come to Ottawa the week of December 8, 1997, to meet us and to see the sights of the national capital. Chris Froggatt from my office took them under his wing and arranged for the family to sit in the gallery of the House while I read Kim's letters into the record as part of the pre-budget debate. After it was all over, we introduced Kim to the media and then had a little pizza party in the leader's office to celebrate the determination and simple eloquence of this unlikely champion of tax relief for rank-and-file Canadians.

How did Kim and Wayne Hicks propose to spend their $3,000 of tax relief?

My husband and I carefully looked at how to best use the money and we decided that the best plan for us was to divide the money into a spend category and a savings category. We divided the money $2,000 and $1,000.

The $2,000 we spent as follows:

1. The first thing this money enabled us to do was to pay our two older boys' dentist bill and gave us the amount needed for our two younger sons' trip to the dentist.

2. The next thing we did was to set aside $200 for one of our sons' visit to the optometrist in October, and to have a new pair of glasses which are badly needed.

3. We bought the extra wood that we will need for winter.

4. We paid off one of our credit card balances thereby easing our monthly payment load, which in turn gives us a bit more money to use toward other bills.

5. The boys and I went shopping for back to school clothing and I set aside money for their school books.

6. I took a trip to the grocery store and bought the items that we needed but could not afford to buy with our weekly grocery money.

7. I paid my mother back the money that she has loaned us over the past few months when we have found ourselves in a bind owing over $800 in Income Taxes.

8. Lastly we decided to take $200 of the money and to spend it any way we wished. We bought Kentucky Fried Chicken and we went to see the movie "George of the Jungle." My husband, along with his regular hours, has had to start working Saturday mornings and also two to three evenings a week to help make ends meet. He only takes one week of his vacation and we use the other week's vacation pay to buy wood. What this means is that we have never taken a vacation trip with our children, but this year we are taking the $125 left from the $200 and we are driving to Pictou, taking the ferry to P.E.I. and driving back across the bridge to N.B. It feels great!

With the other $1,000 that we have left, we for now have put it
into a savings account to use in the case of an emergency or to hope-
fully buy an RRSP, which would give us a start at some future savings.

Was there any member of the House or any bureaucrat at Human
Resources Development or Finance who would have the nerve to
stand up and say that they could have spent that money more wisely,
more carefully, or with more social responsibility? I don't think so.
And how did receiving this tax relief make the Hicks family feel?

The first feeling my husband and I experienced was a sense of relief. It
was as if a weight had been lifted from our shoulders and we could
finally catch our breath.

It meant that we could have the money for those things that kept
having to be overlooked such as trips to the dentist, borrowed money
that couldn't be paid back, or simply a family trip.

It meant for the first time in a very long while that we could have
some guilt-free fun. By this I mean we actually took our children to
the movies and out for supper without sitting there worrying about
"how are we going to get the money to replace what we just spent,
when we didn't have it to spend in the first place?"

But most importantly, after the initial feeling of relief, we felt less
pressure and worry. As a family struggling to get by there is a lot of
guilt and insecurity associated with the pressure of just trying to make
ends meet when there is a lack of money. My husband feels guilty
because, even though he works very hard, he still feels that as a
provider he lets his family down, not only financially but time-wise
also. I feel guilty because as a stay at home mom I sometimes feel that
I am robbing my family of income that we could have if I held a job.
All of this guilt affects our family life – the way we feel, the tension
and stress. Mr. Manning, receiving this money made my husband and
me feel a *lot* less guilty. I actually saw a happier, more relaxed man,
which in turn made our family more carefree and closer than we have
been in a while. I'm not saying that money in itself solves problems,
but it helps to relieve the pressures caused by a lack of it and that in
turn helps to give us a brighter outlook and a happier family.

I have gone to sleep at night with a feeling of being more secure because I know that our kids have been better taken care of and that if a problem should arise we do have money set aside in a savings account. And that means, to us, a brighter future. It makes my husband and me feel a sense of encouragement knowing that we have someone in government who understands our needs and our struggles as a family, and who realizes the heavy tax burden that a family like mine carries, and who is trying to help, and that gives us a sense of hope for our future and our children's future.

■

After the Kim Hicks encounter, we found yet another way to give the tax issue legs. In the spring of 1999 I was involved in a by-election campaign in the auto-manufacturing city of Windsor, Ontario. I was walking through a mall with our Reform candidate, Scott Cowan, and we stopped to talk to a fellow who said he worked in the Chrysler plant. I mentioned the word "taxes" and he exploded like a firecracker! "Taxes? You want to know about taxes? Let me tell you about taxes!" He fished in his wallet for something, and pulled it out. It was a pay stub for his last overtime pay period. "Look at this," he said, pointing to two boxes on the stub. The deductions, mainly taxes, were almost as great as the net overtime pay. "I sometimes wonder who I'm working for," he growled, "Chrysler or the government?"

Then I knew what to do at every factory and office that I visited for the next six months – just go to the coffee room of any work-place and ask the workers if anyone had a pay stub from their last overtime pay period, hold it up, and say, "Look at these tax deductions, compared to your take-home pay. Do you think you are getting value for the taxes you're paying?" (This invariably elicited angry comments about how the government wasted taxpayers' dollars.) "If we could get those deductions down, it would be just like a pay raise, wouldn't it?" (Nods of agreement.) "Then help us make tax relief the number-one issue in the next federal election, and get yourself that pay raise!"

This approach went over so well, we decided to conduct the Great Pay-Stub Rip-Off Contest. We advertised in the papers, on the talk shows, in our householders, and at public meetings: "Send us your pay stub, if you have one that illustrates how badly the government is ripping you off through high taxes." We offered a prize: a free trip to Ottawa, where your tax dollars go to die, and an opportunity to tell your tax horror story on the national stage. The letters flowed in. We collected the best ones, and I read them into the parliamentary record on February 29 in response to Paul Martin's 2000 budget.

There was a letter from a retired couple in Calgary who had paid almost $4,000 in taxes on $28,000 of income. There was the letter from a millwright in Saskatchewan who earned $2,021.67 in overtime pay but got to keep only $1,009.35 – less than half. There was the teacher who had received a $1,000 raise, but because it put her into a higher tax bracket her take-home pay increased by a measly $2.67 per month. There was the fuel invoice from an irate farmer I had met at a turkey shoot in Biggar, Saskatchewan, which showed that he had been charged $605.68 in taxes (federal excise tax, provincial fuel tax, and GST) on a load of fuel costing $531.30. His fuel tax bill was higher than the fuel bill and he was ready to shoot more than turkeys. There was the letter from the Toronto police constable who grossed $61,000 and took home $34,000, and then paid an additional 15 per cent in sales taxes on everything he purchased with his take-home pay. He signed his letter "Completely and Utterly Ripped Off." And then, finally, there was the letter from the ultimate "winner," or should I say "loser," of our great Pay-Stub Rip-Off Contest. His name was Paul Meyer, a structural engineer from Montrose, B.C., and he was sitting in the gallery as I read his letter:

> During the two-week period ending November 05, 1999, I was paid for 80 hours' work, while the following period, I was paid for 80.5 hours' work, having put in a half-hour overtime. The half-hour overtime increased my gross pay by $19.33. Amazingly, this resulted in my federal income tax increasing by $20.13. In effect, I paid [the Prime Minister] eighty cents for the privilege of working a half hour overtime.
>
> I recognize that this is an anomaly caused by "steps" in the tax tables, but the very fact that a "step" could result in an apparent marginal tax rate of 104 per cent tells me that our tax rates are too high.

As a resident of British Columbia with a good salary, my actual marginal tax rate is well over 50 per cent.

I also note that, because it is late in the year, no CPP or EIC deductions were made from my salary, as I have already "maxed out" on both amounts for the year. If it were not for that "anomaly" my apparent marginal rate would have been over 110 per cent.

Our tax crusading efforts reminded my family of Walt Disney's animated version of the old story of Robin Hood, to which we assigned modern identities. "Taxes, taxes, beautiful taxes," croons Prince Jean, as he sits in his castle counting the revenue collected by his notorious taxman, Sheriff Paul of Nottingham. "Tax the poor (the Hickses) to feed the rich (how about another grant to Bombardier?)," whispers Sir Hiss, Prince Jean's chief counsellor, who bears a striking resemblance to senior policy adviser Eddie Goldenberg. "Oh, what a capital idea!" chortles Prince Jean, as he orders the sheriff to raise the taxes yet again. But meanwhile, outside the castle, a green-clad Reformer named Robin Hood is stirring up the peasants, and talk of tax revolt is in the air. The minstrels are singing a little ditty behind Prince Jean's back: "He wants to be known as Jean the First, but instead he'll be known as Jean the Worst." Why? Because he's taxing his people and his country to death, driving capital, businesses, jobs, and young people out of the country. Some day, with the peasants in full revolt, King Jean will be forced by his own nobles to sign the Magna Carta, the first legal document in English history to limit the spending and taxing authority of kings. What a lovely tale. If we could afford it, we'd buy the rights to Robin Hood from Disney and pipe the revised version – with Reform subtitles – into the home of every taxpayer in the country.

■

To become a truly national leader in Canada and to function effectively in the Parliament of Canada, it is necessary to understand and speak French with some degree of proficiency. And had I ever become bilingual enough to be as persuasive with audiences in

French as I could be in English, our chances of forging a strategic alliance between Westerners and Quebecers for the reform of Canadian federalism would have been greatly enhanced. I have been criticized frequently for not acknowledging this sooner and doing more about it, but there were just so many other things to do in getting the Reform Party off the ground that I never got around to language training until I'd actually arrived in Ottawa as an MP.

Many years ago I had taken French classes in high school and one course at university, but that was it. Like many unilingual MPs from Western Canada I now signed up for French lessons, beginning with a two-week immersion session under the watchful eye of Elizabeth Gervais at the government's language-training facility at St-Jean-sur-Richelieu, just south of Montreal. I followed this up with French lessons in Ottawa – off and on – for two to four hours per week, but with big gaps when I was travelling. I had several different instructors provided by the Parliamentary Language Training Services branch – all of them pleasant, professional, and anxious to help. The one who probably helped me the most (after 1997) was Louis Bélanger, a professor of French literature from New Brunswick who spent part of his time each year in Ottawa. He was friendly and outgoing, with an interest and curiosity about politics that gave us some common ground.

By 1997 it was evident that my progress, which the media was monitoring, was much too slow. So after the 1997 election, even though I now had the extra responsibilities of leader of the Opposition, I made a renewed effort to improve. This involved going to the Centre linguistique du Collège de Jonquière in Jonquière, Quebec, Lucien Bouchard's hometown and a separatist stronghold in the heart of the Saguenay. Sandra and I would go for a week at a time every four to six weeks, spending four to six hours per day in the classroom and doing assignments.

We lived in the home of a French-speaking couple and participated in various outings designed to get us to socialize in French. Madame Prebinski, the head of the language program at Jonquière, took a personal interest in us, and she once rescued me from some pranksters who were planning a pie-throwing incident. The couple we stayed with, Clairmont Tremblay and Esther Bergeron, were hospitable and, helpful in every way. Clairmont was an excellent cook, and although I am certain that he supported the sovereigntist cause, we never argued over politics. Esther was very much involved with the local hospital, and we found that health care was as much an issue in Jonquière as anywhere in Canada.

Although I made more progress at Jonquière than previously, the strain of trying to fit French instruction in with all my other responsibilities was almost too much to take. On most days, between classes or afterwards, I would be on the phone back to Ottawa for several hours or trying to cope with dozens of e-mails and faxes. On a number of occasions I would have to take a plane back to Ottawa to participate in a vote or an unavoidable meeting, leaving Jonquière mid-afternoon and getting back well after midnight. My progress was painfully slow.

There was of course a humorous side to my efforts to learn French. Our son Nathan accompanied me to St-Jean-sur-Richelieu on my first visit there, and afterwards we took a short holiday together in Quebec to try out my newly acquired skills. But Nathan (who is fluently bilingual) had to rescue me when I tried *en français* to explain to a fellow at the motel that we had come to do some fly-fishing and to see the whales in the St. Lawrence. The fellow kept protesting that we must be crazy if we thought we could catch a whale on a fly rod.

The great thing about going to Jonquière was that Sandra and I would be learning French together, but it took the instructors about fifteen minutes to ascertain that there was *"un petit problème."* Sandra is a very outgoing person who will try anything; she isn't the least bit afraid of making a mistake and perhaps looking or sounding foolish for a time. I am the opposite – a perfectionist whose inclination is not to do something at all if I can't do it well. Put the two of us together in a language class and Sandra (even though she had had no French training at all) would have five words out (three of them wrong, but two of them right) before I could even get my mouth open. By day two, therefore, we found ourselves separated, each with our own professor. Constant conversation and laughter were coming out of the room where Sandra was, and subdued mumblings came from my direction, punctuated by frequent exhortations from the professor that I exhibit more *confiance*. I could just imagine the instructors conferring before the morning session, flipping a coin to see who got whom, with "the loser" getting you-know-who.

Our bifurcated language experience continued outside the classroom. Most mornings we would stop at the Tim Horton's in Jonquière before class. My order would be quite simple, constrained by my linguistic skills: "*Un café, petit, s'il vous plaît, un sucre, une crème. Merci!*" But trying to order for Sandra, waiting in the car, was another story. How do you ask *en français* for a toasted raisin bagel with non-fat strawberry cheese spread and a mocha with three-quarters decaffeinated coffee and one-quarter hot chocolate? I was already traumatized by the time we arrived at class.

But there was also much to enjoy. Our most memorable evening was the night we went to see a spectacular performance of *L'histoire de Royaume de Saguenay* in a converted hockey arena in nearby La Baie. I preferred going to these public events incognito, or simply as an *étudiant* from the language school. But this evening, a municipal councillor I knew spotted me going into the arena. A few minutes later I thought I heard it being announced to the three thousand people present that *Le Chef de l'Opposition du Parliament du Canada* was in the audience. I turned to Sandra and said, "I think that's me he's talking about," as a smattering of cheers and boos came from the largely pro-sovereigntist audience. The show was magnificent – a dramatic presentation of the history of the Saguenay region, from the first encounters between the aboriginals of the area and the French explorers to the recent Saguenay flood. Every small town in every historic region of Canada should send a delegation to La Baie to see how to make its history live. When the performance was over, many of the locals came over to say hello and even talk a little politics. I declined a wager from one fellow who wanted to bet me that Quebec would be sovereign before I could master French. But most of them wanted to talk about the hospital situation in the region or – you guessed it – taxes. A group of truckers, for example, wondered what could be done about the high fuel taxes that threatened to put them out of business. Except for the language difference, I could have been in Fort St. John in northern B.C.

Every time I went to Quebec, from 1992 to 2002, I was actually searching for something that went far beyond ways and means of improving my linguistic capacity. I was searching for a very special someone – LaFontaine!

Driving near Montreal, Sandra and I once passed through the little town of Boucherville, where Louis-Hippolyte LaFontaine was born. He grew up to become the leader of the Reform Party of Lower Canada, fighting the Château Clique and demanding responsible government for the colony. Most significantly, he formed a strategic alliance with his counterpart, Robert Baldwin, leader of the Reform Party of Upper Canada. When LaFontaine lost his Lower Canada seat in the colonial Parliament, Baldwin found him one in Upper Canada, and later, together, they formed the first "responsible government" in Canada. That's why their statues are on Parliament Hill.

I desperately wanted to invite Quebecers – not just the few that came out of curiosity to our small meetings, but millions of them – to see me as Baldwin representing those in English Canada who wanted to change the federal system fundamentally for the benefit of all Canadians. But what we Reformers from outside Quebec wanted to know was, "*Où est LaFontaine?*" Where are our equivalents in Quebec and who are their leaders, so that we can make common cause?

At a personal level, my friend Gilles St-Laurent and his wife, Mychelyne, were my LaFontaine. Gilles believed in exactly the same type of federalism that I believed in, although he had arrived at that position by an entirely Quebec route. Mychelyne had once supported the sovereigntist cause but was willing to give "reform of the federation" a chance, and putting her and Sandra together showed how easily the language barrier could be overcome if there was the will to leapfrog it. When Mychelyne and Sandra first met, each of them was essentially unilingual. But because each wanted to understand the other and brought such enthusiasm to the effort, they could spend two hours together over lunch "conversing," hands waving, playing charades, facial expressions and laughter substituting for words most of the time.

Unfortunately, while Gilles would be my personal LaFontaine, and I appointed him my Quebec adviser, the media demanded a "big name" before it would take Reform's efforts in Quebec seriously. Hence my speeches in fractured French as the leader of the

Opposition asking, "*Où est LaFontaine?*" Hence, when endeavouring to create the Canadian Alliance, my letter to every member of Quebec's National Assembly asking, "*Où est LaFontaine?*" And hence my many inquiries over the years of Quebec journalists, business people, and municipal politicians, "*Où est LaFontaine?*" I never really got a satisfactory answer to this question. If I had – if some prominent Quebecers with a deep commitment to reforming federalism and exceptional communications skills had entered into an alliance with me and Western-based Reformers – Canadian federalism would have been transformed, I am convinced, for the better.

Of course, there are two other possibilities. Perhaps LaFontaine simply doesn't exist, or he exists but I didn't recognize him. It still haunts me that when I asked Quebec journalists or municipal politicians "*Où est LaFontaine?*" their most frequent answer was "Lucien Bouchard." When I would protest and say, "But Bouchard says he wants to leave the Canadian federation, not reform it," they would say to me, "That's your perception. Bouchard's bottom line is a better deal for Quebec, outside or inside Canada. And besides, we can't pick your Baldwin, and you can't pick our LaFontaine."

■

On September 9, 1997, prior to the opening of the thirty-sixth Parliament on September 20, I went to see Chrétien in his Centre Block office. This was the first time we had met since the June election. There had been time for the dust to settle, and by now Chrétien was much more supportive of "clarifying" the federal government's position on what it would do if Quebec made yet another secession attempt. He noted that when the federal government had finally joined in Guy Bertrand's action to affirm court jurisdiction in the secession issue, Lucien Bouchard blustered and threatened to call an election. But he didn't. And when the federal government referred the question of the legality of a unilateral secession to the Supreme Court (after repeatedly telling us that such a course would be unduly "provocative"), Bouchard had again made a great fuss and threatened to call an election. But he didn't. And now the Prime Minister was delighted that his Intergovernmental Affairs minister,

Stephane Dion, was actually writing letters to the Quebec government saying that Quebec secession from Canada could very well lead to the partition of Quebec itself. (When I had used the "p" word prior to the referendum I had been accused of wanting civil war, but of course I was a Western Reformer and Dion was a Quebec Liberal, and that was then and this was now.)

When I endeavoured to turn the conversation onto a more positive track – from Plan B to Plan A, the need to modernize and fix federalism – the Prime Minister was, as usual, less than enthusiastic. When I asked if he had any objection to my discussing with Dion our ideas for the components of a reform package, he said no, but repeated his earlier objections to constitutional packages like Meech or Charlottetown. He also mentioned that he had met with the Atlantic premiers to discuss the upcoming premiers' conference, presumably to try to get their backing for a "distinct society" clause. He said they had asked him what the Opposition's position was on "distinct society" and that he had repeated what I had said in the election, namely that the West had no objections to acknowledging the uniqueness of Quebec's language and culture as long as that acknowledgment did not confer on the government of Quebec constitutional powers not conferred on the other provinces. He seemed to think that this was some modification of my previous position, although I had declared this position on several occasions in the House, once while he was sitting not ten metres away. This meeting was one of the most positive I had had with Chrétien.

What the Chrétien government was actually doing on the national unity front during August and September 1997 was attempting to influence the approach to be taken by the premiers at their Calgary conference on September 14. Chrétien wanted them to come out strongly for "distinct society" and to leave re-balancing of the powers alone. Obviously, we too had wanted to have input to the premiers' position, although we clearly lacked the leverage to influence them. By now I had fairly good relations with a number of the premiers, especially Mike Harris and Roy Romanow.

On Friday, September 12, I met with B.C. premier Glen Clark in Victoria; he frankly confessed that he hated the unity file and had told Bouchard that if Quebec seceded he would have no one to negotiate with. On September 13, back in Calgary, I met with Premier Frank McKenna of New Brunswick. Frank was very close to the Prime Minister but also anxious to find some kind of compromise on the recognition of Quebec's uniqueness that might carry the judgment of his provincial colleagues. I told him that for every word about Quebec uniqueness in their final communiqué they would need parallel text on the equality of citizens and provinces. On the same day I also talked to Premier Romanow on the phone, whose position was "80/20" – that non-constitutional measures would solve 80 per cent of our national unity problem and constitutional measures only 20 per cent. Then on the morning of September 14 I was up early to have breakfast with Premier Harris. I felt that Harris was the most practical and constructive of the lot, strong on the concept of equality and wanting to get on to the re-balancing of the powers instead of endlessly haggling about how to define and recognize Quebec's distinctiveness.

When the premiers came out with their "Calgary Declaration" on September 14, 1997, it was much closer to what Reform had argued for than to what Chrétien had wanted. It included guidelines for consulting the public on seven principles for strengthening federalism: equality of citizens and provinces in law; recognition of the value of diversity, including the uniqueness of Quebec and the role of its government in protecting and developing that unique character within Canada; the principle that constitutional amendments conferring powers on one province must make those powers available to all provinces; and the principle of the federal and provincial governments "working in partnership" while respecting each other's jurisdictions.

On September 24 the Prime Minister spoke in the House on the Calgary Declaration, strongly emphasizing its recognition of Quebec's uniqueness and completely ignoring its declaration of the equality of all citizens and provinces in law. Even as he was speaking, I sent notes to both him and Stephane Dion saying, "If you keep stressing the uniqueness principle and omit the equality principle you will kill support for the Calgary initiative outside Quebec."

Dion nodded, and when the Prime Minister sat down he gave me a thumbs-up signal, whatever that meant.

By November 1997, we had in hand polling data that indicated considerable support in Quebec for the positions articulated by the Calgary Declaration, although few Quebecers knew about the declaration itself. As yet the federal government had done nothing to promote it in Quebec, and of course the Quebec government had no intention of doing so.

On November 25, Reform put forward a supply-day motion in the House endorsing the efforts of the premiers to initiate reform of the federation through the Calgary Declaration and urging the government to start communicating those ideas to Quebecers. The motion carried by a vote of 190 in favour to 71 against, with the government voting with us but the Bloc, the NDP, and the PCs opposing. In the end, the federal government failed to act on the motion. We tried to compensate for the government's inaction to some extent by using our householder privileges to distribute more than half a million copies of the Calgary Declaration in Quebec and by undertaking a "Quebec consultation" on the subject.

Ironically, the Chrétien government was now more interested in Plan B measures than Plan A proposals. Meanwhile, our Plan A work was our highest priority. In May, our caucus Unity Committee, under Val Meredith, issued the first draft of our New Canada Act, which incorporated Reform's best ideas on strengthening federalism – clarifying the division of powers, reforming federal institutions, and democratizing constitutional changes – into a new legislative format. Over the next year, Val and her committee, aided by Gilles St-Laurent in Quebec, conducted extensive consultations using this draft. In the meantime, the premiers continued to flesh out the seventh principle of the Calgary Declaration, which called for respect of provincial jurisdiction, particularly in the area of social services. On August 7 in Saskatoon, the premiers (including Premier Bouchard) unanimously adopted a resolution advocating measures to strengthen the "social union" in Canada. The premiers emphasized that Canada's social union, and the programs that Canadians value most, particularly health care, must be supported by renewed fiscal arrangements that balance provincial and territorial program responsibilities with revenues.

On December 1, 1998, Reform introduced another motion urging the federal government to conclude a social union agreement with the provinces before the end of the year. Then on December 2, just weeks before the federal government introduced its Clarity Bill, we released our revised New Canada Act, containing in statutory form a Part A on reform of the federation and a Part B on contingency planning. Part A was a further elaboration of our proposals for reforming federalism, including specific measures for re-balancing powers, restricting the federal spending power, and creating a dispute-settling mechanism. Part B was based on a private member's bill that Stephen Harper and Scott Reid had put together in the fall of 1996. Stephen's original bill was brilliantly conceived but had received little attention at the time he proposed it. Now revised and incorporated in our New Canada Act, it declared unilateral secession unlawful, provided a federal definition of what constituted a clear question and a majority in any lawful referendum on secession, and defined the course of action to be taken by the federal government in the event such a referendum carried – including terms and conditions to be negotiated and subjected to a national referendum.

I describe all this exhausting and detailed activity to make one simple point. Between 1995 and 1997 the Liberal government was forced to make another 180-degree turn, this time on constitutional issues. It moved from vehemently denying the need for any Plan B to reluctantly proceeding with the Supreme Court reference and adoption of the Clarity Bill; from an anaemic Plan A consisting of nothing more than "distinct society" and veto powers, to grudgingly endorsing the Calgary Declaration and the social union agreement, with their emphasis on re-balancing the powers. This transformation was brought about primarily by the efforts of the provinces and the Official Opposition in Parliament.

As I've mentioned before, my passion and commitment to Canada often gets buried in the technical detail of proposed solutions, so when we finally presented our New Canada Act to a media conference in Ottawa I wanted somehow, in the midst of this policy and legislative morass, to affirm why I was doing all of this – to express my love of Canada.

I reminded the journalists in the room of the biblical story of Solomon and the baby. Two women from the same household each had a baby. One baby died in the night, and both women claimed the remaining child. Each professed to love it and be its true mother. They brought the baby to Solomon to decide the case. He said: "Bring me a sword." He was going to divide in half the child that they both professed to love.

One woman said, "Go ahead."

But the other woman said to the king, "Whatever you do, don't divide the baby." And, of course, Solomon determined in this way that she was the true mother – the one who truly loved it.

A secession referendum, I told the journalists, is a sword that can divide the Canada we Canadians profess to love. It's a two-edged sword that can also divide the Quebec that sovereigntists profess to love. Who really loves the baby? *Those who will not allow this issue to be settled by division and, even if it means some sacrifice of their personal dreams, resolve to settle it another way.*

Solomon I am not, but the New Canada Act was my best effort to settle it another way.

■

It is probably misleading to call much of the speaking that goes on in the Canadian House of Commons "debate." In a debate, facts and arguments are presented and tested in the light of other facts and counter-arguments – and certainly this occurs on the floor of the House. But in a truly open debate the participants are also free to alter their positions in the light of what is being said. It is this freedom that gives weight and meaning to a true debate, and, unfortunately, it is almost entirely missing from the Canadian House of Commons due to the constrictions of excessive party discipline. Much of what is called debate in the House is really a series of soliloquies in which MPs vigorously present and defend their positions without any hope of influencing the other side or any intention of being influenced themselves by what is said. Nevertheless, every member participates in these exercises, so allow me to share with you some of my experiences.

Besides the big Throne Speech and budget debates, two debates where I felt the MPs went about their business most conscientiously were those in the fall of 1997 dealing with changes to the Newfoundland and Quebec school systems. In essence, the resolutions proposed a process for doing away with the old religious school systems in both provinces and re-establishing them on a non-sectarian basis. They raised such issues as respect for provincial jurisdiction over education and for the rights of religious minorities. As they were constitutional amendments, how we treated them would establish precedents, so members on all sides approached the matter conscientiously. Reform used these debates to establish "tests" that we felt any constitutional amendment should meet: the Test of Democratic Consent (has the amendment been ratified by a majority of the people whom it affects?), the Test of the Rule of Law (is the proposed amendment and amending process legal?), and the Test of the Canadian National Interest (is the amendment and any precedent it might set in the general interest of all Canadians and not just that of the province or interest to which it specifically applies?). I also used the debate to say how I thought religious minorities should conduct themselves in order to best preserve their rights.

In the end, a narrow majority of our members voted for the Newfoundland amendment and against the Quebec amendment, mainly on the grounds that the former had been ratified by a provincial referendum while the latter had not. But the debates involved in arriving at these positions were among the best I witnessed in my time in Parliament.

Ever since I had arrived in Parliament I had wanted to give a major speech outlining in detail the defects of the Canadian Senate, the ineffectual efforts that had been made to reform it, and the Reform Party's proposals for making the Senate Elected, with Equal numbers of Senators per province, and Effective powers to represent regional interests (our Triple-E Senate proposal). But there were several major obstacles in my way. The Chrétien government had no interest in Senate reform and would never permit even a take-note debate on the subject. And until Reformers arrived in the House, successive Speakers had deemed it "unparliamentary" to criticize "the other place" in the Commons. We intended to challenge this.

The one occasion on which debate on the Senate could not be frustrated by the government or the Speaker was when a bill came before the House in which the Senate was specifically referred to. I asked our troops to keep their eyes open for such an opportunity and, lo and behold, one day it presented itself. The bill establishing the new Territory of Nunavut provided for a senator to represent that vast northern region. This was my chance, and as leader of the Opposition, with unlimited speaking time on bills, I intended to make the most of it. When I announced my plans to the caucus, a collective groan went up from my colleagues. While they were all in favour of my tearing a strip off the existing Senate and promoting the Triple-E, some of them knew they would be expected to sit through my entire oration, and this one promised to be a "bladder buster."

Nevertheless, on April 20, 1998, I rose in my place with a solid phalanx of Reform MPs behind me to give the speech, entitled "The Case for Reform of the Senate." We had given an advance copy to the media, and the morning papers had already reported on some of the more colourful sections. Speaker Gilbert Parent himself, not a deputy-speaker, had come to preside, and I had to keep an eye on him because he might try to shut me down if I crossed the line of what he considered "parliamentary."

First I presented "The Case Against the Status Quo Senate" – that it had been wrongly designed in the first place; that it was a compromised House tainted by patronage; that the work, travel, and spending habits of many (not all) of its members were despicable; that it had often proven unwilling or unable to address ethical misconduct by its members; and that its cost far outweighed its benefit to Canada. This was for starters; I was just getting warmed up. Next I presented "The Case For and Against Abolition of the Senate," concluding that the problem with abolition was that it would leave Canada with a one-house parliament in which southern Ontario and southern Quebec would have an absolute majority of the seats, to the detriment of the West, Atlantic Canada, and the North. Which brought me to "The Case for Reform of the Senate." Under this heading I reviewed in detail the "Two Trails to Senate Reform": the Meech Lake–Charlottetown Cul-de-Sac, and the Western Trail to Senate Reform, which featured our constitutional amendment for establishing a Triple E-Senate. I concluded with a "Challenge to Act" aimed at the government, the House, and those senators prepared to lead.

As I got into describing the unethical and wasteful practices of certain senators that disgraced the institution, I could see Speaker Gib Parent edging forward in his great chair with a cautionary look in his eye. So I would raise the level of abstraction to twenty thousand feet until he relaxed, and then return to the assault a few minutes later. Gib slid back and forth on his seat for most of the speech, but he didn't attempt to shut me down, for which I was thankful.

Of course, the government members were not happy with my remarks either. Most of them would have loved to have become appointed and unaccountable members of "the other place" – the joke being that in the United States you had to win an election to get into the Senate but in Canada all you had to do was lose one. When I came to the place in my remarks where I wanted to read into the House record the defective Senate reform proposals of the Meech Lake and Charlottetown accords, and compare them with our Triple-E amendment, the Liberals even refused the customary consent to have *Hansard* include these references without my actually having to read them word for word. And so I read all my references – pages and pages of legal text – into the record. I read them as fast as it was possible to speak, until one of my members slipped me a note saying that the French translator was in danger of strangling to death if I didn't slow down.

I ended by dividing Canadian senators into two categories – the reputable and the disreputable, the sheep and the goats, if you will – with an appeal to the reputable senators to launch their own Senate-reform initiative before Canadians called for the outright abolition of the entire institution.

For the most part, the Senate was infuriated by my talk, and for the next year it was more than my life was worth to venture down to the east end of the Centre Block alone. But I personally got more satisfaction out of this speech than almost any other I had given in the Chamber. Effective regional representation was not only a subject with which I was intimately familiar, but one that I felt passionate about. The *Hansard* record of this speech would also provide our Senate election candidates and campaigners in Alberta virtually everything they would need to know as background for the senatorial election scheduled in that province for the fall. If one took into account all the research and communications preparations that went into that speech, it would work out to about one hour of preparation for every minute of speaking time, and the speech lasted over ninety minutes.

■

Each year the parliamentary calendar provides a certain number of "supply days." On these days, the various opposition parties can propose a motion to be debated – and sometimes voted on – by the House. Sometimes an opposition party proposes a supply motion that even the government will feel obliged to support. Such motions are an example of "leading from behind," and they generally enhance the standing of the opposition party proposing them. Reform's supply motion calling on the House to endorse the Calgary Declaration and for the government to make an effort to communicate its content to Quebecers was an example of this. Similarly, on June 8, 1999, Reform's family critic, Eric Lowther, managed to put forward a motion affirming that, as far as the federal Parliament was concerned, marriage was to be defined as the union of a man and a woman. The motion carried by a vote of 216 in favour to 55 against, with most government members voting for it, but the Bloc, the NDP, and the PCs divided.

Usually, however, the strategic political objective of an opposition party in proposing a supply motion is to find something that the public and the government's own backbenchers support, but which the Prime Minister and the Cabinet oppose. In order to defeat the motion, the government will then have to put the screws to its own members, causing internal division and embarrassment, and alienating voters in the process. This is exactly what happened on April 28, 1998, when the Liberals forced their members to vote against the

Reform motion calling for the compensation of all the victims of Hepatitis C who had contracted the disease from tainted blood; on February 2, 1999, when the Liberals directed their members to vote down a Reform motion calling for the government to take action to uphold a Criminal Code provision dealing with the possession and distribution of child pornography, which had been struck down by the B.C. courts; and again on March 9, 1999, when the Liberals directed their MPs to vote down a Reform motion calling for an end to tax discrimination against single-income families.

Our most effective supply day involved a motion that clearly demonstrated the difference between the government's professed commitment to ethical government and its actual practice. Early in 2001, it was becoming abundantly clear that the ethics counsellor was *not* independent of the Prime Minister and that he should be reporting directly to Parliament (as promised in the Liberals' 1993 Red Book). Reform put forward a supply-day motion: "That this House adopt the following policy from Liberal Red Book 1 and call for the implementation of it by the government: 'A Liberal government will appoint an independent Ethics counsellor to advise both public officials and lobbyists in the day to day applications of the Code of Conduct for Public Officials. The Ethics counsellor will be appointed after consultation with the leaders of all parties in the House of Commons and *will report directly to Parliament.*'"

After a most curious debate, in which Liberals advanced ethical arguments for opposing their own commitments to ethical government, the Liberals voted against their own 1993 election promise. The motion was defeated 142 against to 123 in favour.

9

LIBERAL ETHICS

UPON BECOMING LEADER OF THE OPPOSITION IN 1997, I continued to do a lot of thinking about moral authority. How did a government or a political leader acquire the wisdom and credibility to carry the judgment of Canadians on decisions in which "right" and "wrong" were involved? How could a government vest moral authority in others, such as an ethics counsellor or a regulatory tribunal? And how do political leaders or parties or governments lose whatever moral authority they may already possess?

During my time as leader of the Opposition, three individuals came to Ottawa who had more "moral authority" to speak on the subjects that brought them there than any of us in Parliament. Vaclav Havel, president of the Czech Republic, came on April 29, 1999, to argue that the West had a moral obligation to intervene in Kosovo to stop the human rights atrocities being committed by the regime of Slobodan Milosevich. He described as a "Canadian ethic" the principle that the security of individuals takes precedence over the security of states, argued that the NATO alliance of which both Canada and the Czech Republic were a part should intervene "for ethical reasons," and declared his personal conviction that "human rights, human liberties, and human dignity have their deepest roots outside this earthly world," in the convictions of "our conscience, the ambassador of eternity in our soul." Havel had an authority to speak on this subject that none of us could match. When it came to fighting human rights abuses and the curtailment of freedoms by the Communists in his own country, he had put his own life on the line, suffering persecution and imprisonment. Havel had earned the right to speak authoritatively about a moral obligation to defend human rights and liberties.

The second individual who possessed a similar authority, and certainly not because he had sought it, was the Reverend Dale Lang, father of seventeen-year-old Jason Lang, who was shot down by a deranged fellow student at his high school in Taber, Alberta, on April 28, 1999. Aline Chrétien and a number of MPs (myself included) had attended the memorial service, conducted at the school by Reverend Lang near the spot where his son had so tragically died. He had spoken then about the destructive reality of evil, with the authority of someone who had just experienced that reality in a terrible way. But he also spoke of the transcending power of genuine love to overcome evil with good, and demonstrated this in his actions and attitude towards the students of Jason's school, including his son's killer. When he and his wife, Diane, came to Ottawa to share their experience at the Parliamentary Prayer Breakfast, his words were infused with a moral authority that was palpable and undeniable.

Nelson Mandela, whose life had become a symbol of moral authority earned through suffering, also came to Ottawa while I was leader of the Opposition. He addressed Parliament on September 24, 1998. Like all MPs I was anxious to listen to him and meet him. In all my study of political history and practice, there are two events that I would unabashedly describe as "political miracles." The greatest political miracle of the nineteenth century, in my judgment, was the fact that the Americans fought a terrible and prolonged civil war and still survived to become a strong, united country. And the greatest political miracle of the twentieth century would have to be Nelson Mandela emerging from prison after twenty-seven years and, instead of mobilizing his followers to wreak a terrible revenge on the practitioners of South African apartheid, choosing to participate in a process of healing and reconciliation.

Sometime after their visits I asked my political scientist friend Dr. John Redekop for his thoughts on how an ordinary Canadian politician, without any of the life experience and sufferings of a Vaclav Havel or a Dale Lang or a Nelson Mandela, could acquire sufficient standing with Canadians to be credible and useful on issues of ethics and morality. In response, he advocated the cultivation of truthfulness, transparency, sound judgment, humility, gracious acceptance of criticism and rejection, patience (since the acquisition of moral authority takes time), congruency of personal values and public stances, and consistency over time. If these are the prerequisites for gaining moral authority, most of us have a long, long way to go.

■

Every now and then in a legislative chamber some lawmaker will suggest that it is all right to "bend the rules," or even to ignore or break the rule of law now and then, in order to achieve some more important objective. Whenever such suggestions are made, I feel my hackles as a legislator starting to rise, and there were several occasions during the thirty-sixth Parliament when my hackles were standing straight up on end.

We legislators, whatever else we may do, are in the business of making "rules." For us to ignore or bend the rules for our own personal or political purposes, or even for supposedly idealistic purposes, is not only hypocritical, it undermines our own authority. We pass statutes that usually contain sections dealing with enforcement and penalties – often a fine or imprisonment for any citizen who breaks that law. For us, of all people, to entertain the idea that there are certain circumstances under which the rule of law can be ignored or broken is hypocritical, dangerous, and a threat to peace, order, and good government.

When some of my own members became so incensed about the misplaced focus of the government's gun control legislation that they considered advising constituents to disregard the law, they came perilously close to stepping over that line. When the Prime Minister and the government played fast and loose with rules governing conflict of interest, fair hiring and contracting, and the ethical use of taxpayers' money, they definitely crossed that line.

But in the thirty-sixth Parliament, on February 10, 1998, I had a much more dramatic encounter with this phenomenon. The Bloc had introduced a motion that read: "That this House recognize the consensus in Quebec that it is for Quebecers to decide their own future." The Bloc was of course incensed that the question of the legality of unilateral secession had been referred to the Supreme Court. They denounced it as an attempt by the federal government to subjugate the democratic will of the people of Quebec to a federal constitution that they refused to recognize, asserting that they placed "the democratic voice of the people of Quebec above the Constitution of Canada." Bloc members made it clear that they would support a unilateral declaration of independence in violation of Canadian constitutional law, on the grounds that they did not approve of that law and that the democratic will of Quebecers was above it. I then asked Duceppe how he reconciled this position with the principle of the rule of law and whether the rule of law would be a governing principle in any independent Quebec. He answered that he didn't accept the rule of law when it was the law of Canada, but that in the new Quebec, when Quebec made all its own laws, the "true rule of law" would prevail.

When it was my turn to speak, I cautioned the Bloc about opening a door they might never be able to shut. Once you have taught the people of Quebec that there are exceptions to the rule of law, I asked, how will you answer those Quebecers (the northern Cree, the Mohawks, militant members of the English minority, for example) who tell you, "We don't approve of *your* law, and we have a right to unilaterally break it on the same grounds that permit you to unilaterally break Canadian law"? Having taught Quebecers to take an axe to the supreme law of Canada, what will you do when they turn around and take that same axe to the supreme law of Quebec?

■

You can tell a lot about the ethics of a leader and an organization by observing how they deal with accusations of wrongdoing. And there was no evidence that the Chrétien government had learned any lessons from the Krever and Somalia inquiries with respect to accepting and discharging its responsibilities in the face of such allegations. In fact, the outcomes of these inquiries seemed to reinforce the government's thinking that if it constantly denied any responsibility and then delayed or obstructed the investigations long enough, the media and the public would grow weary of the exercise and the government could ride out the storm with little political damage.

That this was now becoming standard procedure for the Chrétien government was confirmed the next time it was implicated in misdeeds. In November 1997, the federal government hosted the Asia Pacific Economic Conference (APEC) in Vancouver, attended by various heads of state from Pacific Rim countries, including President Suharto, the ruthless and corrupt dictator of Indonesia. In an effort to avoid any embarrassment arising from demonstrations by human rights activists, the Prime Minister's Office had taken a direct interest in security arrangements for the conference. From later testimony, it would appear that officials representing the Prime Minister had given the RCMP the distinct impression that the Prime Minister wanted demonstrations kept to a minimum and that embarrassment of the Prime Minister and the government was to be avoided at all costs. During the conference, an incident arose in which pepper spray and other forceful tactics were used by the RCMP to disperse a student demonstration. This received extensive media coverage and led to questions in the House as to whether the tactics used had been excessive and on whose orders the RCMP had been acting.

At that point, if the Prime Minister had personally assumed responsibility for the actions of his officials, acknowledged that they and the RCMP might have been overly zealous but that they were only trying to maintain security and Canada's reputation as a safe place for international conferences, the whole affair would have been over in three days. But the Prime Minister and the government did nothing of the kind. At first, they tried to make light of the whole incident. The Prime Minister joked, "For me, pepper, I put it on my plate." Then when the allegations of wrongdoing wouldn't go away, the Prime Minister denied that his office had any responsibility for what had happened and shifted the blame largely onto the RCMP.

As is often the case in large organizations, the ethical standards of the leader are very readily adopted by his lieutenants. Solicitor General Andy Scott, who was responsible for the RCMP, should have taken a more independent view of this incident from the outset, but instead he fell into line with the Prime Minister. An indiscreet conversation between Scott and a friend on an airplane to Saint John – in which he predicted that the RCMP would probably have to "take the fall" for the pepper-spray incident – was overheard by NDP MP Dick Proctor, eventually leading to Scott's resignation on November 23, 1998, one year after the APEC altercation. By now, what should have been a minor incident had become a *cause célèbre*. An inquiry had been launched, but it had been undertaken by the RCMP Public Complaints Commission, a body whose chairperson was appointed by the Prime Minister and which lacked the authority to call the PMO to account. Chrétien refused to testify before the commission; the head of the review panel resigned citing interference from commission chairperson Shirley Heafey; the two remaining APEC panellists also resigned; and the hearings were finally restarted in February 1999 under the able chairmanship of Ted Hughes, a former judge and B.C. provincial conflict-of-interest commissioner. Chrétien again turned down requests to testify. In November 1999 the inquiry's chief counsel resigned, and in August 2001, the 453-page APEC Report was finally completed, more than three and a half years after the pepper-spray incident that had precipitated it.

The process represented by the report had cost $10 million and produced twenty-one non-binding recommendations. While Justice Hughes criticized the RCMP for poor planning and procedures, he also found that Jean Carle, one of the Prime Minister's top aides at the time, exerted undue pressure on the police by ordering the removal of protesters camped at the APEC conference site. Justice Hughes called for legislation to ensure that the government could not arbitrarily meddle in security planning, but the government and the Prime Minister's new appointee to the position of RCMP com-

missioner both rejected the recommendation. It was Krever and
Somalia all over again.

■

The ethical management of taxpayers' dollars requires that governments make a conscientious effort to avoid wasteful expenditures and
refrain from using taxpayers' dollars for partisan political purposes.
Both these criteria were continually violated by the Chrétien government, and the incident that brought this most dramatically to
light was the Program Integrity Audit of the Transitional Jobs Fund
and other programs at Human Resources Development Canada
(HRDC), otherwise known as the "billion dollar boondoggle."

In late 1999 a random internal audit of 459 files at Human
Resources Development Canada – files that represented roughly $1
billion of federal "grants and contributions" – revealed some disturbing facts. It turned out that 15 per cent of the projects to which
funds had been disbursed did not have an application on file from
the sponsor; 72 per cent had no cash flow forecast; 11 per cent had
no budget proposal; 11 per cent had no description of expected
results; 87 per cent of the files showed no evidence of supervision. In
addition, 37 per cent of the 459 files contained evidence of such
gross mismanagement that auditors had to do a second investigation
to see whether they should call in the police.

This information might never have seen the light of day, except
that Laurie Throness, a dedicated Reform researcher in the office of
the Opposition, had gotten wind of it and, on January 17, 2000, submitted an Access to Information request to obtain a copy. On
January 18, the department called a press conference on the subject,
and on January 19 it released the audit. To cap it off, HRDC sent us a
letter dated January 20 saying that they hadn't received our request
until January 21. We knew we were on to something.

The internal audit we had requested covered a random sampling of
HRDC projects. If 8 per cent of all files reviewed showed evidence of
gross mismanagement, and 87 per cent showed no evidence of over-
sight of any kind, how much more mismanagement existed in the

thousands and thousands of unexamined files and projects financed by HRDC and other departments? There is a line that runs through the entire federal budget entitled "Grants and Contributions," and the total budgeted expenditure under this heading for all government departments for the following year was more than $13 billion. If the $1 billion "tip of the iceberg" at HRDC was as rotten as the random audit indicated, how much more rot and mismanagement existed beneath the surface?

Persistent and methodical questioning of HRDC minister Jane Stewart by Reform MP Diane Ablonczy over the next four months turned up even more disturbing revelations. Not only was there gross waste and mismanagement of funds by the department, particularly when it came to the Transitional Jobs Fund, but there was also mounting evidence that funds were being systematically allocated to projects for the political benefit of the Liberal Party and its members. Duchess Foods, a prosperous company looking to expand, received nearly $2 million in grants and loans to move thirty kilometres from one low-unemployment riding (Hamilton) to another – Jane Stewart's own riding. The move was 90 per cent funded by the federal government. RMH Teleservices was supposedly lured to the minister's riding using $1.6 million in taxpayers' dollars. The company later acknowledged to the press that it would have relocated there anyway, and the HRDC grant was simply "icing on the cake." Most disturbing of all, it became clear that the Prime Minister himself was part of the problem. Access to Information requests turned up a memo from an aide to the HRDC minister declaring that "we have no choice" when it came to approving money for a hotel project in the Prime Minister's riding that did not meet the department's qualifications. Another search turned up a request directly from the Prime Minister's Office to Canada Economic Development for Quebec Regions for $200,000 to finance a fountain in the Saint Maurice River in the Prime Minister's riding. This request from the Prime Minister was made several weeks before the group sponsoring the project had even applied for funding and gave new meaning to the concept of a "money order."

As the evidence of wrongdoing mounted, the Prime Minister, the HRDC minister, and the government as a whole reacted in a manner that by now had become completely predictable. At first the Prime Minister and the minister denied that a problem even existed. The HRDC minister told Parliament that "everything was in order" even when she had the audit on her desk saying that everything was definitely *not* in order. Then the Prime Minister endeavoured to trivialize the issue, saying that "administrative problems of this nature occur all the time." On February 9, 1999, in the House, he claimed that the auditors had found only "two problems in seven files, and an overpayment of $251.50." According to him, the media and the Opposition were making a mountain out of a molehill. As the questions and allegations persisted and began to focus on the relationship between the Transitional Jobs Program and the Prime Minister's own riding, the Prime Minister sought to justify everything that had been done – including the errors – in the name of job creation and economic development. He claimed that by lobbying the HRDC minister for grants and contributions for his riding, he was just doing what any MP would do. To back up this contention, each day in Question Period he would list HRDC grants that had been given to the ridings of Opposition members, as if this somehow justified his own activities. When an Opposition MP would ask the Prime Minister a question on HRDC grants to the PM's riding, Don Boudria, his House leader, would hand him a sheet from a big black binder, and the PM would reply by listing any HRDC grants that had been given to that MP's riding. But when Deborah Grey asked for a copy of the information that "Binder Boy" was handing to the Prime Minister, so that the Opposition could check the proportion of grants and contributions going from HRDC to Liberal ridings, the government maintained that it could not provide a riding-by-riding breakdown of HRDC grants. Once again, the government was moving from denial mode, to justification mode, to obstruction and cover-up mode. Eventually, in another blatant contradiction, the government did indeed provide a riding-by-riding list for the whole country.

In October 2000, Chapter 11 of the auditor general's report confirmed much of what had been alleged about mismanagement of taxpayer funds at HRDC. The boondoggle at HRDC did a great deal to further weaken any pretence the government might still have made to running an "ethical" government. With an election coming, there would be a golden opportunity (I thought) to drive this point home to the voters. But before that could happen, another incident occurred that was even more revealing about the Prime Minister's approach to public and private ethics. The media labelled it "Shawinigate."

■

Jean Chrétien is a career politician whose personal and political interests have become tightly intertwined. He is also a product and a practitioner of what Reformers call "the old politics," one of the hallmarks of which is the explicit, conscious, and constant use of taxpayers' money for partisan political purposes. Chrétien not only saw nothing wrong with such practices, he boasted about them. For example, on October 15, 1993, just prior to the election that would make him Prime Minister, the *Montreal Gazette* reported on his personal campaign for re-election in the federal riding of Saint-Maurice in these words: "In each public appearance in the region Wednesday night and yesterday, Chrétien reminded [the voters] that he will probably have enormous clout as prime minister to pull government strings. 'When a dossier for Saint-Maurice lands on a cabinet minister's desk . . . need I say more?' he said to rounds of laughter during one meeting yesterday."

Knowing of the Prime Minister's proclivities in this respect, Reformers paid close attention to federal government grants in his riding. These investigations turned up two significant correlations: one between the timing of grant announcements in the riding and the 1997 election (a relatively close shave for the Prime Minister, who won by only 1,601 votes with 2,013 spoiled ballots), and the other between grants/contracts and donations to the Prime Minister's own re-election campaign.

The Auberge des Gouverneurs in Shawinigan received a $600,000 grant on March 13, 1997, just a month before the 1997 election call. The Prime Minister was pictured along with the project's promoter on the front page of the PM's April householder. A fax from an official of the Human Resources Department, obtained under Access to Information, told the story: "This project has been announced by the

P.M. Its approval by the Minister is URGENT." The auditor general later confirmed that the grant had been announced by the Prime Minister four months *before* it was approved by the department.

It soon came to light in the press that the owner of the hotel was a businessman from Europe with a shady past, having admitted in writing to misappropriating nearly $1 million from his business partners. At the time he received financial assistance from the federal government he was under criminal investigation for fraud in Belgium. None of this, however, seemed to bother the Prime Minister – he launched his 2000 election campaign from the convention centre attached to this hotel, also built with taxpayers' dollars. In May 2001 the Auberge des Gouverneurs filed for bankruptcy.

Altogether, nearly 40 per cent of the donations to the Prime Minister's personal campaign for re-election in 1997 were received from companies that had benefited from federal grants or contracts. Which brings us to the case of the Grand-Mère Golf Club and the Auberge Grand-Mère.

The story begins with a document signed on March 1, 1994, by the Prime Minister, required under the "Conflict of Interest and Post-Employment Code for Public Office Holders." He declared: "I was a Director of the Grand-Mère Golf Club (previously 161341 Canada Inc.)" and "I hold a third of the shares of J&AC Consultants Inc., a private company of which the portfolio is managed by a third party without ties of dependence and without right of regard on my part." Behind this apparently straightforward declaration of interests was a tangled web of shadowy business and political decisions, blatant misuse of political influence, apparent conflicts of interest, dubious associations, and questionable financial transactions involving public money.

The Grand-Mère Golf Club is nestled at the north end of the village of Grand-Mère, Quebec, in the Prime Minister's riding. It was purchased in 1988 by Mr. Chrétien and two business partners through their numbered company, 161341 Canada Inc., along with the business (not the building) of the nearby Auberge Grande-Mère while Mr. Chrétien was a lawyer in a private firm. (Mr. Chrétien had resigned from Parliament in February 1986 and was re-elected in December 1990.)

Consolidated Bathurst, a large pulp and paper company of which Mr. Chrétien was a director at the time (it would also donate $5,000 to Mr. Chrétien's personal campaign in 1997), sold the company's golf course to 161341 Canada Inc. for $1.25 million. Over the period from 1988 to 1993 the sewer system failed, the clubhouse burned down, and a combination of bad weather, poor management, and competition from other clubs led to losses of approximately $2 million.

The Auberge Grand-Mère is a century-old hotel located at the head of the lane leading to the golf course. The inn historically served golfers at the Grand-Mère course and was even described on the incorporation records as a hand-in-glove "golf club and auberge" operation.

On April 16, 1993 (six months prior to the election of Mr. Chrétien as prime minister), Mr. Yvon Duhaime purchased the business of the Auberge Grand-Mère from 161341 Canada Inc. for about $250,000, and a year later he purchased the inn building itself from Consolidated Bathurst for $225,000. Mr. Duhaime owned L'Hôtel des Chutes in neighbouring Shawinigan, which had been mysteriously destroyed by fire the previous year. He also had a criminal record for impaired driving and assault, which would later become relevant.

According to Jean Chrétien, on November 1, 1993, three days before being sworn in as Canada's twentieth prime minister, he sold his holding company's shares in 161341 Canada Inc. to Akimbo Development Corporation for $300,000 plus interest. The only evidence of this transaction was a handwritten bill of sale scrawled on a single sheet of paper, a copy of which was made public by the Prime Minister on March 27, 2001, after weeks of intense questioning on the subject by the Opposition. The original document failed to materialize even after an expert handwriting analyst from the United States cast doubt on the authenticity of the document's date. To this day there is no corroborating evidence or testimony that would clarify where, when, or under what circumstances the unusual agreement was written.

Akimbo Development Corporation was owned by Mr. Jonas Prince, a Toronto real estate developer and former CEO of Delta Hotels. Mr. Prince stated to the media that he only bought an "option or right" to purchase the shares. It was later revealed that he never signed the corporate records of 161341 Canada Inc. held at the company's headquarters in Grand-Mère, nor did Akimbo ever participate in any matter involving 161341 Canada Inc. or its assets. Though he was eventually obliged to pay for the shares, Mr. Prince clearly did not consider himself an owner.

Nor was 161341 Canada Inc. itself sure who owned the shares. In the Commons on March 22, 2001, the Prime Minister declared: "I had sold my shares on November 1, 1993. It was very clear." But the very next day a spokesman for 161341 Canada Inc. was quoted as saying, "We approved the sale. Except that in our books, the sale never materialized."

Even the Prime Minister's friends didn't believe that he had sold the shares. Melissa Marcotte, daughter of one of the founding partners of 161341 Canada Inc., was quoted as saying on March 23, 2001, "I wasn't even aware that he didn't sell his shares. I said to Jaimie [her brother and the general manager of the Grand-Mère Golf Club], 'How come you didn't ever tell me? I'm upset. He never sold them (according to the corporate records) and I said he did.'"

The media speculated that the Prime Minister's original intention was to build a Delta Hotel by the golf course, but when he discovered that the Delta in nearby Trois-Rivières had a restrictive covenant preventing the construction of another within fifty kilometres, he was unable to proceed. However, without full disclosure by all the parties involved, there was no way of proving this.

Although the public can only guess exactly when or under what circumstances the sale of shares in 161341 Canada unravelled, it is known that on January 27, 1996, the Prime Minister personally phoned Ethics Counsellor Howard Wilson at his home on a Saturday night to announce that the share sale had fallen through. Though the shares had been legally offered for sale by J&AC Consultants (the Prime Minister's holding company) and should therefore have reverted automatically to the blind trust originally set up under that name in March 1994 "without right of regard" by the Prime Minister, somehow he became aware of all the details.

The ethics counsellor informed him that he had two choices: he could recover the shares and declare publicly that he owned them, or he could resell them. The Prime Minister did neither. Though he promised the ethics counsellor he would resell them, they actually remained unsold for three more years, until October 14, 1999. And their status remained unreported to the public until January 23, 1999, when investigative journalist Andrew McIntosh broke the story in the *National Post*. During this six-year period, any business transactions involving the golf course lands or the Auberge Grand-Mère could have materially affected the value of properties and shares still effectively owned by the Prime Minister.

It will never be known whether Mr. Chrétien would ever have resold the shares or publicly declared his continued ownership of them if the media had not broken the story. Nor is the public ever likely to learn whether the ethics counsellor would eventually have called him to account. Since the story first became public, Mr. Chrétien has steadfastly maintained that the actual share certificates remained in the possession of Akimbo – although the media reported Mr. Prince as saying that they had been returned to the original owner. Mr. Prince, a reputable businessman, was understandably upset by the public attention focused on this transaction, and the Opposition believed him to be more credible on the subject than the Prime Minister.

However, just because the shares sat in limbo did not mean that the Prime Minister was inactive on the Grand-Mère file during that period. Just a month after the Prime Minister phoned the ethics counsellor, he became actively interested – using the influence only a Prime Minister can exert – in securing investments in the Auberge Grand-Mère.

What was his motivation? The local newspaper, *La Nouvelliste*, mused on March 25, 1997, "Prime Minister Jean Chrétien had dreamed, many years ago, of establishing a hotel worth $6 million on the extremity of the golf course near Route 55. He even envisioned a CP hotel, reputed across Canada." Could it be that a Delta hotel by the golf course would have been acceptable, but after the Delta deal fell through he resorted to the next best alternative? Without full disclosure, who knows?

Whatever his reasons, from the outset it was obvious that the Prime Minister had an inordinate interest in the welfare of the inn.

The Opposition maintained that this was due to his continuing interest in the value of his shares in the neighbouring golf course. The attractiveness of his shares to potential purchasers would be enhanced if a hotel project on or near the golf course proceeded. He would also have known that the value of those shares to a potential buyer might decline if a hotel project did not proceed and the golf course business continued to languish.

The Opposition claimed that the Prime Minister had a financial interest in the golf course, proven by the fact that in November 1997 Akimbo paid the Prime Minister $40,000 "as payment in settlement of our agreement." Akimbo claimed it had merely purchased an option and had chosen not to follow through. The Opposition maintained that since Mr. Chrétien knew that at the very least there was a dispute over the shares and that they would eventually revert to him if he failed (or neglected) to find a buyer, he had a financial interest in the company and therefore a motive to lobby for money for the inn.

Clearly, the Prime Minister was knowledgeable about matters being managed by his "blind" trust when he phoned the ethics counsellor about the shares. Nevertheless, he later boldly declared that he had had nothing to do with the matter because his shares and personal business affairs were all in the hands of the blind trust managed by his lawyer. "It is all dealt with by the person who manages the trust of my own affairs. I do not ask them any questions. I do not have the shares. All my assets are controlled, like other members of the Cabinet, by the trustee and the trustee decides what to do. I make it my point not to ask any questions," he said in the House of Commons on March 23, 1999. The contradiction between his actions and his words appeared to escape him.

It soon became apparent, however, through questioning in Parliament, leaks to the press, and Access to Information requests that the Prime Minister was deeply involved in activities having at least an indirect impact on the value and saleability of assets in that "blind" trust.

The Government of Canada operates an Immigrant Investor Program, which is a ready source of investment capital held by immigrant entrepreneurs who want to obtain Canadian citizenship. Investments at the time were made in allotments of $350,000. The program, federally administered in the rest of Canada, in Quebec was administered by the province. The program was so successful there that a provincial briefing note boasts, "Since the beginning of the program Quebec has received nearly 46% of funds transferred to Canada. Between the years 1994 and 1998 . . . Quebec received nearly 65% of all funds, reaching to 81% in 1998."

Just a month after he reported that the share sale had fallen through, on February 28, 1996, the Prime Minister held a private meeting with an immigrant investor and a Montreal investment broker at 24 Sussex Drive to discuss an unnamed hotel. The investor was charged just four months later by the RCMP with trying to bribe senior immigration officials. According to the press, the charges were suddenly dropped in September 1998 because the case was "tied in with demands for disclosure that could have shed light on certain unsavoury goings-on at the Canadian diplomatic mission in Hong Kong."

It was later revealed that Yvon Duhaime had arranged the meeting, and that it had indeed addressed the financial situation of the Auberge Grand-Mère. No surprise – after all, what immigrant investor wouldn't want to be associated with helping the Prime Minister of Canada?

But that wasn't the Prime Minister's story. When he was confronted by the media, during the election campaign in November 2000, with his role in obtaining the immigrant investment, he denied it, saying of the foreign investor, "He has not invested a damn cent in that. The investment was made by three organizations and you never write about it." Then he listed the three, the first being the caisse populaire, "a local organization." He seemed to be well briefed about investments in the inn.

In fact, one week after the 1996 meeting with Chrétien, the first $350,000 instalment of what would amount to $2.35 million from immigrant investors came to the inn, through the local caisse populaire. When Mr. Chrétien was confronted with this in the House of Commons on February 7, 2001, he excused himself by saying, "Mr. Speaker, the investor fund is managed by the provincial authorities. I was not aware that there was any investment there." Even here the Prime Minister did not tell the full story.

Provincial records state that the investments were to be managed by local brokers, not the provincial government – brokers like the one from Montreal who accompanied the immigrant investor the Prime Minister met with in his own home on February 28, 1996. He had to have known that the broker was key to the arrangement, and it further strains credulity to accept that he was ignorant of the immigrant investment in the Inn.

But the Immigrant Investor Program was not the only federal program tapped for funds to assist Grand-Mère–related projects. Other avenues were also being explored whereby taxpayers' money might be used to bolster the finances of people in a position to help the Prime Minister. On March 19, 1996, Human Resources Development Minister Pierre Pettigrew selected three firms from the Saint-Maurice area (Mr. Chrétien's riding) from a list of seven firms to submit proposals for a large contract with the Canadian International Development Agency (CIDA). One of the three pre-qualifying companies was a business named Transelec Incorporated, controlled by the Prime Minister's friend Claude Gauthier.

On August 27, 1996, Transelec was selected by a CIDA committee as the winning bidder on the $6.3-million contract to bring electricity to a rural area in Mali, West Africa. Two weeks after receiving notification that his was the winning bid on the CIDA contract, on September 9, 1996, Mr. Gauthier incorporated a numbered company, 3293475 Canada Inc. Two weeks later his company paid $525,000 to 161341 Canada Inc. (the Chrétien-related company) for a parcel of undeveloped land beside the Grand-Mère Golf Club, enabling that company to pay off a seven-year-old line of credit. Seven months after, during the 1997 federal election campaign, Transelec donated $10,000 to Mr. Chrétien's personal election campaign.

In October 2000, the auditor general released his study of the process by which Transelec was selected. It was a damning report, concluding that the company should not even have been selected for pre-qualification, because it did not meet the minimum requirements for relevant experience, and also because it was not fully Canadian-owned at the time it submitted its bid. When another Canadian company had protested the legality of the award, CIDA officials had simply ignored the protest and awarded the contract.

But Mr. Gauthier had not yet finished winning taxpayers' dollars to bolster his capacity to conduct business. There was always the Transitional Jobs Fund, the scandal-prone job-creation fund that favoured Liberal MPs from Quebec, giving many generous grants to generous Liberal contributors.

Which brings us to the link between the Transitional Jobs Fund and investments in the Prime Minister's riding. The Opposition had applied under Access to Information for details about a man who was charged and convicted of influence-peddling, using federal government grants, around the time of the 1997 election. The ethics counsellor refused to release relevant information, the Opposition appealed for help, and for two years the information commissioner fought the ethics counsellor until he was forced to reveal, just prior to the 2000 election campaign, that he had conducted interviews at the time demonstrating that there was a routine political approval process in Quebec for the Transitional Jobs Fund. The grant applications, along with detailed, sensitive private information about applicants, were vetted by presidents of Liberal Party riding associations, as well as other good federal and provincial Liberals, before receiving approval from the minister.

Though the office of the ethics counsellor himself had discovered this unethical practice, he said nothing, and in fact struggled to prevent its disclosure. The documents show that the unnamed employee in the minister's office involved in this network was also the one to actually lay the approval documents before the minister for his signature, but the minister, of course, denied any knowledge of this seedy business.

On April 4, 1997, just prior to the federal election, a company in the Prime Minister's riding named Aérospatiale Globax received a Transitional Jobs Fund grant of $2.04 million and almost immediately gave $4,000 to the Prime Minister's personal election campaign. Less than a year later, a Globax subsidiary named Placeteco that molds plastic parts for helicopters in Grand-Mère, despite assistance of $114,000 taken from the Globax grant, was in the throes of bankruptcy and its owners were seeking to unload it. Who should end up "rescuing" it but the Prime Minister's friend, Claude Gauthier?

An HRDC staffer commented about Placeteco in an e-mail obtained through Access to Information: "The subsidy being an interesting element for a future buyer, the Office of the Prime Minister wishes that HRDC does all that which it is legally possible to do because if the sale does not take place, a bankruptcy and layoffs are expected." And what did HRDC do, ever willing to comply with the "wishes" of the Prime Minister? Just before the close of the fiscal year on March 27, 1998, it created two trust funds (an exclusive privilege – no others were created in the nation for this purpose) to hold the Globax grant. The trusts were created through the good offices of another prime ministerial friend, Grand-Mère lawyer Gilles Champagne, who is now serving his second consecutive federal political appointment on the board of Canada Post.

These trust funds held the cash over the end of the fiscal year and paid it out again in the new year, contravening Treasury Board requirements that such government funds "lapse" at the end of each fiscal year. When the director of Labour Market Initiatives and Operations at HRDC travelled from Ottawa to Montreal in June 1999 specifically to discuss all seventeen of the Transitional Jobs Fund grants in the Prime Minister's riding, she was horrified to learn of the existence of the trusts and wrote, "I was not aware of this before as I would have been against this approach considering that this is not according to financial administrative procedures." A draft briefing note went further, saying that, as an official had approved it without the proper signing authority, "it would appear that this section of the Financial Administration Act was not respected." Although spending authority for the funds in the trusts had lapsed and did not technically exist, the cash had been paid out anyway, the interest alone on the money was recovered, no one was charged or even disciplined, and the trusts were finally shut down.

What all this demonstrated was that extraordinary efforts were being made to use HRDC's Transitional Jobs Fund to support dubious investments in the Prime Minister's riding, including investment by those with interests in the Auberge Grand-Mère and golf course. A link was now established between the billion-dollar boondoggle at HRDC and Shawinigate.

The Opposition and the media continued to explore this link. It is a mystery (or is it?) how Claude Gauthier, who first received a $6.3-million CIDA contract and then acquired land belonging to the Grand-Mère Golf Club, suddenly appeared on the scene ready to rescue Placeteco and receive $1.19 million of the original Globax grant from one of the trust funds. Regardless of how he learned of the opportunity, he entered into negotiations with compliant HRDC staff, the cash grant became a condition of purchase, and on June 17, Mr. Gauthier became the proud owner of Placeteco. Within six months (December 10, 1998), Placeteco declared bankruptcy, repudiated the requirement of the grant to maintain a certain number of jobs, and the company was started anew. The company's 155 jobs were whittled down to just 62.

Meanwhile, back at the golf course, Mr. Yvon Duhaime was again in the picture. In fact he had been there all along. It will be remembered that he'd been the operator of the Auberge Grand-Mère since 1993. But he owed money on the inn (which he had purchased from Consolidated Bathurst in December 1994), and the business was failing, which would have further depressed the potential value of the Prime Minister's shares in the golf course and increased the difficulty in unloading them.

On April 12, 1996, three months after he let the ethics counsellor know that the sale to Akimbo had fallen through and just six weeks after he met with immigrant investors, the Prime Minister of Canada phoned Mr. François Beaudoin, the president of the Business Development Bank of Canada (a federal Crown corporation), on behalf of Mr. Duhaime, who was desperately in need of a loan. On May 29, Mr. Chrétien met Mr. Beaudoin at a 24 Sussex Drive reception and again raised the issue of a possible loan to the Auberge Grand-Mère and Mr. Duhaime. On September 16, 1996, Mr. Duhaime's initial application for $3.5 million was turned down by the BDC. Even so, Mr. Duhaime persisted, though his criminal record should have prevented him from getting a BDC loan. On February 20, 1997, Mr. Chrétien called the BDC president yet again.

But by now Duhaime wanted more than a loan from a government agency to stay afloat; he wanted government grants, which would also enhance his prospects for the loan. On April 22, 1997,

Yvon Duhaime and the Prime Minister's faithful constituency assistant Denise Tremblay (Ms. Tremblay was a copious letter-writer who responded to every local request for money with an immediate assault on the appropriate federal department; she was later appointed to the Veterans Review and Appeal Board at a salary of up to $90,000 per year) met with local officials of the Human Resources Development office to discuss a Transitional Jobs Fund grant for Mr. Duhaime.

The local officials of HRDC were obviously impressed that an applicant for a Transitional Jobs Fund grant was accompanied by an assistant to the Prime Minister, although they must have been familiar with her, given that the Prime Minister's constituency office was located just down the hall in the same building. On May 28, 1997 (four days before election day), a project to reconstruct the Auberge Grand-Mère was announced at a press conference in the hotel by Mr. René Fugère, a representative of the Prime Minister, with broad hints that a federal grant might soon follow. And it did: $164,000 was obtained for the Auberge Grand-Mère, but again, arms had to be twisted to get it.

On June 5, 1997, an e-mail from Minister Pettigrew's assistant, obtained under an Access to Information request, said that although restaurant jobs at the Auberge Grand-Mère were not eligible for Transitional Jobs Fund financing, the Prime Minister had already "suggested" the provision of funding during discussions with Duhaime. The e-mail concluded, "It is a difficult decision [when] we depart from regional guidelines. Sometimes, difficult decisions have to be made, but in this case, we have to maintain the proposed level of financing. I would like to give another answer, but I have no choice."

The fact that Mr. Duhaime had received significant help from René Fugère in securing the grant for the Auberge Grand-Mère attracted the interest of the media and the Opposition. We subsequently learned that this mysterious figure was helping companies in the Prime Minister's riding obtain government grants, though he was not registered as a lobbyist as required by law. The Prime Minister admitted in the House that Mr. Fugère occasionally represented him on a volunteer basis at public functions, so his personal connection with the Prime Minister could not have been lost on local public servants. A further storm of controversy erupted when the press revealed that Mr. Fugère's company had also represented the Auberge Grand-Mère, and had been paid $11,500 by its owner for "computer consulting work" just ten days after receiving $100,000 of its grant.

Mr. Fugère became the subject of a third RCMP investigation into grants in the Prime Minister's riding after the ethics counsellor himself requested an inquiry on May 19, 1999, for a breach of the 1985 Lobbyist Registration Act. The press reported a year later that the investigation had been dropped, not because Fugère was exonerated but because the RCMP had received an opinion that the act was so ill defined that there was no probability of conviction. (There has never been a successful prosecution under the sixteen-year-old law.) The minister responsible for the act announced a standing committee review, but the Liberal-dominated committee took yet another year to recommend, in typical fashion, "further consultations" on the enforcement provisions of the act. Two businesses in Mr. Chrétien's riding that received grants with Mr. Fugère's help subsequently went bankrupt (Celebrity Boats and the Auberge des Gouverneurs, Shawinigan).

Meanwhile, Mr. Beaudoin, the president of the BDC, was under increasing pressure to help Mr. Duhaime. Mr. Beaudoin's reappointment (with its undisclosed six-figure salary) was up for renewal on January 26, 1998, and the Prime Minister held the power to take away his job. Finally, on September 15, 1997, despite the fact that he was in default on existing mortgages and had accumulated more than $300,000 in unpaid debts, Yvon Duhaime received a $615,000 loan at a 25 per cent rate of interest from the Business Development Bank of Canada. This was $200,000 more than the maximum amount reluctantly recommended in a memo of July 15 from the local branch of the BDC, leaked to the press. The memo read: "You will find attached the documentation submitted in support of the recommendation for the above loan. It's about a project to expand a hotel by 24 units. Following intense negotiations, the promoter has been successful in obtaining important support of all possible assistance from government and financial organizations. The chances of success of the project are relatively acceptable, but the global risk for

the BDC is very high. We are aware that the financing structure recommended does not meet the normal policy or criteria of the Bank."

Notwithstanding the above, in February and March of 1999,
Industry minister John Manley told the House on five separate occasions (on February 2, 3, 9, and March 18 and 23) that the loan was
dealt with in the "normal" course of business. Then, late in May, BDC
president Beaudoin, increasingly uncomfortable with political interference in the affairs of the bank and noting that the Grand-Mère was
in default on its loan, said that he asked the chairman of the board to
consider calling the loan of the Auberge Grand-Mère. Documents he
deposited in court allege that his powers were immediately curtailed
by the board of directors, and on October 1, 1999, a termination
agreement was concluded between Beaudoin and the BDC.

When the Prime Minister was publicly confronted about the
aggressive lobbying effort in support of Duhaime, his office at first
indignantly denied it. Spokesman Peter Donolo said, "The BDC is an
arms'-length Crown corporation. The government does not get
directly involved in the lending decisions of the BDC. Decisions for
that are made entirely by appropriate officials within the BDC." But
later, during the federal election, the Prime Minister admitted that he
pressured the man over whom he held the power of reappointment.
Echoing his Industry minister, he said, "It's the normal operation."

But more was still to come. It became public in April 2001 that a
Montreal judge, a judge who was a regular Liberal Party donor,
appointed by federal Cabinet order in June 2000, and who had once
been a partner in the legal firm representing 161341 Canada Inc.,
had approved a court clerk's authorization to allow BDC officials to
search the home of Mr. Beaudoin to seize and destroy any documents related to clients of the BDC, and "more specifically the
financial file of the Auberge Grand-Mère . . ." This highly unusual
order, later overturned on appeal and termed a "fishing expedition"
by a Superior Court judge, was given at a Saturday hearing, without
prior notice to Beaudoin's lawyer.

What is the overall significance of this tangled web of disclosures
involving the actions of the Prime Minister, his business friends and
supporters, and officials of the government of Canada? Here in a
few points is the bottom line:

- Chrétien and partners bought the Grand-Mère golf course and the business of the Auberge Grand-Mère in 1988 through their numbered company, 161341 Canada Inc., for $1.25 million. Under their ownership the golf course had lost about $2 million by 1993.

- After his election as prime minister in November 1993, Chrétien declared his interest in 161341 and its properties, but said he had sold the shares to Akimbo. But this share sale fell through (which was declared in January 1996) and the shares were not sold until October 1999. During at least half of this six-year period, Chrétien was still the effective owner of the shares whose value could have been affected by any transactions or development affecting the golf course lands or the business of the Auberge Grand-Mère.

- The Prime Minister's friend Yvon Duhaime purchased the business of the Auberge Grand-Mère from 161341 (the Chrétien-related company) in April 1993 and the inn itself from Consolidated Bathurst in 1994. He subsequently used his political influence to secure an investment in the Auberge Grand-Mère of $2.5 million from the Immigrant Investor Program (March 1996), a $615,000 loan from the Business Development Bank of Canada (September 1997), and a Transitional Jobs Fund grant from HRDC (in July 1997). All of these injections of funds from federal programs or institutions could have materially affected the value of the Auberge Grand-Mère and the adjacent Grand-Mère golf course still owned by the Chrétien-related company.

- The Prime Minister's friend Claude Gauthier won a $6.3-million CIDA contract through his company Transelec in August 1996 and one month later, through a numbered company, paid 161341 $525,000 for land beside the Grand-Mère golf course. Then, in 1998, Gauthier acquired another company, Placeteco, which received $1.2 million in Transitional Jobs Fund grants and declared bankruptcy in 1998. All of these transactions affected Gauthier's capacity to buy land from 161341 (the Chrétien-related company), and could have materially affected the value of the shares of that company.

- Actions by officials of the HRDC department (through Transitional Jobs Fund and other HRDC grants), the Immigrant Investor Program, and the Business Development Bank of Canada – acting through the Prime Minister's business friends, Yvon Duhaime and Claude Gauthier, and their companies – all could have materially affected the value of shares and properties in which the Prime Minister had an interest.

And the final disposition of the Prime Minister's shares? The Prime Minister's lawyer was finally able to find a buyer. On October 14, 1999, Akimbo finally accepted and sold the shares for $290,000 to Louis Michaud, another long-time owner of 161341 Canada Inc., in a rather complicated purchase agreement. The amount included the $40,000 payment earlier received from Akimbo, plus two payments of $125,000 to be made over five years (although Mr. Chrétien chose to take both payments immediately at a $35,000 discount). In the end, the Prime Minister received close to what he would have been paid over the four annual instalments agreed to in the original bill of sale, without interest.

The Prime Minister's ethics counsellor, Howard Wilson – faithful to the end – declared, "There's been no financial gain for the Prime Minister." He chose to ignore completely the cost to the taxpayers of the attempts to protect the Prime Minister from financial loss and the constant use of political influence to direct the investment of taxpayers' dollars in the Prime Minister's riding. When the Prime Minister's alleged conflict of interest in pressuring the Business Development Bank became an issue in the 2000 election campaign, the ethics counsellor simply exonerated his boss, declining to comment at all on the larger ethical questions that Shawinigate evokes.

What does Shawinigate tell us about the Prime Minister's view of how to stimulate economic growth and real job creation in depressed regions, when he claims that this was the objective and the rationalization of the misuse of public funds in the Saint-Maurice riding?

What does Shawinigate tell us about the Prime Minister's personal interests and priorities when, at a time when he should have been totally preoccupied with the big issues and pressing affairs of state, we discover his constant and inordinate preoccupation with failing hotels and shares in golf courses and associations with the cast of characters who played supporting roles in the Shawinigate

affair? Could it really be that while Vaclav Havel was addressing the
Canadian Parliament in April 1999 on the moral foundations of an
ethical intervention in Kosovo, our Prime Minister was preoccupied
with finding an ethical justification for calling the head of the
Business Development Bank to get a loan for Yvon Duhaime?

What does the cloud of near-truths, half-truths, and untruths
that greeted media and Opposition attempts to get to the bottom of
Shawinigate say about the Prime Minister's commitment to "transparency" in government? And what does Shawinigate reveal about
the nature and practice of "Liberal ethics" and the Prime Minister's
commitment to "ethical government"?

Is it ethical to use the influence of the Office of the Prime
Minister for the personal and partisan purposes intertwined by
Shawinigate? According to Liberal "ethics" it is. Is it ethical to use
the influence of the Office of the Prime Minister to misdirect and
misuse taxpayers' dollars for such purposes? According to Liberal
"ethics" it is. Is it ethical to withhold information, to stonewall, to
pressure public servants, and to hide behind a subservient ethics
counsellor and self-serving definitions of the public interest for such
purposes? According to Liberal "ethics" it is. And how does the
practice of such ethics establish the moral authority required by a
prime minister and a government to deal with major moral issues in
the future? Liberal ethics has no answer to that question!

∎

If one studies the ethical pronouncements made by the Prime
Minister and other government officials in explaining and defending
conflict of interest (the 1994 Dupuy affair), patronage appointments
and grant awards (from Senate appointments to Transitional Jobs
Fund grants), suppression of truth and unwillingness to accept
responsibility (the Krever, Somalia, and APEC inquiries), the misuse
of taxpayers' dollars for political purposes (the billion-dollar boondoggle at HRDC), and the misuse of the influence of the Prime
Minister's Office (Shawinigate), one can discern the shape and
content of "Liberal ethics." These Liberal ethics, as practised and

articulated by our Prime Minister and his apologists, now occupy a prominent place in our political culture. Obviously they believe in them and are anxious to pass them on to others, in particular up-and-coming young Liberals who must be properly schooled in such matters. It would not surprise me, therefore, if someday soon a brochure appears announcing the First Annual Liberal Ethics Conference. Perhaps you would like to attend.

It will be held, of course, at the Auberge Grand-Mère in Shawinigan, and it will be followed by an Ethical Golf Tournament at the nearby golf course.

The conference will begin with a keynote address by the Prime Minister's friend Bill Clinton. Mr. Clinton will speak on Ethical Behaviour in High Office, with a special session for parliamentary interns to be held afterwards.

A high ethical tone having been set for the conference, delegates will then be invited to attend various workshops dealing with the practicalities of implementing Liberal ethics. A workshop on the Ethical Use of Liberal Friendships will be led by two of the Prime Minister's best friends. One will discuss the ethical extraction of loans from Crown corporations for the ethical refinancing of financially challenged hotels. The other will discuss the ethical levering of CIDA grants for other noble purposes, such as the acquisition of golf course properties near to financially challenged hotels. An anonymous mystery guest will discuss the ethical transfer of shares from important Liberal persons to other persons using not-so-blind trusts and other ethical devices.

Human Resources Minister Jane Stewart, drawing upon her vast experience and aided by "Binder Boy" (the former minister of Public Works), will lead a workshop on the Ethical Use of Departmental Slush Funds to Support Projects in Liberal Constituencies. Former Chief of Defence Staff Jean Boyle will lead a workshop on the Ethical Use of Shredders. This session will include a demonstration of new macro-shredding techniques that allow whole boxes of documents (such as boxes of Somalia Inquiry reports) to be shredded without even opening them. One of the Prime Minister's personal lawyers will lead a workshop on the Training of Seeing-Eye Dogs for the Ethical Guidance of Blind Trust Clients. Another of the Prime Minister's lawyers will lead a fun session on the Ethical Drafting of Bills of Sale on the Backs of Napkins.

Over lunch, the Prime Minister's personal ethics counsellor, Howard Wilson, will address delegates on the subject of the Ethical Application of Whitewash. (The luncheon address was to have been given by renowned British writer and politician Jeffrey Archer on the Ethics of Communications – a View from the Other Side. Unfortunately, Mr. Archer was unable to get permission from British prison authorities to attend the conference.) The Prime Minister will then honour Mr. Wilson by naming him Liberal Ethicist of the Year and presenting him with the prestigious Lap Dog Award. The luncheon will conclude with special entertainment – the Prime Minister, accompanied by Bill Clinton on the saxophone, singing an ethical rendition of "I Did It My Way."

The early afternoon will feature workshops of an even more practical nature. A Liberal senator will lead one on the Ethical Acquisition of Political Appointments. A schedule will be provided of approximately how many dollars and man-hours of political work must be donated to the Liberal cause in order to be ethically qualified for Liberal appointments, ranging from Senate seats to positions on the National Blueberry Picking Advisory Board.

The highlight of the afternoon, however, will be a special plenary session on the Ethics of Party Patronage, expected to excite much interest and discussion among the delegates. A brief backgrounder on the session explains: "In Liberal ethics, nothing is more noble and right than the earning and disposition of patronage. But the distribution of patronage raises serious ethical issues which delegates will be encouraged to examine using the famous Harvard Case Study Method. Suppose that Liberal A helped win an election by redrawing constituency boundaries (gerrymandering) to maximize the Liberal vote. For this he was rewarded with a consulting contract to assist Elections Canada in establishing fair electoral practices in a Latin American country. Suppose also that Liberal B helped finance a successful Liberal campaign by effectively threatening to have government work withdrawn from various accounting, legal, and architectural firms unless they contributed more generously to the Liberal cause. For this he was rewarded with a Senate appointment. Suppose further that Liberal C helped win an electoral victory by organizing an effective campaign to slander certain opposition candidates. For this he was rewarded by being appointed ambassador to the Vatican. Each good Liberal – the gerrymanderer, the bullying bagman, and the slanderer – has served the Liberal cause well, and the good deeds of each have been rewarded by patronage. But ethical questions arise: Were the great principles of justice and equity respected in the distribution of this patronage? Did the patronage awards fairly and honestly match the service rendered to the party? Was a more ethical distribution of patronage possible? For example, if after open and honest debate the delegates decide that the bullying bagman was overcompensated, while the contributions of the gerrymanderer and the slanderer were undervalued, a resolution would be in order directing the PMO and the ethics counsellor to give greater weight in future to the value of gerrymandering and slander. Only by such constructive feedback between the recipients and distributors of patronage can the justice and equity of patronage distribution be improved."

The First Annual Liberal Ethics Conference will then conclude with the First Annual Ethical Liberal Golf Tournament at the nearby golf course. Special prizes – donated by appreciative recipients of Public Works contracts – will be given for the most discreet use of a "foot wedge," the most creative alteration of a score card, and the best lie after a tee shot. Liberal ethics will of course govern the tournament, the most important rule being that, regardless of the weather, circumstances, and individual scores or performances, in the end "the Prime Minister must appear to have won." News releases to this effect have already been prepared.

10

THERE'S NO PLACE
LIKE HOME

ALL OUR FIVE CHILDREN HAVE BEEN HEAVILY INVOLVED IN
team sports – the three girls in synchronized swimming, and the two
boys in hockey and football.

For the girls, the challenge was "to make the national team." In
particular, to find the resources – physical, financial, emotional, and
spiritual – to overcome such obstacles as self-doubt, fierce competition, heavy time demands, nagging injuries, criticism and discour-
agement, major financial costs, and physical fatigue, in order to
compete internationally for Canada.

Sometime in the fall of 1987, we had a family meeting. Sandra
and I explained that I was thinking of doing something different –
getting into national politics. The younger children had no idea
what this meant, so Sandra said, "It's like trying out for the national
team." The reaction of the kids? "Go for it!"

Candidates for public office are often discouraged by the fear of
exposure of their personal life to public view and criticism, abuse by
political opponents and the media, the drain on personal financial
resources, and the challenge to family relationships caused by the
demands of public life. These strains are severe enough if one is a
member of the governing party, but in that case at least there are the

compensations of the support systems that come with being in power and the opportunity to actually accomplish something. If, however, one is part of an opposition party, particularly a new party, which is less capable of providing support and opportunities for accomplishment, the strains are even more severe.

For all this, Sandra and I can say that our marriage and family have largely overcome these strains, not through any beneficence of the Canadian political system, but by drawing heavily upon the resources of family, friends, and faith.

■

Sandra and I were married in 1967 and have raised five children: Andrea, born in 1968, Avryll in 1971, Mary Joy in 1974, Nathan in 1977, and David in 1980. At the time the Reform Party was founded, Sandra was a homemaker and mother, I was a management consultant with political interests, and we were all living busily and happily on an acreage near St. Albert, Alberta. When, in 1987, I was elected the first leader of the Reform Party of Canada and wound up my consulting practice, we found ourselves fully dependent for our family income on the uncertain cash flow of a fledgling political party (for which I was initially also the chief fundraiser), supplemented from time to time by our personal savings, which were not large.

In 1989 we found it necessary to move from Edmonton to Calgary to be closer to the Reform Party's national office. In 1992 we moved again, this time to Calgary Southwest, where I intended to run in the next election. By this time, Andrea had been accepted into law school at the University of Windsor and Avryll was enrolled in a general studies program at the University of Calgary. Mary Joy was in her last years of high school, and the two boys were enrolled at Glenmore Christian Academy. Over the next few years, while I was spending an increasing amount of time either travelling or in Ottawa, it was left to Sandra to raise, support, and ride herd on these dear children as they found their place in the world. At the same time, Sandra was also feeling the pressure to return to the workforce in order to help finance our growing educational expenses and the rising costs of my "political habit."

Besides encouraging our children's spiritual, educational, and athletic development, Sandra and I have also encouraged each of them to live and work in a Third World country. Thus Andrea worked with street children in Manilla, Avryll at an orphanage in Katmandu and a refugee camp in Zaire, Mary Joy with Societé internationale missionaire in Niger, Nathan in Palestine and Irian Jaya, and David in Kathmandu and at a hospital in Nigeria.

Andrea is now married to Howie Kroon, the CFO of a forest products company, and they have two children, Benjamin and Joshua. Andrea operates her own legal research and consulting practice out of her home. Avryll is married to John Fuller, a chartered accountant and tax consultant in Grande Prairie, and they have three children, Emanuel, Abigail, and William. Avryll, having obtained her RN from Mount Royal College and her B.Sc. in nursing from the University of Alberta, continues to work as a community nurse. Our youngest daughter, Mary Joy, earned a Bachelor of Commerce degree from the University of Calgary, worked in London and Moscow, then obtained an MBA from Harvard and now works as an investment analyst with Soros Fund Management in New York.

Of our five children, Sandra and I believe that the demands of our political life have had the greatest impact on our two boys, since they were the youngest when I began my full-time political involvement. The move from our acreage in St. Albert to suburban Calgary was quite a shock for them both. With the help of friends familiar with the rivers and trails of the eastern slopes of the Rockies, so readily accessible from Calgary, I gradually persuaded them that we now had access to a bigger acreage – all of southwestern Alberta and southeastern B.C. Over the next ten years, horseback riding in the Rockies became Sandra's and my favourite escape activity. And for the boys and me, fly-fishing in the mountain rivers and streams helped keep us in touch with each other and the great outdoors.

Nathan studied furniture making at a technical school in Calgary and then in New Bedford, Massachusetts. He subsequently decided that woodworking was a great hobby, but a tough way to make a living. He returned to university to study classics and languages, most recently at the University of Perpignan in southern France. He plans to go on to post-graduate studies and perhaps a teaching career.

David, athletic like the other children, made the Bishop Carroll High School football team as its first-string quarterback in his senior year. From an early age, he decided he wanted to be a doctor, and to that end he is completing his undergraduate degree in human biology at the University of Toronto.

All our children have studied music, but for the boys music became a very important element in their lives. With their cousins, Jordan and Jered Stuffco, they formed a band in 1993, and in 1995, as The Buicks, they played their first show. They later recorded two CDs. Together, the boys created the lyrics and music for many of the band's original songs, shared the joys and the pains of trying to "make it" in the highly competitive music world, learned a lot about themselves, and formed a special bond with their cousins that will last a lifetime.

I should say that my first encounters with my two sons-in-law were not auspicious, and we are fortunate that their first impressions of the Manning clan did not chase them away. The night that Avryll first brought John to our house in Calgary I had just returned from a long political road trip. I was dead tired and determined to unwind by watching an Edmonton Oilers hockey game on TV with Nathan. (Despite living in Calgary, the Oilers continued to be our favourite hockey team – after all, we'd lived in Edmonton during the Gretzky era.) It being near Christmas, Nathan and I had just put up the Christmas tree, but it was one of those trees with a twisted, off-centre trunk that would not stand up straight no matter what we did. We therefore anchored it temporarily with several pieces of rope tied to various articles of furniture, and retired to watch the game.

We had just settled in when, to our mild consternation, Avryll arrived with John. Sandra, who is highly perceptive about these sorts of things, whispered something about "I think this is Mr. Right." Nathan and I absorbed this intelligence but assumed she was talking about one of the Oilers' new acquisitions. We greeted John, ascertaining fairly quickly that he was a Calgary Flames fan, but magnanimously deciding not to hold that against him.

To Sandra's dismay, I neglected to turn off the TV so that I could continue to monitor the game out of the corner of my eye as the evening progressed. I was so tired, however, that I began to nod off, and the sleepier and less conversational I got, the more Sandra tried to compensate by talking more and faster. John was looking quizzically from one of us to the other – me sinking deeper and deeper into my chair and semi-consciousness, and Sandra almost bouncing off the ceiling in her efforts to animate the discussion. To further confuse things, from where he was sitting John could just see the newly erected Christmas tree. He was just about to interrupt the conversation to say "I think your Christmas tree is going to . . ." when the whole thing crashed to the floor. By now Avryll was thoroughly mortified, convinced that John would think she came from a totally dysfunctional family. Fortunately, he gave us a second chance to make a better impression.

After their marriage, John and Avryll suspected that Howie Kroon, John's friend and boss at the accounting firm where they both worked, would be a good match for Andrea. So they conspired to set up a first date, casually asking Andrea and Howie to join them at a Calgary Flames game. At the last minute, Andrea became suspicious that this was a "set-up" and declined to go. Not wanting to let a good hockey ticket go to waste, I volunteered to take her place. Thus it was that Howie's first date with a Manning was not with Andrea, but with me. This time, however, I must have made a good impression because Howie kept coming back.

With such a large (by today's standards) and active family, and considering the respective ages and stages of each of the children during the period from 1987 to 2001, it will be appreciated that our principal focus as parents during these years was on providing the financial, emotional, and spiritual support required to enable them to grow into adulthood. And it was Sandra who carried the bulk of the load. There was little time or money left for her to pursue any other interests independent of the family – such as her interest in music, furthering her education, or developing her own career. My ability to contribute to the support and development of the family, including Sandra's needs, was severely constrained by the endless demands of my political work. And Sandra's ability to join me in the political work was restricted by the need for at least one of us to be fully committed to the family.

The challenge for Sandra and me, particularly after I was elected to Parliament in 1993, was to maintain the integrity of our own relationship and the family under these difficult circumstances. Looking back, however, the family itself was a part of the solution, not part of the problem. Our family, our children, and our relationship with each other became our most important resources – together with our friends and our faith – for dealing with all the other pressures.

■

The challenges a family entering federal political life can expect to encounter are considerable. For us, they included the increased workload, schedule, and pace of political life; the debilitating pressures of being apart for days and weeks at a time from those you love; the constant financial challenges; the insecurities, particularly disconcerting for children, of a "shifting home base"; and the challenge of coping with attacks from external opponents – and from those within – amplified and sustained by the media.

Critics might say that since I chose to involve myself in politics through the creation of a new party – which was itself highly critical of traditional political structures and personalities – I hardly have the right to complain about the personal or family pressures generated by such an approach. Perhaps they are right. Critics might also say that many of the pressures described were "self-inflicted," and to some extent they are right again.

It would also be a great mistake to imply that the only thing participation in public life brings a family is stress. It also brings all kinds of opportunities for a family to expand its understanding of life, its capabilities, and its horizons – knowledge of our country and its people, new friends, insights into major public issues. Our family has been forever changed by our political involvements – and, according to our children, overwhelmingly for the better. If asked whether I would do it all over again, I would definitely answer YES!

My point in describing the stresses encountered by our family as a result of the Reform adventure is neither to complain nor to elicit sympathy. Nor is it to imply that the burdens of public life to which our family was subject were extraordinary or particularly unfair. My sole purpose is to demonstrate that they can be overcome by resources available to most of us, and that the positives can definitely outweigh the negatives.

Some of the challenges of political life can be mitigated simply by planning and time management. But by far the most important help has come from our immediate and extended family, true friends both within and without the party, and faith in the providential care of a loving God.

■

My workload and schedule were determined first of all by the fact that I was the leader of a new political party that had to be built from scratch. Because we were trying to build and expand a new national party in the second-largest nation, geographically, in the world, this involved several hundred thousand kilometres of travel a year to attend meetings and events in three hundred federal constituencies, from Vancouver Island to Newfoundland.

Once I was elected to Parliament in 1993, the workload expanded to include the responsibility of leading a parliamentary caucus and participating in parliamentary affairs in Ottawa, while still giving direction to the party's national office in Calgary and representing a Calgary constituency in the House of Commons. Doing all this meant, among other things, a 5,800-kilometre weekly commute from Ottawa to Calgary and back.

By the time I became leader of the Opposition in 1997, I was spending about fifty days a year in Alberta, mainly Calgary, where Sandra and some of the family were still located; about one hundred days a year in Ottawa, geared to the parliamentary calendar; and about two hundred days a year on the road. This workload and schedule would reach its zenith during the campaigns of the Charlottetown Accord, the Quebec referendum, Zero in Three, Reform's Fresh Start, the United Alternative, and of course the federal elections. During these periods, even the most routine matters – from going to the doctor or dentist to remembering the birthdays of family and friends – were neglected. Immediately after the 1997 election, for example, we were ticketed by the police because the insurance and registration were overdue on our car, and neither of us had noticed. This sort of thing happened a lot.

Conscientious staff people can help a great deal. In our case, a working partnership between Sandra and Ian Todd made sure that the needs of our family were met. Ian was my executive assistant but he was also our friend, and when it came to balancing family against work demands, he put our personal and family needs ahead of everything else. (Not all executive assistants do that.)

Sandra and Ian were careful to carve out family time from my schedule and insist that it be respected. The two would go through logistical nightmares to ensure that the whole family had time together on Sundays and at holidays like Christmas or Thanksgiving. And on the weekends when I was home Sandra would schedule fishing times with the boys when we could get away together.

Our family was also blessed with the help of a number of dear friends who were willing to play a special role in the lives of our boys, for which Sandra and I can never thank them enough. They taught my sons things that I was unable or unavailable to teach them and gave them opportunities we could never have given them on our own. These people included Bruce Robertson, the committed high school teacher and former rock musician who taught both boys to play guitar; Johnnie and Beth Andreason, who taught the boys the art and science of fly-fishing; and Short Tompkins and Bob Sorenson, who have flown us to fishing places in the mountains so isolated and so special to the boys that I am not permitted even to hint at their location.

Like most parents, we have found that "quality time" is directly proportional to "total time" spent with your children. Teenagers, as part of the process of finding their own identities, often appear to be pushing their parents away. However, just when you think the kids want you to get lost, an opportunity will emerge to share a truly meaningful experience together. The problem is that those occasions seem to happen randomly and when you least expect them. They are impossible to plan or schedule. You will "be there for your teen" at those special times only if you are "there," period.

For the boys and me, these "special times" often occurred when we were on fishing or family outings together. One winter weekend, for example, Sandra encouraged Nathan and me to sneak away from Calgary to go skiing for three days in Fernie, B.C. We decided to a take a backwoods route through what is known as "the Gap" in the Livingston Mountains and follow a forestry trunk road south to the Crowsnest Pass highway. Normally this trunk road is closed in the winter, but it looked to us as though it had been recently travelled, so off we went.

About thirty-five kilometres from the last ranch on the western side of the mountains, and about thirty-five kilometres from our destination, we slid off the road, and no amount of digging or jockeying our four-wheel-drive vehicle could get us out. There was nothing we could do but bundle up in our ski clothes and start the trek back to the nearest ranch. It was already late in the day, so our immediate destination was a deserted campsite we had passed earlier.

By the time we made the campsite, it was dark and getting colder. Fortunately, when we had driven by earlier, Nate had noticed a woodpile almost totally buried in snow. With the help of our flashlight, we managed to locate it again, dig out some firewood, and start a fire in a stove in one of the open cook shacks. We spent the night talking, stoking the fire, trying to get a little sleep – imagining we were David Thompson and Alexander Mackenzie on a winter expedition. Although there are wolves and cougars in that part of the country, we encountered neither, and we were struck by how perfectly still and peaceful everything was.

At about five in the morning we started off again. We hiked through the Gap, following the Old Man River as it cuts a notch through the Livingston Range, when a cowboy photographer, out in a pickup truck to take pictures of the mountain vistas at dawn, saw us and stopped. He gave us a ride to the nearest ranch, and at about eight o'clock we knocked on the door of Vern and Ida Dennis, who took us in, gave us a great breakfast, and let us use their phone to round up a tow truck from Pincher Creek.

After phoning Sandra, I also phoned the office. Ron Wood, my media man, couldn't help but observe that if this had all happened a hundred kilometres further south and I were an American politician, he would be on the phone embellishing the story and getting us a nice clip on the evening news. "Congressman and Son Survive Ordeal in the Rockies" would be the headline, with the fine print explaining how politician and son had overcome packs of wolves, cougars, and a howling blizzard to return unscathed to the home fires of civilization. I told Ron no dice, and Nate's and my "night near the Gap" adventure remains one of those special times together that neither of us will forget.

Despite the best efforts, there will still be occasions when you simply cannot be in two places at once, and hard decisions have to be made. In the spring of 1998, for example, David was graduating from high school in Calgary. My heart sank when I learned the date of the ceremony. It clashed with the date when I was scheduled to give one of the most important public addresses of my political life – the keynote address to the Reform assembly in London, Ontario, at which I would challenge the party to embrace the United Alternative concept. Ian checked and rechecked the schedule. The only way I could do both was to attend the ceremony with David in Calgary and then take the red-eye flight from Calgary to Toronto in order to get to London in time. We knew the political logic – I had to be fresh and at the top of my game for that speech because it affected the very future of the party and my leadership. Ideally, I should be there a day or two early to work the delegates. But there was no way I was going to miss David's graduation. There is a weighty sentence in the Sermon on the Mount that says if we put relationships first, our relationship to God and our relationships with other people, that He will take care of subsidiary concerns (my translation of Matthew 6:33). I would put David's graduation first and trust that I would have the stamina to do a good job on the speech. And so Sandra and I attended the ceremony, bursting with pride at David's accomplishments, which included high marks and being named MVP of his football team. Then we caught the red-eye for Toronto, got to London in time, and the speech went off without a hitch.

Faith in the principle of putting relationships first, and trusting God that secondary matters will also be taken care of, is easy to profess but hard to practise. But to the extent that it is practised, such faith goes a long way towards mitigating the pressures of workload, time, and pace on marital and family relations.

■

There is no doubt that participation in public life is much more bearable for those who are independently wealthy. For those who aren't, adequate salaries, expense allowances, and pensions are essential. These stipends should be established by independent commissions that take into account the real costs of participating in public life (costs that have rarely been calculated and analyzed with accuracy). It should also be borne in mind that for anyone with an excessive debt load or undisciplined spending habits, things will only get worse (if they are honest), not better, once they are in the public arena.

Abstract principles, however, are no substitute for personal experience. In 1987, I owned a small, modestly profitable consulting practice, and Sandra and I held clear title to our acreage and home near St. Albert. When I wound up the consulting practice, we agreed that I could use its retained earnings to help support the new party while its own fundraising got up to speed. But I solemnly agreed that the family house and acreage would be in Sandra's name and would not be mortgaged for political purposes.

On many occasions during its building years, the Reform Party was desperately short of cash, and we had to utilize our own resources to cover a portion of my expenses. This practice gave the impression to some of our key party people that I and my family were wealthy and could afford to carry a significant portion of the leader's expense load indefinitely. More important, it kept the party from establishing a proper expense allowance mechanism, the absence of which continued to create problems for key personnel, including MPs engaged in political work, long after the start-up years. And, when combined with the ever-increasing expense of supporting our large family through the higher education years, it saddled Sandra and me with an ever-increasing debt load. By 1993, despite our original good intentions, our home was mortgaged to the hilt.

When the Reform Party finally did achieve parliamentary party status after the 1993 election, my income and my expenses connected with parliamentary work were provided from the public treasury, not from party contributions. But there still remained the problem of covering expenses for partisan political work, which couldn't properly be charged to the taxpayers. Accordingly, the executive council of the party established a Leader's Expense Account to cover expenditures for items ranging from travel to dry cleaning. This account was to be audited annually.

In 1994, shortly after fifty-two Reformers were elected to Parliament, we established our Pay, Pensions, and Perks Committee and vigorously attacked what we considered excessive expenditures by the government. At the same time, a small group of caucus and executive councillors who chafed under my leadership decided to attack my Leader's Expense Account, all in the name of fiscal responsibility. Various stories were leaked to the press about this account being used to provide me with a secret pension and other "perks." None of this was true, but the reports were damaging and disconcerting, especially to my family.

By this time, Sandra was expected to attend more and more public and televised functions with me, and to "look the part" of the partner of a national political leader. And as our pollster and communications people pointed out, she had a better "public persona," particularly on television, than the wives of most of the other leaders. In the crass terms of political calculus, she was a positive political asset, both to me and to the party. But there was no way Sandra and I could meet these increased wardrobe and personal services expenditures out of our own pockets. It was when the attacks on this use of the Leader's Expense Account started to focus on Sandra specifically that she withdrew almost completely from doing political work – to my sorrow and the party's loss – and resolved to return to work.

Sandra obtained her real estate licence and began selling in Calgary with Coldwell Banker's Ram Realty agency. She undertook this new venture with virtually no help from me and spent many stressful hours learning the ropes of the real estate business while still carrying all her responsibilities at home. For the next five years she would attend almost no political functions. Because of this, my own effectiveness was reduced, and we were apart even more.

Friends who knew what we were going through did what they could. Everyone in politics needs friends like Cliff Fryers, Harry Meyers, and Ken Kalopsis, who will take you aside and, instead of lobbying for their pet policy position or asking for a favour, will say: "I want to know how *you* are doing – how Sandra and the children are doing – and if there is anything I can do to help." We had other friends like this, particularly in Calgary and Vancouver, who actively and generously helped our family to get away together at critical times. Ironically, these people, to whom we owed the most at a personal level, were invariably the ones who never asked anything from us or from the party for themselves – not a single thing, over many years – only that we keep on doing what we were doing to "change the system."

All of our children did everything in their power to meet our financial obligations by paying as many of their own educational expenses as possible. The girls all had jobs, sometimes two jobs at a time, plus their university studies. Nate had a furniture-making enterprise and worked at a downtown hotel as a banquet server. David was into "selling" – everything from Regal Christmas decorations to Cutco knives.

Our children have never complained about the effects on them of my participation in public life. On the contrary, they saw it as an exciting and necessary activity for the good of the country and themselves. Perhaps the greatest indication of their support came in a family teleconference call in February 2001. The MP pension issue was raging again. I had advised my colleagues such as Deborah Grey that they should buy back a position in the government plan while there was still opportunity to do so, since it had never been my intention as leader that our MPs should end up with no pension at all. But I felt that I was in a different position. I was still very much opposed to the Liberal pension plan in principle and had led the opposition to it since 1993. My inclination was to continue to opt out of it, but, as I explained to the children, this meant giving up a potential pension of at least $3,000 per month and all the medical insurance benefits that went along with it. I would be going on sixty by the time I left Parliament, which would leave Sandra and me with very few years to rebuild our financial base. I had also just had a bout with prostate cancer, which made the health picture a little uncertain. If anything happened to our health, the kids would not only have to send us to Shady Pines (as they had often threatened to do) but they might end up having to *pay* for Shady Pines, which was quite another proposition.

Howie and John, the accountants, and Mary Joy, our financier, spelled out the financial pros and cons. Obviously if security and family finances were the only considerations, I should opt in. But the whole gang felt there was more involved here. There were all those people who had supported me down through the years who would be profoundly disappointed if I were to opt in. The children were unanimous. They supported our desire to forgo the pension, and if there were negative financial consequences down the road, they undertook to help us deal with those when the time came.

In the final analysis, financial stresses and strains are part of a bigger issue – personal security – and for our family, personal security has come to rest on a broader foundation than the family bank account or balance sheet. It rests rather on the personal faith of each member of our family in the providential care of a living God, difficult as it is sometimes to practise this trust. I am not really talking here about "going to church as a family," important as that can be, and finding security there. Nor am I talking only about being committed to a particular creed or set of beliefs. I am talking more about being committed as individual members of a family to seeking and maintaining a personal relationship with God through coming to know, trust, and take direction from the person of Jesus Christ. The establishment and maintenance of this relationship then deepens and enriches our relationships with each other and the world at large. It makes our marriage more secure – a three-way commitment, each of us committing our lives to God as well as to each other. It has led Sandra and me to see each of our dear children and grandchildren as a gift and trust from Him. It has led each of us to seek His calling for our lives, and as we grow together to realize that it isn't so much that God calls us to particular vocations (although He certainly can do that) but that He calls us to be certain kinds of persons. It is this relationship that enables us to believe there is purpose and meaning in everything that happens to us – in the bad as well as the good. It is in this relationship with Him, and with each other through Him, that we find meaning and the resources and the security to meet and endure whatever challenges and trials – political, financial, emotional, physical – come our way.

Many years ago, when I was first entering the federal political field, on Sunday nights we would sometimes have what we called "home church." I might read a story from the Bible and the children would act it out. Or we would go around the circle and ask each person what challenges they were facing that week so that some other family member could pray for them. But mostly we would sing. And one of the favourite songs – simple and adaptable to every situation – was "He's Got the Whole World in His Hands." We would improvise verses on the spot. Were Sandra and I worried about family finances? Well, "He's got family finances in His hands." Were Andrea, Avryll, or Mary Joy facing a big swim meet? Well, "He's got all the Sisters in His hands." Were the little brothers getting on everyone's nerves? Well, "He's got Nathan and David in His hands." Did our favourite hockey team lose on Saturday night? No matter. "He's got the Edmonton Oilers in His hands." Did illness or trouble threaten someone we loved? Well, He's got that person and that situation in His hands as well. In fact, He's got Canada – and the whole world – in His hands.

■

If "home" is the base of the family, constantly moving can be a major source of family stress. We made six moves in the course of thirteen years to accommodate my political career – not counting my taking up residence in the Travelodge and at Stornoway in Ottawa. There are not many women, particularly women who attach supreme importance to providing a secure home base for their family, who would put up with such instability and transience. Sandra not only did so, but she did it with grace. We worried about the effect these moves would have on the children. But we also learned to appreciate that our "home" is not so much a place as it is a relationship with each other. As a family, we still aspire to one big, central place where we can all congregate together on a regular and familiar basis. But in the end it is the relationships that make a house a home.

At a family get-together over Christmas 2001, I asked our children specifically for their assessment of the impact of my involvement in national politics on their own lives. I also asked them to be frank (something they are quite capable of being without encouragement). Without exception, they expressed the view that Sandra and I overestimated the negative impacts of our political involvements on the family and underestimated the benefits. It was an assessment we were glad to hear.

The shift in our home base that disturbed me the most and was hardest of all on dear Sandra was our move into Stornoway, the official residence of the leader of the Opposition in Ottawa, in June 1997.

Federal spending throughout most of the 1990s was out of control, and the Reform Party was crusading for more fiscal responsibility. As previously mentioned, I had said several times that the federal government should either sell Stornoway or turn it into a bingo hall and apply the proceeds to reduce the deficit. Even after becoming Leader of the Opposition, I was all for selling Stornoway and moving into something much more modest, if the federal government would provide it. But the government had no intention of doing so. We then discovered that the entertainment and driver/security budget for the leader of the Opposition was attached to Stornoway, not to the leader's office. If I did not move into Stornoway, the Reform Party itself would have to pick up the cost of entertaining and housing official guests of the Opposition at hotels, as well as the cost of maintaining a driver who could double as a security man. The executive council of the Party made it abundantly clear that it was unable to carry such expenses and voted strongly for me to move in.

By now the media sensed the dilemma that the move was creating for me and the newly elected Official Opposition. Questions about Stornoway dominated our news conferences. To further complicate matters, while our Western members considered Stornoway to be a symbol of the "establishment" we were trying to replace, many of our eastern Ontario supporters considered it a part of the Canadian political heritage and interpreted my reluctance to live there as a form of Western disrespect. We began to get letters and calls demanding that we move in, alongside the steady stream of letters and calls damning us for even thinking about it. A decision had to be made in order to lay the matter to rest. So on June 20, after a caucus meeting at which two-thirds voted in favour of moving in, I announced that Sandra and I would make Stornoway our Ottawa residence.

Even after the decision was made, it continued to be a source of annoyance for us and for the party. The decision was political, not personal, and Sandra had been left out of most of the discussions, even though, next to me, she was the person most directly affected. At the time, she was still working in real estate in Calgary, and she couldn't just pack up and come to stay with me in Ottawa. So even when we did officially "move in" to Stornoway, for the most part I would be there by myself.

Both of us were also well aware that the media would be watching like hawks to see whether we demanded any makeovers of the kind that Maureen McTeer, Mila Mulroney, and Aline Chrétien had undertaken. Stornoway had been vacant for four years and was in quite a mess, primarily due to leaks in the roof. We nevertheless resolved not to ask for anything to be done (other than the erection of a Canadian flag on the property) and to leave the renovations and decorating up to the National Capital Commission personnel responsible for the official residences. Even the furnishings were left up to them, and the media who had staked the place out waited in vain to get a shot of the arrival of the moving van with our effects. All we brought to Stornoway of our own belongings were a few suitcases of clothes and a box of pictures of the family. Daily at first, and then weekly for months, the media filed Access to Information requests seeking details of any capital or operating expenditures. When these showed nothing untoward, the *Vancouver Sun* ran stories anyway on our extravagant expenditures. To their credit, the National Capital Commission took it upon themselves to correct such stories and to set the record straight. What should have been a positive and exhilarating experience, especially for Sandra – the opportunity to move into a historic home in beautiful Rockcliffe Park – had been turned into a headache.

Eventually of course there was a positive side to the Stornoway affair. The National Capital staff did everything in their power to make our time there enjoyable, and three people in particular made Stornoway both an official residence and a home. Evie Robarts, Ian Todd's wife, became our chatelaine, managing the household and making sure our social schedule meshed smoothly with all my other commitments. She recruited Mary Beth Howitt to serve as the Stornoway chef, and Mary Beth's culinary skills and down-to-earth friendliness soon won many compliments from our visitors, friends, and family. And my old friend Sam Okoro came to be our driver and security man, living in the apartment above the Stornoway garage. Among the three of them, our every need was met, and soon we were able to put the official residence to the use for which it was intended.

We wanted to use Stornoway for public service. We held an open house for the neighbourhood to get to know our neighbours and to show some Western hospitality. There were Christmas parties for the parliamentary staff and their children, barbecues for the media, which included a bingo game, receptions for various charities, and a summer garden party for more than 350 new Canadians on July 1. Most useful from my perspective were the numerous "Critic Dinners" held in the Stornoway dining room. These dinners, suggested by Randy White, involved asking the chief Opposition critic for each portfolio – Defence, Finance, External Affairs, etc. – to identify eight key experts or interested parties in his or her critic area and invite them to Stornoway for dinner. At such dinners, the critic and I would ply them with questions, and they would have an opportunity to get to know us and our policy positions. On top of the official and political use of Stornoway, our family members were able to gather there on several occasions, and Stornoway, for at least a few days, became the "home" it was originally meant to be.

■

The political arena is notorious for attacks on participants from political opponents and as a result of political infighting. Because of the personal and emotional dimensions of these attacks, the media consider them far more newsworthy than any positive proposal to solve a public problem. An attack on your position or behaviour by an opponent or internal critic will usually be picked up by the media, amplified, and broadcast to the entire country, a phenomenon that deters many people from entering politics.

A party like the Reform Party, which was created to challenge the positions of the traditional parties on at least a dozen fronts, was itself involved in heavy-duty criticism of the traditional political establishment, for which I make no apology. They had it coming. But I made it a point to focus our attacks on the *positions* and *policies* of our opponents, not the people themselves. On the few occasions when I departed from this rule in the heat of battle – as when I suggested after the Quebec referendum that the Prime Minister must have had "a screw loose" to pursue such a misguided strategy – I genuinely regretted it.

During my own time in federal politics I was attacked by both Prime Minister Mulroney and Prime Minister Chrétien as "an enemy of Canada," guilty of traitorous activity for challenging their positions on Quebec and national unity; by Sheila Copps as a racist ("Canada's David Duke," the American Ku Klux Klan leader); by other Cabinet ministers as a bigot, an extremist, and a religious fanatic; and by various other leading lights of the Liberals, Conservatives, and NDP as anti-French, anti-immigrant, anti-aboriginal, anti-women, anti-gay, anti-disabled, and an enemy of the old, the sick, the young, and the poor. Often these attacks would be made in comments to relatively small numbers of people, but because they were "newsworthy" – even a lie from a Cabinet minister is "newsworthy" – they would be picked up by the media. It always amazed me how my liberal and socialist critics in particular could declare their undying concern and affection for all mankind in general, and yet work up such passionate hatred for a few people (like me) in particular. But that is for them to explain. In general, such attacks became routine for our family and largely a matter of indifference, to be responded to by myself if at all by rebuttal and counterattack.

To be fair to the media, if a politician does not use family members as "props" for political purposes, the media will usually leave them alone. But if the politician attempts to gain political yards using family members, the family becomes fair game.

The personal attacks that hurt, and the ones that affected us most as a family, were the ones that came from internal sources. They caused tensions between Sandra and me because of the way I responded or often failed to respond to them, and they frequently poisoned, or robbed us of, the little precious time we did have together.

For example, in 1994, shortly after my election to Parliament, two Western-based columnists of a national newspaper, fed by a disgruntled caucus member, published a series of columns impugning my leadership generally and specifically alleging abuse of my Leader's Expense Account. Three of these four articles appeared on successive Saturdays, days that Sandra had carefully carved out of my schedule as family days in Calgary. So what were supposed to be days of relaxation and togetherness with the boys would start with an early-morning telephone call from our media people in Ottawa sounding an alarm, several hours spent preparing rebuttals, phone calls to key people who might react badly to the misinformation in the columns, letters to the editor, and interviews.

These damage-control exercises would in turn generate more phone calls and requests for comment, which in turn would require follow-up. If I was at home, most of the day would be spent on the phone or at the computer and fax. If we had planned a day trip to the mountains, Sandra and the kids would try to go ahead with the planned activity, but I would be forever on the cellphone, or stopping at hotels or the condos of friends for conference calls or to review draft press releases. Our children grew to resent these kinds of intrusions, and to lose any respect they might have had for the journalists and insiders responsible, but there was little we could do to prevent them.

In the case of the expense account attack, on April 6, 1994, in the midst of our Easter break from Parliament, Stephen Harper and several other caucus members went public with their criticism. Even though procedures existed for handling any complaints about the use of party funds, Stephen went to the media, not to the caucus officers or the Management and Planning Committee of the party's executive council, all of whom were justifiably furious.

By the time I returned to Ottawa on April 11, a special caucus meeting had to be held to "clear the air." It went on for almost five hours. Stephen professed not to know what all the fuss was about, saying that he was being "unfairly accused." In the end, the caucus meeting established improved procedures for dealing with complaints, but, more important, it brought to light some deeper and more serious concerns that had been simmering for some time. Many caucus members poured out their frustrations about the workload, the financial pressures, and the accusations of ineffectiveness from media commentators. In particular, they expressed the need for more open and closer relationships with each other and with me as leader, to alleviate the atmosphere of suspicion and mistrust that allowed machinations like Stephen's to breed and flourish.

By the time the meeting was over, I had been going eighteen hours, and I made the mistake of giving Sandra, who had come to Ottawa with me for a few days, only a cursory description of what had happened at caucus. This was my habitual way of dealing with the stress – keeping my feelings to myself, and dealing coldly with the problem at a strategic level. Part of Stephen's attack had been directed at Sandra, and this was definitely *not* the way to alleviate her pain and frustration. What Sandra wanted from me was to be defended vigorously and to be intimately involved with me in dealing with the issue. I was always talking about the West "wanting in"; well, she "wanted in" too. She wanted me to share my feelings with her, not retreat within myself, and she suspected that that was also what some of the caucus were trying to tell me.

At this point I didn't think things could get much worse in terms of Sandra's pain and frustration. But they did. The next day, while leaving the Centre Block, she slipped and reinjured a knee she had torn up in a skiing incident just ten days before. This additional accident left her on crutches and needing to return to Calgary immediately. I went back to the hotel, read a three-page letter from Sandra pouring out her heart, and sat alone.

This whole issue – which really wasn't about expenses at all – was the most painful experience our family had endured to date. What made it particularly hard to endure was that it was initiated not by an external opponent, but by one of our own. I felt that if I couldn't do better to protect the family and meet Sandra's needs in such situations, it wasn't worth being party leader or an MP. That night, I took off my House of Commons pin – given only to MPs – threw it into my briefcase, and never put it on again until the day I left Parliament.

The ability of the modern politician to handle the stress of public life, including the attacks of external and internal foes, very much depends on the people around him or her. The character and abilities of your partner, your friends, and your close associates are crucial. Do they compensate for your weaknesses, or do they ignore or reinforce them? My tendency is to deal with external and internal attacks by ignoring them, suppressing my feelings rather than expressing them, turning inward rather than sharing my frustrations with others, and responding to attack mainly on the intellectual level. Fortunately for me, my circle of family and friends includes people who compensate for all these tendencies.

Sandra is sensitive and emotional, expressing the feelings that I tend to bury. And she is outgoing and relational, reaching out to other people even in times of stress, rather than withdrawing.

And then there are my friends like Cliff and Leslie Fryers. Cliff insists more strongly than anyone I know on "honesty" in relations and communications. At many of the critical decision points of my political career, it was Cliff who would tell it exactly like it was and ask the hard questions. "If you keep wearing 'fiscal responsibility' like a hair shirt, you, Sandra, and half the caucus will end up old, sick, and in the poorhouse." "When Stephen attacks the expense account, this is why he does it, this is who it hurts, this is who will believe him and who won't, and here's what we should do about it!"

And when it came to asking not, "How is this attack affecting the party, or the caucus, or the campaign?" but, "How is it affecting you and Sandra and the children?" it was invariably Cliff who made it his business to raise these questions and insist that they be addressed by us and by others. Because Cliff does not suffer fools or self-deception gladly, he can appear from a distance to be cold, detached, and confrontational. But those of us who get to know him close up and earn his trust have never had a more true or loyal friend.

And then there were Rick and Michelle Anderson. Most people know the strategic side of Rick, but there is another side – a warm, friendly, thoughtful, and generous person who has never lost sight of the "relational" side of politics – something I often neglected and which Reformers, in our ideological and policy zeal, often forgot altogether. Did a new staff person need a place to stay or a tour around Ottawa? Rick would arrange it. Should a dinner or lunch be held to honour some person or achievement? Rick would suggest it, and often pay for it. Did caucus members need hockey tickets, perhaps to give a visiting son or daughter the thrill of seeing the Ottawa Senators at the Corel Centre? Rick would find some tickets or give you his. Did Sandra and I need to get away from the Ottawa fishbowl for the weekend? The welcome mat was always out at Rick and Michelle's place in Merrickville. Was I under attack in the media? It was Rick who would spend hours on the phone and flood the Internet with e-mails supplying the other side of the story. Frequently, in the course of defending me, Rick himself became the target of completely unfair and undeserved abuse. One of my regrets is that I never really came vigorously and publicly to his defence, the way he always came to mine.

The other chief resource that I had to assist me in coping with such attacks was the example of my parents. My father spent his entire adult life in public office, a major portion of it during the Depression, when the desperation of the times added a viciousness to politics that has seldom been seen since. He, too, was a founder and leader of a "new party" that challenged the status quo, and from 1935, when he entered the Alberta legislature, to 1968, when he left, there was not an insult or political attack known to the Liberal, Tory, or Socialist mind that he did not endure and overcome. His basic approach was to persevere in the course that he felt best for Alberta, to trust in the scriptural admonition "Vengeance is mine, saith the Lord," and to ignore 98 per cent of the attacks altogether – a strategy that I learned and practised almost to a fault.

My mother also was no stranger to the slings and arrows of political life, much of her experience coming in an era when the wife of the politician was expected to endure every calumny in complete silence. My mother, however, has never been silent and has always been a very shrewd judge of character, particularly political characters, of which she has seen every shape and variety over her fifty years in public life. She can "smell a rat" among professed friends more quickly than anyone I know, and her "early warning" signals to my father on who could be trusted and who could not stood him (and me) in good stead in anticipating political attacks from unexpected quarters.

There hardly arose an issue or a problem during my time in federal politics that my father and I had not discussed in some form or another years before. His death in February 1996 from a form of lung cancer deprived me of both my father and my most senior political adviser. I was campaigning with Joe Peschisolido in a Toronto by-election campaign when I learned that he had passed away. Ian and I caught the first plane home to Calgary, where comforting my mother was my first priority. Because politics and my father were so intertwined in my own mind and heart, I couldn't separate the two, even at the time of his death. I remember thinking that if Reform was going to go "all the way" and form a government, I wanted him to live long enough so that I could give him a small office adjoining the prime minister's office, just as he did for me when he was premier of Alberta.

My father's funeral on February 23 in Calgary was a celebration of a life that touched tens of thousands of Albertans for the better, none more so than mine. Now all the political attacks and insults large and small that he endured over the years seemed so minuscule in relation to what people remembered of his character and achievements that they faded into complete irrelevance.

At the funeral service, our girls each paid tribute to their Grandpa and the boys helped carry the coffin. In a brief address I paid tribute to his sense of balance – the balancing of his fiscal conservatism with his concern for the well-being of people, which had propelled him into politics in the midst of the Great Depression. I also paid tribute to a greater legacy that he left his family and the province, his example of how to integrate your faith and your work – in his case, the work of government. I told the story of the man who said he liked going to a certain church because nothing they did or said there interfered with his politics, his business, or his religion. That was *not* my father's idea of faith. His view was that your faith, if it was real, had to influence your politics, your business, and your religion. And if it did, you ought to say so. He left both a political and a spiritual legacy, for our family as well as an entire province.

In my father's judgment, the best advice that could be given to families thinking of exposing themselves to all the challenges and dangers of political warfare – advice he gave to me – was that spoken by King George VI to worried citizens and families in his famous wartime address: "I said to the man who stood at the gate of the year, Give me a light that I may tread safely into the unknown. And he said to me, put your hand into the hand of God, and that shall be to you better than a light, and safer than a known way."

■

When Sandra and I were married in 1967, our view of marriage, rooted in our Christian faith, was to make our relationship with each other as deep and lasting as possible. During the period from 1987 to 1993, when we were building the Reform Party, I was on the road almost constantly, but at least we had a home base to which I always returned. But from the fall of 1993, when I was first elected to Parliament, until the fall of 1998 – a period of five years – Sandra and I were apart for longer periods of time than we had ever experienced before. Both of us agree that this was the most difficult time of our political and married life.

During Sandra's "time alone" she had to cope on her own with most of the needs of the children, plus the need to augment our family finances. While Sandra felt very much alone at her end of the country, I felt very much alone at my end, despite the multitude of people in my life as a politician. With no family in Ottawa I would spend almost every night either at my parliamentary office or at my desk in the Travelodge. Even after I moved into Stornoway in 1997, because of the need for Sandra to maintain her real estate practice, she had to remain in Calgary. So I would sit at my laptop in the study of that empty old house, and think to myself, "I might as well still be in the Travelodge and have avoided all the flap of moving here. Whether I'm here or there, Sandra and I are still apart."

The times Sandra and I did have together were precious and just long enough to remind us what we were missing by being apart.

Sandra was frequently in tears as I left for the airport. She would explain that the tears came because her feelings on those occasions were "deep," not necessarily because she was sad. But I felt awful for what I was putting her through, and there seemed nothing short of getting out that would truly remedy the situation. The only times I ever seriously considered quitting federal politics were as a result of seeing the negative effects that my long absences, the financial burdens, and the stresses of political life were having on my family and on the woman I love.

We relied more or our personal faith than on anything else to help us cope with separation. There really was no other remedy. During these years, the Hebrew word *mizpah*, inscribed on the inside of our wedding rings, was our most frequent prayer: "May the Lord watch between you and me when we are apart."

By the time of the 1997 federal election, Sandra was able to spend the entire seven-week campaign period together with me. At long last we were able to work together politically and, despite the pressures, it was one of the happiest periods of our political life. By the fall of 1998, with both boys through high school, two of the girls through university and married, and Mary Joy on her own, Sandra put her real estate practice on hold and came to live with me in Ottawa for the first time since I had been elected. Fortunately for us, our marriage had survived five years of being apart. We knew of half a dozen other MPs and their spouses who had been less fortunate. Sandra and I truly enjoyed "doing politics together," our only regret being that the opportunity to do so was all too short.

From a personal standpoint, my greatest single source of inspiration and help for coping with the pressures and assaults of public life has been Sandra herself – lover and friend, wife and mother, heart and soul of our family, committed Christian, partner in life and politics, all embodied in one lovely and dynamic person. Are the pressures of time and work becoming overwhelming, threatening health and family? It is Sandra, working with Ian, who will rework my schedule to relieve the pressure. Is it necessary for us to shift our "home base" yet again? It is Sandra who will do everything within her power to create a real home for us, no matter where it is we have to live. Are the rising costs of remaining in politics straining the family budget to the breaking point? It is Sandra who will roll up her sleeves and earn the additional income required. Am I becoming dull, distant, and one-dimensional – totally preoccupied with some public issue? It is Sandra who will bring fun, music, physical exercise, and friends into the situation to restore a sense of balance. Do we have to shake five hundred more hands after the umpteenth Leader's Dinner? It is Sandra who best understands that "the speech" is only a small part of such evenings and leads the way from table to table communicating to each guest with her smile and her interest the fact that we really do treasure their presence and support. Is our pace and work schedule crowding out family, friendships, relationships, including our relationship with God? It is Sandra who will fight to maintain all of these. Do I need straightforward advice on a speech, or a position I am thinking of taking, or a person I am thinking of trusting – advice rooted in intuition, sensitivity to people and situations, and spirituality? Sandra will provide it.

I first encountered the concept of self-sacrificial love – the great ideal of the Christian faith – in my study of Christian theology. But it is in Sandra's life that I have most often seen that concept worked out in practice. The great danger to such a person of course is that their self-sacrificial service will be taken for granted by others, even by those who benefit from it most, or, worse yet, taken advantage of by others in the selfish pursuit of their own objectives. I sometimes ask myself, "What is Sandra getting out of this besides criticism, work, and strain?" The answer is usually "precious little," unless someone makes it their business to ensure that she is noticed, respected, honoured, and appropriately rewarded for the invaluable contributions she makes. I should have made this my business far more often than I did.

There is no greater human resource for coping with the pressures and the strain of politics than an understanding and supportive partner. In fact, if your partner in life is not able or prepared to be your partner in politics, better to stay out of politics altogether, or at least to wait until circumstances change. And if God has blessed you with a partner like Sandra, take care of your partner at all costs. In the final analysis, that responsibility should be even more important than taking care of your constituents or "the national interest." If I had ever made it to the Prime Minister's Office, the country would have had a remarkable "first lady" unlike anyone who has ever occupied that unofficial office before. As it is, no matter what, Sandra has always been and will always be my "first lady."

11

THINK BIG

On Sunday, May 23, 1998, Sandra and I were driving daughter Avryll and first grandson Emanuel to the Calgary airport for their flight home to Grande Prairie when the car phone rang. It was our son-in-law Howie announcing that our oldest daughter, Andrea, had just given birth to Benjamin Nathaniel Kroon – six pounds, fifteen ounces. Yahoo! In the excitement I almost drove our Jeep off the road. It had been a long and hard delivery, but mother and baby were doing well, and father Howie was also expected to recover. All of us were thankful and ecstatic, and soon the communications lines were buzzing as the good news was spread to family, friends, and even total strangers.

Little Benjamin was about four hours old the first time I saw and held him. It is never easy to break bad news, but I felt it my duty as his grandfather and a federal parliamentarian to advise him that his share of the national debt, plus his portion of the unfunded liability of the Canada Pension Plan, amounted to about $40,000. The little fellow took it well. In fact, he didn't say a word. It was only when I told him that the Liberals were promising debt and tax relief, but not in his lifetime, that he started to cry.

Five days later I stood before 2,000 people – 1,200 of them delegates – at the Reform Party's 1998 National Assembly in the city of
London, Ontario, and initiated a process that would eventually give
birth to a new federal political party, the Canadian Reform
Conservative Alliance. The delivery of this new political baby
would also prove to be long and hard, but at the time I had high
hopes for a safe birth and a bright future. There are various means
whereby a political family can grow, but one of the most important
is through wise marriages and births, without which the family
withers. I wished to communicate this concept to Reformers,
Conservatives, and anyone else who would listen.

The speech I gave to Assembly '98 called upon Reformers to
rededicate themselves to "rekindling the national dream" of a new
and better Canada. To achieve that dream we needed to grow bigger
and stronger, and to do so more rapidly. I then invited assembly delegates to direct the leadership of our party to organize a special
"United Alternative" convention. Its first purpose would be to
gather under one federal political roof representatives of all
Canadians who shared four fundamental principles: fiscal responsibility, social responsibility, democratic accountability, and reformed
federalism. Its second purpose would be to define a platform and a
political action plan for electing a majority of members to the House
of Commons committed to those principles and that plan. In other
words, I was challenging Reformers to initiate the building of a
bigger and broader political tent in which more Canadians would
feel at home, in order to create a principled, governing alternative
to the federal Liberals.

At the heart of this proposal was the task of "building alliances
and coalitions" among people who shared certain common principles and goals – an activity that I believe will become as central to
the politics of the early twenty-first century as "reforming" was to
the last decade of the twentieth. Over the next three years we
would discover just how difficult a task that was.

My speech had been a long time in the making and drew upon the
thinking and contributions of many others who had come to similar
conclusions by different routes. Thirty years before, I had helped my

father write a book entitled *Political Realignment*. Its thesis had been that a change in the alignment and structure of the federal parties on the conservative side of the house was necessary to create a principled alternative to liberalism and socialism. What goes around, comes around. The day after the June 1997 election, in the disappointment of having failed once again to break through east of Manitoba, my own campaign team had begun thinking of alternative strategies for overcoming our own limitations and the problem of vote-splitting with the Conservatives. Immediately after the 1997 election we conducted assessment meetings with candidates, campaign managers, and workers all over the country. One of the principal findings? That grassroots members of both the Reform and Conservative parties, particularly in Ontario, wanted their leaders to find some way to stop the vote-splitting that handed seats to the Liberals by default. Thus, the "United Alternative" campaign, under the direction of MP Jason Kenney and party organizer Nancy Branscombe, was set up to solicit grassroots ideas on how this might be accomplished. This campaign received as much input from provincial Conservatives and disgruntled federal Conservatives as it did from Reformers. The effort, however, was organized and financed by Reform, with the findings to be reported to the Reform Party's annual assembly in London in May 1998.

Meanwhile, out West, Klein Conservatives such as Rod Love and Thompson MacDonald were thinking along the same lines. On January 9, 1998, they met in Thompson's Calgary office in Bow Valley Square to discuss ways of getting Reformers and Conservatives to work together. Four months later, on May 6, 1998, at Winnipeg's Manitoba Club, Rod and Thompson would meet with Cliff Fryers, Rick Anderson, and a small group of Conservatives from across the country, who were in Winnipeg to celebrate Gary Filmon's tenth anniversary as premier. The group included several Manitoba Conservatives, Peter White of the federal Tories, and Mike Burns, a PC fundraiser from B.C. Eventually all of these people would find themselves working together on the United Alternative Steering Committee, but that evening the conversation was exploratory and cautious. They agreed that they would meet again to advance the

United Alternative concept if the Reform Party's upcoming assembly encouraged its leadership to do so.

From January 22 to 27, 1998, I held a series of meetings with key Reformers to plan our future. According to my notes, this was the first time that the United Alternative was considered as a serious option. On March 17 I had a friendly meeting with Ontario premier Mike Harris at the Ottawa airport to discuss the prospects of making common cause to bring common sense to Ottawa. On March 23 Sandra and I met with Hal Jackman and a number of other prominent Torontonians on the University of Toronto campus. The United Alternative option was a major part of that discussion.

At this stage, the leadership of the federal Conservatives, in particular Jean Charest, was hostile to any talk about an accommodation with Reform. But in March 1998 rumours surfaced in Ottawa and Quebec City that Jean Charest would soon be leaving the Conservatives to assume the leadership of the Quebec Liberals. Suddenly the concept of "political realignment" was very much in vogue. On March 25, I spoke to the caucus and to members of our executive council by teleconference. When I told caucus that I would rather that we "crashed and burned" trying to create a principled government than settled indefinitely for our present position as Opposition, there was nodding of heads and applause, except from a fearful few.

Two days later, at a press conference in Vancouver, I announced my intention to invite Reform's May assembly to pursue the United Alternative option. I tied my announcement to the speculation of the last few weeks concerning the future of Jean Charest: "If it is acceptable for the leader of the Progressive Conservatives to leave his party and join the provincial Liberals to create a united alternative to the separatists in Quebec, then it should also be acceptable for many other people to consider leaving traditional party allegiances to band together to create a united alternative to the stagnant Liberals in Ottawa."

On May 24, with the assembly only three days away, Sandra and I had secluded ourselves at Sibbald Flats just west of Calgary in a beautiful log cabin owned by our friends Rollie and Pam Laing.

With the Rocky Mountains in the distance for inspiration, and a mountain of memos and briefing notes on the table, I sat down to finalize my address to the Reform assembly. Jean Marie Clemenger was at her computer in Ottawa and Jennifer Grover was on line from Kelowna. People like Rick, Cliff, André Turcotte, Harry Meyers (chairman of the party's executive council), and the caucus officers were only a phone call away, and all ready to help. This was how we did "big speeches."

The challenge to Reformers to participate in a great political gathering with others who were of like mind was not hard to formulate. Nor was it difficult to explain why this initiative would be in the national interest, or to wax eloquent on the possibilities if this venture were to succeed. The hard part was realistically to assess the risks to the party and to myself of going down that road.

The risks of having our Reform principles diluted or the word "Reform" abandoned would be diminished to the extent that Reformers vigorously and actively participated, in large numbers, in the United Alternative convention and process. And as for the risks to myself:

> Do I risk the position of leadership which you have given me this past eleven years? The frank answer to that question is Yes! But if I as your Leader consider that risk worth taking – if the result to be gained by such risk taking is the creation of a governing party based on Reform principles under the great banner of Reform – why should that risk cause us to hesitate?

At the time these words were written I had been the leader of the Opposition for less than a year, and now we would risk it all by pushing the envelope yet again. Would it be worth it? Of course it would be worth it if it helped us make the transition from an opposition to a governing party. But it would also be worth it if, as a result, we could gain the confidence of four million voters, win at least a hundred seats in the House, push the Liberals into a minority position, more strongly influence the future direction of the country, and by that means get Canada on the road to a better and brighter future.

The day following my speech to the London assembly, the delegates voted on both my proposal and my leadership. When the votes
were counted, my leadership was endorsed by 81 per cent (down
somewhat from the previous assembly), but the United Alternative
resolution carried by a vote of 91 per cent in favour. We had a strong
mandate to proceed. I had paid a price to get it, but the price had
not been too steep.

As I made my way out of the crowded London Convention
Centre, there was the ever-enthusiastic Kory Teneycke. Kory had
organized the Reform Youth bus tour for the 1997 campaign and
was currently working for us in Ottawa. I asked him to give me dates
that would provide maximum opportunity for university students to
attend the United Alternative convention. "That would be
towards the end of the first Reading Week in 1999," he said. And
that is how the dates for the first United Alternative convention,
February 19–21, 1999, were determined. The United Alternative
was, above all, about the future. Those to whom that future
belonged would have maximum opportunity to attend.

■

Even before the London assembly, the media had begun to refer to
the movement to create a bigger, broader alternative to the Liberals
as a movement to "unite the right" – a label that was both unfortunate and inappropriate. What we were aspiring to do was much
more than that and was not accurately described by such a phrase.

In the spring of 1998 I asked our pollster, André Turcotte, to
conduct a national public opinion survey asking Canadians to try to
position themselves on the "left-centre-right" spectrum. Of those
polled, 34 per cent were unable to do so. Another 39 per cent positioned themselves at the centre (meaning neither left nor right), a
clear indication that they found the choices expressed this way
quite meaningless. Of the remainder, 17 per cent placed themselves
"on the left," with only 10 per cent locating themselves "on the
right." Even among our supporters, 45 per cent of Reformers couldn't
position themselves on the axis at all, and only 9 per cent placed
themselves on the right, while only 15 per cent of PC supporters

positioned themselves on the right. As André observed, "When political commentators refer to 'uniting the right,' they are unknowingly referring to uniting the 10 per cent of the electorate who consider themselves on the right of the political spectrum – surely not a strategically profitable exercise for either the Reform Party or the federal PCs."*

This and similar surveys confirmed my view that to build a *governing alternative* to the Liberals – not some right-wing NDP eternally destined to opposition status – we needed to do far more than "unite the right." We needed to unite fiscal and social conservatives who attached a high priority to free enterprise and individual autonomy, small-d democrats committed to democratic accountability, and reform-oriented federalists committed to re-balancing the federation – all under one roof. This was the bigger objective that I invited Reformers and others to support under the banner of the United Alternative.

Of course, Canadians do not come in neatly tied ideological packages labelled "conservative," "democrat," or "federalist." Real people are much more complicated, real politics is much more messy, and uniting real people for real political action requires uniting them on more than ideological grounds. Thus, in organizing support for the first United Alternative convention, my team and I had at least three big lists of potential "allies," not just one. Yes, we had potential ideological allies – prominent fiscal conservatives, social conservatives, small-d democrats, reform-oriented federalists, with the organizations to which they might belong and the publications they might read. And we appealed to them to join with us.

I also had a second list of potential allies, including many of the same people but organized geographically, because there are many Canadians who put geography – the region in which they live – ahead of other political considerations. This list included "movers and shakers" in Atlantic Canada who wanted a new, market-based approach to regional development; the *troisième voie* people in Quebec – soft nationalists and discontented federalists who rejected

---

* Preston Manning and André Turcotte, "3-D Politics: A Renewed Canadian Political Discourse for the New Millennium," June 1998, unpublished.

both the separatism of the Bloc and the status quo federalism of the
federal Liberals; the supporters of the Common Sense Revolution in
Ontario, not all of whom could be described first and foremost as
fiscal conservatives; and Western Reformers, who themselves represented a unique but internally consistent coalition of interests across
the four Western provinces.

And then I had a third list of potential allies, which was "organizational" – again overlapping the other two lists, but including people
who needed to be appealed to first and foremost by appealing to
their "group." This list included the Campbell Liberals in B.C.
(then in opposition); the Klein Conservatives in Alberta; the new
Saskatchewan Party people in that province, headed by former
Reform MP Elwin Hermanson; the Filmon Conservatives in
Manitoba; the Harris Conservatives in Ontario; the Action démocratique in Quebec; the four provincial Conservative parties in
Atlantic Canada; some but not all of the constituency associations of
the federal Progressive Conservative Party of Canada; and of course
the members and constituency associations of the Reform Party itself.

It was my belief that there was enough common ground among all
these individuals and groups to enable them to work together at the
federal political level. There was no insurmountable reason why
fiscal and social conservatives couldn't work together, as long as
they let democracy mediate their differences. There was no reason
why Atlantic Canadian movers and shakers couldn't work together
with Common Sense Revolutionaries in Ontario and Western
Reformers – in fact, each of these regional groups needed allies in
other parts of Canada to get its positions effectively addressed by the
federal government. There was no insurmountable reason why
provincial political interests across the country couldn't work
together under one federal banner to replace the federal Liberals.

And if anyone doubts that this was the breadth, depth, and scale
of the coalition-building exercise that my friends and I undertook in
launching the United Alternative effort, let them examine the
huge files of correspondence, telephone calls, speech notes, media
advisories, and meeting notes that we began to accumulate once the
Reform assembly had approved the UA initiative. My own files
include An Open Letter to Newfoundland, An Open Letter to the

People of the Maritime Provinces, and summaries of a meeting of Atlantic Canadian Movers and Shakers at Stornoway on April 21, 1998. They include letters to all the Atlantic Canada MLAs, letters and phone calls to former New Brunswick premier Frank McKenna, and notes from a meeting with P.E.I. premier Pat Binns, whom I tried to persuade to host the second UA conference, at Charlottetown, the birthplace of the federation. Those files include an *"Où est LaFontaine?"* letter and address sent to every member of the Quebec National Assembly, letters and phone calls to Jean Allaire and members of the Action démocratique, notes from meetings with Rodrigue Biron and his sovereigntist friends, and notes from a meeting with Claude Ryan at his apartment. And those files also include notes from separate meetings with both Pierre Marc Johnson, the former Parti Québécois premier, and his brother, Daniel Johnson, the former Quebec Liberal premier, inviting them to appear on stage together at the first UA convention to declare that reformed federalism was the only way to reconcile the tensions within the Canadian family. (Pierre Marc was sympathetic but Daniel was very cool, still believing "distinct society" to be the solution.) Huge files exist on all the communications between Reformers and the Harris Conservatives, particularly at the constituency level. The Harris Conservatives, headed by Tony Clement, proved to be the strongest ally of the United Alternative process among all the provincial Conservative parties, followed closely by the Klein Conservatives in Alberta. We published an Open Letter to Ontario Taxpayers. Letters and phone calls concerning the UA went to all the Conservative MLAs west of the Manitoba-Ontario border, to all our Saskatchewan Party contacts, to all the B.C. Liberal MLAs, and to a list I maintained of "Big British Columbians" – residents of B.C., including Gordon Campbell, Gordon Gibson, Mel Smith, and many others, who had spoken out against the crippling polarization of B.C. politics and who were coalition builders in their own right. And in addition to all this there was the stream of correspondence, e-mails, Reform newsletters, "dashboard" tapes, demon-dialer messages, and other communications that flowed among my office, national office, caucus, executive council, and our Reform membership.

Happily, all these communications bore fruit, particularly at the grassroots level. Rank-and-file Canadians – Reformers, Conservatives, Nunziata Liberals from Toronto, members of other parties, people who were not members of any party, and young people, especially – were signing up by the score to attend the first United Alternative convention in Ottawa in mid-February 1999.

■

On the night of Thursday, February 18, 1999, the night before the first United Alternative convention was to begin at the Ottawa Convention Centre, a very special group of people joined Sandra and me at Stornoway. They included most of the members of the United Alternative Steering Committee who had worked so hard to bring this event to fruition. The committee had included five Reformers – Cliff, Rick (assisted by Lisa Samson), Jason Kenney, Ken Kalopsis, and Nancy Branscombe – and sixteen non-Reformers from across the country. Our guests included people as diverse as Quebecers Rodrigue Biron and his gracious wife and blunt-speaking Albertans like Rod Love. They included a few who had visited Stornoway before, when Joe Clark was the leader of the Official Opposition. They included people who would eventually support me for the leadership of the Alliance, and others, like Peter White, Rod Love, and Bob Dechert of the Tory Blue Committee, who would never do so. But this was no time to worry about that. First we had to have something bigger and broader to lead; then we could fight about who should lead it. As each person left, I gave them a copy of Christopher Moore's book *1867: How the Fathers Made a Deal*,* on the founding of Confederation. Inside I had written, "With sincerest thanks for your leadership of the UA convention, and for creating the possibility of a New Deal for Canada for the 21st century."

More than 1,500 delegates registered for the convention, 57 per cent of them Reformers, 43 per cent non-Reformers. More than three hundred youth delegates – fifty of whom arrived from Atlantic

---

* Christopher Moore, *1867: How the Fathers Made a Deal* (Toronto: McClelland and Stewart, 1998).

Canada after an eighteen-hour bus ride – added a zest and energy out
of proportion to their numbers. The convention began at 6:30 p.m.
with Deborah Grey and Ontario Transportation minister Tony
Clement serving as co-chairs. Alberta premier Ralph Klein was
present to give the opening address.

A few minutes before things got underway, Sandra and I went
backstage to greet Ralph and thank him for coming. Ralph had been
very little involved in the planning of the UA convention or in
building the coalition behind it, but he had not discouraged his
MLAs from participating, and several of his key people – Rod Love
and Thompson Macdonald, in particular – had been deeply
involved. To his credit, Ralph had been the only Conservative
premier to publicly endorse the convention and agree to attend.
Unlike Premier Harris in Ontario, who had been privately supportive but publicly constrained, Premier Klein risked very little by
endorsing this initiative, since over half his provincial support came
from Reformers, and in Alberta the Reform Party was far more
significant than the federal PCs.

In his address, Ralph made two telling points. First, that those
issues that presented a moral dilemma of a personal nature should be
left to the internal moral compass found within every Canadian and
not made issues of party or government policy. And second, that we
must not allow the principle that all provinces should be treated
equally (in law) to deny recognition of Quebec as "different." This
latter point was identical to the Reform position, but the first was
seen as a warning shot across the bows of social conservatives. Ralph
did not say what should be done on moral issues that the state
cannot avoid – like those raised by the genetic revolution – but this
was not the time for addressing such dilemmas. Premier Klein left
the hall to thunderous applause, his presence truly appreciated by
the delegates, myself included.

Delegates spent the whole next day debating resolutions designed
to define the "principled ground" on which a United Alternative
might be built, and working on a final resolution outlining a political action plan. Prominent spokespersons presented the various
options for action. Reform MP John Reynolds presented the case for
uniting behind the Reform Party. Gordon Gilchrist, a former PC

With the RCMP's March West commemorating the 125th anniversary of the North-West Mounted Police ride across the prairies, June 1999.

Dave Buston

Going over my notes backstage before the United Alternative I speech, February 1999.

United Alternative I speech, February 1999.

Speaking at the Alliance
convention, February 1, 2000.

Dave Buston

Celebrating the new party name, Canadian Alliance, January 2000.

Ian Todd and me "Doing Business Day" in Ottawa, 2000.

Sandra working the phones during the PM4PM Campaign, May 2000.

Helping each other get ready
during the PM4PM campaign,
May 2000.

George Pimentel

Dave Buston

Admiring the view in Writing on Stone Park, Alberta, 2000.

Election 2000 with leader Stockwell Day.

Waving farewell to Corel Centre fans on the night before my last day
in the House of Commons.

Walking to the House of Commons for my farewell speech, January 31, 2002.

Farewell celebration with Sandra and the "Iron Snowbird,"
MP Deborah Grey, friend and co-labourer, January 31, 2002.

Tom Hanson/CP

My last day in the House of Commons.

MP, made the case for uniting behind the federal Progressive Conservative Party. PC Mario Annecchini and Reformer Joe Peschisolido made the case for a merger of the two federal parties. Stockwell Day presented the case for the creation of a new political party, the option I personally favoured, and did so with passion, speaking without notes. And Hal Jackman made one of the most impressive presentations of the day, arguing for "the local unity option," the adoption of measures that would facilitate riding-based actions to recruit and select common candidates.

That night Sandra and I arrived at the Ottawa Congress Centre early enough to hear Rodrigue Biron, the former Parti Québécois minister from Quebec, give an excellent talk on Quebec's openness to a third way. He hoped the United Alternative could provide it. The national media tended to dismiss both Jean Allaire, who had spoken earlier, and Biron as "old warhorses," but delegates and viewers in English Canada were impressed to hear Quebecers presenting perspectives other than separatism or status quo federalism.

Rodrigue concluded his presentation by introducing me. I welcomed the delegates and applauded their efforts to define principled common ground. I stated that I was at this convention to unite with others to lower federal taxes, heal the health care system, and achieve other common objectives aimed at bettering the lives of Canadians. I truly believed, I said, that they were there for the same reasons.

I quoted a Mr. Blackwood of Nova Scotia, one of the lesser known participants in the Confederation debates. In reference to the union proposed by the Fathers of Confederation, he said: "We may establish what will be called a union, but will it be a union of the heart?" Any new political union, I said, must involve a union of the heart as well as the head.

I spoke of the necessity of building alliances for tax relief and health care reform and national unity, not on the brittle foundation of cold and impersonal political calculations but on the relationships of heart and mind and hand that characterize the building and strengthening of a family.

I concluded by asking the delegates to come with me in their mind's eye to the Railway Committee Room of the House of

Commons to view a reproduction of Robert Harris's famous composite painting of the Fathers of Confederation at the Quebec and Charlottetown conferences. There are thirty-six people in the picture – some sitting, some standing – including representatives of six provinces and a dozen political groups, some in government and some in opposition. But not everyone is in the picture who might have been or should have been. Some were invited but wouldn't come. Some could have come but decided to stay on the sidelines until they were certain of the outcome. Others are not in the picture at all because they simply weren't invited. It is my dream, I said, that some day – just once, perhaps to begin the new millennium – this country could have *one big family meeting*, a meeting like we've never had before. It could be a political convention like this one – perhaps "Charlottetown 2000" – but one at which every region and every principled interest committed to redefining our politics and our federal union was truly represented. If they so decided, it could very well be the founding convention to redefine or establish the governing alternative to the Liberals that this convention would be proposing the next day. No doubt someone would capture that Big Family Meeting in a photograph or on videotape. And years later someone in your family might see it and ask, "Were you at that Big Family Meeting that changed the course of Canada for the twenty-first century?" I want to be able to say – don't you want to be able to say? – "*Oui, j'étais là.* Yes, I was there."

The next day the convention approved a political action plan to create a new federal political party, its constitution, principles, and platform to be determined at a second United Alternative convention to be held prior to June 30 of the following year. My job would be to encourage Reformers to participate fully in the development of that party, to communicate its potential to Canadians at large, and to do so "from the heart."

■

Following the closing ceremonies of the first UA convention and a brief media conference, I hurried over to the West Block, where a special meeting of the Reform caucus was already in progress under

Deborah Grey's chairmanship. I had never stood on ceremony at caucus meetings, and there was no pause in the meeting as I slipped in and took my seat at the head table. For once, however, it bothered me that caucus didn't seem to realize what a significant political event had just transpired and the crucial role that Reform leadership had played in bringing it about. The convention and its decisions were of course the only topic of discussion, and as usual the most fearful members of caucus spoke first. Then, as also usually happened, the stronger and more positive members gave their assessment, so that at the end of the session it was clear that a majority were prepared to move forward in support of the conclusions of the convention. It bothered me personally, however, that the basic mood of caucus was sombre – on a day when Reformers should have been inspired by the success of the convention and looking forward to the future with positive expectation. Later, when I shared my concern with Sandra, she asked, "Did you tell them you were disappointed?" When I said "No," her comment was that "speaking from the heart" includes sharing your disappointments as well as your hopes, and that I should be doing more of that with our own people, not just the public at large.

By contrast, my meeting with the executive council was much more upbeat. On the issue of building a bigger and broader tent, the party appeared to be running ahead of the caucus, and the rank-and-file members were ahead of both.

My next immediate task was to complete my "Report to Reformers" on the UA convention. This discussed why a United Alternative was needed, the proceedings and conclusions of the convention, and a description of the follow-up grassroots process to develop a platform, a constitution, a communications and election readiness plan, a fundraising effort, and a plan to reach out to members of other parties. In my report I made it equally clear what, in my view, the United Alternative was not. It was not the death of Reform or an abandonment of our mission, as some had suggested. It was not a takeover of Reform and it was not just about Ontario. It was not top-down – the rank-and-file members would have a chance to vote on the initiatives proposed at each stage. It was not just about "uniting the right" and it was not yet a "done deal." I then recommended to Reformers "that we proceed to the next step to explore the ways we can build this newer, bigger political home, and that we continue to participate in the UA effort while withholding judgment on joining into a new party until its constitution, principles, and platform are available for scrutiny." The report then spelled out the actions that the party intended to take to facilitate a full and frank discussion of the UA option among Reformers, and to conduct a party-wide referendum on whether Reformers wanted to continue to support the initiative or not.

Shortly after the first UA convention, the Reform Party's executive council announced the rules for a party-wide referendum to be held via a mail-in ballot, with the results to be announced on June 10, 1999. The question on which members would be asked to vote was: "Should the Reform Party of Canada continue with the United Alternative process – Yes or No?" For the referendum result to be valid and binding under the Reform Party's constitution, at least 25 per cent of the membership eligible to vote would have to cast ballots, and a "Yes" vote would require a double majority – a majority of the total votes cast, and a "Yes" vote in a majority of the provinces and territories.

For the next four months, in addition to my duties as leader of the Opposition, I participated in a coast-to-coast campaign to discuss, explain, and defend the United Alternative process and objectives to Reform Party members and anyone else who would listen. The executive council of the party (all volunteers) and its national office staff became fully engaged in organizing local and regional conferences and in preparing for the party-wide referendum. At the same time, the United Alternative Steering Committee had a huge job to do in preparation for the second UA convention. Almost all of my key staff and many key members of caucus were engaged in this activity as well, while still discharging their duties in Parliament and the constituencies. To those who criticized us for spending as much time on this political work as on our parliamentary work, I responded by saying that the Opposition has two main functions: to hold the government of the day accountable, and to put in place a credible alternative to the government. The United Alternative effort was our approach to discharging this important second responsibility.

In speaking to Reform members on the subject – the people who could actually vote "Yes" or "No" on continuation of the UA process via the mail-in referendum ballot – I made it clear that the party belonged to them, and that the final decision on the UA belonged to them. But as their leader it was also my responsibility to inform their discretion and give them my own judgment on the proposal. That I would then proceed to do, urging them to vote in favour of the UA process.

At the same time, as I criss-crossed the country on behalf of the UA, I wanted to keep communicating the UA concept to the general public, because if they became enthusiastic about it as the way to get enough seats and votes in the Parliament to lower taxes and fix health care, then the Reform membership would feel more comfortable about endorsing the concept. Thus, many of our UA referendum meetings had a public meeting first to which every-one in a community was invited, and then a meeting for Reform Party members afterwards.

During this period we also worked hard at broadening the coali-tion of interests that the United Alternative was seeking to unite. This meant innumerable phone calls, letters, small meetings with provincial and municipal politicians and with those publications and interest groups representing fiscal conservatives, social conser-vatives, small-d democrats, and reform-oriented federalists in every part of the country. The more I worked on "broadening the coali-tion" under the UA banner, the more vulnerable I became to the attacks of critics who accused me of "abandoning Reform princi-ples." On October 13, 1999, I therefore used my reply in the House to the government's October 8 Throne Speech to restate the com-mitment of myself and Reform to our principles – everything from the principle of fiscal responsibility to political realignment. The speech was later published and widely distributed under the title "Strong Roots, Bright Future," and it helped to reassure Reformers that I was committed to advancing their principles through the UA, not watering them down.

Building support for the UA also meant seeking to involve more and more federal Conservatives in the process. Much of this we left to our provincial Conservative friends, particularly in Alberta and

Ontario. I also made several direct appeals to the leader of the federal Conservatives, Joe Clark. On October 29, 1998, just after Joe had resumed the leadership of the federal PCs and more than three months before the first United Alternative convention, I wrote him a letter. I congratulated him on his election, raised the obvious necessity of creating a viable alternative to the Liberals, and invited him to bring his ideas on how this might be done to the United Alternative convention in February. Joe had already told a press conference that those desiring an alternative to the Liberals should simply unite behind his party, so I told Joe that if he honestly believed that, he should "come and argue that position at the UA convention," and added, "There are those who think you must lead this effort. There are those who believe it must be me. There are those who believe it cannot be either of us. What I propose is that, once this United Alternative has been created, if you think you are best qualified to lead it, then put your name forward, and let the grassroots members and supporters decide. I am prepared to accept their judgment, Joe, and I invite you to join me in doing so."

Joe would have none of this, however, and the first UA convention came and went without his participation, even though I offered him a speaking slot on the Saturday night with national television coverage of whatever he might choose to say.

Notwithstanding Joe's coolness and public dismissals of the UA concept and process, there were prominent Tories, such as Hal Jackman in Toronto and Doug Mitchell in Calgary, who firmly believed Joe and I should get together to talk. I was willing, but Joe was reluctant, and there was always the problem of meeting without raising expectations we couldn't satisfy, or arousing the suspicions of our members that some backroom deal was in the offing. Finally, Doug Mitchell arranged for me to go to Joe's residence in Ottawa on the afternoon of Sunday, May 30, 1999, for a chat.

I drove the short distance from Stornoway to Joe's, knocked on the door, said hello to Maureen and Catherine, and followed Joe to the lower level of their split-level home. Joe and I knew each other well enough, even though we have disagreed on many things, that there was really no awkwardness in meeting like this and getting down to business. I raised the question of co-operating where we could in the House with respect to Question Period, supply days, and issues like Kosovo. We had a fruitful discussion on some particulars, including pushing together for parliamentary reform. But I could tell from the beginning that Joe actually wanted to talk about the UA, so we soon got on to it. Joe appeared to believe that Reform's strength had passed the point of diminishing returns and that the UA proposal was born out of desperation. But he also recognized that vote-splitting was a real problem – for both of us – that simply couldn't be ignored. He didn't disagree with the four political options raised at the first UA convention, he simply believed that uniting behind the federal PCs was the best one. He seemed to believe that being a former leader of the Opposition and a former prime minister gave him some status and appeal with the public, particularly in Quebec, that would eventually bear fruit. He remained committed to running 301 federal PCs in the next election.

I felt that Joe was deluding himself on a number of these matters, but there was little point in my saying so, when even his Conservative friends had had no success in changing his opinions. I kept probing to see if there wasn't some political ground related to the UA on which we could agree. What about the UA as a possible meeting ground for Quebec and the West on constitutional issues? Joe had little to say about the West, but a great deal to say about Quebec. He seemed to believe that Bouchard could be persuaded to give only token support to the Bloc the next time around, and to regard the PCs under Joe as a better ally in Ottawa. I was skeptical, but I took the time to explain our New Canada Act, the thrust and content of which seemed to surprise Joe a little. What about Jackman's proposal for local co-operation? Joe said there was no enthusiasm for it among his people. What about Mike Harris as a possible broker between Reform and the Conservatives? Joe didn't dismiss the possibility but mentioned voters who would vote for him (Joe) but not for Mike. Finally I asked whether there was any point in trying to carry on a dialogue on this subject. Joe said yes, there was, but it should be done in neutral forums where smaller groups of people could discuss the options and the obstacles frankly in greater

privacy than they could at big, public conventions. We agreed that
he and I should talk again after the results of the Reform referendum
were known and after the Ontario and New Brunswick provincial
elections. Two hours after my arrival, I took my leave. I felt that the
visit hadn't done any harm, but that Joe's unwillingness or inability
to "seize the moment" could not easily be remedied.

On June 10, 1999, the results of the party-wide mail-in referendum were tabulated in Calgary: 60.5 per cent of the participating
members had voted "Yes" to continuing with the UA process. It
wasn't overwhelming, but it was enough to carry on. "Proceed, but
proceed with caution," was the message from the members. Out of
64,649 ballots issued to eligible members, 32,099 valid ballots had
been cast, for a 49.7 per cent response rate, well over the required 25
per cent minimum required under the party constitution. The proposal to carry on with the UA process had received majority support
in all jurisdictions except Saskatchewan and the Territories.
Another milestone was passed. There would be another United
Alternative convention in Ottawa, on January 28–29, 2000, with
Reformers fully participating. Stay tuned!

■

Three days later I was back in Calgary for a few days' break. David
and I decided to go fishing and that night we camped on Chinook
Lake, a small jewel of a lake nestled beneath Crowsnest Mountain.
The next day was warm and sunny, and, after fly-fishing for trout in
the lake and on the Crowsnest River, we headed for Badger Lake on
the prairie near Vulcan to try fly-fishing for pike. Dave landed a
good-sized one with a big hairy black fly designed to look like a
floating dead mouse. We then headed back to Calgary, David
driving the Jeep, The Buicks' music pounding through the stereo,
satisfied with ourselves and the world. The car phone rang (this was
getting to be routine) and it was son-in-law John from Grande
Prairie. He said that he and Avryll had been fishing too, and that
they had caught a big one – seven pounds, nine ounces – which they
intended to keep. Her name was Abigail Mary Fuller, and mother
and baby were doing just fine. One of the ways a family grows is

through wise marriages and births. Our family was certainly growing in this way; would our political family do likewise?

■

The second United Alternative convention was about as positive and stimulating a political experience as one could wish for. All of our hard work and meticulous planning was coming together. For me, it meant that I was about to realize at least one dream I had talked about, that dream of gathering a large group of Canadians together at one big meeting, Canadians who shared certain common principles but found themselves divided into different political camps, to discuss the idea of rejuvenating our political foundations for the twenty-first century.

Co-chairs Tom Long and Val Meredith opened UA II by presenting the 1,400 delegates with an agenda for building the framework for a new coalition. But first a panel of pollsters delivered some encouraging news: the UA concept, properly presented to the public, had the potential to attract greater support (nationally, and in Quebec as well) than either Reform or the Progressive Conservatives on their own.

Over the next two days the delegates would debate and decide on a Declaration of Policy, a constitution to govern the new party, and a name. The national networks and regional media were out in full force to cover the proceedings, with lights, cameras, and microphones recording every word. The free national publicity was worth its weight in gold.

Several key participants made major speeches during the proceedings. On the evening of January 27 it was Stockwell Day, Alberta's Finance minister, hammering home the theme that it was fiscal reform – in particular tax relief – that would unite Conservatives and Reformers across the country. Stockwell also performed a karate kick on stage, which generated more media attention than the speech. Then on January 28 it was Tom Long, one of the chief architects of Mike Harris's two Ontario election victories, who delivered a blistering analysis of why the federal Conservatives under Joe Clark could not provide the principled alternative to the

Liberals required by the country. He received five standing ovations. Both Tom and Stockwell were already viewed by many of the delegates as potential leadership candidates, and both enhanced their stature by their speeches to UA II.

I kept my own participation in UA II to a minimum. I would have a chance to give a major presentation at the Reform assembly to follow, but at the UA convention it was important for me to keep a lower profile, so participants and media would not misinterpret this new entity as simply a new "Manning vehicle."

If an observer had looked around during this convention – beyond the debates and media scrums and resolutions – he would have seen and felt something else going on, something critical to successful coalition building. It was the melding of different political cultures, and it was astutely observed by the *Globe and Mail*, which made note of the "weatherbeaten western farmers in cowboy hats rubbing shoulders with Tom Long who looked like he just walked out of a Harry Rosen ad." By and large, Western Reformers and Harris Conservatives were culturally as well as ideologically compatible, and this compatibility held great promise for the future.

The other highly encouraging dimension of both UA conventions was the youth participation. For both conventions, Sandra and I booked into a downtown hotel and turned Stornoway over to delegates, mainly young people from out of town. Our own children, the girls' husbands, and their peers were all present, and the convention debates carried on late into the night and around the breakfast table the next morning. There was a feeling that they were participating in the birth of something new and historic – the same feeling that had prevailed at the birth of the Reform party ten years before.

The last major item of business for UA II was the selection of a name for the new entity. It had to incorporate the idea of Reform (we didn't want to lose the word), it had to appeal to Conservatives, and it had to convey the idea of people coming together in a bigger, broader coalition or alliance. Not surprisingly, after heated debate, glitches in the electronic voting, and changes in the order of the words to avoid an embarrassing acronym, the name of "a new party for a new century" was decided. It would be the Canadian Reform Conservative Alliance – or Canadian Alliance for short.

■

My participation in the second United Alternative Convention was modest and mainly behind the scenes. For much of the proceedings I sat with my fellow delegates from Calgary Southwest, voting on the various motions but not participating in the discussion at the microphones. But when the convention concluded at about 2:00 p.m. on Saturday, January 29, 2000, I couldn't have been more pleased with the results.

For Reformers, however, the work of the weekend was not yet done. A one-day Reform assembly had been scheduled to follow immediately after the UA convention to officially receive and discuss its resolutions before passing them on for assessment and approval by the Reform Party membership. That process began on Saturday afternoon when the product of the second United Alternative convention was formally conveyed by Jason Kenney to the delegates of the Reform assembly.

That night I spoke to the delegates. While my speech was addressed first and foremost to Reformers, it was televised nationally and therefore also needed to reach a broader audience. This would be the first exposure of many Canadians to the concept of the Canadian Alliance.

Since this one-day Reform assembly was still a formal national assembly under our constitution, the delegates – among whom were many of those skeptical about the UA process – would again have an opportunity to vote for or against my leadership. Their assessment this time would no doubt be very much dependent on whether or not they approved of the Canadian Alliance initiative.

In January I had written a letter to the entire Reform membership spelling out my position with respect to the UA initiative. I had indicated that I regarded the initiative as the best option for achieving a reform-oriented government after the next election. I had said that I would be a candidate for the leadership of the UA if it was approved by the party, and if it failed to win the approval of the party I would step down as leader. Knowing that I had already taken these positions, the media labelled that night's address to the assembly the most important speech of my political life.

It was Thompson MacDonald who reminded me that this also had to be a speech from a leader. People would be looking for direction and resolve, not simply the management consultant's assessment of the pros and the cons. And it was Rick Anderson who suggested the approach I adopted in making this speech. "What you have to do," he said, "is gather Reformers around the fire, relive all the things we have done together, and then show how that has prepared us for the challenge that still lies ahead."

In searching for a theme I reached a long way back. When Sandra and I were living on our acreage in St. Albert and our children were young, I would sometimes tell them "Canada stories." One was "Canada is people" – I'd tell them about the great variety of people, from aboriginals to recent immigrants, who made Canada their home. Then there was "Canada is North" (received with some skepticism), in which I told of the adventures of the Northern explorers and endeavoured to present ice, snow, and frigid temperatures as national treasures. And then there was "Canada is BIG!" – in which I tried to convey the immensity of our country and everything in it. Some time after the first UA convention I began to stress the fact that we live in a BIG country – easily illustrated no matter where you are in Canada – and dealing with the future of Canada requires us to think BIG. With the help of Jennifer Grover, Bob van Wegen, and Thompson MacDonald we brought these three streams of thought together for my Reform assembly speech. I would gather Reformers around the fire . . . and challenge them as their leader to think *big* about the future.

My team had arranged for 2.5-metre Styrofoam letters spelling out the words "THINK BIG" to be erected on stage. The stage was kept dark while delegates were taking their seats, but soon the giant letters were lit with yellow spotlights, and Sandra and I stepped out between them. The effect was dramatic, and, judging by the wild reception, I had already made my point. We were off to a good start.

I began by reliving the major steps we had taken together: the 1987 Western Assembly, where it all began; the Founding Assembly in Winnipeg; publication of the first Reform Blue Book (policy platform); the 1988 federal election; the 1989 Beaver River by-election, which gave us Deborah Grey; the Alberta Senate election, which sent Stan Waters to the Senate; the 1991 Saskatoon assembly, where we became truly national; the first rallies in Ontario and Atlantic Canada; the first forays into Quebec; "Know More" and the Charlottetown referendum campaign; the breakthrough 1993 federal election campaign that sent fifty-two Reformers to Ottawa; the Fresh Start campaign and the 1997 federal election campaign; and the swearing in of Reformers as Her Majesty's Loyal Opposition.

What a ride! What a journey! And what were the characteristics that distinguished our decisions and actions along the way? Change, change, constant change. Application and reapplication of our principles to new situations. Constant expansion of our base. Always pushing the envelope. The exercise of courage, raw courage – always accepting risk rather than avoiding it, always THINKING BIG rather than thinking small.

I then described the United Alternative option that lay before us, which many in that audience had helped create, and challenged everyone to approach it with the same commitment to change, reapplying our principles, expanding ownership, and pushing the envelope that had allowed us to accomplish great things together in the past.

Our task, I told them, was to dislodge the Liberals. It wouldn't be easy. They occupied a secure position on what we might think of as Taxation Mountain. They would be routed only by a coalition of forces operating under a single banner. And those forces would have to abandon the safety of the trenches they presently occupied to charge up the sides of the mountain. It could be done. It had to be done. And when it was done, and people asked us how we had taken the mountain, we would tell them: We were thinking BIG!

The next day, the Reform delegates voted on whether to endorse my leadership once more. For those delegates who disapproved of the Canadian Alliance package, this was their opportunity to express themselves. When the votes were counted, I had won the approval of 75 per cent. I was using up my political capital, but the Canadian Alliance concept was now very far advanced.

That weekend we launched the second and final Reform referendum campaign, in which Reformers would be challenged to vote "Yes" or "No" on whether the Reform Party of Canada should adopt the new constitution and the policy declaration of the Canadian Reform Conservative Alliance. I would be urging Reformers from one end of the country to the other to THINK BIG, VOTE YES!

∎

During the campaign to secure support for the UA among Reformers, there had been various members of caucus, the executive council, and the membership at large who opposed the initiative, some quite vigorously and viciously. They also attacked my leadership with increasing ferocity. Under such circumstances, a leader is often advised and tempted to label such people "dissidents" and "rebels" and to discipline or even expel them. I did my best to resist this temptation, not just to maintain caucus and party unity but also for another quite different reason. Any leader who professes a Christian commitment must be particularly careful about ever labelling any of his associates or followers "rebels," because our faith is quite clear on how "rebels" are to be treated. They are to be treated as God himself has chosen to treat us when we rebel against Him – with repeated offers of reconciliation and forgiveness, not judgment and expulsion.

During the UA campaign I was particularly reminded of this because, in my personal meditations, I had been studying the life of Moses, one of the greatest political and spiritual leaders who ever lived. In his writings, Moses describes four great revelations or insights that he received concerning the character of God. In the burning bush that was never consumed he saw God as Eternal. In the Red Sea, where Pharaoh's chariots were destroyed, he saw God as Warrior. On his first journey to the top of Mount Sinai he saw God as Lawgiver. But on his second journey to the top of Mount Sinai he saw God as Goodness, who, while still maintaining the standards of the Law, is also "the compassionate and gracious God, slow to anger, abounding in love and faithfulness, maintaining love to thousands, and forgiving . . . *rebellion* . . ."*

Moses had been given these insights into the character of God so that he might model Him to his people. But shortly afterward, when Israel rebelled against his leadership in the desert, Moses forgot all about this last revelation and reacted in a manner completely contrary to it. Tragically, in so doing he disqualified himself from leading Israel into the Promised Land.

I knew I might not be given the privilege of leading Reform supporters into the Promised Land of political success, for a number of reasons. But I resolved in my mind and heart that it would *not* be because I had treated so-called dissidents and rebels in such a way as to split the party and discredit my Christian profession.

On a broader canvas, the more I learn about the proper relation between faith and work – in my case, political work – the more I am convinced that God is much more concerned about what kind of person we are and are becoming through our experiences than He is in any mission that we might undertake on our own or to which we feel "called." The story of Moses kept me reminded of this principle throughout the UA campaign and helped me cope with the internal dissent it generated.

■

The Reform assembly of 1998 had got the United Alternative ball rolling by directing the party leadership to proceed with the UA initiative. The first UA convention in February 1999 had laid the foundational principles and proposed a plan of action for fleshing them out into a party constitution and platform. The first Reform referendum of June 1999 had given us the green light to proceed with the process, but to proceed with caution. The second United Alternative convention of January 2000 had completed the task of developing the constitution, principles, and platform for a bigger and broader political vehicle – the Canadian Reform Conservative Alliance. Now, while the caucus officers prepared for a major assault

* *Exodus*, 34:6-7.

on the ethics and conduct of the Chrétien government in the House, my other weary team prepared for one more campaign – the second Reform referendum, through which Reformers would decide once and for all whether to join the Canadian Alliance.

By this time, criticism of the Alliance concept was receiving far more attention than the efforts to build it. This was in keeping with the prevailing principle of media communications in Canada: that negative is more newsworthy than positive, and evidence of disunity is more newsworthy than efforts to unify. The principal internal critics of the Alliance concept included a group of Reformers (a few MPs among them) calling themselves GUARD – Grassroots United Against Reform's Demise. The critics also included the Liberals, the Clark Conservatives, and some of the media, like the *Ottawa Sun*, which amplified to the sky the opinions of any professed Reformer who attacked the concept. But as soon as we got out among the public to explain the Alliance to voters, there was a noticeable enthusiasm. As is often the case in Canadian federal politics, the voters appeared to be ahead of the partisans.

It became apparent that the best way to persuade Reformers to support the Canadian Alliance was to demonstrate its saleability to the Canadian people. And so for the next six weeks that is what I did. I went on the road, covering thirty-five major centres and telling the Canadian Alliance story to every public audience, Reform gathering, and media conference that would listen. It was just like an election campaign, with the same opportunity to measure the results at the end of the day.

At each meeting, I would elaborate on one or two of the major policy commitments of the Canadian Alliance draft platform, such as the commitment to a 17 per cent single rate of income tax. This was particularly important to the general public, whose interest was not so much in the internal mechanics of creating the Canadian Alliance (conventions, constitutions, referendums, etc.) but in what the CA might do for them. In Calgary, I also issued a challenge to Joe Clark to participate in three debates, on our contention that it was the Canadian Alliance and not the Progressive Conservative Party of Canada that truly represented the principles and aspirations of twenty-first-century conservatives in Canada. The joke in

Calgary was that if Joe were arrested by the Liberals and charged with being a conservative, there wouldn't be enough evidence to convict him.

On March 9, 2000, it was THINK BIG again – this time a televised address to the Empire Club in Toronto. By now, Stockwell Day had made it known that he would be seeking the leadership of the Alliance if and when it was formed, and I welcomed him to the race, which was still "unofficial." The prospect of a good leadership contest was stimulating positive media interest again, but I still had to focus on convincing Reformers to support the CA concept.

In the midst of this referendum campaign I got another phone call from family that helped put all we were doing in perspective. I was at my Ottawa office on February 28 when son-in-law Howie called to say that Andrea had just given birth to Joshua Jacob Kroon, seven pounds, twelve ounces. Once again – thanks to God, healthy parents, and a good medical system – mother and baby were doing fine.

The "end of the day" for the second Reform referendum campaign came on March 25. Sandra and I were in Calgary, along with most of the rest of the team, where the mail-in ballots were being counted under the strict supervision of Returning Officer Jack Pike, Deputy Returning Officer Troy Tait, and independent auditors appointed for the vote. Judging from the response we had received on the campaign trail, my guesstimate was that the party membership would vote in favour of the Canadian Alliance proposal by at least two to one. But this would make it very close, as a two-thirds majority was required to carry any proposal affecting the Reform constitution, which this one did. There was really no way to be sure of the final outcome. The opposition to the Alliance concept by the minority had been vocal, and amplified by some of the media to the point where the press gallery assumed it would be nip and tuck, with everything on the line for me, as the leader who had pushed it this far.

On March 25, 2000, the room at Calgary's Metropolitan Conference Centre was packed with media and Reformers, and the atmosphere was tense with excitement. All the announced candidates for the Alliance leadership contest were there: Stockwell Day; Frank

Klees, the Harris Conservative from Ontario; Joe Peschisolido; and MP Keith Martin. Jocelyn Burgener, an Alberta Conservative MLA, and Peter White were in the chair, "O Canada" was sung, and the chairs reminded the crowd and the television audience that the question to be decided by the Reform referendum was: "Shall the Reform Party of Canada adopt the new Constitution and the Policy Declaration of the Canadian Reform Conservative Alliance – Yes or No?"

They also reminded the audience that, to succeed, the Referendum needed to pass three tests: (1) more than 25 per cent of the membership would have to cast ballots; (2) a majority affirmative vote would have to be achieved in at least six of the eleven provinces and combined territories; and (3) more than 66.7 per cent of the total ballots cast would have to be cast in the affirmative. With the explanation complete, I came to the podium with the vote tally sheet in my hand.

I told the audience that 48,838 members had cast ballots in the referendum, representing 66.5 per cent of the eligible members. The referendum had passed the first test!

I told them that a majority of members in every single province and in the Combined Territories had voted in support of the Canadian Alliance. The referendum had passed the second test!

Finally, the result that we had all been waiting for – the vote required to create a new party and the new government for a new century. Of the ballots cast, 91.9 per cent had been cast in the affirmative. It was an overwhelming vote of confidence by Reformers in the concept of the Canadian Alliance. The audience roared its approval.

■

Upon the completion of the March 25 referendum, the Reform Party of Canada ceased to exist and the Canadian Reform Conservative Alliance officially came into being. How did I feel about it? The same way I felt about the growth of our family through the birth of our children, the marriages of our daughters, and the births of our grandchildren. The family as it had once been was no more, but something new was being born, and the family was growing bigger and better.

On March 27, 2000, I resigned as leader of the Opposition to contest the leadership of the Canadian Alliance, vacating both the leader's office and Stornoway at the same time. There must have been a "last day" in the leader's office and a "last night" at Stornoway, but I neither remember nor recorded them.

How did I feel about it? What did it matter? It simply had to be done to give the United Alternative and Canadian Alliance concepts legitimacy. Commentators like Jason Moscovitz of the CBC would later repeat several times that if I had known what lay in store with respect to the leadership I would never have launched the UA process to begin with. But I had crossed that bridge more than three years ago. A rereading of my speech to the 1998 Reform assembly will show that I knew very well the risks that pursuing the UA created for my leadership, and that I chose to take them anyway. There will be no political progress in this country of any kind if so-called leaders always take the course of action least risky to themselves and their own careers.

On March 27, I advised the Speaker of the House of Commons, Gilbert Parent, that, effective immediately, all Reform members of Parliament should be recognized as members of the Canadian Alliance. Deborah Grey would serve as interim leader of the Opposition until a leader of the Canadian Alliance was chosen. That vote would be concluded on July 8, 2000. The leadership campaign was about to begin.

12

PM4PM

The day following the Reform membership vote endorsing the Canadian Alliance, my team met around the boardroom table at Cliff Fryers's offices in Calgary to initiate yet another campaign – my bid for the leadership of the Canadian Alliance.

No one at that table assumed that, since I'd been the chief architect of the Canadian Alliance, the leadership was mine for the taking. Rick Anderson, in his systematic way, sketched out the dangers and the challenges – the danger of complacency among my core supporters, particularly in caucus; the backlash against me among those who opposed the CA initiative; the attractiveness of the simple argument that a new party needed a new leader; the potential of other possible contenders to sign up large numbers of PCs or to mobilize interest-group support; and the "carnival queen" character of "one-member one-vote" leadership contests. It was Rick's assessment that, in order for me to win, we had to sell another 50,000 memberships – 5,000 memberships per week over a ten-week period – to people who would commit to voting for me. It was as simple and as stark as that. If we couldn't do that, despite all our past accomplishments and no matter what else we did well, I would lose.

With these sobering facts on the table, we then proceeded to hammer out a simple campaign strategy. Phase I involved putting together the campaign organization and funding, and calling the entire membership list and beyond to identify my supporters. In Phase II the entire emphasis would be on selling memberships and getting out the vote.

■

Our planning had included some rough estimates of the cost of the campaign in dollars and cents. But there were other costs to this whole exercise that remained largely unaddressed. These were the "human costs" that we had already incurred during the creation of the Canadian Alliance, and which the leadership campaign would now add to. To this could be added the cost of the "fatigue factor" among my own team members.

Since the exhausting federal election campaign in the spring of 1997, we had taken on the increased responsibilities of the Official Opposition in the House of Commons. In addition, we had organized two big Reform assemblies, each requiring a virtual campaign to secure Reform approval of the UA process, then two United Alternative conventions, each again involving extensive campaigning, and finally two nationwide party referendum campaigns, the last of which had taken me to thirty-five cities and towns across the country. Darrel Reid, my chief of staff, had also run as a candidate in the 1997 election, and as early as the fall of 1997 he had come to me requesting a brief leave of absence. He warned that we were "burning our people out" at an alarming rate, himself included. We took the prioritized "to-do list" for myself, the leader's office, the caucus officers, and the party and cut off the bottom third of the items. But it was like chopping off the tail of a chameleon, and within three months it had grown back, now even longer than before. Our House leader, Randy White, was going eighteen hours a day, and in the spring his health gave out (a gallbladder attack), putting him on the sidelines for weeks. And Darrel advised that he would be leaving in order to take a senior position with a respected national interest group, Focus on the Family.

All of the caucus officers, the senior officers of the party, and key staff people in Calgary and in Ottawa had been doing double duty for months – carrying out their normal duties associated with managing the affairs of the Official Opposition and running the Reform Party, while also handling the multiplicity of tasks thrust upon them by the UA process. Many were "running on nerves" and were stretched to the breaking point.

And what about the group around my leadership campaign table and their partners and families? Ian Todd had been keeping eighteen-hour days for three years, and since he and Evie had been married, they had been apart more days than they had been together. Ian now had two cellphones, one for incoming and the other for outgoing calls, and often he would be on both at the same time. Rick Anderson had been across the country as many times as I had over the last two years, attending innumerable meetings, writing innumerable memos, and taking more abuse than any of us, usually from people whose own contributions to the party paled in comparison to his own. Several weeks before, he had been taken to the hospital with a suspected heart attack. It turned out to be simple exhaustion, but it was a sobering warning to the entire team of the toll that constant campaigning can take on our health. All during this time, Rick's wife, Michelle, was looking after three active youngsters, running one of the largest riding stables in eastern Ontario, and still showing up time and time again at political gatherings to hear speeches she could have recited in her sleep. Cliff Fryers had set aside his lucrative law practice and was now holding down two unenviable jobs – chief of staff to the leader of the Opposition and Chairman of Everything Else related to the Reform Party and the UA process – while commuting weekly between two cities more than 2,900 kilometres apart. Cliff's wife, Leslie, was managing partner of another major Calgary law firm and staunchly supportive of everything Cliff and I were trying to do. Cliff and Leslie also had two young people at home. Over the last two years, Ellen Todd, Mona Helcermanes-Benge, and Jennifer Grover had organized, scripted, and publicized more "events," large and small, in all parts of the country, under every conceivable circumstance, than all the rock concert organizers in the country combined.

Similar things could be said about each MP, staff person, and volunteer around that leadership campaign table, and the one descriptive phrase that applied to everyone, including Sandra and myself, was that we were all "dog tired." And it was no longer the kind of fatigue that could be remedied by a good night's sleep or a week's holiday.

As invariably happens when a large organization is challenged to move in a new direction – even an organization committed to "reform" – there are those who disagree with or fear the proposed change and resist it every step of the way. These included Reform MPs like Dick Harris, Lee Morrison, Darrel Stinson, and Myron Thompson. There were other MPs who had become dysfunctional or unhappy within the existing organization and used the UA challenge as an excuse to vent their frustrations against their colleagues and the leadership, MPs like Jake Hoeppner, Allan Kerpan, and Jim Hart. Jake was consumed by his focus on Wheat Board reform to the exclusion of all other considerations; Allan hated travelling to Ottawa and refused to spend any time there; and Jim (along with several others) wanted to get back into the MP pension plan and blamed me for mishandling that issue. We also had former and present executive councillors who resisted the UA initiative for various reasons.

Then there were key people whose support I had lost "along the way." In January 2000, just before the second UA convention, Jason Kenney had come to visit me at Stornoway. He felt that I had given him neither the recognition nor the positions that his abilities and efforts warranted. This genuinely surprised me because I liked Jason, had encouraged his candidacy, and admired his values and abilities. I had given Jason – a new MP – a position in my shadow cabinet over the strenuous objections of my House leader, who felt he was too much of a lone wolf and too obsessed with social conservative issues. I had given him the position of Revenue critic so that he could promote tax reform – one of his primary interests – but Jason really wanted the Finance portfolio. I had also put Jason on the UA Steering Committee. I did what I could to reassure Jason, but, while he remained completely dedicated to the UA/CA effort, he became less and less supportive of me personally.

And then there was Randy White. Randy was like the girl in the nursery rhyme: "When she was good, she was very, very, good. But when she was bad, she was horrid." Randy had a prodigious capacity for work and for organization that I decided to take advantage of by making him a caucus officer, over the objections of those who saw only his other side. That other side made him resentful and unco-operative when things didn't go his way. It also compelled him to try to dominate every group of which he was a part, and when he couldn't dominate it, to "blow up" at the rest of the team over even minor issues. Randy especially resented Cliff Fryers, who simply couldn't be bullied, and Chuck Strahl, whose easygoing personality won him more support among caucus colleagues and staff than Randy's hard work did for him. Nevertheless, for several years Randy served me and the caucus well, and I had hoped that this relation-ship could be maintained and expanded once the CA was a reality. As the second Reform referendum neared, however, Randy remained equivocal about the CA, and as Cliff and I were spending more and more time out of Ottawa, I could tell that the rest of the caucus officers were increasingly reluctant to be "left alone with Randy." It was imperative that the House leader sing from the same song sheet as the leader, strategically, and it became apparent that Randy and I did not. It was also imperative that the caucus officers who would be in charge when I resigned to run for the Alliance leadership be completely dedicated to working together as a team during that delicate transition period. In late January 2000, there-fore, I called Randy into my office and told him I wanted to make a change. I invited him to become a senior critic with special respon-sibilities for several of the justice issues in which I knew he had a keen interest, until the referendum and leadership contest were over. But I didn't want him to continue as House leader during this critical period, when caucus unity and complete commitment to the CA were essential. Predictably, Randy "blew up," insisted that he was being "fired" and not just moved to another important position, stormed out of the room, and told the media that he had been pushed out because he did not support my leadership bid. All of this was also part of the "cost" – the human cost – of bringing the Canadian Alliance into being, and a significant portion of it was being paid by me in terms of potential support for my leadership bid.

For every high-profile member of our caucus or executive council who objected to the UA process, or took the occasion to express opposition to my leadership for whatever reason, how many rank-and-file members might be in the same boat? Media predictions that I was well ahead in the leadership contest were cold comfort: every major media prediction with respect to the UA up to this point had been wrong. I had to wonder, when I looked at my faithful team gathered around Cliff's boardroom table, did this group – and did Sandra and I – have enough strength left to conduct a full-blown national leadership campaign against fresh and well-endowed opponents, while keeping enough in reserve to fight the federal election campaign that would follow soon after? Only time would tell.

■

On Monday, March 27, Sandra and I formally launched my leadership campaign with a rousing kickoff at the Canadian Pacific Railway Pavilion in downtown Calgary. The pavilion replicates a nineteenth-century railway station, and our campaign train was ready to roll. Many of my friends, family, and campaign team, including the Calgary Southwest gang, were in attendance. The mood was relaxed and upbeat as I gave a short speech entitled "Ready for the Job." I positioned the leadership campaign as more than a contest to choose the first leader of the Alliance; it should be a campaign to choose someone qualified to be the next prime minister, a leader of change and a builder of principled coalitions. I presented my credentials and invited support for my "PM4PM" campaign.

I must confess that this type of speech was not easy for me to give. I was not used to asking directly for personal support and I felt awkward and presumptuous doing so. In the past, my approach to soliciting political support for myself – as any Reformer who has door-knocked with me in Calgary Southwest can attest – was oblique rather than direct. If you as a voter had a concern about taxes, health care, or unaccountable politicians, Reform had a solution to that concern, and I was the representative of Reform and that solution in my riding. It was a "soft sell" – much too soft in the opinion of many of my advisers, who insisted that I must make a much more direct appeal for support in the leadership contest.

On launch day, I also released the names of my 51-person National Campaign Committee, chaired by Cliff Fryers, with Phil von Finckenstein as my campaign manager. We also released the first 52 names on a "Friends of PM" roster, which we intended to augment weekly. This latter list grew to more than 650 names of friends dedicated to me personally – from Paul Arnold in Victoria, B.C., to Leonard Barron in St. John's, Newfoundland – and became one of my most treasured possessions. I also launched the *www.pm4pm.com* Web site before heading to Ottawa for the first-ever Canadian Alliance caucus meeting on Wednesday, March 29. On that same day I made my first Question Period appearance sitting beside the new Opposition leader, Deborah Grey. Deborah was as feisty and as steady as always. She would do just fine.

When we knew we would be vacating Stornoway, Sandra made arrangements with our friend Sam Okoro – my former driver and security man – to rent a room in his condo. Sam used to live with us at Stornoway; now we were living with him. On Thursday I opened our eastern PM4PM campaign headquarters in downtown Ottawa, where volunteers were already preparing to phone the 75,000-name Reform membership list. Sandra and I then flew to Toronto and drove to Burlington. To our mutual delight, we were doing this campaign together. We stopped at a Swiss Chalet for dinner, where a man came up to our table and asked if I would answer a question for him. "Certainly," I said, preparing to wax eloquent on some great issue of public policy. "As a politician, you must attend hundreds of political dinners where they always serve chicken because it's cheap," he said. "So what are you doing having a chicken dinner when you don't have to?"

That night, along with Frank Klees, the Ontario PC Cabinet minister who was expressing interest in the CA leadership, I participated in the first annual general meeting of a Canadian Alliance constituency association. The Burlington meeting elected both Reformers and Progressive Conservatives to its board of directors. These were grassroots people who had once battled each other in federal election campaigns but who now hoped to work together to defeat the Liberal incumbent. I was given a very kind introduction as "the architect of the Canadian Alliance" by former PC candidate Mike Kuegle, and both Frank and I received standing ovations. It was a great start to building the CA coalition at the riding level, and to the leadership race.

By Friday afternoon, Sandra and I were back in Calgary at the national office in time to file my nomination papers (signed by 300 paid-up members), along with the required leadership affidavit and a $25,000 deposit. This entitled us to receive the official Reform – now Canadian Alliance – membership list, which was immediately transmitted to our Ottawa office so that the volunteers could start phoning on the weekend. On Saturday, Sandra and I opened our western PM4PM campaign headquarters, under the supervision of the indefatigable Anne and Harold Davenport and Lenora Southgate.

To this point, the media coverage for the Alliance generally, and for myself in particular, had been positive and generous. Sandra and I were spending every spare moment on the telephones, recruiting key supporters and workers. In fact, the whole thrust of the initial weeks of the campaign was to nail down key supporters among the existing membership and our new allies, and to build up an organization extensive enough to sell the new memberships required to win.

■

On October 5, 1999, four months before the second UA convention, I had met with Tom Long in Toronto. He wanted me to meet Washington consultant Mike Murphy, for whom he had a very high regard. He also expressed the view that a strong, competitive leadership race was necessary to personalize the new party and make it exciting. He felt that if the race ended up as simply a 100-per cent acceptance of my initiatives, with myself ending up as the leader by acclamation, the public would assume this was simply Reform with a new name. A vigorous leadership contest was therefore essential, and if I won it, that would be to my advantage and that of the party. When I asked about potential candidates from the Harris camp, he acknowledged that as yet there were no visible candidates in sight.

The Ontario PCs were interested in the new party, but not yet energized by it.

Although some members of my own team worried about the risks of a wide-open, vigorous leadership contest, most agreed that it would certainly be good for the Alliance and would also provide an opportunity to "re-brand" me in the eyes of the Ontario electorate. Additional leadership candidates from the Reform camp wouldn't really contribute much to broadening the Alliance and would feed the rumours of internal dissent. What was really required were two or three strong candidates from the Conservatives. Stockwell Day was interested and was being encouraged to run by Ralph Klein. On March 5, 2000, I called Stockwell at his home and told him that I thought it would be good for the Alliance if he were to run. At this time, the outcome of the second Reform referendum was still not known, but Stockwell indicated that if the members voted "Yes" then his hat would be in the ring. He also said that he was approaching this decision prayerfully in consultation with Christian supporters.

Since both Stockwell and I were from Alberta and appealed to many of the same people, a contest between just the two of us would have limited national appeal. What the Alliance leadership race required above all else was a strong and credible candidate from the Harris Conservative camp in Ontario. I had told Tony Clement that his candidacy would be most beneficial and welcome, and that if he were to win it fair and square I would be pleased to be his Western field marshal. But with the re-election of the Harris government in June 1999, Tony felt he owed it to Mike and his electors to serve out the mandate, and that the timing simply wasn't right for a shift into federal politics.

Early in March, Frank Klees, the PC party whip at Queen's Park and minister without portfolio in the Harris government, publicly expressed interest in the CA leadership. I contacted Frank as well, and he appeared on stage as a possible leadership contender at a number of events that month. Frank apparently had the backing of a significant number of his colleagues at Queen's Park, and he was scheduled to make a formal announcement of his candidacy on April 6 at a news conference in Toronto. But just minutes before the news conference, concern over his ability to finance his campaign and a fear that strings were attached to the pledge from one of his chief backers caused Frank to withdraw. This change of mind caught his colleagues by surprise. The Alliance leadership contest was already underway, but still there was no credible candidate from Ontario.

At this point, Tom Long came under intense pressure to step up to the plate. He was well known to the Ontario Conservatives, having played a key role in reorganizing the party under Mike Harris, launching the Common Sense Revolution, and managing their two successful provincial election victories. He had also played a key role in the creation of the Canadian Alliance, and his speech to the second UA convention had impressed many delegates from across the country. In February, after the convention, Tom and his wife, Leslie, took a short vacation during which they assessed the pros and cons of Tom's letting his name stand. In Tom's judgment, the cons outweighed the pros, the strongest reason for not running being the fact that Leslie was expecting and due to deliver in mid-June – right at the peak of any leadership contest. Tom did, however, feel passionate about the need for an alternative to the Liberals. After the Klees withdrawal, Tony and Tom conferred again, and concluded that one of them had to run. By the next day, Tony and his wife, Lynne, had again decided that the time simply wasn't right for them, which left the decision solely up to Tom.

In the end, Tom told me afterwards, Leslie and he concluded that if they could make a difference, they should try. Or, as Leslie put it, "What are we saving ourselves for?" Tom rightly felt that his candidacy would be a bridge for Conservatives who were looking for a way to reconcile their past loyalties with their urge to "do something" to rid the country of the Chrétien Liberals. He also hoped to use the campaign to spark a national debate about committing Canada to the goal of vaulting over the United States and the rest of the world in terms of wealth creation and quality of life. He and Leslie made the decision to "go for it" on a quiet Sunday morning in early April. It was to be their last "quiet morning" for the next three months.

By mid-April the list of leadership candidates for the Canadian Alliance consisted of myself, Stockwell Day, Tom Long, Joe

Peschisolido, Keith Martin, and John Stachow. John was a single-issue candidate who wanted to use the CA leadership race as a platform to promote his views on monetary reform, and Joe later withdrew in support of my candidacy. Keith hoped to use the leadership race to challenge the CA to take a more definitive position on reforming health care.

■

Sandra and I spent much of April attending dozens of small coffee parties from one end of the country to the other. These were organized by existing members and their object was to sell more memberships, recruit more workers, and raise more funds for the PM4PM campaign.

During this period I virtually disappeared off the national radar screen while Stockwell and Tom were getting daily headlines, but I really had no other option. Unlike the other candidates, I had just come off a national tour in my campaign to win the second Reform referendum on the CA. The capacities of staff, volunteers, and available venues were stretched to the limit, and it was simply not feasible to do yet another tour of this kind now. Some of my supporters also wondered why I wasn't making major "policy announcements" and engaging in policy debate. But I was at a disadvantage on this front as well. Over the last year I had talked "policy" – Reform policy, Alliance policy, public policy – until I was blue in the face, and there was hardly any major policy issue on which I had not made major pronouncements. But when Stockwell or Tom made even a simple announcement of their support of some policy to which the CA was already committed, it was "newsworthy," marking the first time the national media had heard them speak on the subject in this new context.

So Sandra and I found ourselves on the coffee party circuit – three or four per day for weeks. A typical party would start with the host giving a brief, scripted, but low-key introduction. Then Sandra, who has always been better than me at these types of gatherings, would say a few words to put people at ease. I would give my "Ready for the Job" remarks, with a few modifications to adjust to the audience or the location or the issue of the day. Then the host would open it up for questions. While these parties were well attended and quite useful in terms of getting volunteers and donations for my campaign, in another respect they were disturbing. There was no real sense of urgency among my supporters. Many of them had been at party meetings, conventions, or town halls where I had spoken before. To them this was just another meeting. Many of them assumed that I would win the leadership of the Canadian Alliance because I had proposed and promoted it. Time and time again the questions raised were about policy (our members always ask me about policy) or organization or what was going on in Parliament, rarely about the leadership contest.

To try to bring these discussions into better focus, Sandra began to play the role of "friendly heckler," raising pointed questions about me and the other candidates that no one else would raise. I had to remind the guests repeatedly that leadership contests for political parties are carnival queen contests: "You can be ugly as sin, but if you sell enough tickets [memberships] you get to be the Carnival Queen. We have to sell tickets if I am going to win." People would laugh, and acknowledge that this was true, but the sense of urgency and commitment to selling memberships on a scale required for me to win was missing more often than not.

■

The chairman of my leadership campaign was my faithful friend and caucus colleague Diane Ablonczy. Diane and I had been on the same side of every campaign the party had undertaken since 1988. At this time she was also the Official Opposition critic for Human Resources Development, and she had been distinguishing herself in the House by her incisive and methodical questioning of HRDC minister Jane Stewart over the "billion-dollar boondoggle."

MPs John Cummins and Mike Scott served as liaisons between the campaign team and my caucus supporters, with John Reynolds and Jay Hill assisting in B.C., Monte Solberg in Alberta, and Inky Mark in Manitoba and Saskatchewan. Since Deborah Grey was now interim leader and leader of the Opposition, she had to remain neutral, but I knew that in her heart and her prayers she would be pulling for me.

When it came to recruiting support from among the caucus, I was again in a unique and delicate position. I had helped every one of these people get elected to Parliament, just as every one of them had helped me in some way at one time or another. I needed and wanted their support, but I also respected their freedom to make their own choices without fear of intimidation or recriminations. With the exception of those who were openly antagonistic, I talked to each MP in person or by phone during March and April and simply asked for their support. In the end, about thirty (half the caucus) declared in favour of my candidacy. About half of the rest wanted to remain neutral or uncommitted for the time being, and the remainder divided their support between Stockwell and Tom.

There is nothing like a leadership contest to test priorities, loyalties, and the true quality of the members of a political caucus, and the contest for the leadership of the Alliance was no exception. The reactions of some caucus members profoundly disappointed me. On the other hand, the reactions of others surprised and impressed me.

For example, I called up one MP to ask for his support and he made it clear that he would only support me if I supported his efforts to opt back into the MP pension plan. The leadership of the Alliance and the country was completely secondary, in his mind, to this personal consideration. Needless to say, I lost that MP's support. On the other hand, the vast majority of MPs I called, including some who had never been happy with the critic assignments I had given them, asked for nothing at all in return for their support. Needless to say, those MPs made me proud as punch.

In my seven years of leading the Reform caucus, I had never consciously used intimidation to get my way. In particular, I had never knowingly permitted the party machinery to be used to threaten the renomination of an MP as a way of compelling compliance with my wishes as leader. But once the Alliance leadership contest was underway, several MPs reported to me that they had received what could only be interpreted as "intimidation calls" from a fellow MP and organizers connected with Stockwell's campaign. The message was simple: "Come with us, or we'll use the church vote in your riding to take away your nomination." Whether Stockwell had authorized these calls I did not know, but the fact that they were being made caused me great consternation. Anyone who would use the "church vote" as a threat and a club, particularly against a fellow believer, discredits the Christian faith as much as he discredits his political cause. And any MP who is given a measure of authority, such as responsibility for caucus management or managing a campaign, and uses that authority to intimidate others disqualifies himself, in my opinion, from being given greater authority. If he uses even small measures of authority to intimidate, imagine what he'd do if given substantial authority such as that of a Cabinet minister? At the same time, any MP who would allow himself or herself to be intimidated by such threats is a disappointment to me. What would that MP do if faced with bigger and bolder threats from interest groups that are much better organized and financed than the "church vote"? In the Alliance leadership campaign several MPs whom I would never have suspected of being susceptible to this kind of intimidation succumbed. And others whom I might have suspected of being susceptible refused to be bullied. Sometimes you cannot tell what kind of metal people are made of until they are tested in the fire.

While I very much appreciated the support of my caucus colleagues, I experienced a similar reaction from them to that which I experienced at the coffee parties. They did not seem to realize that I was engaged in the fight of my career. I needed each of their campaign teams to sell 500 to 1,000 memberships in the next ten weeks. Some of course had never sold that many on their own behalf, let alone for somebody else. Others were so consumed with their parliamentary duties that they couldn't conceive of mounting such an effort on top of everything else they were doing. And others simply weren't engaged in the leadership contest. In the past I had always been fairly successful in motivating this group to undertake adventures on behalf of the party, but I was not nearly as adept at motivating them to campaign for me personally.

■

Seven weeks into the campaign, we held a full-blown campaign team meeting in the Lord Elgin Hotel in Ottawa. On several fronts there was good news. Our telephone canvass of the 75,000 Alliance members who held membership cards at the beginning of the race showed 32 per cent undecided, 21 per cent supporting Stockwell or Tom (with Stockwell leading Tom by almost two to one), and 47 per cent (or about 32,250 votes) supporting me.

And on the financial front, I was amazed and humbled by the level of support. We had set an initial budget of $500,000 and were already well on our way to exceeding that. The fundraising had been kick-started by several substantial contributions from people who had supported me for a long time, plus generous donations from newer supporters who appreciated the UA/CA effort. But particularly gratifying were the hundreds and hundreds of smaller donations from all over the country, many of them from people who, because of their financial circumstances, really shouldn't have been giving to a political campaign at all. Many of these contributions contained notes of encouragement or remembrances of past events and campaigns. These are some of my fondest and most treasured mementoes from the PM4PM campaign. Before the campaign began, I was acutely conscious that any cost overrun in the leadership campaign would be my responsibility alone. When I asked my son-in-law Howie Kroon to be my personal representative on the fundraising and comptrolling committee, I gave him only one instruction: the campaign *must not* finish in the red. Even though this meant saying no to many possible expenditures, especially in the last two weeks, Howie (and the whole team) did their duty, and ours was the only leadership candidate campaign that was debt-free when it was all over.

All of the foregoing good news, however, was overshadowed by one stark and disturbing fact: we were not selling new memberships at anywhere near the rate necessary to win. Although Tom had started late, he had a strong membership sales effort going among the Ontario provincial PCs, and he was investing heavily in the use of telemarketing to recruit new members. Even a 5 per cent return on 500,000 telemarketing calls could yield up to 25,000 memberships. Stockwell had not only all his provincial PC connections in

Alberta and other provinces but a very extensive recruiting drive going on through evangelical and conservative Catholic churches, various para-church organizations, and pro-life groups. Jason Kenney, Stockwell's campaign manager, was especially well connected to these groups. Both Stockwell and Tom, but especially Stockwell, had the potential to sell 25,000 to 40,000 memberships using these techniques. But to date our campaign, while doing a great job among the existing members, had sold only 1,600 new memberships. We had always assumed that the leadership vote would go to two ballots. For me to win on the second ballot, I would need to have more than 43 per cent of the total vote on the first ballot and a 10 per cent lead over the second-place finisher. There was no way we could get to these numbers at the rate we were going. The revised target for membership sales was set at 25,000. We would have to sell about 800 memberships a day over the next thirty days. So far, on our best day, we had sold only 275. The rest of the meeting was spent on ways and means of turning this around.

■

As far as we could tell, the membership sales effort being made by Stockwell's team was focused on two main groups: Progressive Conservatives who could be persuaded to join the Canadian Alliance and help pick its new leader; and a particular segment of the Christian community, namely, evangelical Protestants, conservative Catholics, and the pro-life organizations. I had my friends and associates among the PC crowd as well, but I was still regarded by many of them as the outsider who had wrecked their federal party. Our best bet on the PC front was that Tom and Stockwell would split this vote evenly among themselves. The bigger problem for me personally was how to deal with the approach Stockwell, Rod Love (Stockwell's campaign manager), and Jason were taking to the Christian community. Many of my religious convictions were similar to Stockwell's but I had always resisted campaigning directly for the "Christian vote" for reasons I have already explained. I invited people of Christian convictions to participate actively in the broader political arena and to make their influence felt there rather than carrying partisan politics into the spiritual arena, where its presence would ultimately do more harm than good. I was opposed to selling party memberships at religious services and to making "appearances" for political purposes at worship or prayer services. I was also opposed to plugging the membership lists of churches and para-church groups into our campaign's demon-dialer and mass-mailing systems or to inviting "prayer support" from Christian "prayer chains" and then using their telephone lists to solicit funds and votes.

Stockwell's team, however, appeared to have none of these reservations. Some of the more naive and overly zealous of Stockwell's supporters were even promoting him as God's personal choice ("the Lord's anointed," to use the Old Testament phrase) to lead the party and the country, and attacking anyone who opposed him as an agent of the forces of darkness. Because these believers felt they were guided by personal revelations and the spirit of God Himself, they were impervious to reason and evidence that might moderate, balance, or alter their inner convictions.

In response, we had three choices. One was to play the same game. The second choice was to maintain the position I had always taken – to appeal to Christian believers to involve themselves in the politics of their country and to support my campaign if they so chose, but not to make them the specific target of a "spiritualized" appeal. The third choice was to actually make an issue out of the approach Stockwell was taking and to challenge the Christian community to seriously assess the dangers it represented to its own unity and reputation. I drafted a letter gently making this case – suitable to be sent to Christian leaders, churches, and para-church groups across the country. Sandra and I consulted with Christian friends and advisers to discuss this option. In the end, we decided that to raise the issue – particularly in the midst of the leadership race – would divide the Christian community even further, and bewilder and appal the broader political community. I decided not to send the letter, and to respond to concerns on a private basis only. Some might argue in retrospect that this was a costly decision, but I am convinced it was the right thing to do, and that the short-run cost to myself and my leadership will prove to be nothing in comparison to the long-run cost to the Christian community of embracing Jason's and Stockwell's approach.

■

The one part of the campaign that brought the candidates into contact with each other was a series of all-candidate town halls and TV debates. The first of these was held in B.C. at the CA's first regional conference in that province, in Kamloops, on Saturday, April 8. This successful "trial run" was then followed by three official leadership town halls and three CBC-TV debates organized by the national council.

The town hall debate that stands out most in my memory was the last one in Montreal. By then we all had our "pitches" down pat, the audience was exuberant, and we were all relieved that it was the last debate. No surprises, but almost.

Having advanced the venue, Ian Todd was standing at the back of the hall watching the crowd come in when his eagle eye spied two men and a woman walking conspiratorially together. In a clear plastic handbag carried by the woman Ian thought he spotted a clown's nose. Suddenly it clicked – Les Entartistes, the "pie throwers" of Quebec, whose specialty was planting pies in the faces of politicians at the most awkward times. Ian knew from their Web site that I was on their list. In fact, whenever I visited Montreal I carried a fork in my suit coat pocket, so that if they got me the camera shot might show me prepared with fork in hand rather than "in shock and outrage," the reaction they were hoping to inspire.

Having detected the enemy, Ian organized our defence. He spotted the Entartistes' cameraman, who was also carrying a boom mike and posing as CBC crew. (Les Entartistes specialized in capturing their dastardly deeds on video for distribution to the networks.) Ian located Sam Okoro and told Sam not to let that particular cameraman get anywhere near "the boss." Kory Teneycke, Andrew Stec, and other loyal PM4PM supporters, under Ian's direction, then quietly and efficiently surrounded the pie-armed enemy, effectively preventing them from getting anywhere near me and stealing the show.

■

The essence of political competition is to shamelessly promote your own strengths and to ruthlessly expose the other candidates' weaknesses. But in the competition for the Alliance leadership, we were still in the process of building a coalition. So while we were competing to lead this political enterprise, we were also in a very real sense partners in building and expanding it. Coalition building requires you to draw attention to the strengths of the team and to minimize its weaknesses. The CA membership was very conscious of this and demanded a positive, high-road leadership race to ensure unity at the end.

Trying to compete and build a coalition at the same time created a peculiar, contradictory dynamic. It made the campaign rhetoric, particularly at the debates, surreal, characterized by shadow boxing and the pulling of punches rather than by honest and hard-hitting debate aimed at bringing to light the real strengths and weaknesses of each contestant. The success of the whole had to take precedence, or at least appear to take precedence, over individual capabilities and ambitions, giving rise to an impression among the voting members that the leadership was a sort of three-for-one sale. No matter which candidate they picked, the others would be there to help, so the differences between the candidates weren't that important. Stockwell's inexperience on the national stage would be compensated for by my experience. My awkwardness on television would be compensated for by Stockwell's camera appeal. The potential unattractiveness of the Alberta candidates to Ontario would be compensated for by Tom's Ontario credentials. Tom's unfamiliarity with the West would be compensated for by Western allies like Stockwell and myself. If it's "one for all and all for one," does it really matter which of the Three Musketeers leads the charge?

Tom and I were much more conscious of this dimension of the leadership contest than Stockwell, because we had been much more deeply involved in the creation of the Alliance, particularly in

Ontario. This had a distinct impact on how we conducted our campaigns and on the eventual outcome.

■

As the competition became more intense, the behind-the-scenes manoeuvring and "below the radar screen" scuttlebutt became more and more personal and negative. Stockwell's camp, in particular, now included hundreds of people who had never been involved in federal politics before, or who had been involved only through pro-life interest groups, few of which had gone through the lengthy coalition-building exercise that brought the Canadian Alliance into being. They were more willing to say and do things that, while advantageous to Stockwell in the short run, might permanently alienate people whose continued support of the Alliance was critical to its long-term success. While Stockwell publicly maintained that he was pursuing an "agenda of respect," I was increasingly depicted as a unilingual has-been who couldn't win Ontario and a "closet Christian" who hid his light under a bushel. But the more damaging attacks, from the standpoint of the long-run health of the Alliance and its capacity to break through in Ontario, were directed towards Tom Long. He was increasingly depicted as a Bay Street boy and Johnny-come-lately who was suspect on the social conservative issues.

Early in May, the Campaign Life Coalition published on its Web site a critique of the Canadian Alliance leadership candidates, including a piece penned by the president of "Families for Day." It criticized Tom Long for having several prominent homosexuals on his campaign team, naming names and exposing them to media inquiries and personal abuse. What made the attack particularly offensive was its focus on *persons* rather than their positions or actions. When Stockwell was confronted with this attack he personally distanced himself from it. But he appeared unconcerned about the damage done to the reputations of individuals or the Alliance, and he refused to take responsibility for what one of his chief allies was doing on his behalf. This refusal to accept responsibility for wrongdoing was the tip of the iceberg, the magnitude of which would become apparent only with the passage of time. Stockwell denied that he held any personal prejudice towards gay people, and when he later became leader of the Alliance he included at least one gay employee on his personal staff. This was then pointed to as evidence of Stockwell's tolerance, whereas in Tom's case it was "exposed" as evidence that he was in league with the devil. The hypocrisy of all this – which became evident only after the leadership race was over – did more to damage Stockwell's "Christian testimony" among those who knew the facts than any other single act of the campaign.

Less than ten days before the first ballot, yet another incident occurred that further damaged the credibility of the Alliance leadership contest and Tom Long's campaign in particular. Tom had assigned the recruitment of Quebec supporters for his campaign to Conservative organizers in that province. He had established quality-control guidelines as to how this was to be done and assumed that they were being followed. But after the deadline for selling memberships had closed, someone leaked the information to the media that there had been a huge upsurge in Quebec memberships in places as remote as the Gaspé, where *L'Alliance Canadienne*, let alone the name Tom Long, were hardly household words. For a brief moment this was welcomed as good news. But subsequent inquiries by the media and the national office disclosed that many of these "new members" had been signed up and paid for without their knowledge or consent. Opponents of the Alliance were quick to scream that the Alliance itself was practising the "old politics" that it so loudly decried, and Tom's campaign was dealt a fatal blow among members for whom the integrity of the democratic process was everything.

The Gaspé incident revealed the vulnerability of a new political party organized as hastily as the Alliance to skulduggery of this type, particularly in areas where we were not properly organized on the ground. But in retrospect, the Gaspé incident also revealed something else that I came to truly appreciate only after the campaign was over. Although Tom himself had nothing to do with the actual incident, other than to authorize PC organizers to recruit on his behalf, he accepted full responsibility for what had happened and for the actions of his Quebec allies and subordinates. He accepted responsibility in the media rather than attempting to distance himself or hiding behind his campaign manager. He apologized to the party and its members, and he called each of his fellow candidates – myself included – and apologized to us. His acceptance of responsibility was total, not hedged with conditions or disclaimers. It was the difference between Tom's handling of the Gaspé incident and Stockwell's handling of the gay attack that told me that Tom would make the more responsible and conscientious leader of the Alliance, if one had to choose between the two.

At the same time, my own campaign team was receiving more disturbing information on Stockwell, mainly from observers and participants in Alberta provincial politics. The problem was deciding what to do with this information, without descending into the mudslinging game to which politicians in a hotly contested election are so easily enticed.

The federal Liberals, with the help of the provincial Liberal Opposition Office in Edmonton, were beginning to compile a file on Stockwell, going right back to his days as the principal of a Christian school in central Alberta and including all his pronouncements and activities as a provincial MLA and minister. The rumour was that it would contain dozens of juicy items to be dragged out at the appropriate time during any federal election campaign should Stockwell become the Alliance leader. Of course, the Liberals had done the same thing with me years before. But the difference now was that most of their ammunition on me had been fired and was no longer newsworthy, whereas Stockwell represented a shiny new target.

The news that disturbed me even more was a story drifting around the Edmonton legal community that a lawsuit in which Stockwell was engaged with Lorne Goddard, a Red Deer lawyer, was a "scandal in the making" because of the nature of the dispute and the amount of taxpayers' money that was being spent on Stockwell's defence. The rumour in political circles in Edmonton (and it appeared inconceivable that the national media had not yet picked this up) was that Ralph Klein had two reasons for backing Stockwell as the leader of the Alliance, neither of which had anything to do with uniting the right or the welfare of the country. Ralph was well aware of Stockwell's lawsuit and did not want it blowing up during the provincial election that he hoped to call later that year. If by then Stockwell had moved on to the federal scene with a different political party, it would be easier to distance the provincial Tories from the fallout. In addition, if in the future Ralph himself wanted to move away from provincial politics, he did not want Stockwell (or any social conservative) to be in a position to become the next leader of the Alberta Conservatives and premier of the province. One sure way to accomplish this was again to encourage Stockwell's move to the federal scene. To some observers and participants in Alberta provincial politics, this was the only way to explain how Ralph could go to the first UA convention, solemnly warn the delegates against pushing the social conservative agenda to excess, and then come out in support of the one Alliance leadership candidate most likely to do so. It was also the only way to rationalize the actions of Rod Love, the premier's right-hand man. Rod's antipathy for the social conservatives among Reformers and Conservatives was well known, yet here he was running Stockwell's leadership campaign, a principal component of which involved mobilizing the church vote. The prediction was that Rod would get Stockwell safely deposited in Ottawa, 2,800 kilometres from Edmonton, and then drop him like a hot potato (which is exactly what happened).

All of this should have come out in the leadership contest. There should have been an opportunity to separate fact from rumour and truth from lies. Stockwell should have been given an opportunity to address in the light what was being whispered in the shadows. Alliance members should have been given an opportunity to see how Stockwell (and other candidates) handled the stuff of which Liberal smear campaigns are made. But how could this come about? If I, or any of the other candidates, tried to raise these issues, it would be seen as self-serving mud-slinging, in complete contradiction to the coalition-building exercise to which we were all committed and the high road we had all pledged to walk.

Strategists like Rick Anderson and pollsters like André Turcotte, who could see the Alliance being blindsided by Stockwell's baggage during a federal election if it wasn't dealt with in advance, attempted to raise this subject in the last few weeks of the campaign. But because they were associated with my leadership, they were not only ignored but vilified for doing so.

■

So, in this kind of campaign, how can the truth – good and bad – about a candidate be brought out into the open so as to assist the members to make an informed choice? My own view is that participants in the political process – party members, political executives, candidates, financial contributors, voters, and even the media – must give much more attention to exercising what the business and professional worlds call "due diligence." This means making an actual effort to get the facts, cross-check the facts, and assess the facts concerning the individual candidates *before* making a decision. In other words, perform the "due diligence" on candidates for political office and their claims that any prudent employer would automatically do before hiring any individual for a responsible position. Perhaps the political marketplace requires a Due Diligence Bureau to perform the same function as the Better Business Bureau.

Were you thinking of supporting or opposing me in the Alliance leadership contest based on whether I would be able to carry Ontario? There are unaligned pollsters who have examined that question in detail, and your due diligence might include consulting their findings. Is such-and-such a rumour true, half-true, or false? Check it out – go to the source. Were you thinking of supporting or opposing Tom Long on the basis of whether he is a bona fide Common Sense Revolutionary or a Bay Street boy? Ask the people he worked with for years in federal and Ontario provincial politics. Were you thinking of supporting Stockwell mainly because he was part of a provincial Progressive Conservative government and you are a provincial Conservative in Manitoba or Ontario? Well then, make a phone call to several of his caucus colleagues in Alberta – the people who know him best – to get their assessment of his strengths and weakness.

Two years later, with the Alliance in shambles, these same people would lament, "But we didn't know he believed this," or, "We didn't know he might do that . . ." And how is it that they didn't know?

Due diligence was absent. And let none of us think that we can let journalists or commentators exercise our due diligence for us. The newspapers and television networks play a vitally important role in our political system, but they also have their own agendas and their own competitive interests and battles to fight. The Toronto newspaper wars, for example, which were going on during the Alliance leadership contest, had a direct effect on the volume and slant of the coverage given to our race. The *National Post* was championing the Alliance and desperately wanted a credible Ontario candidate. When he appeared in the form of Tom Long, the instant and extensive national coverage given to his candidacy caused his campaign to spiral upward farther and faster than anyone had expected. But too fast. When expectations are raised too high too quickly, disillusionment can easily follow. With Tom seen as "the *Post's* candidate," the *Globe and Mail*, the *Toronto Star*, and the *Toronto Sun* naturally set out to "put him in his place." And when Tom's candidacy got into trouble over the Gaspé incident, the attacks of the opposing papers and the scrambling of the *Post* to distance itself from Tom accelerated the downward momentum. Most often the media are players in the game, and rarely the dispassionate and objective analysts that the public sometimes assumes them to be. "Due diligence," therefore, must include more than collecting newspaper clippings or channel-surfing. "Due diligence" also means subjecting media stories about various candidates to rigorous analysis. The missing ingredient in the 2000 Alliance leadership race was "due diligence," and we all paid a price for its absence.

■

During the last few weeks of the campaign, the exchanges between Stockwell's camp and mine became more pointed, although the underlying issues at stake never got a proper airing in front of the tens of thousands of Alliance members who would soon be voting. To the charge that Ontario wouldn't vote for me, we argued that I had won almost two million votes in Ontario in the last two elections, more than on the Prairies, and more than the Conservatives and NDP. The real problem in Ontario was vote-splitting, and the creation of the Alliance addressed that. We also distributed an Angus Reid poll showing that when Ontario voters were asked who they would prefer to lead the Alliance, I led Stockwell two to one. Ontario voters are suspicious of novelty, preferring the devil they know to the devil they don't know. To the charge that I was "attacking" or allowing others to attack Stockwell's social conservative views, our answer was no, I had attacked no one. But it was imperative that Stockwell demonstrate his capacity to handle such issues as abortion, gay rights, family values, and the use of referendums in moral decision making *on the national stage*. So far, Stockwell had not done so, and it was important that he do it *before* rather than *during* a federal election campaign. And to the oft-repeated mantra that "a new party needs a new leader," I countered that what a new party like the Alliance needed above all was an *experienced* leader. An old party can get away with a new leader because the public assumes there is experience in the party. But a new party like the Alliance – which, unlike Reform when it started out, would be claiming that it had the capacity to form the next government – needed an experienced leader, particularly if it wanted to crack Ontario. Nor was experience in Alberta provincial politics sufficient to cope with the demands of national politics. The national stage was far bigger and more diverse than any provincial stage. The Parliament of Canada was a very different chamber than the Alberta legislature. The national press gallery was a much more aggressive animal than the docile Alberta press gallery. And the federal Liberal Party was a powerful, arrogant, national party with all the resources of the Government of Canada at its command. Fighting it was a very different proposition from competing with the weak and ineffective opposition parties in Alberta. Stockwell was needed and wanted on the Alliance team, where he would *get* national experience. But he was not yet ready to lead it.

As voting day, Saturday, June 24, drew closer, the pace of telephoning by volunteers and demon-dialing to identified supporters on our membership lists reached frantic levels at the Ottawa and Calgary campaign headquarters and call centres. By now, all of our children, with the exception of Mary Joy in New York, were heavily involved in the PM4PM campaign. David, our youngest son, put his

salesmanship skills to work at the Calgary office, where the tele-
phoners would give him the "undecided but movable" calls to
handle. Andrea and Howie were focused on ensuring that the campaign finished in the black. Nate was also working the phones in
Calgary, while Avryll and John did what they could to boost support
in the Peace country. Mary Joy, though absent, offered moral
support and encouragement by phone and e-mail.

The night before voting day, the party had organized one last
leadership event at the Telus Convention Centre in Calgary. The
vote to be conducted the next day would be a one-member, one-
vote affair in which members would vote either at polling stations
established in each riding or by telephone in the more sparsely pop-
ulated ridings. By now, the Canadian Alliance membership was
around 200,000, making this the largest political leadership vote
ever conducted in Canada. While a one-member, one-vote election
is more democratic than a few thousand delegates electing the
leader at a delegate convention, such a convention – with its
hoopla, last-minute speeches, and floor demonstrations – makes
much better television. The Alliance hoped to get the benefit of
both approaches by holding this convention-style event the night
before the actual vote.

The room was jumping with sign-waving supporters, packed with
media, and tense with excitement – exactly the kind of venue that
gets my democratic juices flowing. Each of us was given twenty-five
minutes for an introduction, demonstration, and speech – however
we wanted to use the time.

Tom spoke first, his content strong and substantive but his delivery subdued. Stockwell spoke next, preceded by a vigorous demonstration, but his energy level was surprisingly low and the content
uninspiring. When it was my turn, I sensed that the crowd wanted
a "barn burner" and I did everything in my power to give it to them
under the headings of "Think Hard," "Think Ahead," and "Think
Big." As part of our demonstration, my supporters carried into the
room the original 2.5-metre-high "THINK BIG" letters from my
first Think Big appeal at the Ottawa Convention Centre five
months before. The theme, the speech, and the demonstration res-
onated perfectly with the mood of the audience, and the media gave

me the highest score for the evening's performance. Of course, that score would mean little or nothing in the next day's voting, but it greatly boosted the morale of our troops.

My own fondest recollection of that evening was not my own speech or the reaction to it, but the short speech preceding it given by my introducer, Donna Kline. Donna is the wife of our pollster, André Turcotte, and the story of how this talented and dedicated couple – he from Quebec and she from Ontario – came to be at the leadership vote for the Canadian Alliance in downtown Calgary was itself an inspiration to anyone interested in assembling a principled coalition of Canadians.

André had been a student in Blair Williams's political science class at Concordia University and had been introduced to Reform through Rick Anderson. I first remember meeting him in 1994 during the taping of an electronic town hall meeting when we were looking for guests, in particular a bilingual federalist from Quebec. By then André was a pollster with Pollara in Toronto, but beginning to branch out on his own. I retained him to do some polling and focus testing for Reform. His first survey identified all the negative perceptions of myself and Reform that we didn't want to hear about, and our executive council wanted to fire him. But I admired his willingness to tell us what we needed to hear as distinct from what we wanted to hear, and I was impressed by his sensitivity to public opinion and political trends in both Quebec and English Canada.

He became our official party pollster, as well as a trusted friend, but Sandra and I had only recently come to know his wife, Donna. She was a young professional, a mother of two, born in Scotland but raised in Ontario, and initially quite skeptical about both myself and Reform. At the same time, she was precisely the type of person that the Canadian Alliance and its leader had to reach out to in order to succeed, and her willingness to endorse me as the leadership candidate best qualified to win Ontario was something special.

Late in the afternoon of Saturday, June 24, my family and all of the campaign team members who were in the West (half the crew were working the Get Out The Vote [GOTV] machinery from the Ottawa office and had remained there) assembled at the Hyatt

Hotel adjacent to the Telus Convention Centre in downtown Calgary, where the voting results would be announced. There had been all sorts of glitches with the telephone voting, and the usual logistical problems of establishing and operating polling stations all across the country. Our campaign pulled volunteers off our own GOTV effort to help with the election-day workload of the national office. But, by and large, the national office staff and volunteers did an amazing job organizing a national democratic leadership vote across the second largest country on the face of the earth.

Finally the votes were counted, and the results announced to the assembled crowd in the Convention Centre confirmed our greatest fears. The first-ballot standings were 44 per cent for Stockwell (53,249 votes out of 120,557 valid ballots cast), 36 per cent for me, 18 per cent for Tom, and less than 2 per cent for Keith Martin and John Stachow.

Jason, Rod, and Stockwell had run a very effective campaign, particularly in terms of new membership sales and getting those votes out. For this they deserved full marks. But what devastated our team was the fact that only 60 per cent of the total Alliance membership had voted. A large proportion of the non-voters were my supporters, who, despite all our urgings and dire warnings, apparently assumed that the outcome was a foregone conclusion. And instead of Stockwell and Tom more or less evenly dividing the non-Manning vote between them, Stockwell led Tom by more than two to one. The Gaspé affair was as disastrous to our campaign as it had been to Tom's. As Peter White later observed: "The Manning camp was stunned, the Day camp exultant, and the Long camp, having seen the writing on the wall, stoic in defeat."*

The chairman announced that, in accordance with the election rules, since no candidate had received a 50 per cent plus one majority, Tom, Keith, and John would be dropped from the ballot and a second vote would be taken between Stockwell and myself, two weeks hence on July 8, 2000. "Profoundly disappointed" was probably the best way to describe my own reaction, that of my family, and

---

* Peter G. White and Adam Daifallah, *Gritlock: Are the Liberals in Forever?* (Toronto: Canadian Political Bookshelf, 2001), p. 196.

the mood of my campaign team, but we still had a decision to make concerning a second-ballot campaign.

The next morning, Sandra and I and key members of my campaign team met for breakfast. Rick and Cliff had obviously been talking, and Rick began by saying that the chances of recovering on the second ballot were virtually nil, and therefore I should seriously consider withdrawing immediately. While I agreed that the contest had in all likelihood been lost, I told the group I felt we should continue. First, the CA resolution establishing the leadership contest had called for balloting to continue until one candidate had a 50 per cent plus one majority. It was important as a precedent to honour the terms of convention resolutions to the letter, and I felt we should do so. Second, I didn't like the idea of "quitting," even if the chances of winning were very remote. How many times during our election campaigns had I arrived at the campaign headquarters of some Reform candidate who had just taken a poll showing that he or she was running a distant second with time running out? What did we do in those circumstances? Did we sympathize with the downcast candidate and agree that there was little point in carrying on? No, we would urge the candidate to finish the race and hold out that last straw to which all losing campaigns cling, that "something might turn up" to turn things around. Third, we all knew that, it being summer with virtually nothing else exciting going on in Ottawa, another two weeks of campaigning would garner for the Alliance and the eventual winner millions of dollars of free media coverage. It would be in the interests of the Alliance that the leadership campaign continue for another two weeks. I had only one stipulation, and that was that we not get into a frantic spending spree during the next two weeks that would put our campaign into debt. Cliff sensed that my mind was pretty well made up on the subject. He would call the campaign crew in Ottawa and tell them my decision, and we turned our minds to planning the next two weeks.

There is nothing more draining than completing a losing campaign. We met with Tom Long, whose disappointment was as deep as ours and compounded by a large campaign debt that Tom would now have to pay off by his own efforts. Tom and I had grown closer throughout the campaign, and he generously agreed to support me on the second ballot. Key members of his campaign team – Sandra Buckler, Mark Spiro, Jeff Naphin, Michael Fraser, Stephen Waters, Rachael Barkey, and Andrew Wallace – would be driving over to my Ottawa campaign headquarters the next week to join forces with my crew. We also met with Tom's consultant friend Mike Murphy, who had come up from Washington for the first-ballot vote. Mike's advice was to organize a high-profile, last-minute "blitz of the country," featuring Tom and me campaigning together in Ontario and the West and demonstrating the type of teamwork that the Alliance required at the highest level to succeed. Ian and Ellen went away to organize this tour, while I met with my Calgary campaign crew to gear them up for one more frantic round of demon-dialing and call-centre activity. Everyone was down, but we were also determined to see this through to the end.

The next two weeks are just a blur in Sandra's and my memories. Ian had organized yet another tour. What I didn't know at the time was that his wife, Evie, was very ill – her illness obviously stress related – and the strain on Ian of trying to care for her and me at the same time was almost unbearable. Rick and Sandra Buckler organized a launch event at the Royal York in Toronto on June 29 where Tom would announce his support of my candidacy. John Reynolds flew in on the red-eye from Vancouver to chair the meeting, and Belinda Stronach – who had been extremely supportive throughout – gave a substantive introduction in which she clearly explained why she wanted the Alliance and my candidacy to succeed. Tom gave a short but impressive presentation, introducing me as the leadership candidate who could win Ontario.

The CBC organized one last televised debate between Stockwell and me, which took place at the Centrepointe Theatre in Nepean on July 5. It had the largest television audience of any of the Alliance leadership debates, confirming my view that continuing the leadership race would increase the Alliance's national exposure. Prior to the debate, at which nothing new was really said, there had been a discussion among my people as to whether I should "take the gloves off" to expose Stockwell's potential liabilities as a national leader, and the intimidation tactics that were now being used even more aggressively to get more of the caucus to fall into line behind his campaign. One such intimidation threat to an MP had actually been put into a letter by one of Stockwell's key workers (a very foolish thing to do), and it would provide the ammunition for the argument that under Stockwell's leadership, if these tactics were used, the Alliance caucus would be in danger of splitting. At this late stage, however, I thought that such an approach would make little difference to the outcome of the leadership contest and only lead to lasting bitterness within the Alliance after it was over. I had that letter in my suit coat pocket during that last debate, but I never used it.

For the last few days of the leadership contest, Ian had lined up two helicopters for our Ontario blitz and two helicopters for an Alberta blitz. One would be used by Tom and me, accompanied by Ian and Sandra Buckler. The other would be used by the media. The media like helicopter rides, and we had no problem getting takers. Half the helicopter time had been donated, which made the cost manageable. Tom and I had fun those last few days – I could imagine what it would be like barnstorming Ontario and the West with him in a federal election campaign. We worked well together. On this trip, which we called the Whirl-Win Tour, Tom would introduce me as the best candidate, in his judgment, to lead the Alliance. And, speaking as someone who had managed two successful provincial election campaigns in Ontario, he stated his conviction that with the Alliance I could break through in that province.

There was no time to organize big events or crowds, so the venues were hastily organized get-togethers at the acreages or farms of key supporters – preferably in the country or the suburbs or near airfields, so the helicopters could get in and out: Jack Hurst's acreage in Newmarket, Eddie and Lianne Long's place in Terra Cotta, the Georgian Flight Academy in Barrie. All the time we were on this mini-tour, my exhausted campaign crews in Ottawa and Calgary, beefed up by the presence of many of Tom's volunteers, were re-calling the membership list, focusing on known supporters of Tom and myself and those who had neglected to vote in the first round. Tom, Sandra, Ian, and I flew to Calgary, where the Western-based choppers met us and our small media entourage. Then it was off to Medicine Hat where Monte and Deb Solberg had organized a last-minute event. We were flying over country I knew like the back of my hand, and I gave Tom and Sandra Buckler the condensed version of the history of the Old West. The small crowds we were meeting now were subdued. They were there out of loyalty, not out of any illusion that the campaign was going our way. There were no daily briefings now from Ottawa or Calgary. I was getting very little information about anything. This is a characteristic of a losing campaign on its last legs, when your campaign crew doesn't have the heart to tell you that the hoped-for miracle isn't happening. At the Edmonton Municipal Airport, the people in the crowd were almost all familiar to me. All our relatives were there – the Carters, the Stuffcos, the Harrisons – as well as a few MPs and many old friends.

But the event I remember the best on that last-ditch tour was flying into Drumheller on that last afternoon, on the edge of the Alberta badlands. The badlands of Alberta are a deep gash of strange rock formations cutting across the prairie and appearing out of nowhere when approached from the ground. Tom and Sandra had not seen them before, and from the air the view is spectacular. We were riding in a black, streamlined chopper, with red decals, that looked like something out of the "Air Wolf" TV series. We swooped in on a small crowd hastily assembled by our PM4PM team in the Crowfoot constituency. Front and centre was Doug Fawcett, long-time president of our Crowfoot riding association, who had been with us from the very beginning. He had worked his heart out for me, for Reform, for the Alliance, and for his old friend Jack Ramsay. In the early days, he and Jack had been charged with mischief for dropping Reform pamphlets on small towns in the riding out of an airplane, but now Jack was facing a much more serious charge – an accusation of attempted rape from an incident thirty years before, when Jack had been with the RCMP. Jack's career, and all he and Doug had worked for, appeared to be in tatters, and now, on top of that disappointment, it looked like Doug would be on the losing side of the CA leadership race. Nevertheless, there he was. Smiling as always, leading the cheering, trying to rally the troops for one last stand. We landed, spoke briefly, and left. The pilot circled low one last time over the crowd. Doug was again cheering frantically, waving goodbye.

On Saturday, July 8, the volunteer-manned polling stations for the CA leadership vote opened and closed at staggered times across the country. The tele-voting system was in operation from noon on July 6 to the close of voting at 5:00 p.m. MDT on July 8. This time the national office expected fewer problems than on the first ballot. By now Tom and I were back in Ontario. We had chartered a campaign bus and, with Ian as wagon-master and with our closest friends on board, we made a short visit to various polling stations around Toronto. We then met together again in a room in the Regal Constellation Hotel, where the results of the second ballot would be announced to a crowd gathered in the Constellation Ballroom. Once again, the family had gathered round, and most of the campaign crew from Ottawa had made the trip to Toronto. Tom and a number of his key people were there as well. The ballroom downstairs was crawling with media. They were as anxious to capture the pathos of my loss as they were to capture the excitement of Stockwell's victory.

Shortly after 9:00 p.m. we got the results from Calgary. There had been no miracle. The final totals gave Stockwell Day 64 per cent of the 118,487 votes cast, and me 36 per cent. For me, it was over; for Stockwell, it was just beginning.

Sandra and I made our way down to the ballroom. Each network had a camera on Stockwell and Val and one on me and Sandra. The announcement was made. Wild cheers from Stockwell's crowd; embarrassed silence from ours. I had prepared a short speech for the occasion, hastily written by hand on both sides of a single sheet of paper. It was time to give it.

In Canadian politics, few of us have had the opportunity to participate in the creation of one new political party, let alone two. Sandra and I want to thank all of you for the honour and privilege of doing that.

I am a reformer and a conservative, but above all a democrat. All of us are democrats, and election contests always test our faith in democracy. It is easy to believe in democracy when the vote goes your own way. But the real test of our commitment to democracy is our acceptance of the results when the vote goes the other way.

Tonight I accept the judgment of the members of the Canadian Alliance. I congratulate our new leader Stockwell Day and move that the decision of our members be made unanimous. To Stockwell and Val, Sandra and I offer you our best wishes, our support, and our prayers that you will be guided and sustained in your new responsibilities.

And now for a few thank-yous. Before I thank anyone I want to thank God and my Saviour Jesus Christ for the opportunity of serving you all. To Sandra and my family, to my campaign team and supporters, to my fellow candidates, especially Tom Long, thank you.

And to Ian Todd, my friend and tireless associate, without whose daily – even hourly – help I could not have coped with the challenges of the last eight years – thank you.

I concluded with an appeal for unity and then was whisked away for a few brief interviews with the main TV networks. Sandra and I later made our way slowly out of the hall and upstairs, where campaign team members and supporters were gathering to commiserate with each other and with us. The night is still just a blur in my memory. I felt I had let these people down, but they felt that they had let me down. Sandra carried the ball on the thank-yous because now I really didn't know how to say thank-you. At dozens of planning meetings and post-campaign functions over the years I had tried again and again to find the words to thank these people who had given so much of themselves, their time, their money, their families, and their lives to me and to Reform, and now to the Alliance. The words always seemed so totally inadequate. But that hadn't bothered me much because I knew in my heart how I was really going to thank them. I would thank them by making their political dreams come true, by delivering to them what they really wanted – the New Canada that we had pursued together for so long. But now, there was no way I could deliver that ultimate thank-you to them.

Neither Sandra nor I wanted the evening to descend into despondency. This was a time to mourn, but it was also a time to recognize the deep and abiding friendships that our many campaigns together had forged, and to celebrate our accomplishments together. About the transition from Reform to the Canadian Alliance I remarked that "the operation was a success, even though the doctor died." This led to more outlandish comments and observations, and much laughter amid the tears. And the evening ended with a surprise. Ken

Kalopsis and Nancy Branscombe, whom Reform and the Alliance campaign had brought together, announced the formation of a new and better alliance: they intended to marry. The room erupted with cheers and best wishes all around. I had begun and ended many a reform-oriented speech with the observation that in life and in politics "something old is always dying but something new is being born." This was as true that evening as it had ever been before.

■

The following day, after another brief session with Cliff and Rick, Sandra and I returned to Ottawa. I was still a member of Parliament, and I had told the Alliance membership that I would run in the next election, whether I won the leadership or not. But at this point, all Sandra and I wanted to do was to escape.

Rick – always helpful, always supportive, always looking ahead – handed me a memo, which I still have, entitled "Options." It listed all the things I could do with my newfound time, while still playing a modest and supportive role in Parliament and the caucus – from recreation, to family time, to writing a book, to expanding my intellectual horizons. For the benefit of those misguided souls who believe that from the moment I lost the leadership people like Rick were plotting a "comeback" on my behalf, there is not a word in that memo on that subject. There never was, nor is there now, any plot on the part of the PM4PM team to destabilize the new leadership of the Canadian Alliance or seek to regain the Alliance leadership for me or anyone else by such tactics.

Back in Ottawa, Sandra and I dropped in unannounced at our campaign headquarters. How many people had spent literally hundreds of hours in this place over the last three months? We ordered pizza, sat on the floor, and had a time of tears and laughter with the staff and volunteers who were doing the cleanup. Some of Tom's people were still there, to the bitter end. I attended the special Alliance caucus on July 12 and a get-together for staff and caucus in the Confederation Room of the West Block to welcome the new leader. I was asked to speak and, after thanking them all for the past privilege of being their leader, told them they should be encouraged by the new structure, the new leadership, and our excellent prospects for the next election. I also told them that the greatest gift they could give Stockwell would be to unite and pull together over the summer so that all our efforts could be focused on fighting and winning the next election. I had a meeting with Stockwell (more fully described in a later chapter), at which I offered to provide whatever advice or assistance he asked of me. Sandra and I then got on the plane for Calgary and home.

Sandra had been devastated by the experience, and I didn't know how to comfort her. I feared that she was feeling that all the work, and all the sacrifice she had been called upon to make in order to build the party had now been wasted or lost. But as we talked, she assured me those were not her feelings at all. I expressed the concern – thinking strategically, as usual – that Stockwell, based on what I had seen in the campaign, might make errors in judgment that would prevent the dream of the Alliance from being realized. But Sandra, who has a much more intuitive grasp of people and situations than I, said that her fear was "that the dream would be sidetracked by someone who was not what he appeared to be." She was also devastated because, just when we had "hit our stride" in finally working together as a couple, it was all over. There was nothing I could do to address her intuitive misgivings about Stockwell, but I did resolve that whatever the future held in store, we would do it together.

During that last week in Ottawa I also distinctly remember experiencing two sensations that I had never really felt before in federal politics. First, I felt embarrassed by my failure to accomplish something. I had been in many political battles before – some of which we had won, and many of which we had lost. But I never felt any personal embarrassment over not wining any seats in the 1988 election, or losing by-election campaigns, or even by the failure to "break through" in Ontario in 1997. Somehow this defeat was different. I would meet people on the street – Liberals, civil servants, media people, staff, our own supporters, strangers – and feel I owed them some sort of explanation for what had happened. But I didn't really know what to say, and neither did they. It was, in short, embarrassing.

Second, it was during that week that I "lost my political voice."

For years my political opponents had wished I would shut up – shut up about Western alienation, shut up about the deficit, debt, and taxes, shut up about the lack of democracy in Parliament, shut up about reforming federalism – the list went on and on. To encourage me to shut up they would often ignore what I said, or try to drown me out with ridicule or counter-messages. Through it all, I had never lost my political voice. But this week, and in the months to come, I found it almost impossible to speak on the old themes, or even new ones, with any kind of enthusiasm or authority. When I was leader, I could say with absolute conviction that Reform and the caucus was committed to this principle or that policy. The certainty of that conviction, and the awareness that I was speaking on behalf of so many others as their leader, gave me strength and authority. But now if I were to speak, where would that strength or authority come from? I really wasn't certain. I still didn't know what the new leader's bedrock convictions were – certainly not sure enough to assure others about them. Nor did I know for sure whether the newly formed Alliance would stick together, or stick to the positions that it had committed itself to. And I was reluctant to speak "just for myself" on any public issue, because that would make me appear to be distancing myself from my leader and colleagues. I had been used to speaking in Parliament dozens of times per year, sometimes at length, on every issue of importance to Canadians, but after July 8, and for the rest of my time in Parliament, I scarcely uttered a word. And out in the rest of the country, whereas I had been used to speaking several hundred times a year at functions large and small, I found myself turning down almost every invitation because I was no longer certain what I should or could say. "Losing my political voice" – not through any act of my opponents but through a decision of my own party – was one of the strangest and most unsettling experiences of my political life.

■

After all the effort involved in creating the Canadian Alliance, and the strain of the leadership contest, Sandra and I needed to get away. Where better to find solitude than in the Rocky Mountains?

On August 10 we bundled up our duffle bags and drove into the mountains southwest of Canmore, Alberta. There we joined a small group of adventurers for the purpose of riding by horseback from Mount Sharpe in Alberta, over the Great Divide, to Fort Steele near Cranbrook, B.C. The group included Chuck Hayward and Brian Smith – friends we had made during the RCMP's "Ride West," Cleve Cooper, an assistant RCMP commissioner, Norm Rolf, a retired judge, Anders Oksfold, a mounted policeman from Norway, Cam Ostercamp, a skilled farrier, Warren Webber, a veterinarian, and Neil Grey, our troop doctor.

We hoped to relive some of the adventures of legendary North West Mounted Police Sergeant Sam Steele, who in 1887 led a contingent of Mounties from Fort Whoop-Up in southern Alberta, through the Rockies, to the confluence of the Kootenay and Wild Horse rivers, where he built the first NWMP fort in British Columbia.

For ten days we rode the trails over the Great Divide via the Spray and Palliser passes; along the Albert and Palliser rivers; over Sylvan Pass and down the middle fork of the White River; up the Lussier River, over Nickle Pass, and down Wild Horse Creek to Fort Steele. Our trip gave us a small taste of all those early riders must have experienced. At least we had a map; they had only the stars and their instincts to guide them.

Two days from Fort Steele we decided to take a "shortcut" over Nickle Pass into the Wild Horse Valley. We got up one side of the mountain – twenty riders and ten pack horses – only to find there was no trail down the other side, and night was coming on. Chuck (seventy years old but steady as they come), Brian, and Cam undertook to find a way down. The mountain had been logged years ago, and there were "benches" wide enough to ride along – but they led nowhere. What to do? One by one, we got on to one bench, dismounted, sent our horses over the edge, and hoped that they would stop on the next bench. Then we slid down the mountainside behind them and repeated the process until we found a trail halfway down. Later an outfitter told us you can't bring horses over that pass – but we did. When we finally made it to a hunter's camp, everyone had a feeling of accomplishment. These mountains aren't "obstacles," they are opportunities for people to find out what they are made of.

Two days later we put on old red NWMP uniforms and rode in formation into Fort Steele, where we presented the original Union Jack from Fort Whoop-Up to the head of the local RCMP detachment.

Sam Steele was a reformer, getting the NWMP to move beyond the cavalry traditions of days gone by and to adopt practices more suitable to the Canadian West. This included replacing the pillbox hat with the western Stetson. In his honour, Sandra and I wore our Stetsons as we rode into the parade square. We completed our "musical ride" to the sound of Purcell's "Trumpet Voluntary" and brought our horses to a halt in a large semicircle around the flagpole. The flag was presented and accepted. Mission accomplished.

That night, as we unrolled our sleeping bags in the same barracks where Sam Steele's men slept 112 years before, I was reminded of J. Monroe Thorington's "The End of the Trail." It is just as applicable to riding the valleys and scaling the peaks of democratic politics as it is to riding the mountain trails of the Canadian Rockies:

> And so we come to the End of the Trail. What, after all, has it amounted to – this riding in the wilderness, this mad scrambling on inaccessible crags? If you ask us, "Of what use?" perhaps we shall only smile and remain silent, answering not at all. If your curiosity be aroused, perhaps you will go and see for yourself – and find the answer we might have given. That for a little moment we have transcended ourselves; and, upon a mountain top, looking off across the vastness of the glorious earth, have felt ourselves apart from the sham and pettiness of daily life, and have come a little nearer to the Unfathomable Presence.*

---

* The End of the Trail," by J. Monroe Thorington, in *Tales from the Canadian Rockies*, ed. Brian Patton (Toronto: McClelland & Stewart, 1984), p. 288.

13

OPPORTUNITY LOST

———━━■━━———

ABOUT A WEEK AFTER THE CONCLUSION OF THE ALLIANCE leadership race, Stockwell and I met, at his request, at the Rideau Club in Ottawa. This was the first of several meetings over the next year that all followed the same pattern. Stockwell, cordial and friendly, would ask in the most general way for "advice." Except at one meeting, he never seemed to have strategically significant questions, and he never took notes. What surprised me at our first meeting was what he *didn't* ask about. Unlike Tony Clement or Tom Long, Stockwell had been involved only peripherally in the organization of the United Alternative conventions and the creation of the Alliance. I assumed he would want to know how the whole thing was "stitched together" – the ideological, geographic, and organizational components – in order to consolidate, manage, and strengthen it. But he never asked about the composition of the Alliance, leaving it for me to gently hint that this might be something for him to consider.

What further surprised me was that Stockwell didn't have questions about senior staff or the human resource requirements of a federal opposition party. His entire political experience had been with the governing Conservative Party in Alberta. The ministers of a governing party have at their disposal the services of scores of civil servants and consultants who provide advice and support on any subject at any time. But an opposition party is much more dependent on its own leadership and a very small cadre of overworked and underpaid staff. If Stockwell was aware of his absolute dependence on either the existing staff, some competent people whom he could bring with him from Edmonton, or preferably some combination of the two, he gave me no indication. I suggested that he might want to surround himself with competent people to ensure that he had the advice and support required to function in his new role.

The only other subject that I raised was whether it was wise for him to be in a rush to get a seat in Parliament. I reminded him that Reform had been able to inflict serious damage on the Conservatives in 1992–93 with the leader campaigning hard outside Parliament while the Tory members were tied to the House. And now, with the media already so interested in him, he could probably get almost as much attention campaigning outside the House as in it. Also, the more he remained outside the House prior to the election, the less able the Liberals would be to gauge his effectiveness. Their tendency would be to underestimate his and the Alliance's potential and, feeling no real sense of urgency, to perhaps delay calling the election until the spring of the following year. Stockwell gave no indication as to whether he agreed or disagreed. (It was only much later that I learned of the efforts that he and Rod Love were exerting to facilitate the resignation of Jim Hart from his B.C. seat so that Stockwell could get into the House as quickly as possible.)

After covering a number of other subjects in a general way, we parted, but I had no real sense of whether I had been truly helpful, or whether Stockwell was merely going through the motions of consulting with the former leader to be able to say that he had done so. Later, when I conferred with Tom Long and several others who had been asked by Stockwell for "advice," I found that they, too, had been left with same sense of uncertainty. The fact that key members of the Harris Conservatives also felt this way was exceedingly dangerous. Stockwell might hold the West with or without my advice, but he was absolutely dependent on the advice and support of the Harris Conservatives to make a breakthrough in Ontario.

One year later, Rod Love, who had become Stockwell's first chief of staff in Ottawa, when asked why he no longer supported Stockwell for leader of the Alliance, put it much more bluntly. He said that Stockwell was simply unable to seek or follow advice. But in July 2000, when Stockwell asked me to serve as a senior adviser, I had no idea that this might be the case. Over the next few months, I was not involved in providing advice to the new leader on anything substantial – not on shadow cabinet assignments, staff resources, issues before the House, or election strategy. This did not bother me particularly, as it was Stockwell's prerogative to seek advice from whomever he wanted, and I understood his desire to put his own stamp on the Alliance. What did disturb me, however, was Stockwell's "communication" on the subject of my advisory role. When asked if Manning was giving him advice or involved in strategic planning for the election, he would say that I was. But this was simply not true. In the end, it was errors in judgment, combined with misleading communication, that lost Stockwell the support of some of the strongest and most ethical members of caucus.

■

The days immediately following Stockwell's election as leader were heady days for the Alliance. Both he and Joe Clark won by-elections on September 11. Stockwell was easily elected in the B.C. riding of Okanagan-Coquihalla (the riding Chrétien once referred to as Coca Cola–Okinawa) with 70 per cent of the vote, and he celebrated the fact by arriving at his first news conference as a member of Parliament on a jet ski, dressed in a wetsuit. Joe, on the other hand, had received 53 per cent of the vote in Nova Scotia's Kings-Hants riding, but minutes later received the news that two of his caucus had defected to the Liberals.

Stockwell was sworn in on September 19. He was led into the Chamber by Deborah Grey and Chuck Strahl and took his seat for the first time as leader of Her Majesty's Loyal Opposition, with me seated beside him. I made it a point not to say much to him, remembering my own desire to be left alone just before Question Period in order to concentrate on my lead questions. Stockwell nonetheless surprised me by asking me a question, namely, "Which camera are we on?" If the party wanted a leader who was conscious of media opportunities, Stockwell was certainly the man.

As expected, the Question Period staff found Stockwell a different kind of person to work with from me. I always worried about content, while Stockwell's preoccupation was presentation. I tended to stick to a strategy approved first thing in the morning and rarely deviated from it, while Stockwell was much more flexible, sometimes changing the theme for the day and the Question Period lineup at the very last minute. Staff who came into my office in the half-hour before Question Period usually found me eating a quick lunch while poring over my questions, while they might find Stockwell sitting at his desk with an electric razor in his hand.

On balance, since Question Period has become, first and foremost, a media-driven communications exercise, Stockwell's approach was probably more effective than mine. His facility in the French language also meant that we were at last getting more coverage in the French media, especially on television. But once again there was a small cloud on the horizon, generated by Stockwell's difficulty in taking strategic advice, and this one became a big cloud hanging over the Alliance's election fortunes.

There is a danger that the drama of Question Period poses to overconfident Opposition parties. They might be tempted to rise to great heights of righteous indignation over some failure of the government, and then dare it to call an election on that issue. This strategy can make for great theatre in the short run, and it might even be advisable if the Opposition party is truly prepared to fight an election. But it is decidedly unwise even to think of going down this road if the government is looking for an excuse to call an early election and the Opposition party is unprepared for it. This was the state of affairs in the early fall of 2000. Despite warnings from Rod Love and others, on September 25 Stockwell challenged the Prime Minister to "call an election based on his record of being the highest-taxing leader in the G-7 countries." In twenty seconds, the Alliance leader had handed the government an excuse to call an early election and deprived himself the right to criticize that premature election call as politically motivated. The Liberals could now say, "It was the Canadian Alliance who demanded an early election; we simply acceded to their request." This is what Chrétien did. On October 22, 2000, he called the federal election with almost two years left in the government's mandate.

■

The Alliance membership had chosen their new leader for his obvious strengths – experience as a senior minister in the government of Alberta, communication skills suited to television, a strong personal following, particularly among social conservatives, and a facility in the French language. At the same time, Stockwell had never sat in the federal Parliament and had little experience in national politics, no experience in leading an opposition party, no in-depth appreciation of the composition and culture of the party he had been chosen to lead, and no experience in fighting a national election campaign against the Liberal Party of Canada (a very different proposition from competing with the anaemic Liberal Party of Alberta). Stockwell therefore had to spend the weeks following the leadership vote getting elected to Parliament, getting to know the Canadian Alliance caucus, learning the ropes of being on the opposition and not the government side of the House, and assembling a parliamentary staff. Very little time or energy was spent on consolidating and building the Alliance or on planning to fight a national election campaign as an alliance of ideological, regional, and organizational interests united by a commitment to a principled platform. As a result, by the fall of 2000, the Canadian Alliance was unprepared to jump into an election fight.

Very little of this, however, was evident to the public, the media, or the membership. Stockwell and the party were still receiving extensive media coverage, and the Liberals looked tired and lethargic by comparison. On October 18, 2000, with the help of Jim Ginoux (one of Mike Harris's key fundraisers) and Peter White, the Alliance held one of the largest fundraising dinners ever organized by a political party in Toronto. The official Canadian Alliance election platform document, "A Time for Change," was already rolling off the printing presses. It offered "New Leadership for a New Century." The campaign advertising emphasized not the personalities and capabilities of the Alliance as a whole, but the personality and capability of the leader. It offered Stockwell Day's Plan for Cutting Government Waste, Stockwell Day's Fair Tax Plan, Stockwell Day's Plan for Health, Stockwell Day's Plan to Keep Our Communities Safe, and Stockwell Day's Agenda of Respect for All Canadians.

By mid-October I had not heard anything from the national campaign team as to what, if anything, I was expected to do. Many of our MPs – including Deborah Grey, our most effective grassroots campaigner, as well as Tom Long and other high-profile Conservatives in Ontario whose involvement was crucial to our electoral success there – were experiencing the same difficulty in finding out how, if at all, they would fit into the national campaign effort. On October 20, two days before the election call, I faxed a memo to the national campaign office in Ottawa wishing Stockwell and the team every success in the upcoming campaign and suggesting a few spots where I might be of help, but I had difficulty getting anybody to make a decision on my request.

A month earlier, Stockwell had issued a press release listing the members of the Canadian Alliance national campaign team, but by election day the real decision-making authority appeared to rest with three small groups, none of which really agreed with the others and one of which wasn't even on the list. There was Jason Kenney, whose official title was national co-chair, and several of his friends, referred to by the rest of the team as "the Catholic mafia" because of their common religious background and interest in pushing the social conservative agenda. Then there was Rod Love and Hal Danchilla from the Klein camp in Alberta, although Rod seemed strangely detached from the campaign. The tension between Rod and Jason on strategic matters was obvious and a cause of some consternation to staffers, who simply wanted to know who had the authority to make decisions. And then there was Stockwell's immediate family, including his wife, Val, and son, Logan, who seemed to have a major influence on Stockwell's decisions, comments, and day-to-day activities. I knew nothing of all this at the time, only that I (and others) were having trouble getting any clear direction from the national team. Eventually, Hal Danchilla gave me the

go-ahead for four campaign excursions on my own – not connected
to the national campaign effort – to help in ridings where my connections and support might be useful.

■

On Sunday, October 22, Jean Chrétien announced that the federal
election would be held on November 27 and that the campaign would
be a competition between "two different visions of Canada."
Stockwell was not immediately available to respond because of his
declared practice of not doing political work on Sunday. His campaign
would begin the next day. At the time the election was called, a Leger
and Leger poll showed national support for the Liberals at 48 per cent,
with the Alliance at 21 per cent, the Bloc at 10 per cent, and the
Conservatives and the NDP each at 8 per cent. On the day the election was called I was in Calgary preparing to do battle in Calgary
Southwest, with no instructions to do anything else.

According to the campaign plan, the emphasis during week one
was to be on government waste and high taxes. On October 23 I
joined with the other Calgary candidates at a kickoff rally where we
hammered away at these themes. At the same time, the Leader's
Tour was kicking off the national campaign in Ontario with an
event outside the HRDC offices in Hull, reminding voters of the
waste of taxpayers' dollars by Jane Stewart and the billion-dollar
boondoggle. The national campaign continued to emphasize these
themes throughout the week as Stockwell blitzed various parts of
Ontario before heading out across the country.

There were a few opening-week glitches. On October 24
Stockwell visited Quaker Technologies to make the point that high
taxes were driving high-tech entrepreneurs out of the country, only
to find that the owner of Quaker had come from the United States
– an illustration of "brain gain," not "brain drain." The next day, at
Niagara Falls, Stockwell declared that because of Liberal high taxes,
Canadian capital and jobs were flowing south, just like the Niagara
River – only to be told by startled locals that the Niagara River actually flows north. Fortunately, these glitches were not bad enough to
seriously damage local campaigns or dampen enthusiasm.

Of more concern to me personally, and of far more ominous import for the national campaign, was the fact that Stockwell appeared to be "flying solo" in Ontario, the province where the Alliance leader should have been campaigning as the head of an Alliance team that included the most prominent and influential of our allies among the Harris Conservatives. However, no serious effort had been made to consolidate their position within the Alliance, or to secure their participation on the national tour. Even at the field level in Ontario it was apparent that Harris's first-string organizers and campaigners had not been recruited or integrated into the Alliance campaign.

On day five of the campaign, the Leader's Tour rolled into Calgary for an event at Petro Canada Square. The optics of this location served to remind Albertans of the Liberals' infamous National Energy Program – which extracted $100 billion from the Western petroleum sector through federal taxes and price-fixing – and the possibility of a repeat raid through the imposition of "green taxes" as part of the Kyoto Accord. The theme of the rally was taxes – to demand an end to excessive Liberal taxation and to promote the Alliance's 17 Percent Solution. By the time Stockwell got to Calgary, however, the "tax message" had become muddled. Jason and Stockwell had endeavoured to explain to the national media that, due to the Liberals' reallocating some of the existing federal surplus, there would not be enough revenue to give our single rate of tax to all Canadians until the fifth year of an Alliance administration. This generated unnecessary and damaging headlines accusing the Alliance of backing away from its position. At this stage of the campaign, the apparent contradiction of the Alliance's basic tax relief message was not fatal in itself. But if the leader's trumpet continued to "give an uncertain sound" on an issue as fundamental to the Alliance's success as tax relief, it would quickly erode voter confidence in our program.

In Calgary, our local organizers had done their job, and a large and enthusiastic crowd had assembled at Petro Canada Square to welcome Stockwell and the national tour. Surrounded by our Calgary-area candidates, I briefly reviewed the Liberal tax record and introduced Stockwell as a proven tax-cutter. Stockwell bounded from the campaign bus and gave me a warm bear hug (I am not a hugger) in front of the cameras before delivering his speech. This ensured that the picture in the papers and on television would be one of us working together as a team. If only it were true. When one of my fellow candidates who knew the real situation asked about the "hugging scene," I replied, "We hadn't seen each other in quite a while."

■

The second week of the campaign began on an encouraging note. Polls were showing that national support for the Liberals had dropped 3 per cent while support for the Alliance had surged 7 per cent.

While our national campaign had had its problems in the first week, Chrétien's lacklustre performance was raising more questions about the Liberal government's capability. By this time, Rick Anderson, Jim Armour, and Ian and Ellen Todd had been asked to join the national campaign team to beef up its strategic and logistical capability. Now, with the public expressing doubts about "Liberal competence," would have been a perfect time to hammer the government record of fiscal mismanagement and ethical failures.

On October 31 and November 1, Sandra and I made our first expedition outside of Calgary to assist other Alliance campaigns. We first visited Victoria to speak on behalf of Alliance candidate Brian Halsor in his battle with Environment minister David Anderson. We then did the media rounds in Vancouver and participated in several events in support of candidates like Kerry Lynne Findlay, an articulate and hard-working lawyer with an excellent chance of taking Vancouver Quadra from the Liberals. From what I saw of the constituency campaigns in B.C., they were proceeding well.

Our candidates were picking up signals similar to those revealed by the national polls, suggesting that there was considerable public disenchantment with the Prime Minister's perceived lack of competence, integrity, and accountability. Many voters were aware of the "billion-dollar boondoggle" at Human Resources and the Shawinigate shenanigans. "Why then," our candidates were asking, "is the national campaign not vigorously attacking Chrétien and the Liberals on this ground?" Stockwell was resisting a direct attack on the Prime Minister, saying he wanted to pursue an "agenda of respect." But in private, and when talking only to key supporters, Stockwell, Jason, Rod, and most other Alliance spokespersons expressed nothing but contempt for Chrétien and the Liberals. Almost everyone, including the media, knew that the so-called "agenda of respect" was a slogan, not a principled position. Stockwell later abandoned the "agenda of respect" rhetoric and went on the offensive. But by then it was Stockwell's alleged weaknesses and mistakes, not Chrétien's, that had become the focus of media and public attention.

While I was in B.C., the campaign of the Alliance candidates received another disconcerting jolt. They awoke on October 31 to read a big, bold headline in the *Globe and Mail* proclaiming "Alliance supports two-tier health care." The story was based on an interview with Alliance campaign co-chair Jason Kenney. Health care in Canada was the number-one concern of a majority of voters, but the way the health care issue was handled by the Alliance's national campaign and leadership put the Alliance, rather than the government, on the defensive. In Jason's interview with the *Globe* he had not even used the words "two-tier medicine." He had simply expressed the view that there would and should be a place for private capital and facilities in the health care system of the future. Exactly the same point has been made since by authorities as diverse as the Senate committee headed by Liberal Michael Kirby, former Conservative deputy prime minister Don Mazankowski in a report to the Alberta government, and former NDP premier Roy Romanow in a report to the federal government. But in the context of the election campaign, the *Globe*'s misrepresentation of Jason's remarks was seized upon by the other parties as evidence that the CA had a hidden agenda for destroying Medicare through whole-sale privatization.

In the fall of 2000, according to the pollsters, more than one-third of Canadians actually agreed that there should be an expanded role for private capital and facilities in the health care system, as long as the quality of the public system could also be maintained. This was the time to stick by Jason, to hold the Chrétien government accountable for its role in the deterioration of health care in Canada, and to sell the Alliance position that quality and affordable health care for all Canadians would be attainable if a new balance were struck between federal and provincial responsibilities and between public and private resources. Instead, the CA leadership back-pedalled furiously, muddled the message, disappointed its supporters, and created doubt and suspicion in the minds of voters on the number-one issue in the election.

Sandra and I spent the latter part of week two of the campaign in Ontario, opening Scott Reid's campaign headquarters in Kanata and spending a day with Sean and Lisa McAdam in Hastings-Frontenac-Lennox and Addington. (It took me an hour to memorize the full name of the riding.) Sean had several small campaign headquarters spread throughout the riding, including one in a converted coin car wash facility in Bancroft. Over the door was a big sign that said "Loonies Only," which had to be carefully covered up before the media arrived. Political parties, particularly new ones, have enough problems with loonies without inviting them in during an election. We then took a swing through southwestern Ontario, where candidates like Nancy Branscombe in London and Reg Petersen in Cambridge were waging vigorous constituency campaigns. Sean, Nancy, and Reg were all experienced candidates who had been very active in putting together the Canadian Alliance at the local as well as the national level. They had worked hard for several years in addressing the vote-splitting problem with the Conservatives at the constituency level and had good prospects for winning their seats. They were optimistic, but there was a growing uneasiness among their workers that negative back-feed from the national campaign – such as the two-tier health care headlines – was adversely affecting the riding campaigns. At the beginning of week two, the day after Jason's comments, the Liberals had released Red Book III. Even the media panned it as an unexciting extension of previous Red Books, with a heavy emphasis on spending more taxpayers' dollars on everything from soup to nuts. The ridings were well equipped to pound away at the doorsteps on the distinction between Liberal spending and Alliance tax relief. But when they got to the doors, the question was, "What's all this about two-tier health care?"

■

The highlight of week three of the campaign was the leaders' debates, on November 8 in French, and in English on November 9. My biggest worry in the days leading up to the debates was that the Liberals, or some of the media hostile to the Alliance, would do something to further destabilize the Alliance campaign in order to put Stockwell on the defensive. Sure enough, something "happened" during this period that had this effect.

A newspaper obtained a copy of the CA candidates' briefing book and professed to see a discrepancy between it and the party's platform on citizen-initiated referendums. The party's position was that 3 per cent of the total number of eligible electors in the previous election, petitioning the chief electoral officer, could trigger a national referendum on the subject of their petition. The Liberals and others immediately translated this into the accusation that the CA had a "hidden agenda" to allow 3 per cent of the electors to trigger a referendum on abortion. The supposed vulnerability to abuse of the CA Citizens' Initiative and Referendum Law was further exaggerated over the next ten days when the comedy show "This Hour Has 22 Minutes" collected more than one million "signatures" through an Internet referendum on a proposal to change Stockwell Day's name to Doris Day. (This was one of the most hilarious incidents of Election 2000, which badly needed some comic relief.)

Once again, instead of clarifying the CA position on direct democracy – one of the fundamental tenets of party policy – the CA leadership retreated. By mishandling the referendum issue, it turned one of the party's greatest strengths – its commitment to direct democracy – into a liability. Under intense questioning, Stockwell appeared unfamiliar with all the research and debate that had gone into the Reform/Alliance direct democracy measures over the past ten years, and he waffled on the percentage required to trigger a national referendum under the CA proposal. Instead of back-pedalling, this would have been the time to boldly ask Canadians to take a stand for more democracy in their national political affairs. Which was more democratic and respectful of the will of the Canadian people – to allow a handful of Supreme Court justices, or a score of deputy ministers, or even a couple of hundred parliamentarians to decide certain important public issues, or to allow millions of Canadians to have a direct say on the matter if they desired to do so? And what would be wrong with letting half a million Canadians initiate a referendum? If that group was out to lunch on some contentious moral or social issue, their position would be soundly defeated by an overwhelming majority in the referendum itself. If their position was capable of carrying the judgment of a majority, why shouldn't it be put to a vote? Are Canadians so immature politically, as many of our elites maintain, that the country would allow itself to be torn apart by divisive referendum debates on controversial subjects? This has not been the experience elsewhere. Switzerland is one of the most stable democracies in the world, despite major ethnic and religious differences in its population. Yet its referendum laws allowed 100,000 people to initiate a referendum in 2000 on whether the country should have an army. Which federal parties – the Liberals? the PCs? the NDP? all of them? – have so little faith in the judgment of the Canadian electorate that they would deny them a direct say on anything except who should represent them in Parliament? Why should voters trust such parties when such parties obviously do not trust the voters?

The "22 Minutes" mock-referendum provided the material for a perfect object lesson in the potential of electronic democracy, as well as the necessity of safeguards to prevent the abuse of referendum laws. The Alliance should have thanked "22 Minutes" for raising the issue, and then explained to Canadians in a good-natured way exactly what would have happened if the "22 Minutes" electronic referendum had actually been presented to the chief electoral officer under the Alliance's proposed federal referendum law. It would, of course, have been rejected – rejected on at least three grounds, all of which would be instructive to Canadians and future petitioners. First, its subject matter (changing an individual's name) is in the provincial, not the federal, jurisdiction, and the petition would have been rejected on that ground. If you are going to initiate a national referendum on something under a federal law, you'd better know your country's constitution. Second, the measure the "22 Minutes" referendum sought to enact – changing the name of an individual by a collective vote – violates the Charter of Rights and Freedoms and so would be rejected on that ground. And third, when the chief electoral officer performed the spot audit required to verify the authenticity of the petition's "signatures," it would have revealed many multiple entries (people who voted more than once). The petition would then have been rejected on that ground as well, with the sponsors being subject to a fine and barred from submitting future petitions for a specified period. These are the safeguards necessary to protect the integrity of any referendum process and to prevent the abuses that its critics so greatly fear. On the positive side, however, the mock-referendum illustrated the enormous potential of the combination of television and the Internet for soliciting the input of millions of people in a very short period of time on any subject that captures their interest. What if that potent combination of television and the Internet were harnessed, with appropriate safeguards, to soliciting timely public input on some issue of real significance to Canadians? Why shouldn't Canada be in the forefront of exploring the potential of electronic democracy, instead of ignoring or denying it?

I watched the leaders' debates with my workers in Calgary Southwest. In Calgary, there was minimal interest in the French debate, and the fact that Stockwell did not participate very actively caused little concern. With respect to the English debate, the general consensus in our campaign headquarters was that Stockwell had done reasonably well. We were further encouraged when the Ipsos-Reid poll published on November 13 showed that Liberal support had dropped to 40 per cent, and that Alliance support was either holding or up slightly to 28 per cent.

The two nagging concerns I had about the English-language leaders' debate were the relatively strong showing by Joe Clark and Stockwell's flashing of a "prop" during the debate proclaiming "No Two-Tier." If a leader wants to retain the confidence of his support team during a campaign, he simply must not "surprise" them. Stockwell had apparently spent several days with his advisers in intense debate preparation, but had never once indicated to them that he would use such a prop, or sought advice as to its appropriateness. While it may have struck viewers as amateurish, its overall effect on voters was probably minimal. But the effect of this stunt on Stockwell's own campaign team was unsettling, just as it was entering the final and most critical phase of the election. Use of this prop also violated the debate rules painstakingly negotiated among the networks and the parties, and it would create credibility problems the next time the Alliance had to negotiate similar arrangements.

Notwithstanding the problems encountered by the Alliance's national campaign during the first three weeks, the Liberal campaign had not gone smoothly either. As one commentator put it, "Day is not gaining ground, but the Liberals are losing it." The last two weeks would tell the tale as to whether the great opportunity represented by Election 2000 could still be seized.

■

In the midst of all this, I had to cope with a personal crisis: prostate cancer. During all of my previous years in federal politics – despite the never-ending travel, lack of proper exercise, and irregular diet – I had never been seriously ill. For this, Sandra and I were immensely thankful to God and to our devoted staff, who did everything possible to guard my health, especially during times of intense stress. It is apparently a well-documented phenomenon, however, that people who live with stressful responsibilities for a long time and then are suddenly relieved of them often become ill when their immune system – no longer stimulated by the daily adrenaline rush – takes a holiday.

Once the Alliance leadership contest was over, I had gone to our family doctor, Dr. Ken Cody, for my regular physical examination. As part of the exam, Ken included a PSA test – a simple blood test that (while not infallible) is a good early warning of the possibility of prostate cancer. This time when the result came back it showed a slight "jump" in the PSA rating. Ken referred me to a Calgary urologist, Dr. Bill Hyndman, who sent me to the Prostate Cancer Institute for a biopsy. The institute is a not-for-profit research centre funded primarily through private donations and open to the public, and it just happens to be in Calgary Southwest. Its president, Phyllis Kane, the staff, and the volunteer counsellors were extremely helpful in providing Sandra and me with both information and moral support as we endeavoured to learn all we could about prostate cancer.

After the biopsy, I went to see Dr. Hyndman again to review the results. While sitting in his examination room, I glanced up on the wall and saw that his specialty certificate had been granted by the Royal College of Physicians and Surgeons "under authority granted to it by the Parliament of Canada." Knowing what I did about the Parliament of Canada, this did not particularly bolster my confidence, but the more I got to know Bill Hyndman the more I became convinced that I was in extremely good hands.

Dr. Hyndman said that the first biopsy indicated a problem, but it was inconclusive. If I had prostate cancer it was in the early stages, and he ordered another biopsy to focus more specifically on what he suspected was the problem area. By now the federal election was underway and I had to juggle this challenge with my campaign responsibilities, while endeavouring to keep my medical condition confidential until we knew exactly what the score was. I have seen campaigns where political opponents have started or amplified rumours that such and such a candidate had a fatal disease, and I didn't want that happening to me.

Sandra and I were campaigning in the Ottawa area that first week in November when the call from Dr. Hyndman came with the results of the second biopsy. The bare facts were that I had prostate cancer, that it was likely still at an early stage, that I had several treatment options, from radiation therapy to surgery, and that we should make a decision as soon as I was back in Calgary. I have since been asked by many people what were Sandra's and my initial feelings and reactions to the news that I had cancer. About all I can say is that the news had no dramatic impact on either our mental state or day-to-day activities, probably because of two factors – our faith in the providential care of God, and our past experience in the political arena, where receiving and dealing with "bad news" is a very frequent occurrence.

When I received the first "bad news" represented by the PSA and biopsy test results, it struck me about the same as Ian coming in one morning and saying, "We've got a nasty editorial in the *Toronto Star*, and you'll have to deal with it." All you can do is assess the problem and the potential damage, decide on a course of action to address the problem, and then implement it. If it works, fine; if it doesn't, then we'll worry about that later.

To Sandra and me, whatever the physical or political dimensions of "assessing and addressing the problem" may be, there is also a spiritual dimension, which is the most important of all. I believe there is much truth in something a palliative care specialist in Calgary, Irene Kehler Huff, once told me: that people generally handle the challenges of serious illness and the prospect of their own death in much the same way that they handle the challenges of life and living. If you are angry at how life is treating you, you will be angry at illness and death. If your family is your greatest source of support and comfort in life, your family will probably be your greatest source of strength when death threatens. In our case, Sandra and I had committed our lives to the providential care of God a long time ago. Whatever happened, for good or for ill, we considered ourselves to be in His care and keeping, even if we couldn't understand the "why" of it all. It was this faith that sustained us when the CA leadership race did not turn out as we had hoped, and it was this faith that sustained us in coping with prostate cancer.

We decided on surgery – a radical prostatectomy. I tend to like "radical" solutions to serious problems. We then went on with the election campaign and didn't really think or talk about prostate cancer again until December. Then, with the election behind us, I entered Calgary's Rockyview Hospital (again in my riding) for surgery. Six weeks later, I was back in my seat in Parliament, minus my prostate gland but with excellent prospects for a complete recovery, thanks to caring and skilful doctors and nurses, the constant support of Sandra and our family, and the will of the One who ultimately holds our times and lives in His hands.

■

Week four of the campaign began with the Liberal minister of Citizenship and Immigration, Elinor Caplan, who was in trouble with Jewish voters in her own riding because of the government's support of anti-Israel resolutions at the United Nations, accusing Alliance supporters of being racists, bigots, hostile to immigrants, and deniers of the Holocaust. At the same time, Stockwell was in the Toronto area trying to advance the Alliance's tough law-and-order policy, but the racism flak from Liberal artillery – aimed particularly at Toronto's multicultural community – filled the political skies. For some reason, the national campaign also chose this particular time to address aboriginal issues, including the proposed abolition over time of the reserve system and the aboriginal income tax exemption. This had the unfortunate effect of providing more fuel for the racism allegations.

I spent almost all of week five visiting ridings in Edmonton, Hamilton, Toronto, and Peterborough, and I ended the week on Vancouver Island. In Edmonton, Sandra and I were picked up and transported to a number of riding events by the irrepressible Jenni Byrne, whom I had first met on the Reform Youth Bus in the 1997 campaign. In Edmonton Southwest, the campaign headquarters of Alliance candidate Tim Upall, a young and personable Sikh, had been vandalized. But no national headlines appeared alleging racially motivated attacks when it was an Alliance candidate who was the victim. In Hamilton I spent some time with Leon O'Connor and his family; Leon was a committed Alliance candidate with an aboriginal background whose life had been threatened after Stockwell's venture into aboriginal policy. If one is going to make major pronouncements on aboriginal policy, it is better done by a coalition of Alliance spokespersons that includes aboriginal people. But Leon had not been asked to help roll out the Alliance policy in this area.

In Toronto, I got far more publicity for the Alliance by appearing as a "guest comedian" on "Open Mike with Mike Bullard," and on TSN's "Off the Record with Michael Landsberg," than I did by appearing at election events. Unbeknownst to me until we arrived, Michael's other guests included a fellow whom I thought to be a burned-out NHL hockey star, who kept agreeing with almost every point I made. It turned out that he was Ron Jeremy, said to be one of the world's most famous adult-film stars.

On November 14 the CBC aired a "documentary" on Stockwell's religious beliefs, alleging among other things that Stockwell thought human beings and dinosaurs had existed on the earth at the same time. (When I was asked about this the next day, I replied that if one observed the Chrétien Cabinet long enough one might very well come to that conclusion.) Any response to the effect that Stockwell's personal religious beliefs were nobody's business would only make things worse. Since he frequently used his religious views to court political support from those who shared them, those views were fair game. But – without getting into the evolution-versus-creationism debate and ways of justifying or reconciling the two per-spectives – the CBC documentary deserved to be attacked by fair-minded persons, no matter what their political or religious per-suasions. It is important for the public to know what are the most deeply held values, including religious convictions, of those involved in their public affairs. But if the media are going to inves-tigate the beliefs of one leader, they should do the same for all the leaders. And once a television network steps onto this ground, it should not be surprised when, at the next CRTC licensing hearing, lawyers representing faith communities want to question network executives and producers on their values and convictions, in partic-ular the value base from which they presume to interpret and judge the values of others.

Three generations of the Manning family have wrestled with the issues that surround the interface of religion and politics. We have been subjected to dozens of attacks on our religious convictions by political and media opponents. Veteran MPs like Deborah Grey and Chuck Strahl have also managed for years to avoid media-planted land mines in this area, while still maintaining a strong Christian testimony. Nevertheless, our advice on how to handle the attack on Stockwell was not sought.

In virtually every riding, candidates were doing their level best to deliver the central message that "It Is a Time for Change." But more often than not, developments in the national campaign were hurting rather than helping their local efforts. In riding after riding, it was being reported that Stockwell's religious views had become more of an issue than Chrétien's ethics, that misrepresentations of Alliance health care policy had become more of an issue than Liberal mismanagement of health care, and that allegations concerning the Alliance's so-called "hidden agenda" were more discussed than its real agenda. At the same time, attacks directed towards Stockwell were becoming more vicious. Veteran constituency campaign managers insisted that the national campaign had to make some sort of "strategic adjustment" to turn things around in the last ten days of the campaign.

The Alliance leadership, perhaps because there was so little time to plan, had decided to run an essentially personality-centred campaign similar to the one that had worked for Stockwell in the Alliance leadership contest. One of the downsides of such a strategy is that it encourages your opponents to focus all their firepower on the leader, and it takes an exceptional individual or special circumstances to withstand those attacks. If a party says that its leader is the solution, its political opponents will do everything in their power to discredit that leader and to make sure that he becomes "the problem," which is what happened to the Alliance and Stockwell in Election 2000. Another downside to personality-centred campaigns is that if they go "off track" during an election, there is very little you can do to rescue them. If an issue-based campaign goes sideways, because you picked the wrong issues or your messages weren't quite right, you can always refocus on better issues and new messages. This mid-course adjustment will strike the media and the public as a shift from your original strategy, but not a complete abandonment of it. But if a personality-centred campaign goes sideways, what can you do? If you move away from promotion of the leader as your primary focus, it will be evident to everyone that you are abandoning what you initially claimed was your greatest asset.

■

On November 21, the media reported an alleged statement by an Alliance candidate in Winnipeg describing the increasing number of Asian immigrants as an "Asian invasion." This statement should have been dealt with by a sincere and immediate apology by the candidate – something she was quite prepared to do. And Inky Mark, our respected Manitoba MP, who is himself of Chinese descent, was quite prepared to help mend fences with the Asian community. Instead, the national campaign team forced the candidate to withdraw, only to have her express second thoughts about having retreated under duress. Their response turned a one-day story into a three-day story during the critical last week of the campaign.

Meanwhile, Chrétien's Shawinigate shenanigans had finally become a campaign issue, with both Stockwell and Clark hammering away at the Prime Minister's integrity and self-serving "ethics." At the constituency level, this change in direction was welcomed by Alliance candidates, who had wanted to make Chrétien's integrity, or lack of it, an issue from the very beginning but had been constrained from doing so by the now abandoned "agenda of respect."

In Calgary, the main worry now was in Calgary Centre. Eric Lowther, the Alliance candidate there, was one of our very best MPs, particularly when it came to handling the delicate moral and ethical issues that had proven to be such a minefield for us. In Calgary Centre, however, the Liberals and the NDP, as well as the gay community, were now lining up behind Joe Clark, and the whole focus of their attack was not on Eric but on Stockwell Day. Now it appeared that Eric's seat might be lost due to factors largely beyond his control.

During the last ten days of the campaign I witnessed something I had rarely seen before: shock and bewilderment, bordering on fear, among some of our troops at the nature and intensity of the Liberal attacks on the Alliance and its leader. Some of the newer members from the Christian community, whom Stockwell had made a special effort to recruit into the party, had never been involved in a federal election campaign before. In ridings like Peterborough, where a tough, veteran campaigner like Nancy Branscombe had been replaced by a candidate more acceptable to the evangelical community (Nancy subsequently ran in London), the new group was largely unprepared for the type of campaign in which they were now embroiled. They seemed unable to grasp the fact that if you use religion to secure a political base, your opponents will seek to undermine that base by attacking your religion. Campaigners were also saying things like, "This is the dirtiest federal campaign in Canadian history. Things are being said about Stockwell and our candidate that have never been said before." But the reality is that any time a Liberal or Conservative administration is truly threatened by an opposition party, that party and its leader will be subject to every attack imaginable. Certainly this was the experience of Reform and myself. In federal politics in Canada, there is nothing new under the sun; even the dirt and the mud are recycled. Our new members should have been made acquainted with these past experiences and instructed on how to minimize exposure to enemy fire. Those constituencies with completely new candidates and campaign teams, with little or no effort to get a balance between veteran workers and raw recruits, with no real "alliance building" at the local level, with no guidance on how to handle the religion and politics issue, and with little appreciation of the hard-earned lessons of previous campaigns, generally suffered accordingly.

With less than a week to go, a federal election campaign that had failed to come to grips in any meaningful way with any major issue of concern to the general public careened to its conclusion. It was characterized by faux pas and desperate last-minute appeals on all sides. In a moment of uncharacteristic frankness, Chrétien mused that he liked dealing with East Coast Canadians better than Westerners, especially Albertans. This of course made for bold headlines in all the Alberta newspapers and caused Liberal candidates to run for cover. Two days later, the Edmonton Journal, quoting unguarded comments by Alliance MP Ken Epp, added the "phasing out of Old Age Security" to the Alliance's hidden agenda. This time it was Alliance candidates that looked for cover.

On November 24, three days before the election, I made my last campaign speech, introducing Stockwell Day at our last big Calgary rally as "a proven tax-cutter, a friend not an enemy of the provinces . . . and our democratically chosen leader." On November 25, Chrétien gave his usual last-minute warning to Ontario about the dangers of minority government, and on November 26 Stockwell made a last-minute appeal to Ontarians – via a pre-recorded province-wide telecast – not to give Chrétien a blank cheque. Some commentators couldn't help but observe that November 26 was Sunday, and that this telecast therefore constituted "campaigning on Sunday." On this insightful and helpful note, the federal election of the year 2000 ground to a merciful end.

∎

On Monday, November 27, members of my family came to our condominium in Calgary Southwest and we walked over to my campaign headquarters to watch the results. As the results from Eastern and Central Canada appeared on the television screens, the disappointment was deeper and more palpable than in 1997 – the initial prospects for an Alliance breakthrough had been so much brighter. Nothing in Atlantic Canada and nothing in Quebec (a bilingual leader was supposed to change this). And although our vote totals were up, we earned only two seats in Ontario, not the forty that Stockwell's team had been predicting at the beginning of the campaign. Three cheers for Scott Reid and Cheryl Gallant, our new Ontario MPs, for swimming against the tide. But once again, the media desks were projecting a Liberal majority government even before the Western vote had been counted. Encouraging news from Manitoba as Brian Pallister (the former PC leadership candidate) and Vic Toews (the former attorney general of Manitoba) were added to the Alliance caucus. Even better news from Saskatchewan, as the Alliance captured ten of that province's fourteen seats. And then the solid returns from Alberta and British Columbia, the Alliance capturing twenty-three out of twenty-six seats in Alberta and twenty-seven out of thirty-two seats in B.C. Sixty-six seats in all, but even the Western results were tinged with disappointment. Close races again in Anne McLelland's Edmonton riding and David Anderson's Victoria riding, but still narrow victories for these Liberal ministers. A victory in Richmond, B.C., and in Port Moody–Coquitlam, regained for the Alliance by a young up-and-coming member named James Moore. But no breakthrough in Quadra or the other Liberal- and NDP-held ridings in Vancouver. And saddest of all, Eric Lowther defeated by Joe Clark in Calgary Centre. In Election 2000 the federal Tories suffered their worst federal election defeat since Confederation – only 12.5 per cent of the popular vote nationally – but Joe's win would be seen as a great victory, and together with eleven other Tory seats mainly in Atlantic Canada, the federal PCs would retain official party status. My own re-election in Calgary Southwest, with 34,529 votes and 65 per cent of the popular vote, was greeted with whoops and cheers. But my supporters in Calgary Southwest are by and large "big picture" people, and tonight the big picture was even more disappointing than it had been in 1997.

The final results would show the Liberals with 172 seats, up 17 from 1997; the Alliance with 66 seats, up 6 from 1997; the Bloc with 38 seats, down 6 from 1997; the NDP with 13, down 8 from 1997; and the PCs with 12 seats, down 8 from 1997. The final popular vote totals, compared with the standings in the polls when the election was called, showed the Liberals at 41 per cent, down 7 per cent; the Alliance at 25 per cent, up 4 per cent; the Bloc at 11 per cent, up 1 per cent; the PCs at 12 per cent, up 4 per cent; and the NDP, as they started, at 8 per cent. Total voter turnout, reflecting the public's general dissatisfaction with the election as a whole, was 61.5 per cent, 15 per cent lower than in 1988, when Reform first broke on the electoral scene. And most galling of all, an Ipsos-Reid post-vote survey found 66 per cent of respondents agreeing that Mr. Chrétien "doesn't have what it takes anymore to lead the country"; 59 per cent disapproved of the way that Chrétien was doing his job; and 58 per cent agreed that the Liberals were arrogant and corrupt. The Canadian people had been prepared to reject Chrétien and vote for a principled alternative; they just did not perceive that alternative in Stockwell Day and the Canadian Alliance.

■

About five days after Election 2000, on the Saturday night, I walked over to my now deserted campaign headquarters, unlocked the door, went in, and sat down at one of the long tables that once supported our telephone bank. There is nothing quite so desolate as a campaign office after the campaign is over. But this had been the Calgary headquarters of my PM4PM campaign as well as my Calgary

Southwest re-election campaign, and there were still plenty of reminders of both endeavours. I instinctively looked into the wastepaper baskets still full of election material. My first political job as a teenager had been to check the garbage cans outside campaign offices on the day after provincial elections, because my father and his chief organizer wanted to know which materials, so painstakingly prepared and distributed by the party's central office, had been used or discarded by the local candidates. If the main campaign has been going well, all the centrally produced material featuring the leader and the platform will likely be used. If it hasn't gone well, you will find half of that material in the storage rooms or the garbage cans, the local candidates having switched halfway through to personal brochures of their own design and manufacture.

Just as I visited the deserted Commons Chamber late at night and found myself envisioning what that Parliament might be like if a democrat occupied the prime minister's chair, so on this night I found myself envisioning the Alliance campaign that might have been, and might yet be at some future time. Pure nostalgia? Perhaps. But I prefer to think of it as historically informed idealism – looking back, in order to get a clearer perspective on what may still be possible in the future.

The public purpose for which the Canadian Alliance had been created was to bring into being a better Canada through a principled alternative to the federal Liberal Party. This "better Canada" – as defined by the Alliance's principles and policies – would be a nation where public moneys were used wisely, not wastefully, where federal taxes and debts were reduced to competitive levels, where both economic growth and environmental conservation were national priorities and practical realities, where health care and other essential services were provided on an effective and efficient basis, where federalism and democracy were renewed and revitalized, where personal and national security were strengthened, where integrity and high ethical standards were restored to national politics, and where Canada's international responsibilities were pursued with renewed purpose and credibility.

The immediate political objectives of the Canadian Alliance had been to win four million votes and at least one hundred seats in the federal election, driving the Liberal government into a minority situation so that the Canadian Alliance would, in effect, be "driving the bus from the back seat." The campaign strategy that I and my team had envisioned for achieving these political objectives was a logical and focused extension of what we had been working on for the past three years. It had four essential components.

Our first priority would have been to affirm and consolidate the Alliance at the leadership level, the strategic level, and on the ground. This would have meant putting together a visible and credible leadership team at the very top – with recognizable, credible regional generals in Atlantic Canada, Quebec, Ontario, the Prairies, British Columbia, and the North – of which the newly elected leader would be the commander-in-chief. Affirming and consolidating the Alliance would also have meant cementing relations with all those ideological, organizational, and regional interests that had helped bring the Alliance into being, and engaging them at every level – in particular the constituency level – in a national election campaign.

Our second priority would have been to make a supreme effort in the House and with the media to position the leader, the caucus, and the party as reasonable, competent, and more ready for a greater role in national affairs than we had ever been before. This would have been our chance, if we could have mustered the necessary self-discipline, to re-brand the party and, if necessary, its leader – to shed the "extremist" and "eccentric" vestiges of the Reform image, and to reposition ourselves, particularly in the eyes of Ontario voters, as broadly based, experienced, and ready for greater responsibilities. "Ready for Change" might have been our initial theme, linking the public appetite for a change from Liberal arrogance and inaction to our willingness and capability to work for constructive change.

Our third priority would have been election readiness. Immediately after the leadership vote, we would have accelerated election preparations in the field, from nomination meetings to volunteer training to heavy-duty fundraising. Unlike Stockwell and his team, we would not have been on a steep learning curve. We would have been more than ready to capitalize on the momentum and excitement generated by the successful creation of the Alliance and its leadership contest to energize the federal campaign itself.

And fourth, our election plan would have been designed to take full advantage of our past experience, expanded resources, and new circumstances. Our greatest strength in the Charlottetown referendum and the 1993 election campaign had been a large and motivated "grassroots army" of about 130,000 people. As a result of the campaign to create the Canadian Alliance, and the subsequent leadership contest, we now had the opportunity to mobilize and deploy an even larger grassroots army of more than 250,000 members and potential volunteers. Our greatest strength in the 1997 election and the United Alternative campaigns had been a competent and experienced campaign management team capable of running effective *national* campaigns, leader's tours, and advertising campaigns. In planning for Election 2000, the aim should have been to harness these two great strengths together to advance the fortunes of the Alliance.

The 2000 election plan would also have been a plan for running an issue-based campaign, the type of campaign our party was best suited to conduct. This would have required identifying and assembling ammunition on the three issues we were capable of fighting for most effectively, and where the Liberals would be at the greatest disadvantage. In the spring of 2000 (subject to the latest polling results, and any late-breaking developments) we anticipated that our three best issues would likely be government waste, high taxes, and integrity in government.

The most challenging and potentially exciting aspect of the 2000 election plan would have involved our intention to campaign as an alliance or coalition, something we had never done before. If the Canadian Alliance really was a "principled coalition" of fiscal conservatives, social conservatives, small-d democrats, and reform-oriented federalists, how could we have presented and explained this coalition so as to maximize support from its constituent parts and the public at large? If the Canadian Alliance really was a national alliance that linked together Atlantic Canadian movers and shakers, reform-oriented federalists and nationalists in Quebec, Common Sense Revolutionaries in Ontario, and Western Reformers, how could we have presented this face of the Alliance in a national election campaign? In Ontario, where a big breakthrough was imperative, how could we have effectively demonstrated – on television, through literature, and at public rallies during a campaign – the strength and capability of an alliance among provincial Conservatives, Reformers, and disillusioned federal Conservatives and Liberals?

Perhaps when the alliance and coalition builders of the future finally discover how to do this, one night in the not too distant future, Canadians will switch on their television sets to witness an election campaign event unlike any in recent memory. On that national stage will be some twenty-first-century Tupper or Tilley from Atlantic Canada, some twenty-first-century Cartier from Quebec, some twenty-first-century Macdonald from Ontario, and some twenty-first-century George Brown from Canada West – one of them the first among equals in the Great Coalition created to bring into being the New Canada of the twenty-first century.

At present, Canada has no truly national party, and as yet no viable principled governing alternative to the Liberals. I am convinced, however, that such an alternative will emerge, and that it will be built and operated on the principle of alliance or coalition building. Such a party will then conduct, for the first time since the Confederation election of 1867, a national election campaign in which its leaders and candidates campaign as a true alliance or coalition for change. Its issue-driven platform will appeal to the various components of the coalition, but its greatest strength will be the commitment and determination of its leaders and members to work together to achieve their common goals. Perhaps its leader will even repeat the words of Sir John A. Macdonald in an address in Montreal during the 1867 campaign, when he said: "I am now ready to defend the union of Conservatives and Reformers in Upper and Lower Canada, Nova Scotia and New Brunswick . . . [and elsewhere]. When the object is a good one, coalitions are praiseworthy."*

I turned off the lights in my campaign office for Election 2000 and locked the door for the last time. But in my mind's eye I could still see the light of a campaign that might yet be shining somewhere up ahead.

---

* From the campaign speeches of John A. Macdonald, the *Montreal Gazette*, August 1867, as quoted in *Canadian Party Platforms 1867–1968*, compiled by D. Owen Carrigan (Toronto: Copp Clark Publishing Company [no publication year available]).

14

THE DOWNWARD SPIRAL

THE CANADIAN ALLIANCE EMERGED FROM ITS LEADERSHIP contest with national attention, the largest membership by far of any federal political party in Canada, a new leader, the capacity to raise an election war chest of $25 million, upward momentum in the polls, and the opportunity to win more than 4 million votes and at least 100 seats in the forthcoming federal election. This was the status and potential of the vehicle to which our members handed Stockwell Day the keys on July 8, 2000.

Five months later, when Election 2000 was over, the optimism and enthusiasm of the majority of Alliance members and supporters had turned to deep disappointment. The golden opportunity to drive the Liberals into a minority position, or even opposition, had been lost. Despite the enormous investment of time and energy required to bring the Canadian Alliance into being, and despite spending more money on the 2000 election campaign than Reform had done in the 1988, 1993, and 1997 federal elections combined, very little progress had been made.

Seven months after the election, following a series of embarrassing incidents all directly or indirectly involving Stockwell Day, thirteen Alliance MPs, including some of the most experienced and respected members of caucus, lost their confidence in the judgment and integrity of the leader and were suspended from the caucus for saying so. (Six of these members eventually returned, but seven joined with the PC members in the House to create the Progressive Conservative–Democratic Representative Coalition.)

At an emergency caucus meeting held in Calgary on July 17, 2001, close to forty of the fifty-three remaining members of the Alliance caucus were prepared to support a motion of non-confidence in the leader unless Stockwell agreed to resign and permit a leadership review. This he reluctantly agreed to do. After a long period of delay in which the national council of the party established the parameters for a new leadership contest, Stockwell resigned as leader in December 2001. In January 2002 he announced that he would seek to regain the office he had just vacated. With the Alliance now below the PCs in the national polls, its coffers bare, its caucus and national council divided, and its membership down from more than 200,000 to less than 70,000, the leadership contest commenced, with no candidates from Ontario or points east. In March 2002, Stockwell Day was replaced as leader by Stephen Harper. In April 2002, six of the seven Democratic Representative Coalition MPs applied for readmission to the Alliance caucus. And the massive job of rebuilding the fortunes and capacities of the party began anew.

During the two-year period from March 2000 to March 2002, public opinion polls showed that support levels for the Canadian Alliance had dropped from more than 30 per cent nationally at the conclusion of the CA leadership race and the beginning of the election campaign, to 24 per cent at the end of the November 27, 2000, federal election campaign, to 7 per cent nationally in the Gallup poll of March 2002.

■

What went wrong? The superficial explanation is that the Alliance was wrecked by internal dissent fomented by those who would not accept the change in the leadership. But in reality, public confidence in the party and the leadership was already in serious decline before any of the internal dissent was evident. Nor does that explanation honestly address the real reasons why some of the most able and conscientious members of an Opposition caucus and national council felt it necessary to distance themselves from their party's leadership, even if it meant jeopardizing their own positions and careers.

On more than one occasion, senior caucus members had tried to discuss what they perceived to be "the problem" with Stockwell Day himself. But they were left with the impression that either he simply didn't understand what was being said to him, or he rejected it and felt that they owed him unquestioned loyalty, regardless of their concerns.

Four incidents in particular led deputy leader Deborah Grey, House leader Chuck Strahl, deputy House leader Grant McNally, and Stockwell's chief of staff, Ian Todd, regretfully and with great personal anguish, to resign their positions in mid-April of 2001.

After a month of avoiding any detailed discussion of "the reasons why" they left – because of the damaging effect this could have on the confidence of the rest of the caucus and party – on May 15, Chuck Strahl stood before the national media and carefully read the following statement:

> Today, a few more of us have made the difficult decision to speak out about one of the major impediments to fulfilling [the Alliance] dream, which is the leadership of the Alliance itself. We realize that by speaking out, there are implications, including the fact that we will be suspended from caucus. But we are convinced that over the past few months the current leadership has exercised consistently bad judgment, dishonest communications, and lack of fidelity to our Party's Policies. Since we do not wish to be associated with such practices, we have chosen to speak out today in an effort to bring about change.

Standing with Chuck as he read these words were some of the party's most trustworthy and long-standing MPs, including Jay Hill, the straight-shooting Peace River MP with a reputation both in and out of caucus for "telling it like it is," and B.C. MP Val Meredith, who had actively supported Stockwell in the leadership race. Other MPs in the group included Grant McNally, Art Hanger, Jim Gouk,

Jim Pankiw, and Gary Lunn. And although she remained in the caucus for some weeks after, this statement was later endorsed by the first lady of Reform, our former caucus chair, the co-chair of the United Alternative conventions, the first interim leader of the Canadian Alliance, and our longest-sitting member in the House, Deborah Grey.

Chuck had been one of the consummate "team players" in caucus and in the party, both as a Reformer and in his initial efforts to serve under Stockwell's leadership. As such, he was still extremely reluctant to elaborate on the "consistently bad judgment, dishonest communications, and lack of fidelity" that had made his continued support of the leader impossible. This of course made it possible for Stockwell's defenders to maintain that these were false and specious charges, that their motivation was simply resentment of the change of leadership, and that the "disloyalty" of the "dissidents," as they came to be labelled, was the real cause of the Alliance's difficulties.

In my judgment, the assessment by Chuck and the so-called Group of Eight concerning the root causes of the Alliance's difficulties was accurate. But a fair assessment requires specific examples of what precisely was meant by "poor judgment," "dishonest communications," and "lack of fidelity" on the part of Stockwell Day, so others can understand that they were part of a pattern that was at the root of the growing loss of confidence in Stockwell's leadership.

A Deal with Jim Hart

In July 2000, with the new leader anxious to get into the House as soon as possible, it was announced that Jim Hart, the Reform MP from Okanagan-Coquihalla, would resign his seat to make way for Stockwell to run in a by-election. Jim resigned, and Stockwell was subsequently brought into the House in the by-election of September 11, 2001. It all seemed quite routine. What most of us didn't know at the time is that Jim had asked for a payment of $50,000 to compensate him for a severance package that he would have received from the House of Commons had he not run in the general election, and to compensate him for loss of salary following his resignation. Rather than finding some other supportive MP who would give up his seat with no strings attached, the leader's office, through Stockwell's chief of staff, Rod Love, entered into negotiations with Jim. A deal was struck. The money was to be paid by the party, but by the time the election was called Jim had not yet been fully paid. He then hired a lawyer and threatened to go public unless payment was made forthwith. The party subsequently paid Jim in full two days after the election call.

It is a criminal offence for an MP to accept money or a reward to quit Parliament or for anyone to give money or a reward for that purpose. An RCMP investigation later concluded (the results were never officially made public) that the Hart deal involved compensation for lost income but not a payment to resign, and no charges were laid. Jim's financial situation was such that his actions, while not commendable, were at least understandable. But for the newly chosen leader of a party like the Alliance, who had pledged to do politics differently and with integrity, to have even the remotest connection with such an arrangement was a gross error in judgment. A slightly different interpretation of the circumstances or the relevant section of the Criminal Code by the authorities could have meant criminal charges and, upon conviction, Stockwell's disqualification from sitting in Parliament.

All of this was kept under wraps at the time, but five months later (with the media investigating another matter involving Stockwell and party finances), it all came to light. Instead of taking responsibility for what had happened, Stockwell and the leader's office maintained that it was the party – not they – that had negotiated the deal. This forced party co-chairman Ken Kalopsis to publicly declare: "All I know is that the negotiations were handled by the leader's office and the party was asked to pay that amount, again by the leader's office, and the party consequently did that." Other members of the national council declared that they were faced with a *fait accompli* on the eve of the federal election and felt pressured to pay, to avoid causing the party and Stockwell political embarrassment.

An error in judgment on the part of the leader had led to a bad decision, which in turn led to dishonest communications to avoid responsibility, deflect criticism, and shift blame to others. It was to become a pattern of behaviour that would be repeated.

The Goddard Lawsuit

Even before the Alliance leadership race, I had heard about Stockwell's involvement in what was called the Goddard lawsuit. I was surprised that the media hadn't dug into it during the leadership contest, and that the Liberals hadn't tried to raise it during the election. (They joked that they were "saving it for later.") At the heart of this suit was a letter that Stockwell had written in April 1999 to the Red Deer *Advocate*, while he was an Alberta MLA and Cabinet minister. The letter criticized Red Deer lawyer Lorne Goddard, who was also a school board trustee, for representing a pedophile charged with possession of child pornography. Goddard filed a civil defamation suit to the tune of $600,000, and the rumour was that the costs of defending Stockwell were going through the roof. These costs had the potential to become an embarrassing political issue for the Klein government because they were being borne by the Alberta taxpayers through an insurance plan designed to protect MLAs from lawsuits.

Sure enough, this all hit the fan less than a month after the federal election, when Stockwell settled out of court for $60,000. Three weeks later the Alberta government released documents that showed the prolonged efforts to defend Stockwell's position had run the total costs up to $800,000, and that the suit could have been settled for minimal costs eighteen months earlier if Stockwell had agreed to do so. More than half of the $800,000 went to pay for Stockwell's legal defence, the bulk of which was handled by the Calgary law firm of Bennett Jones. Stockwell had finally agreed to settle only after receiving a letter from the executive director of the Alberta government's Justice department directing him to do so or cover his own legal fees.

Members of the Canadian Alliance, including myself, have advocated that governments and the courts should come down like a ton of bricks on child pornography and the predatory practices of pedophiles. But there are ethical and effective methods of advancing this position in the political arena, and attacking a lawyer who is defending a client before the courts is not one of them. The fact that Stockwell wrote the letter in the first place was an error in judgment, made worse by the prolonged and expensive effort to defend the indefensible with taxpayers' dollars. Not only did this event tend to discredit whatever else the Alliance might say on the pornography issue, it made it difficult for Alliance members in the House to keep up the attack on Liberals' misuse of taxpayers' dollars. The Liberal rebuttal was simply to point to Stockwell's "personal boondoggle."

But the damage didn't stop there. Once again, an error in judgment was compounded by communications intended to mitigate it. At first Stockwell defended his actions by saying that people who knew the facts would not hold the costs against him, and that he had no choice but to use the taxpayer-funded insurance fund to defend himself. On January 18, a news conference was scheduled to enable Stockwell to clear the air. Party officials fully expected him to offer an outright apology to all concerned. Instead, Stockwell said that, while he was sorry for the costs, he had acted in good faith and stood by his principles. When pressed by reporters, he stopped conspicuously short of admitting an error in judgment or offering a believable apology. That weekend things got worse when a poll was released showing that three-quarters of Albertans felt that taxpayers should not be on the hook for Stockwell's legal defence, and comments by Klein that "Day should pay his share." Klein, of course, with a provincial election call now only weeks away, was trying to put some distance between himself and his former Finance minister.

It was now almost impossible for Stockwell, or any other Alliance MP, to hold a news conference without questions concerning the Goddard suit dominating the agenda. Finally, on March 5, almost two months after news of the settlement broke, Stockwell issued the apology that should have been made at the outset and offered to try to make amends by contributing $60,000 (from mortgaging his home) to the settlement. By then, however, these actions appeared to be concessions wrung from a reluctant politician by media and public pressure, rather than a sincere effort to rectify a wrong for which he was responsible.

Around this same time, Stockwell called me on the phone saying he wanted my "personal affirmation" in the media. On a later occasion he asked me up to his office and requested the same thing, saying that he had said supportive things about me in the media when I was under attack, and it was time for me to reciprocate. I wanted to be honest with Stockwell, and I told him that I had been handling questions from the media, members, and the public on the leadership issue in two ways. One was by simply not responding, because some of the questions being asked about the wisdom of his actions simply couldn't be answered honestly without giving the impression that I was critical, and that was the last impression he would want created at this time. The other way was to answer them "at 30,000 feet" – to say that the party needed to decide what it wanted to become, where it was headed, and whether the current leadership would build that kind of party. If the leadership was willing and able, it deserved to be supported; if it wasn't, the party would have to address its concerns at the next convention. Stockwell said that it was this sort of vagueness that generated the feeling that I was less than supportive. At this point, I said that I did have doubts as to the answer to these kinds of questions, which is why I preferred to say nothing at all. Stockwell made no serious attempt to inquire as to what those doubts might have been, although on the occasion of his second request I raised with him the matter of errors in judgment and misleading communications result-ing in a general loss of confidence. But Stockwell reinforced the very point I was trying to make when he gave me the distinct impression that he thought I could "make things better" simply by making some statement to the media that I didn't really believe. I felt that he very much underestimated the nature of the problem, and very much overestimated my influence.

The Britton Donation
Even before Stockwell's eventual apology for the Goddard lawsuit, yet another crisis engulfed the Alliance and its leader. In February 2001, rumours began to swirl in Edmonton and Calgary about funds paid to a law firm from the Alberta Risk Management Fund being recirculated as contributions to a political party. In other words, a kickback scheme. Because the fund was operated by the provincial Tories, much of the initial criticism of the use of the fund had been directed towards Klein by Liberal opponents preparing for the provincial election. But by February 19, when the facts behind the

rumour came out, it was Stockwell Day and the Alliance that were implicated.

Media reports alleged that a $70,000 donation had been made to the Canadian Alliance by a lawyer at the same firm that received the lion's share of legal fees incurred in defending Stockwell from the Goddard lawsuit. The lawyer, William Britton, was a partner in Bennett Jones and had no personal involvement whatsoever in Stockwell's defence. But the original cheque to the party had been written on the firm's trust account and a tax receipt had been issued to Bennett Jones. After the matter came to light, an investigation by the firm and a committee of the party's national council concluded that, while the cheque had been written on the firm's trust account, the contribution had actually come from Mr. Britton and the receipt should have gone to him. By now, however, no matter what the facts were or what explanations the firm or the party offered, to the public the whole affair looked like a "kickback": the prolongation of the Goddard lawsuit and the escalation of the legal bills that accompanied it appeared to have resulted in a large contribution by the law firm to the party led by Stockwell Day. This conclusion was false, but the appearance was incredibly bad.

At the root of this dilemma were two more errors in judgment. The first was made by the contributor. Surely warning bells should have been going off in Mr. Britton's head when instructing that cheque to be written. Certainly those warning bells went off when it arrived at the Alliance national office. It was executive director Glenn McMurray who let the leader's office know that a large donation had been received from Bennett Jones, and that this would be reported in the party's regular filing of financial contribution information with Elections Canada. There was also the question as to whether this was an anonymous contribution by the firm on behalf of someone else, because if it was, it couldn't be kept by the party. The latter question was cleared up by contacting Bennett Jones, but the political question of whether to accept the donation at all under the circumstances was left to the leader's office. The short answer, the ethical answer, and the politically prudent answer to that question should have been "return it," with instructions to do so coming from the top. Neglecting to do so was another error in judgment.

Instead, Stockwell first attempted to shrug off the issue by saying controversy "went with the territory" of being a political leader. Then several of his supporters on the national council implied that the fault lay with the party administration, which was most unfair since they were the ones who had sounded the warning. And finally another attempt was made to divert attention from the real issue by charging unnamed "Manning-ites" on the council with releasing information damaging to the leader. The donation was then declared by Stockwell and others to be perfectly acceptable, talking points were issued for caucus members to support this conclusion, and the matter was declared to be "resolved." But, of course, it hadn't been resolved to the satisfaction of many members of caucus, the party, or the public.

The Demand for Loyalty

As the number of incidents undermining confidence in Stockwell's leadership mounted, he began to appeal more and more for "loyalty" from the caucus, council, staff, and membership. The vast majority of Alliance people, including myself, sincerely wanted to give him that loyalty, but it had to be grounded in something deeper than the mere request for it. What kind of loyalty were we being asked to give? Loyalty to principle and policy? Missteps in this area during the election had shaken confidence in Stockwell's own commitment to some of those policies and principles. Loyalty to the party and the concept of the Alliance? But Stockwell himself had virtually forsaken alliance and coalition building, at least for the time being. Loyalty to the people of Canada – our political masters? But the Canadian people themselves were losing confidence in the Alliance leadership. If MPs went home and followed their constituents' wishes, they would find themselves drawing farther away from – not closer to – Stockwell. Which left only one last basis on which to appeal for loyalty: an appeal for loyalty to the leader himself, for its own sake. That kind of loyalty, however, cannot be commanded; it can only be earned.

It was on this loyalty issue that Stockwell made another of those costly errors in judgment. On several occasions – at internal meetings in February and March 2001 – when requesting personal loyalty from his caucus officers and key staff, Stockwell had emphasized the point by saying: "If I kill my grandmother with an axe, I want you to stand up and say she had it coming." On at least one occasion he said this pointedly to Deborah Grey. Whether this was intended to be humorous in a macabre way I do not know. But the last person in the world to whom I would ever make such a statement, if I were trying to engender loyalty to myself, would be Deborah Grey. In effect, Stockwell was saying, "No matter what I do or say, I expect you to get out there and defend and support me. And I want you to support me, not by showing me the error of my ways, but by dishonest communications – by standing up and saying 'She had it coming.'" Deborah Grey was one of the straightest shooters in our caucus. If this was what Stockwell meant by loyalty, Deborah simply couldn't give it and live with her conscience.

Your truly loyal friends are those who tell you what you need to hear, not what you want to hear. I thought of this in mid-February when, in the midst of the Goddard controversy, Stockwell dismissed Phil von Finckenstein, with the implication that he needed more loyalty in the communications department, and hired Ezra Levant as his new director of communications. I had known Ezra since he was a teenager, and his whole family had been extremely supportive of me in Calgary Southwest. Ezra was also a good friend of the Days', especially their son, Logan. I liked Ezra, admired his considerable abilities, and hired him to work in the leader of the Opposition's office as our Question Period coordinator in 1997. He did good work for us, developing questions designed to resonate more effectively with the media and coaching me and other MPs on presentation. But Ezra got us into trouble on several occasions (leading to lawsuits alleging defamation) because of difficulties in discerning, in the heat of battle, that line between "the truth, the spin, and the lie." When Ezra – who described himself as a "Stockaholic" – eventually came to see me in his capacity as Stockwell's new communications director, I reminded him of this difficulty and suggested a way to avoid it. What Stockwell really needed was a check and balance rather than a soulmate. So, after Ezra and Stockwell had agreed on a communications piece, one that was no doubt provocative and very much designed to catch the evening news, would it not be wise for Ezra to do one more thing before giving it to the media? Would it not be advisable for him to go into his office for thirty seconds, close the door, and ask himself just one simple question: "Is it true?"

Whether Ezra ever did this, I don't know, but within days he was embroiled in a nasty controversy with the media over disclosure of his salary, and three months later, he was gone in a cloud of controversy.

The Talk Show Hoax

On Saturday, March 17, 2001, Rahim Jaffer, the likeable and easy-going MP for Edmonton Strathcona, was supposed to be on a national radio show originating from Vancouver's CKNW. Rahim was to participate by telephone from Edmonton. But when the time came to do the interview, Rahim, who was in the coffee shop business, was otherwise engaged opening up a new shop. So his assistant, Matthew Johnston, did the show for him, posing as Rahim. A woman from Edmonton listening to the show apparently recognized Matthew's voice and called in, prompting the show's producer to phone Rahim to confirm that he had actually been on the show. Rahim said "Yes," lying to protect his employee and friend.

The story as told by Rahim in Ottawa, with help from his friend Ezra, was that Matthew had acted entirely on his own. Matthew was then fired but given a generous severance package. Chuck Strahl, the House leader, first learned of all of this from Jason Kenney at a strategy meeting at Stornoway (Stockwell was not then present). Chuck told Jason that Rahim's account had better be the whole truth, because the media would be looking for contradictions,* and if they found any, Rahim would be in even greater trouble. Jason then said, "I wouldn't worry about that; $40,000 buys a lot of silence." The reference to $40,000 was made without any elaboration. The next day the same statement about $40,000 buying a lot of silence was repeated by Ezra Levant to both Chuck and Deborah Grey, who this time demanded an explanation. Ezra then said that

---

* Sure enough, the following week the *Edmonton Journal* ran stories quoting the CKNW producer, Shannon Gunning, and questioning the veracity of Rahim's account of the incident.

it meant nothing, that he was just shooting off his mouth and it was no big deal.

By now Chuck's confidence in how the whole issue was being handled had been thoroughly shaken, and he went to Stockwell, begging him to get to the bottom of the affair before someone did something illegal. The next morning Stockwell told the strategy group that he had asked those involved to ensure that Rahim's description of what had happened was accurate, that he had received assurances that it was, and that the matter was therefore closed. On March 20, Rahim gave his explanation to the House, apologizing to the talk show, his constituents, his parents, and to his fellow MPs for his error in judgment and wrongdoing.

Most of the MPs, myself included, felt terrible that Rahim had gotten himself into this pickle and wanted to give him the benefit of the doubt in accepting his explanation and apology. But once again, an error in judgment had been made, and the confidence of the caucus officers – in how it had been handled and in the integrity of the communications surrounding it – had been badly shaken. For them, living with this worry, wondering what "the next disclosure" might be, and worrying about the integrity of communications emanating from the leader's office on such matters was becoming more and more nerve-racking.

The Spy Affair

On the weekend of April 7, Alliance caucus members woke to headlines that sounded like a "Keystone Cops" spoof. The news was that Stockwell had met with and hired a former "undercover agent" to help get more information on the Prime Minister's controversial golf course and hotel dealings in Quebec. He had been encouraged to do so by two Alliance MPs with a particular interest in investigating the criminal activities of biker gangs, Darrel Stinson and Myron Thompson. The next day, Stockwell acknowledged that he had met the man, but that it was untrue that he had been hired or that the purpose was to dig up dirt on the Liberals. The following day, Stockwell issued another statement saying that no "formal" job offer had been tendered, that he had in fact *not* met the man personally, and if any job offer had been made it was now withdrawn. Myron and Darrel, who had been quite vocal on the agent's alleged meeting with themselves and Stockwell two days previous, went incommunicado for a day, and then emerged to confirm that no such meeting with Stockwell had occurred.

By mid-week, the "agent" in question had been identified as a Mr. James Leigh, a colourful character with legitimate investigative credentials, living in London, Ontario. Despite his reputation as an "undercover man" he was now quite willing to talk to the media. He described as "really cool" his visit late in March to the House of Commons and the offices of the leader of the Opposition, and alleged that his assignment included investigating Alliance MPs who might have been leaking damaging information to the media.

On April 17 I received an e-mail from a James Leigh through my online mailbox on the Canadian Alliance Web site. It was entitled "Witchhunt," included a telephone number and a return e-mail address, and read as follows:

> Mr. Manning: Perhaps I was hired by the Alliance to investigate Anderson and other loyal Preston supporters as well. We should talk, don't you think? I have tapes and witnesses.

I never responded to Mr. Leigh's invitation. Other MPs received similar messages.

By now, the national council of the party was getting concerned. Ken Kalopsis, the party's co-chairman, accompanied by his lawyer, met with Mr. Leigh, who repeated his assertion that his duties were to have included investigating Alliance MPs. Ken then sent a strongly worded e-mail to John Reynolds, the Alliance whip, asking him and Chuck Strahl to look into these allegations and questioning the judgment of any Alliance MP who would have anything to do with Mr. Leigh. John replied that the allegations were completely unfounded and that it was inappropriate for the party to be questioning the judgment of MPs.

The pattern was familiar: errors in judgment, denial of responsibility, and miscommunication in an attempt to explain or cover up, leading to a loss of trust. There is a place for organized and hard-nosed investigations of suspected misconduct and cover-ups by governments, and in our parliamentary system the Opposition has a responsibility to try to bring such misconduct and cover-ups to light. But Myron and Darrel, much as I like them, are not the people to advise the leader on such matters, and hiring a James Leigh is hardly a responsible approach to this challenge. In an effort to get to the bottom of things, House leader Chuck Strahl held a conference call with everyone involved (except Stockwell) during which he asked Darrel Stinson if it was true that Stockwell had known about the job offer all along. Darrel answered that he had kept Stockwell "in the loop" during the discussions with Leigh, "but I'm prepared to take the hit for Stock on this one." How could the leadership of any party, particularly one pledged to doing politics differently, maintain any moral authority if this ethic became the norm?

The Justice Silcoff Affair

Sometimes when a political leader or party is in the midst of a crisis, something else will come up to divert attention mercifully onto something less damaging, or even something advantageous. Governing parties have the resources to create such diversions, but usually the most that opposition parties can do is to take full advantage of such opportunities when they come along. Shortly after the "spy affair" began, such a diversion occurred. But before the Alliance and the caucus officers could breathe a sigh of relief, another error in judgment, compounded by over-the-top communications, landed leader and party in yet another crisis.

On the same weekend that the Keystone Cops story broke, lawyers for the Business Development Bank of Canada sought an order from a Quebec Superior Court judge to search the home of Mr. François Beaudoin and to seize and destroy any documents relating to the finances of the Auberge Grand-Mère in the Prime Minister's riding. This was the same Mr. Beaudoin who had resisted pressure from Prime Minister Chrétien to grant a loan to his friend, Yvon Duhaime, and whose employment by the BDC had been terminated in October 1999. The judge in question, Justice Joel Silcoff, had been appointed to the bench by the Chrétien government the previous

June, and prior to that he had been a partner in the Montreal law firm that represented the Grand-Mère Golf Club.

The peculiar combination of facts and circumstances in this case was enough to suggest, again, that there was something rotten in Shawinigan. The media were suspicious that there was more to the story than met the eye – possibly more evidence of a cover-up of the Shawinigan shenanigans. All the Opposition had to do was to keep asking questions. But Stockwell was so anxious to divert attention away from the "spy affair" that he went over the top in his comments on Judge Silcoff. Instead of keeping the focus on BDC and the Shawinigate connection, Stockwell (with little more than newspaper reports to go on) accused the judge of having an obvious conflict of interest. One would have thought, given Stockwell's recent misadventures with lawyers and the courts in the Goddard suit, that alarm bells would have been going off all over the leader's office. But Stockwell and Ezra were winging it and throwing caution to the winds. Not only should the order be overturned, but the Alliance would file a complaint with the Canadian Judicial Council concerning Silcoff's conflict of interest.

By now the issue in the media was not the Shawinigate connection but Stockwell's attack on the judge. Prominent members of the legal and judicial community rushed to Judge Silcoff's defence, and it was rumoured that the judge was contemplating a suit against Stockwell and the Alliance. By this time the alarm bells truly were ringing all over Alliance offices. Ian Todd, the chief of staff, was still being told that the leader wanted to pursue this initiative – to go after Silcoff – on limited evidence of wrongdoing, despite warnings from Chuck as a member of the Board of Internal Economy of the House of Commons that the House would not cover any legal defence if Stockwell were sued, and despite similar warnings from the party. Finally, after Ian simply refused to proceed, reason began to prevail, and by the next day Stockwell and the Alliance were in full retreat. John Reynolds, the whip, assured the media and the judge that no personal offence had been intended. But more damage (reflected in the polls) had been inflicted on the Alliance.

■

Since the turn of the year, key staff, caucus officers, and members had been carrying out their parliamentary and party duties while at the same time trying to cope with leader-related crisis situations that were occurring about every two weeks. While there were other examples of the same phenomenon, it was the "talk show hoax," the "spy affair," and the attack on Justice Silcoff that proved to be the straws that broke the camels' backs for Chief of Staff Ian Todd, House leader Chuck Strahl, and deputy House leader Grant McNally. In Deborah Grey's case, it was these events plus the peculiar "demand for loyalty" mentioned earlier.

On the morning of April 23, Ian and Chuck literally ran into each other in the foyer outside Stockwell's office. Each had a resignation letter in his hand, and, unbeknownst to the other, had decided that today was the day to present it.

For Ian, the past six months had been particularly harrowing and disappointing. He had taken the position of chief of staff at Stockwell's request but against the advice of most of his friends, who feared it would be a no-win situation. They felt that Stockwell's propensity for errors in judgment could not be managed and that, in the end, Ian would be blamed and suspected of disloyalty if things went from bad to worse. But Ian honestly felt that he might be able to smooth the transition and bridge the gap between Stockwell and my former staff, many of whom were either quitting or being fired.

Because of the crude way the firing was being done, Ian felt that Stockwell and the party were laying themselves wide open to unlawful dismissal suits and damaging political fallout. Nor did Stockwell seem to understand that almost all of the departing staff were more than employees. Most were supporters of the principles and policies of the party who played other key volunteer roles. When they were callously dismissed, he ran the risk of alienating important constituencies within the party and the public. For example, Sam Okoro, the loyal driver and security man at Stornoway, was deeply involved in the black community in Winnipeg and Ottawa and had come to the defence of the party and me time and time again when we were falsely accused of racism. It is understandable that Stockwell might wish to hire his own driver, but the way Sam was fired was unconscionable. He simply got a phone call one day from

Stockwell's office and was told to deposit his keys and cellphone at Stornoway – he was through. No interview, no explanation, no offer of assistance to find something else, and no thank-you. This callous and unfair treatment alienated a good portion of Sam's community when they heard about it, and it could easily have resulted in wrongful-dismissal suit had Sam been so inclined. Moreover, Sam was not the only Alliance employee to receive this kind of treatment. Ian was anxious to get staff relations back on a more professional basis.

In any event, Ian had given it his best shot, and had come, by a different route, to the same conclusion as the caucus officers – to get out. Events now followed swiftly. At 3:00 p.m. on the same day, Deborah Grey told Stockwell that she wished to step back from her position as deputy leader. At a stormy shadow cabinet meeting that evening, the first after the Easter break, MPs angrily demanded answers concerning the "spy affair" and the attack on Justice Silcoff. The following day, veteran Calgary MP Art Hanger called publicly for Stockwell's resignation. At an equally stormy meeting of the full caucus on Wednesday, Stockwell presented the caucus with new officers "loyal" to himself: John Reynolds as House leader, Cheryl Gallant as deputy House leader, Dick Harris as whip, and Garry Breitkreuz as deputy whip. On his way into the meeting that morning, Stockwell had buttonholed Macleod MP Dr. Grant Hill and asked him whether he would like to be deputy leader. A surprised Dr. Hill said yes, if it would help, and found himself being announced as deputy leader a short time later. An election was held to choose a new caucus chairman to replace Deborah Grey, and Randy White was voted in. After a great venting of caucus frustrations, Stockwell was given one week to come up with a "strategic plan" that would get the party back on track. The next day Stockwell fired Art Hanger as the Alliance Defence critic, and relieved Gary Lunn of his critic responsibilities for sympathizing with Art.

During all this turmoil I had deliberately stayed away from Ottawa. I'd gone to check out some fishing spots in Montana with my son Nathan. By now there were a number of veteran Ottawa reporters – Sheldon Alberts of the *National Post*, Brian Laghi of the *Globe and Mail*, Tim Harper of the *Toronto Star*, Julie Van Dusen and

Don Newman of the CBC – who would know exactly what to ask me. They would have taken any one of Stockwell's "miscommunications" and asked me, "Is this true?" If I had said yes or that I didn't know, I would have been lying, which I was not prepared to do. And if I had said no, then I would have made a bad situation even worse. The only position for me to take was that a former leader who was still in the caucus and in the House should not comment on the activities of the present leader.

The next week I returned to Ottawa in time for the Wednesday caucus meeting at which Stockwell was to present his "strategic plan." The whole meeting was bizarre. Stockwell began by giving an election-style address – as if the caucus were a public audience to be persuaded of the worthiness of the Alliance cause, rather than colleagues who were desperately worried about recent events and looking for frankness and reassurance from the leader. The "strategic plan" was then presented in PowerPoint form. But it said nothing about the real difficulties – the errors in judgment and erroneous communications – that were at the heart of the Silcoff incident, the "spy affair," and the lawsuits and threatened lawsuits. It was essentially a plan to prepare for the next election, and MPs didn't know what to think. Were they missing something, or was Stockwell completely missing the point?

When the presentation concluded, almost every MP, including myself, spoke briefly, some trying to improve the plan and others trying to address its deficiencies. But it was no-nonsense Jim Pankiw from Saskatoon who got up and said, "What's going on here? That didn't even touch the problems we identified last week." Randy, as chairman, tried to get the caucus to give unanimous consent to the plan "in principle," but the MPs were having none of it. Art Hanger simply blew up, making it clear that he would not give consent to anything and again demanding Stockwell's resignation.

All of this notwithstanding, Stockwell went to the media thronged outside the Alliance caucus room and told them that the caucus had given unanimous consent to his plan. The talking points already prepared by the leader's office boldly proclaimed that the caucus "unanimously endorsed the steps outlined in a strategic plan presented this morning" and "unanimously supported passing this plan on to the party's national council." Once again, an error in judgment – failing to address the causes of the crisis of confidence in Stockwell's leadership – had been followed by a dishonest communiqué. This pattern seemed to reassert itself more strongly than ever in crisis situations.

It was at this May 2 caucus meeting in Ottawa that some sort of "divide" was crossed with respect to the Alliance's official explanation of its difficulties. In response to the fact that the Alliance was falling steadily in the polls – and that our own constituents were losing confidence – the leader's group would vigorously assert that it was the actions of "dissidents" that were pulling us down. Not the disappointment of the election campaign, not the foolishness of the Goddard lawsuit, not the $800,000 bill passed on to the Alberta taxpayers, not the cloud of kickback allegations, not the "talk show hoax," not the spy we met but never met and hired but never hired, not the over-the-top attack on Silcoff – no, the reason we were down in the polls was because of the expressed concerns of those who wanted the real causes addressed.

A large number of caucus members simply didn't buy this analysis. They regarded it as yet another error in judgment accompanied by a dishonest communication. But unfortunately, other caucus members (particularly the newer ones) did. It was a less painful explanation than the truth, and it shifted the blame for our dilemma on to "others." And the more they repeated it to themselves, the media, and their constituents, the more it became the mantra of the party, making the likelihood that the real causes would ever be acknowledged even more remote.

A few days later, Stockwell, again seeking with Ezra's help to divert attention from the challenges to his leadership, delivered a strongly pro-Israel speech to a Toronto audience. Unfortunately, his Foreign Affairs critic, Monte Solberg, knew nothing about the positions enunciated by Stockwell until he read them in the newspapers the next day. The National Council on Canada-Arab Relations denounced the speech as hate-mongering and threatened a lawsuit. By the end of the week, Stockwell had backtracked, offering an apology of sorts in the House to anyone who had been offended. Now both the Jewish and the Arab communities had been alienated, and our Foreign Affairs critic was left to pick up the pieces. Monte, too, now began seriously to question Stockwell's leadership capacities.

On May 9, Stockwell and the new caucus officers issued an ultimatum. Alliance MPs were told either to support the leader or leave the caucus. As Chuck Strahl said, "It was time to fish or cut bait." So on May 15, Chuck and seven other MPs – Jay Hill, Val Meredith, Grant McNally, Jim Gouk, Art Hanger, Jim Pankiw, and Gary Lunn – held their news conference formally calling on Stockwell to resign and citing his "consistent errors in judgment, dishonest communications, and lack of fidelity to Alliance policies." At this point, none of them had any plan for forming a new group or joining any other group in the House. They just wanted to distance themselves from Stockwell's actions and statements.

Ezra Levant took vehement exception to the reference to dishonest communications and sent Chuck a letter threatening him with a lawsuit. Like so many of Ezra's communications and threats, it went completely over the top. Even the caucus officers loyal to Stockwell now recognized that under the circumstances Ezra was a liability, not an asset, and he was asked to resign.

Over the next two months, the situation continued to deteriorate. An organization called Grassroots for Day was founded by a individual named George Bears to rally support for Stockwell, particularly among the Christian community. It publicly attacked Chuck Strahl, launched a lawsuit against Deborah Grey, issued numerous news releases, and placed hundreds of automated calls denouncing the "dissidents," and doing so in the name of the Alliance's grassroots membership. When the court, in connection with the lawsuit, finally forced Grassroots for Day to file its membership list, it was found to contain the names of three people. The contagion was spreading.

Throughout this time of turmoil, the whole concept of building the Alliance and reaching out to potential political allies was virtually abandoned, except when making a pronouncement on that subject could serve as a diversion from the internal problems. On June 14, Stockwell announced that he would direct the national council to hold a party-wide referendum on whether the Alliance should unite with the Progressive Conservatives. But he failed to advise the caucus or the national council in advance, leading to more confusion and resentment. Corporate contributions to the party had virtually dried up, and contributions from members were also falling. The party was in no position to incur the expense of a party-wide referendum. But Stockwell had apparently not considered this, nor had he consulted with the party's financial officers. Eventually the proposal was watered down to a mail survey to be held in conjunction with a regular fundraising appeal to the membership.

One of the few good things that happened to the Alliance during this period was that Jim MacEachern came to Ottawa from British Columbia to serve as the new chief of staff. Jim was a calm, quiet professional with strong Tory connections as well as a strong commitment to the concept of the Alliance. He was not seen as belonging by association to any one "camp," and this was beneficial. Unfortunately, Jim's arrival almost launched another disaster. The news release announcing his hiring had been "hyped up" to allege that he had held senior positions in the Harris campaign organization and the Campbell campaign organization in B.C. Both issued disclaimers saying this was not the case, causing Jim needless embarrassment: his own credentials were impressive enough without embellishment.

In late May, at an acrimonious national council meeting in Calgary, Stockwell and his supporters insisted that Rick Anderson be suspended from the council because of his criticism of the leadership and support of the "dissident" Group of Eight. Suspension and recrimination, not reconciliation, were becoming the standard method of dealing with dissent, both in caucus and on the council.

By now the media speculation was that the Group of Eight might grow to twelve or more, which would give them official party status in the House if they chose to pursue it. All eyes were on Deborah Grey to see whether she would join the Group of Eight or remain in the no man's land of her present position. Deborah describes this period of her political life as the worst she ever endured. The attacks of Grassroots for Day and others were far harder for her to endure than all the slings and arrows that had been hurled at her by Liberal and Tory opponents over the years. She had prayed long and hard about how to handle the acrimonious divisions that were now appearing among Christian supporters over Stockwell's leadership.

She had consulted friends and colleagues and family. She had surveyed her board, her membership, and her constituents, but the final decision was up to her. On July 17, the Alliance caucus was scheduled to meet in Calgary to address the leadership issue, and it was imperative that Deborah make her position known before then. On July 3 she announced her conclusion that it would be in the best interests of the party and Stockwell himself if he were to resign. Stockwell and the caucus officers then suspended her. She described her feelings at the time as an enormous sense of relief. By now, the Group of Eight had grown to the Group of Eleven with the addition of Monte Solberg, Brian Fitzpatrick, and Andy Burton. With the addition of Deborah and Manitoba MP Inky Mark, its number stood at thirteen as the remaining Alliance caucus members assembled in Calgary for the showdown with the leader.

Stockwell was by now being told by the caucus officers that there would very likely be a vote of non-confidence in his leadership at the Calgary meeting, and that it had a good chance of passing. On July 8, one year to the day after he had won the Alliance leadership, Stockwell made his own counter-proposal. He would take a leave of absence until the next Alliance convention and offer "terms of reconciliation," whereby suspended members would be asked to rejoin caucus, Grant Hill would serve as acting leader subject to caucus and council approval, Ken Kalopsis must resign as party co-chairman, and the work of the Unity Committee (seeking ways of co-operating with the PCs) would continue. Stockwell insisted that the main problem was the split in the caucus, not the leadership factors that lay beneath and behind the split. When Chuck Strahl pointed out that this plan didn't come to grips with the real issue, and that it was also inconsistent with the party's constitution, Stockwell withdrew it. Some of the caucus officers alleged that it had been rejected because the "dissidents" had not been promised their previous positions.

Stockwell now apparently told his inner circle that he had no intention of resigning at all and would tell the caucus so. They erupted in anger, especially Randy White, who had been telling caucus members that Stockwell would agree to resign ninety days before an official party leadership vote at the next convention,

therefore making any non-confidence vote by the caucus unnecessary. The caucus officers were convinced that if Stockwell did not
offer to resign prior to the leadership vote by the membership, up to
forty-two members of the fifty-three-member caucus might support
a non-confidence vote.

Stockwell first implied that he would hang tough, then said he
would offer caucus a choice between his plan and the caucus officers'
proposal. Then, just before the caucus meeting was to begin, he
finally agreed "in the best interests of the party" to proceed with the
caucus officers' plan. Apparently when the plan was presented to
caucus – I was not in attendance – those who had serious reservations about Stockwell's ability to lead thought they had achieved
their objective. Stockwell would be resigning, and the party would
have a chance to reassess him and, if necessary, find a new leader.
What they didn't know was that the national council – itself crip-
pled and divided – would delay the leadership vote for almost nine
months, leaving Stockwell and his supporters in control of the
leader's office and much of the party machinery until December
2001. During that period the underlying problems with Stockwell's
leadership continued to manifest themselves, the lack of progress in
the polls and with the public was blamed entirely on the "rebel
alliance," and the caucus missed its one and only opportunity to
force a more expeditious resolution.

The compromise reached at the caucus meeting in Calgary also
had a negative effect on the Group of Thirteen, the majority of
whom were not convinced that this compromise had resolved anything. They proceeded with plans to give name and substance to
their new group and on July 19 announced the formation of the
Democratic Representative Caucus (DRC) with twelve members
(Brian Fitzpatrick had returned to the Alliance caucus). They
intended to seek recognition as an official parliamentary caucus from
the Speaker of the House, but by now some members felt certain that
Stockwell was on his way out, and that they could return to the
Alliance having made their point. Eventually Jim Gouk, Art Hanger,
Andy Burton, Monte Solberg, and Gary Lunn did so.

The members of the DRC were still committed to "alliance or
coalition building" among "others likeminded" in the federal political

arena. They had been reaching out to the Progressive Conservatives in the House and were making some progress. Key members of the Alliance caucus were also still committed to this concept, and a Unity Committee had been formed to continue to investigate the possibilities. Their efforts had, however, been hampered by the leadership problems, and by the fact that the Tories felt themselves to be on more equal footing in discussion with the smaller DRC group than the larger Alliance caucus. In June, Stockwell had declared that the Alliance was interested in exploring joint candidacies at the riding level, and the Unity Committee had held meetings with PC representatives in Halifax and St. Albert. The DRC also proposed to hold a joint meeting with PC representatives at Mont Tremblant in Quebec on August 17–18, 2001.

I was anxious to encourage all these initiatives, and prior to the Mont Tremblant meeting I wrote an op-ed piece for the *National Post* stating my view that both Stockwell Day and Joe Clark were to be commended for encouraging their MPs to discuss coalition building. Some of the media and the Alliance leadership took this as an endorsement of the DRC. My primary intention at the time was to endorse coalition builders in all the camps, although it was true that I saw a more genuine willingness to pursue this goal among the leadership of the DRC than I did among the leadership of either the Alliance or the Tories. Ultimately what emerged from the Mont Tremblant talks was the Progressive Conservative–Democratic Reform (PC-DR) Coalition, officially recognized as a caucus (though not a party) by the Speaker of the House on September 24, 2001.

While our intentions in proposing and working to create the Canadian Alliance had been to bring all these people under one roof, now there were actually three groups, and the one least likely to be seen by the public as a principled coalition builder, unless its leadership problems were resolved, was the Alliance itself. In August 2001 an Ipsos-Reid poll showed that Stockwell's popularity in Alberta, the province that knew him best and which had most strongly supported the Alliance concept, had tumbled to a record low of 21 per cent from 66 per cent just a year before. It was also clear to me that the public considered all the internal machinations of the Alliance, and even the creation of the PC-DR Coalition, to be "inside baseball" and only remotely connected to real voter concerns.

On December 12 I attended the last Alliance caucus meeting of the year, at which Stockwell made his resignation official. There was still not a hint in Stockwell's address that he recognized the roots of the problem and was prepared to deal with them. Instead, he laid the blame for the Alliance's misfortunes entirely on the caucus revolt of July 17 and the "rebel alliance."

■

The position from which I viewed political events from July 2001 until the spring of 2002 – including those contributing to the down-ward spiral of the Canadian Alliance – was a peculiar and untenable one. I viewed Stockwell's initial weeks in Parliament (September–October 2000) as his supportive but silent seatmate in the House. I viewed the federal election campaign from October 23 to November 27, 2000, principally as the Canadian Alliance candidate in Calgary Southwest, spending only thirteen days outside the riding and none on the national campaign tour. At two post-election meet-ings in Calgary – one with some of our key financial contributors and the other with southern Alberta constituency presidents and campaign managers – Stockwell was asked point-blank why people like Deborah Grey and myself had not been intimately involved in the national campaign. His response was to say that we had been, and to express profound gratitude for our help. The fact that there were several people in the audience who knew that this simply was not true didn't seem to register.

Having been re-elected, I spent the better part of December and January recuperating from prostate cancer surgery before returning to the House on February 5, 2001. I then spent the next year in virtual isolation from the turmoil of the Alliance caucus, serving (at my request) as the Opposition critic for Science and Technology. My chief preoccupation was to participate in the deliberations of the Health Committee on legislation to regulate assisted human reproduction and related research. On January 31, 2002, having fulfilled my promise to supporters to run in the 2000 election and to serve for at least a year thereafter, and having helped the Health Committee to complete its report on a subject I consider of vital importance for the future, I resigned my seat in the Commons to pursue my political ideals and other interests free of the constraints of partisan politics.

During this period I received a growing number of inquiries from the media and from Alliance members and supporters asking what was going on, what could be done to "get the party back on track," and why didn't I personally "do something" to "help Stockwell out" or to "constrain the dissidents."

I found, however, that if I said anything substantive, even privately, concerning the real roots of the problem or what might be done to address them, this was perceived as undermining the new leadership. On several occasions I responded guardedly to letters from Alliance members pleading simply to know "what is going on?" But I suspected that some of my analysis was being passed on to the media as "evidence" of a conspiracy by Manning-ites to undermine Stockwell, so I stopped responding to such inquiries all together. Having carried on extensive and open communications with thousands of party members for almost fifteen years, my voice was now virtually silent and my pen still.

But in my peculiar circumstance, even silence could be misinterpreted, and it frequently was. It is true that, immediately after the leadership contest, some of my strongest supporters urged me to remain in Parliament and "keep my powder dry" in hopes of a future leadership opportunity. But I did nothing to encourage such thinking, and even took a number of concrete steps to discourage it. I announced that I would be leaving Parliament after the Health Committee report was finished, and I did so. I turned down scores of invitations for interviews and commentaries on current public issues and political developments so as *not* to put myself in a position where the media could ask questions about the leadership issue. I announced that I would be pursuing my political ideals and other interests outside the partisan political arena and provided the names of the institutions with which I would be working. There were those in the leader's office and among Stockwell's supporters who were convinced that this was a ruse of some sort. But if they had made even a few simple phone calls to the institutions I had named, they would have found that my arrangements with them were real and substantive and precluded partisan activity for the foreseeable future.

Why didn't I simply urge everyone to respect the democratic will of the members and support Stockwell until the next constitutionally scheduled leadership review? Three reasons. First, as I have often said, if push comes to shove, an elected democrat must put the democratic will of constituents and voters ahead of even the democratic will of the party. Voters and constituents were telling us – through letters, phone calls, and the cold science of the public opinion polls – that they were losing confidence in Stockwell, and if the party didn't do something to change the leadership soon, they would desert the party entirely. Second, while Stockwell still enjoyed the support of a majority of the membership, it was clear by July that he no longer enjoyed the support of a majority of the caucus, which made his continued position as a leader in Parliament unsustainable. It was now apparent to many MPs, including myself, that if things continued with another half dozen incidents in the next year like those of the last year, no leader – Stockwell or anyone else – could recover the fortunes of the Alliance. Time was of the essence; if the leadership was going to be reviewed, it had to be done sooner than the next party convention, which was still a year away. And third, as I have always maintained, respecting the democratic choice of a convention or the membership or the electorate includes an obligation to "inform the discretion" of that convention, membership, and electorate. When the majority of our members put their faith in Stockwell they believed his assertions that he was not only experienced and capable enough to lead the Opposition in Parliament but experienced and capable enough to be the next prime minister. Now those most closely associated with him were finding out, to their immense regret, that this simply was not true. They felt it was their obligation to act on that knowledge – and to inform the discretion of the membership and the public by "telling it like it is." I agreed with that decision, painful as it was to all concerned.

Why didn't I simply make a strong statement in support of Stockwell? I ask, in turn, what should have been the content of that statement? Immediately after the leadership contest I introduced

Stockwell to several audiences as the duly elected leader of the Canadian Alliance, in whom we had placed our hopes for the future. That was true, and I could say it without reservation. During the election, with tax relief being one of our main planks, I introduced Stockwell as a "proven tax-cutter" based on his record as Finance minister in Alberta. This I could do because I believed it to be true. But what could I say on Stockwell's behalf after the exposure of his errors on the national stage? If I had simply given uncritical support – as I was frequently urged to do – this would have left the basic problem untouched, and the decline of the party would have continued. It would also have been grossly unfair to those of my colleagues and friends who were sticking their necks out to tell it like it was. It would also have been hypocritical and, in due course, when the truth came out, would have undermined my own credibility with supporters, the media, and the public. The most I could do for Stockwell under these circumstances was to say nothing.

During this period I received dozens of letters telling me that the problem could be nipped in the bud if I would simply tell "the dissidents" to toe the line and hold a news conference publicly supporting Stockwell as the legally elected leader of the party. The problem with this advice is that it was given in almost complete ignorance of the real roots of the problem. I had talked to Stockwell and had detected no awareness or preparedness on his part to acknowledge the ethical problem he was creating for others. And I had talked to the caucus officers who no longer felt they could serve both Stockwell and their own consciences at the same time. If one were to try to dissuade them from leaving their positions and to support the leader no matter what he did and said, it would be necessary to persuade them to be publicly disloyal to their own principles and consciences. This they rightly considered even more unacceptable than the course of action they chose, and I agreed. The growing unrest in the caucus could not have been nipped in the bud in this way. At best it might have been delayed until the root problems became more clear, by which time the future of the party would be in even greater jeopardy. And the expectation that some news conference held by me in support of Stockwell would have calmed the waters and healed the breach was completely unrealistic as well.

Suppose that I had accompanied Stockwell from the caucus meeting of May 2 and made a strongly supportive statement then to the media crowding the door of our caucus room. The national media are not fools – by this time they themselves knew Stockwell's weaknesses, and they knew that I have never been very good at "spinning a story." They would have waited impatiently for me to finish my "supportive statement," and then Sheldon or Brian or Tim or Julie would have cut to the chase: "Mr. Manning, Mr. Day has just told us that the caucus unanimously supports his plan for moving the party ahead. Is that true?" And what should I have said then? "Yes, it is true," knowing this to be false and that in thirty seconds other caucus members would be spilling out of the room contradicting everything that Stockwell and I had just said? And if I had told the media the truth, for the sake of preserving my own integrity, and said, "No, what Stockwell has just told you is not true. In fact, it is the very opposite of the truth," how could that have possibly helped Stockwell? About the only thing I could do that morning was to do what I did – walk briskly out of the caucus room, right past the scrum, ignoring the pleas of the media for a comment, and saying nothing. This, regrettably, was the position of impotence to which many of the most thoughtful and influential members of caucus had been reduced by the judgments and communications of our leader.

■

Of all the chapters in this book, this one describing the downward spiral of the Alliance has been the most painful to write. During my seven years in Parliament as leader of the Reform Party and of the Opposition I had made my share of mistakes, and endured many crises, including internal ones. But the most serious of these involved fights over policy and strategic direction or major disagreements with the government. The incidents that were now crippling the Alliance had nothing to do with policy positions or strategy issues, yet they threatened the life of the party as it had never been threatened before.

The question arises: Is there anything that can be learned from the root causes and events of this downward spiral that might assist in the recovery of the Alliance, and be generally instructive to all of us who choose to participate in the politics of our country, especially by those of us in politics who also profess a Christian commitment? My answer is yes. The most important lessons in life and politics are learned from our failures rather than our successes, and the more costly the failure, the more valuable the lesson.

Due Diligence

It cannot be stressed enough that in seeking personnel to occupy political offices – from that of a candidate for Parliament to the leader of a party and every staff position in between – it is essential to do "due diligence." And before taking a position in an organization, it is essential to subject it to due diligence as well. Much of the grief that the Alliance endured might have been avoided if Stockwell had done much more due diligence about the party and the people he was being called upon to lead, and if the members and the party had done more due diligence with respect to Stockwell's strengths and weaknesses. This is not to suggest that Stockwell could not or should not have led the party. But both leader and party would have known exactly what they were getting into, the strengths to be exploited and the weaknesses to be avoided and overcome. Since all of us have weaknesses and deficiencies, due diligence will always reveal negatives as well as positives about the individual under examination. Those who do due diligence out of envy or jealousy or the desire to tear someone else down will always use the negatives destructively; but those who do due diligence out of constructive motives will use the negatives to identify those areas in which the candidate or the leader needs help and support from others if he or she is to succeed, and do everything in their power to provide that help and support.

Stockwell had his strengths: his considerable appeal to fiscal and social conservatives, his work ethic, his desire to do well, and his appeal through the medium of television. These could have been great assets to the Alliance. But Stockwell also had his weaknesses and deficiencies as just described – and the failure of the Alliance to recognize and compensate for these cost us all dearly.

In the preceding pages I have given my honest assessment of some of the strengths and deficiencies of the new Alliance leader, Stephen Harper, whom I have known for fifteen years. The positives are impressive: he has a brilliant strategic mind, a sound grasp of public policy, and good communication skills in both French and English. The negatives – his mistrust of the grassroots, his tendency not to be a team player in his earlier years, and the tendency to withdraw – are manageable if they are acknowledged and compensated for by the strengths of others. These comments were actually written before Stephen became leader, and I briefly considered removing them for fear that they would be quoted out of context and misunderstood. But on reflection, I decided to leave them in, because there is no way any party can bolster its leadership at those points where bolstering is required if it doesn't know what those points are. Destructive due diligence seeks out weaknesses and deficiencies in order to attack and pull down. Constructive due diligence identifies positives as well as negatives, and identifies weaknesses only so that they can be addressed and overcome. It is constructive due diligence that I am practising here, to the end that Stephen's leadership may be strengthened and successful.

When to Leave and When to Stay

One of the most difficult situations, in life and in politics, is to discover yourself under the legitimate organizational authority of someone who has lost their moral authority. What do you do in that situation? Do you stay or go? Do you stay and remain silent, compromising your own integrity in the process? Do you stay, but challenge the ethics of those in authority, and run the risk of being seen and treated as a "rebel"? And if you go, do you go quietly and on your own? Or do you take others with you, and again be seen and treated as a "rebel"? And whether you go or stay, do you have any obligation to warn others whose interests are affected by the moral compromises you are aware of but they are not? These are the types of questions members of the Alliance caucus and national council faced when they found themselves under a leader who possessed the legal, constitutional, and democratic authority to hold that position, but had lost a large portion of his moral authority. These are questions that many members of the Liberal Party are wrestling with as they find themselves under the authority of a prime minister who has the legal, constitutional, and democratic right to hold that office, but whose moral authority has eroded to the vanishing point. These are the same questions recently faced by key employees of Enron Corporation when they became aware that the ethics practised by their legal superiors were indefensible but still largely invisible to shareholders and the public. But these are not new questions; they have been with mankind for as long as there have been people in and under authority.

My own view is that the right thing to do under such circumstances is first to make an effort to change the situation from within. But if you are unable to do so, to leave, and to tell others whose interests are affected the reasons you are doing so. This is essentially the course of action that – after much agonizing and soul-searching – Deborah, Chuck, and company took. If they had not done so, the Alliance might still not have addressed or resolved its leadership problems. Of course, those who take this course of action will be labelled as "rebels." Which raises the further question, if you are the one in authority, how do you handle perceived rebellion? Do you bend over backwards to address root causes, looking within yourself as well as at external factors? Or do you adopt a policy of "zero tolerance" to any questioning of your authority, driving the "rebels" out of your own camp whether they truly want to leave or not, and most likely into the arms of your opponents? Of course, the examination of causes, internal as well as external, is the appropriate response, painful as it may be to implement.*

Faith and Politics

There are two ways to deal with the interface between faith and politics. One is to avoid it like the plague and to keep these two areas of human life and experience in separate, watertight compartments.

---

* For an examination of these issues from a Christian perspective, see Gene Edwards, *A Tale of Three Kings* (Wheaton, Illinois: Tyndale House Publishers Inc., 1980). This was the most insightful commentary on these issues that I read during this period, and I passed it on to several MPs.

This is the secular politician's answer to minimizing political-religious conflict, and it is the course that has been followed by most politicians and parties in Canada for the latter part of the last century. I suggest, for reasons discussed earlier – including the violent intrusion of misguided faith into politics represented by Islamic terrorism – that in the twenty-first century it will be increasingly difficult to maintain this watertight separation. The real challenge will be to understand the interface of faith and politics and to manage it wisely rather than foolishly.

I further believe that if those of us who come from the evangelical Christian perspective are honest with ourselves and with our fellow citizens, we should admit that the political activism of many of us in relation to the downward spiral and leadership struggles of the Canadian Alliance has been a disgrace to Canadian politics and a profound discredit to our faith. For professedly Christian interest groups to attack other Canadians with lies and slander, and to attack and even to launch lawsuits against fellow believers for political reasons, is surely a discredit to our faith. For worship services and prayer meetings to be made forums for the sale of political memberships and the raising of funds for partisan political purposes is to risk the corruption of genuine faith with politics and to challenge Christ to overturn such politics, the way he overturned the tables of the money-changers who invaded the temple in Jerusalem long ago. For Christian believers who claim a spiritual ability to discern right from wrong and truth from error to fail to practise that discernment in relation to the actions of political leaders and followers is also a discredit to our faith. And for Christian believers who claim that the ministry of reconciliation is at the heart of our witness to the world to be unable to practise that ministry when politics pits brother against brother and sister against sister is likewise a discredit to our profession.

What is now required is a commitment on the part of responsible Christian leaders to acknowledge these sins of commission and omission and to lead their fellowships in the development of guidelines for the responsible participation of believers in the politics of their country and the parties of their choice. The first of those guidelines should be the one Jesus gave to his original followers when he sent them out on their first "public ministry" – namely, the necessity of learning to be "wise as serpents and harmless as doves."

■

In the twenty-first century, the most important ethical imperative for politicians, business people, and the media to rediscover and reassert will be that of "telling the truth."

The recent collapse of Enron in the United States, and the apparent complicity of its auditors in keeping the truth about the company's finances from the shareholders, the regulators, and the public, underscores this fact. Enron is but the tip of an iceberg. The declining confidence of investors and consumers in business communications will not be reversed until the leaders and spokespersons for business acquire and practise a new and deeper commitment to truth-telling.

In the media business, the "spin-doctoring" of news has become so prevalent and widespread that the public are becoming as cynical about newspaper and TV reports as they are about speeches from politicians. And the awesome capacity of advanced communications technology to create whatever public impression the controller of that technology desires requires a rededication of its use to truth-telling as opposed to other purposes.

After all is said and done, modern politics is 90 per cent communications, and the currency of communications is words and images. The great ethical acid test of politicians is increasingly coming to be not "Are they stealing anything under the table?" (which still needs to be watched) but "Are they telling the truth?" Today, if you ask that question of Canadians in relation to most political utterances and advertising, the most frequent answer is no. Fewer and fewer Canadians believe that their politicians are telling the truth, and this contributes enormously to the decline of public confidence in politics and political institutions.

Canadian poet Duncan Campbell Scott must have been anticipating this debasement of truth by aspirants to political office and their media minions when he asked a century ago:

What manner of soul is his to whom high truth
Is but the plaything of a feverish hour,
A dangling ladder to the ghost of power?

In raising the imperative of telling the truth, I am not being naive. "What is truth?" someone will ask, and we could launch into an endless philosophical or even theological debate. Truth can be multifaceted. Certainly in political discourse there are various sides to every issue and proposal, and proponents can be expected to put the most attractive side forward while opponents will seek to display the worst side. This is persuasive presentation. But there is a line just beyond persuasive presentation where the positive or negative spin morphs into the lie. I would maintain that most politicians know where that line is, and that those who truly don't should be driven from the public stage in the best interests of themselves, their parties, and politics in general. If we stick to the truth as we understand it, or even the positive/negative "spin" on the truth, we are within acceptable limits. But when we cross over that line where the spin becomes the lie, we threaten the integrity of ourselves, our parties, and our institutions.

The most damaging aspect of the "Liberal ethics" described in earlier chapters is its basic disregard for truth – and the willingness to ignore it, bury it, shred it, stretch it, and twist it for political purposes. The most disturbing aspect of the downward spiral of the Canadian Alliance is not the errors in judgment described earlier – regrettable and damaging as these may be – but the false communications that were used to excuse them, justify them, obscure them, or make them to appear to be different from what they actually were.

If there is one area where I failed Stockwell, and where the Christian community failed Stockwell, it was this one. I have several dear, blunt-spoken friends who share my political convictions but not my religious ones. They tell me that because professed Christians have this strong desire not to offend and to "keep peace in the family" at almost any cost, we are not honest and straight with each other when being honest and straight is most desperately required. I am afraid this is true. Christians are instructed by the Apostle Paul to "speak the truth in love." The Greek word for love used here is not *eros* – self-seeking love. We are not to speak the truth in a self-serving way, which in politics we most often do. Nor is the Greek word used here *philios* – familial love. We are not to speak the truth in such a way that we obscure it and twist it simply to keep peace in the family. No, the Greek word for love used here is *agape* – self-sacrificial love. Speaking the truth from this perspective means speaking the truth even if it takes us completely out of our own comfort zone. It means telling it like it is even if it hurts – even if it results literally in our own demise (as it did in the case of Jesus).

When the leaders of Christian churches and interest groups went to see Stockwell during the period of the downward spiral, the last thing he needed to hear from them was encouragement to persevere in whatever he was doing or saying. What he needed to hear – and who would tell him if not his true friends? – was the truth that hurts but saves in the end. The caucus officers tried to say it, and I tried, but we were too "nice" – too "Christian" in the wrong way. When I went to see Stockwell to try to discuss the roots of the problem – the errors in judgment and the dishonest communications that were eroding his moral authority – I should have grabbed him by the shoulders and shaken him until he either acknowledged hearing and understanding what I was saying, or threw me out of his office because he heard, understood, but profoundly disagreed.

The federal political party, and the federal leader, who best grasp and practise in a new and transparent way this pathetically simple ethic of "telling the truth, even when it hurts" will be the party and leader with the moral authority required to rekindle the trust of Canadians in federal politics. Given the high price that the Alliance has paid for failing to practise this ethic with the public and among ourselves, I hope and pray that those who have gone through this experience will become the first to grasp this ethic with a fresh tenacity, and thereby regain the trust of Canadians without which it will be impossible to truly succeed politically.

15

THE SCOUT

IT WAS A SATURDAY MORNING SEVERAL YEARS AGO AND I WAS
flying back to Calgary from Ottawa for the weekend. The plane was
only half full, and as I sat down in an aisle seat I introduced myself
to the gentleman sitting in the window seat. He said his name was
Jerry Potts, Junior. I asked him if he was related to *the* Jerry Potts –
the great Metis scout who guided the old North West Mounted
Police as they struggled to bring peace, order, and good government
to the Western frontier. He said that he was – a direct descendant –
and I felt honoured to meet him. It was the legendary Sam Steele,
one of that original NWMP company, who would write in his autobiography: "In the heat of summer or in depth of winter, in rain, storm
or shine, with Jerry Potts as guide one was certain one would arrive
safely at the destination."

Of course in those days, as is true today, if the troop wasn't going
anywhere, and was content to simply huddle around the campfire of
the status quo, it had little need for scouts. It is the troop that
intends to move beyond the status quo and face the challenges of
the frontier that needs people like Jerry Potts – those who will ride
out ahead of the main company, study the weather and the signs of
the trail, carefully note the dangers and the opportunities that lie

ahead, and report back so that wise decisions can be made on the best course to take. The more unfamiliar the territory and the more uncertain the future, the more crucial the role of the scout.

What does a scout look like? The media may have their preconceptions, but certainly Jerry Potts didn't fit the Hollywood image. Jerry Potts was short, stocky, round-shouldered, and bow-legged, and he dressed in a most peculiar combination of native and white man's clothing. He never used two words when one word or a gesture would do. He inspired confidence, not by his image or his speech, but by his reputation for knowing what he was doing and by demonstrating, day in and day out, his knowledge of the land, its people, and "what lies ahead."

What does lie ahead for Canadians? Let me share a few thoughts on the frontiers that beckon most strongly to me and that I intend to scout in the years to come.

■

I took my leave of the House of Commons on January 31, 2002. After Question Period, there were some kind tributes from John Manley and David Kilgour for the Liberals, Werner Schmidt for the Alliance, Gilles Duceppe for the Bloc, Dick Proctor for the NDP, and my dear friend Deborah Grey and my old adversary Joe Clark for the PC-DR Coalition. Then it was my turn.

I tried my best to acknowledge and thank all those who had joined with me to change the federal agenda. For the last year, however, with the Alliance in such turmoil, what I had really been doing was looking ahead – thinking and applying the analogy of Jerry Potts the scout to the frontiers of the twenty-first century. Those frontiers were economic, social, environmental, international, political, and spiritual, but for my last remarks in the House, I would touch only on the spiritual frontier.

I told the members of the House that they would soon have to legislate on how to regulate the genetic revolution – one of the most exciting and potentially beneficial developments in history. But because this science deals with the beginning and transmission of human life, it cannot help but have moral and ethical dimensions. I think that this is a good thing, an issue not to be avoided but embraced. And I expressed the wish that the members of the House would be open, honest, wise, and successful in their deliberations.

Then I reminded the members of the events that had occurred on September 11, 2001. Our Prime Minister and other world leaders had rightly described those acts as evil and the misguided faith of the terrorists as a counterfeit faith. Such declarations, I said, have the effect of pulling certain aspects of the debate on foreign policy, defence policy, and justice policy onto moral ground. They also oblige us to say by what standards we consider this act to be evil and this policy good, or this expression of faith to be counterfeit and that expression genuine.

In days past, we would have avoided the use of these terms like the plague. But just as it is a mistake to see moral issues where they do not exist, so it is an even greater mistake to fail to see them where they do exist. And again, I wished the members of the House success as they ventured forward on this frontier.

Had time permitted, I would have gone on to say that Canada urgently needs scouts who will explore this frontier and report back to the main company on the safest and surest path to take on the moral and ethical issues that distinguish it. The best scouts may well prove to be those of "mixed blood," like Jerry Potts, through whose veins flowed the blood of his Scottish father (of the same lineage as Commissioner Macleod of the NWMP) and his aboriginal mother (of the same lineage as Chief Crowfoot of the Blackfoot Confederacy). As I explore these frontiers myself I will be looking especially for those whose heritage and experience commingle faith with science, and faith with politics. And with their help, perhaps we can help Canadian politicians find that more solid and dependable ethical trail that must lie somewhere between the amoral, relativistic swamp of Liberal ethics and the rock-strewn path of misguided fundamentalism that caused the Alliance to stumble.

■

In the federal election of 2000, voters repeatedly told the pollsters, and anyone else who would listen, that improving health care was their number-one concern. Canadians want quality health care that they can count on when they need it, regardless of ability to pay. Riding the frontier of health care reform will include addressing the need to increase our commitment to prevention and health sciences research, making health care more "patient centred," controlling health care costs through improved management and the application of market mechanisms to health care organization, finding the right balance between the use of public and private resources, and finding the right allocation of responsibilities between federal and provincial governments.

There has been no shortage of editorials, studies, and reports putting forward various ideas – and plenty of good ones – for achieving these goals, but they have not been acted upon by the federal government. In Alberta, health care reform is proceeding on the basis of recommendations contained in the Mazankowski report, and the federal government – facing a crisis – is finally looking for guidance to the Romanow report. But the less-travelled trails of the health care reform frontier that I hope to scout most thoroughly are its communications and political dimensions. What needs to be done to permit an intelligent national debate on health care reform to occur, and to achieve the political consensus required to actually implement health care reforms?

The reports from any frontier that are most informative are often those that record the experiences and perceptions of the people who live, work, and die there. Almost all the health care reports and studies I have seen in the last ten years discuss health care reform from the perspective of the governments, the health care scientists, the medical practitioners, the policy makers, the administrators, the taxpayers, and the private sector participants in the system – and these are all important. But rarely do you see analyses presented solely from the perspective of the users – the individuals and families whose health care needs the Medicare system is supposed to serve. Certainly few of the health care reform proposals presented to parliamentarians are ever presented in the language or reflect the emotions of health care users.

What I think would communicate both problems and solutions more effectively would be to put them in a book, perhaps entitled

Mr. Mazankowski and Mr. Romanow, Meet the Neighbours. Or substitute your surname for "the Neighbours." The Neighbours are a Canadian family – with children and parents and aging grandparents – and the first part of the book will simply describe through their eyes the challenges they encounter and the benefits they receive from the Canadian Medicare system as it is now. It will include views of health care from the perspective of children and the parents of children; problems encountered in finding a family physician, particularly if they move to a new or remote community; stories of visits to doctors' offices, walk-in clinics, and emergency rooms, including their experiences with waiting lists to see specialists or to get a bed in a hospital. It will include a description of the family's habits and what they are doing or not doing to improve their own health and prevent illness; a description of the impact on the family budget of drug costs and the purchase of health care services such as dental care not covered by Medicare; and their experiences – good and bad – with doctors, nurses, and other health care practitioners. It will also describe their experience with the growing health care needs of aging parents, the need for home care, and the health issues raised for the family by the dying and by the death of a family member.

The second part of the book will then describe how the experience of this family might change *if* the recommendations of the Mazankowski report are fully acted on, or *if* the Romanow recommendations are followed, or *if* other major reforms are actually implemented. Until the various prescriptions for health care reform are translated into the language and experiences of folks like you and the folks next door, and communicated in these terms, I fear that a key requirement for building a broadly based public consensus for health care reform will be missing.

The other communications aspect of health care reform that I would like to scout is our seeming inability to effectively debate and resolve fundamental issues of this kind in the political arena. As the recent federal election campaign demonstrated, the federal political arena is the last place a consensus on health care reform is likely to be forged, unless some fundamental change occurs in the rules of engagement for national debates.

Among the most endearing characteristics of Canadians are our temperance and our moderation. But politicians and interest groups often take advantage of these characteristics in a perverse way that makes productive debate on important issues almost impossible. In Canada, because moderation is so highly valued, the quickest and cheapest way to discredit someone else's position is to label it and its proponent as "extreme." So, if someone proposes a new balance between the use of public and private resources in health care, that idea itself never gets considered or debated on its merits. Instead, its opponents carry it to its extreme, accusing the proponents of wanting to "privatize health care" or "bring in U.S.-style health care." Then they categorically denounce it.

Similarly, if someone suggests that a new division of responsibilities is required between the federal and provincial governments – whether the proposal is for a stronger federal role in achieving national health care standards or a stronger provincial role in health care delivery – again the proposal is rarely debated and evaluated for what it is. Instead, its opponents take the proposal to its extremes, and denounce its proponents as either extreme centralizers or extreme decentralizers.

Where argument over false extremes is the distinguishing characteristic of a public debate, it is impossible to arrive at an informed consensus, on health care reform or anything else. The first prerequisite to achieving a civil society is civil discourse, and the society incapable of the latter will never realize the former.

Real health care reform requires not only dedicated champions and an organized campaign to achieve it. It also requires a fundamental change in how we speak to each other on subjects of importance to us all.

■

The health care frontier is just one segment of a much broader frontier – the social services frontier, which embraces child care, education, social assistance, crime prevention, law enforcement, pensions and elder care, and the alleviation of poverty. To provide love and care to the young, the sick, and the aged; to teach a child or retrain an adult; to address the root causes of poverty, illness, and crime, which mar and destroy so many lives – whether through the services of governments or the activities of the volunteer and non-governmental sectors – is to address some of the most basic human needs of our people.

If Canadians are generally satisfied that these needs are being adequately met, there will be no real appetite for social reform. But for those of us who feel that something more and better than the current provisions of the welfare state are required, there are many social reforms to be investigated and pursued.

Those that attract me the most, and whose application I would like to scout, include:

- The application of marketplace mechanisms to social service financing and delivery, and the encouragement of "social entrepreneurship."
- A re-balancing of the roles of the federal and provincial governments, and those of the public and private sector, with respect to the provision of education, similar to that required in the health care field.
- New approaches to regional economic development – including aboriginal economic development – that rely more on private property, free enterprise, marketplace mechanisms, tax incentives, and tax relief, rather than public ownership, subsidization, and government initiatives.
- Conducting an "issue campaign" on some major social frontier like health care reform, similar to the issue campaigns on fiscal reform that the Reform Party carried out so successfully in the 1990s.

■

Besides acting as an interpreter and liaison between the white man and the Blackfoot, the two most important functions performed by Jerry Potts for the NWMP were forecasting the weather and finding good water for the men and their horses. Failing to anticipate a prairie blizzard or an electrical storm that would stampede buffalo and horses could be a fatal mistake on the Western frontier in the

1870s and '80s. And good water was extremely scarce in the Palliser Triangle, where the NWMP spent a great deal of their time. Today, two of the most critical issues facing Canadians are climate change and the water supply – is there anything new under the sun?

It is our own young people – your sons, daughters, and grandchildren, and mine – who will inhabit the frontiers of the future. They are the ones who will live the majority of their lives in the twenty-first century, just as we have lived most of ours in the twentieth. Whenever I've visited high schools, as I frequently did when I was active in politics, I would ask that next generation of Canadians what kind of Canada they wanted to live in. Well over half the answers I received were related to the environment. Children (my own included) would tell me, "We want to live in a country where we can breathe clean air, drink clean water, grow our food in clean soil, and where our oceans, forests, and wildlife are healthy." Some children would express deep-seated fears about the dangers of environmental catastrophe, ranging from another Walkerton-like tragedy to an irreversible global crisis – not imaginary childhood fears but ones rooted in reality, not unlike the fear of nuclear catastrophe that once gripped many of our generation. It comes as no surprise that environmental conservation is as high a priority to many of the next generation as economic development has been to ours. How to strike the right balance between the two is one of the most critical challenges of our time. So far, we are doing a lousy job of it. Surely we have a moral obligation, as well as a political and economic one, to deal with environmental challenges more vigorously than we have thus far.

It is very likely that wars will be fought over water in this century. In a growing number of countries, sources are already contaminated or drying up, and we are now concerned about the safety of our own water supply here at home. In years to come, pressures will come from all directions, in particular the United States, for Canada to make some hard decisions about what to do with our water: do we sell it or not, and if so, on what basis? When that time comes, if we haven't taken the lead in reconciling the environmental, economic, and moral dimensions of the use and conservation of water, we will be ill prepared to make wise decisions.

Canada is home to many "green leaders" and interest groups –
from David Suzuki to Greenpeace – who have scouted the environmental frontier and returned with reports of what lies ahead.
However, these individuals and groups have so far had little success
in plugging into the priorities of our traditional political community in a meaningful way. Despite all the lip service paid to inte-
grating economic and environmental objectives and policies, we
still proceed with economic initiatives like trade liberalization
without any true idea of the environmental consequences, and
adopt environmental conservation measures like the Kyoto Accord
without any true idea of the economic consequences. At present,
none of the federal political parties, including the ones that I have
helped to create, has the commitment or conceptual frameworks
required to develop and implement a twenty-first-century environmental policy.

So what can be done to change this? In exploring the environmental frontier – particularly from a political perspective – I would
like to help make environmental conservation a much more prominent component of the conservative agenda than it is at present.
The words "conservative" and "conservation" come from the same
root, and free-market mechanisms for wealth creation can also be
harnessed to environmental conservation. But there is much work
to be done before environmental conservation occupies the place it
ought to in the creeds and platforms of conservative parties. If the
opportunity arises, I would be willing to help responsible environmental interest groups and embryonic green parties explore their
political options. Are Canadian "greens" prepared to be essentially
"single-issue people" indefinitely? Or are they prepared to enter into
strategic alliances and coalitions with other interests and parties to
advance environmental conservation on the national and international agendas?

■

Knowledge, and new ways of generating, storing, transmitting, and
particularly applying it, are the raw materials and infrastructure of
the New Economy, the frontiers of which I am anxious to explore

more fully. One of the downsides of active politics is that you use up your intellectual capital with little opportunity to replace it. Preoccupation with the immediate issues of the day crowds out opportunities to study and prepare for the issues of the future.

Science and education are the cornerstones of a knowledge economy, but what would a twenty-first-century science policy for Canada and a twenty-first-century education system look like? What kind of political education and effort will be required to bring them into being? I hope to get some answers as I spend more time at Canada's universities and colleges, where both scientific research and education are the principal preoccupations.

Jerry Potts helped the NWMP prepare the way for the railway, the settlers, the homestead, and the one-room schoolhouse – the four cornerstones of the frontier economy. But what are their twenty-first-century equivalents for Canada as a whole? The government of Canada played a major role in opening up the Old West – securing the land, enabling settlement by facilitating the building of the Canadian Pacific Railway, parcelling out the land to homesteaders from around the globe in 160-acre chunks, and providing the rudimentary educational and other services required to create the beginnings of community. But somehow it was done without smothering and suppressing the enterprise and initiative of the pioneers, or their sense of responsibility for themselves and for their neighbours. Today we seem unable to find or maintain that balance – witness the dependency-creating failures of federal economic development efforts in Atlantic Canada, eastern Quebec, and northern Canada – and yet there must be a solution to permit these regions, and indeed all Canadians, to participate fully in the New Economy.

Everyone acknowledges that science and technology are not only the driving forces of the New Economy, but also the dominant influences shaping modern thinking and societies. And yet to my knowledge there is not a single bona fide scientist in the caucus of any of Canada's federal parties. Canada does not yet have a senior Science minister, and science analogies and scientific reasoning are almost totally absent from the speeches of our parliamentarians. To its credit, the Government of Canada has significantly increased its support of scientific research in recent years, but Canada still does not have an effective decision-making model for telling us whether an investment in big science project A or science infrastructure project B would be the wiser investment of taxpayers' dollars.

Science projects in Canada advance mainly on the basis of the lobbying efforts behind them, and whether they can find an effective champion in the bureaucracy or at the Cabinet table. There is a danger that politically inspired pork barrelling – perhaps we should call it cyberpork – will play as large and detrimental a role in the creation of science infrastructure for the twenty-first century as it did in the building of roads and railways in the nineteenth century. There is no chief scientist for Canada available and accountable to Parliament on the same basis as the auditor general. Parliament itself has no mechanism – other than the cumbersome committee hearing system – for bringing science effectively to bear on its deliberations or its decisions, whether we are talking about legislation to deal with climate change or to regulate the genetic revolution.

To remedy many of these deficiencies it seems to me that one of the first steps must be to establish and expand more consistent and meaningful dialogue between the scientific and political communities. Jerry Potts was a most useful scout because he was also an excellent interpreter. He came to know the ways of the NWMP, he already knew the ways of the Plains Indians, and he spoke the languages of both. I hope to spend some time in the next few years interpreting the political perspective to members of Canada's scientific community, and assisting them to better communicate science and technology to the political community.

■

A respected scout for the Canadian Imperial Bank of Commerce, Jeffrey Rubin has predicted that unless international and domestic confidence in the Canadian dollar is restored soon, within five years "the swooney" will be replaced by the American dollar. There will be no point then in having the Bank of Canada, and Canada will in effect be treated as the thirteenth district of the U.S. Federal Reserve. I agree with this prediction, even though it disturbs me. Increasing numbers of Canadian companies quote prices in U.S.

dollars, pay key executives and employees (not just our hockey players) in U.S. dollars, and report their financial results in U.S. dollars. Increasing numbers of Canadians are putting at least a portion of their savings into U.S.-dollar accounts, investing in U.S. equities, and purchasing U.S. assets as protection against a declining Canadian dollar.

There are three questions to be put to the scout as we sit warming ourselves around the campfire of the status quo. What combination of monetary and fiscal policy might restore confidence in the Canadian dollar? (Rubin says higher interest rates and much deeper tax cuts.) What other actions should Canada take to preserve its sovereignty in the face of globalization and the tendency for monetary unions to follow the creation of free trade areas? And what corporate and personal strategies should be pursued if in fact we are headed towards a single North American currency? These are questions that I personally hope to explore in greater depth in the months ahead, and you might want to do the same.

Based on past experience, the chances of the Chrétien government taking such scouting reports seriously and acting on them expeditiously are not great. This country is gifted with people who have the ability to see ahead. But what good does it do to have such scouts attached to our troop if their insights are rarely acted upon by the national government until the dangers they so clearly foresaw are upon us, or the opportunities they urged us to seize are past? There have been those among us who have long sensed that major economic difficulties lay ahead – loss of markets, jobs, profits, and tax revenue – if Canada did not get its fiscal house in order while our economy was being dragged along by a buoyant U.S. economy. But the warnings and reports of such scouts were largely ignored. In fact, these scouts were chastised for being "extreme" in their predictions and too drastic in their prescriptions for action. "Go slow," was the accepted advice. "Canada has lots of time to get its fiscal house in order." And then came the slowdown and recession, making it much more difficult to do what we should have done years before to improve the fiscal foundations of our economy. Canada needs its scouts on the monetary and fiscal frontiers; but even more important, we need commanding officers prepared to act on their reports when they ride into camp.

■

There are so many frontiers to explore, and some of them are as vast as the planet itself. We live in an age of globalization – of worldwide trade liberalization that is freeing up the flow of capital, labour, goods, and services across national boundaries and increasing our standard of living. But globalization also increases the influence of international agreements and multinational organizations on our daily lives. Canadians and others around the world want more attention paid to the social, cultural, and environmental consequences of these international arrangements. They want to have a say in the terms of these agreements and more control over the multinational corporations and agencies that put them into operation. But how is this democratization of international agreements and activities to come about? At present, international environmental agreements like the Kyoto Accord and international trade agreements like that establishing the Free Trade Area of the Americas are largely negotiated by the executive arms of governments. Heads of state or their representatives meet, often behind closed doors, just as Canada's first ministers did when they negotiated the Charlottetown Constitutional Accord. The public and the legislatures are then presented with an international *fait accompli*, which they are expected to accept and rubber-stamp. Members of the public who question or disagree with the terms have no effective democratic mechanisms to represent their concerns or enable them to participate in the governance of such agreements. And so we have riots in the streets in Seattle and Quebec City or wherever these "international Charlottetown Accords" are to be negotiated or discussed.

Many able and far-sighted people (not enough of them in leadership positions in Parliament or our national parties) are scouting the frontier of globalization and the so-called "democracy deficit," and I hope to ride with them for a while to see what I can learn. If Canada is to be an integral part of any Free Trade Area of the Americas, should we be proposing some Congress of the Americas (not unlike the European Parliament) to provide multinational democratic representation and governance to such a trading block? If so, on what basis would countries like Canada be represented in such a Congress – by population, by GNP, by some combination of both? And should we not be starting to submit international trade and environmental agreements affecting the lives of all our people to some sort of democratic ratification process, as we did in the case of the Charlottetown Accord? The opportunities and the dangers to be scouted on the globalization frontier are many, fascinating, and of importance to us all.

■

Canadians sit in front of their television sets every day and see scenes more horrific than those of any horror movie: people killing each other in the streets of Jerusalem and Ramallah, mass graves in Kosovo and Bosnia, the endless streams of refugees and starving children in Africa, Hindus and Muslims firebombing each other in India. Either we just turn the TV off and go about our business, or we decide to "do something" when and where we can. One of the things we are committed to doing is devoting Canadian resources and personnel to international peacekeeping. It is the international expression of the Canadian commitment to "peace, order, and good government" (POG) that lies at the heart of our national character.

International peacekeeping in the first part of the twenty-first century is likely to be very different from international peacekeeping in the latter part of the twentieth century. If Canadians want to maintain and even expand our commitment to "international POG," we'll have to make major adjustments. We will need to solicit and digest scouting reports from the peacekeeping frontiers of the world, in particular those that might shed light on the following questions. Do we intend to be a permanent part of the International Coalition against Terrorism, and, if so, what should be our role? Is there a significant future role for Canada in Middle East peacemaking (where Canada, under Lester Pearson, proposed the creation of the first UN peacekeeping force), and if so, what would it be? What does

Canada intend to do to improve its understanding of and relations with the Islamic world, and how is such an initiative to be organized? Could Canada's experience with federalism as a mechanism for maintaining unity in the face of ethnic and linguistic diversity be of real help to troubled federations like Nigeria, and if so, how might this experience be exported and applied in a meaningful way? Could and should Canada become a dedicated "exporter" of democratic ideology and technology, given that we are better positioned to do so than former colonial powers like Britain and France or superpowers like the United States? And if the great wars of the twenty-first century are likely to be fought in Asia, among nations armed with nuclear weapons, should we preparing for a role, however modest, in Asian peacekeeping efforts?*

Despite the immensity of these issues, and their possible impact on the peace and security of us all, not one made it on to the political radar screen in the recent Canadian federal election. Lester Pearson must have been turning over in his grave. Because of my limited international experience, I, like many Canadians, have much to learn on all these subjects. But I do know something about the use and organization of "issue campaigns" to change the policy priorities of the federal government. When the time comes to *act* on the scouting reports coming back from the international frontier, and to try to generate a national consensus for action on any of these fronts, my friends and I would be interested in contributing.

■

A political person like myself, who has spent the last fifteen years using the tools of democracy and our federal political institutions to

---

* Restrictions of time and space do not permit me to elaborate on my "adventures in Asia" as Reform Party leader and leader of the Opposition. Given the current relevance of Islamic fundamentalism, nuclear tensions between India and Pakistan, and the rise of China as a superpower, I would like to share with readers in some future publication insights gained from three particular sets of meetings, i.e., discussions with Chinese officials on human rights, discussions with Indian and Pakistani officials on the testing of nuclear weapons, and a long session at the Islamic International University on the political relevance of Islam.

advance a conservative, democratic, and reform-oriented agenda, cannot help but continue to explore the political frontier, even though I will now be riding a non-partisan horse.

Much work remains to be done to complete "the fiscal revolution" in Canada – the controlling of government spending, the consistent balancing of budgets, and the lowering of debts and taxes. But that revolution is well underway, thanks to the pioneering efforts of groups like the Fraser Institute and the Canadian Federation of Taxpayers, various provincial governments led by the Klein and Harris administrations, and the work of Reform and the Canadian Alliance on the federal front. The longer-range question that I hope to help Canadians of all stripes address is, "What lies beyond the fiscal revolution?"

Before Canadians will fully accept and practise the principles of fiscal responsibility and marketplace economics, they must hear our answer to that question. Adam Smith, that great scout of the economic frontiers of the eighteenth century, once raised the question, "To what PURPOSE is all the toil and bustle of the world? What is the END of avarice and ambition, of the pursuit of wealth, of power, and pre-eminence?" He answered it by saying that the purpose and end of wealth creation was not wealth for its own sake, but for the "fortune" and "happiness" of others. So it is in our day that many of the ends to which the wealth of productive societies and the work of governments (including conservative governments) must be directed are "social ends" – the health and education of our people, and the care of those unable to provide or care for themselves, along with the care of the world around us. But much work remains to be done on defining and communicating a conservative philosophy and policy on the soft issues of health care, education, environmental protection, poverty, and chronic underdevelopment. This is a challenge that faces not only conservatives at the provincial government level, to which our Constitution assigns the primary responsibility for many of these matters; the application of conservative values and marketplace mechanisms to social ends is also essential to revitalizing conservatism at the federal level.

Just as "reform" was the right word to describe the political challenge of the 1990s, I am equally convinced that "alliance building" or "coalition building" is the key to advancing our principles in the first decade of the twenty-first century. It is my intention to visit the frontiers of "strategic alliance and coalition building" in business, trade, and in the politics of Europe and the U.S. congressional system, where the successful practice of this art seems to be so much further advanced than in the Canadian Parliament and Canadian federal politics. And I will report my findings on how to build such alliances and coalitions to whatever conservative or reform-oriented political camps in Canada are willing to pursue that objective.

Sam Steele once told the story of a horse that feared the wrong things. Sam rode this horse up a steep mountain trail with a sheer rock wall on the right and a yawning abyss on the left. Safety lay in the horse's staying as close to the wall as possible, but the horse was more afraid of the wall it could plainly see than of the abyss at its feet. It repeatedly shied away from the wall, until its hindquarters slipped over the edge of the trail. Only superhuman efforts by Sam kept it from plunging to its death.

Canadians are often reluctant to try new ideas, and conservatives are afraid to vigorously pursue coalition building, because of certain deep-seated fears. We are afraid that the results of doing something new or different will be worse than the results of doing nothing. Conservatives and reformers are afraid that we will lose either our heritage or our principles if we broaden our political circle through alliance and coalition building. But is it not possible that our fears are misguided, and that by rejecting coalition building we will do ourselves far greater injury in the end than we'd incur if we worked together to seize the day?

Conservatives in different camps fear the clearly visible and imposing obstacles that lie in the way of working together. What they don't seem to see as clearly or to fear as deeply is the yawning abyss of political oblivion that awaits if they don't come to grips with those obstacles and learn how to work together. In helping to outfit Canadian conservatives to ride the political frontiers of the twenty-first century, the wise scout will be looking for horses that fear the abyss of oblivion more than they fear the walls of division.

■

In the summer of 1999, Sandra and I borrowed two horses named Zeke and Willie from an Alberta pioneer family named Gilchrist, who ranch near the Milk River in the heart of Jerry Potts country. For three days we joined the trail ride commemorating the 1874 March West of the original NWMP contingent. It was on this trip that I saw how effective picket lines are in controlling large numbers of horses. A long rope is strung between two strong trees or posts and the horses are tied on each side of the rope, so that if one spooks, it pulls against the rest, who pull back, and the line usually holds. I could have used the picket line principle in managing caucuses.

From the high places above the Western plains – the Cypress Hills on the Saskatchewan-Alberta border, the Sweet Grass Hills of Montana, and Chief Mountain overlooking southern Alberta – a scout can see forever. To the Blackfoot, and Jerry Potts, these places were all sacred – places where the old came to dream dreams and the young to receive visions, including visions of the future. But I doubt that any of the inhabitants of the Old West in the latter part of the nineteenth century could have guessed the shape and strength of the New West that would one day emerge. The Old West was wild and vast, with enormous potential, but it was economically and politically impotent. At the end of the nineteenth century it produced less than 10 per cent of Canada's wealth, had less than 10 per cent of Canada's population, and held less than 10 per cent of the seats in Parliament. The Old West couldn't even defend its own interests, let alone impress its ideas on the federal government or the rest of Canada. It understandably developed an "underdog psychology," which persists in some quarters to this very day.

But ride with me today along the frontiers of the New West and what do we see?* The New West of the twenty-first century will produce more than one-third of Canada's goods and services. It will become home to more than one-third of Canada's population, with B.C. becoming the nation's second largest province by population, and it will control more than one-third of the seats in Canada's Parliament. In the twenty-first century it will be impossible to

---

* Roger Gibbins, Loleen Berdahl, and Robert Roach, *Building the New West: A Framework for Regional Economic Prosperity* (Calgary: Canada West Foundation, 2001).

implement any truly national policy without the West's concurrence, or to form any truly national government without Western participation.

The frontier of the New West is one that I have scouted more thoroughly than any other. I see both dangers and opportunities ahead, and I intend to share my perceptions of these with my fellow citizens – in the West itself and in other parts of Canada – at every opportunity. The dangers are that the West will refuse to shake the underdog psychology of our past and approach the future "thinking small." If the New West takes this approach, it will focus almost exclusively on its own regional concerns, avoid association with "Easterners" for fear of "losing again at the national poker table," and turn inward, even flirting with separatism, building firewalls around itself rather than forging new and stronger links with the rest of Canada and the world. I hope to use my influence to dissuade Westerners from ever heading down that trail.

On the other hand, the West has a glorious opportunity to shake the last vestiges of its underdog psychology and to seize the future by "thinking big." In business, we should learn from the examples of Western entrepreneurs like Jimmy Pattison, Ron Southern, Jim Gray, Izzy Asper, Clive Beddoe, and many others who have built small Western-based enterprises into national and international powerhouses. In politics and government, of course, the New West should use its new influence to raise the agricultural concerns of the Prairies higher on the national agenda, to protect our oil- and gas-producing regions from another raid by the federal government, and to fully develop and promote British Columbia as Canada's magnificent gateway to the Asia-Pacific region. But we should do much more than that. The New West should also use its influence in the federation to address and resolve the problems of the federation as a whole, and to put its brand on Canada.

In future, when I meet Westerners around our political campfires, I will speak of the dangers of thinking small. But the bulk of my scouting reports will focus on the opportunities that lie ahead to form bold new alliances – among ourselves and with people in other parts of the country – in order to advance both regional and national interests. The prairie provinces need to form a strategic alliance among themselves to jointly plan and finance badly needed transportation infrastructure – a Prairie Transportation Authority, which will expand one day into the Prairie-Pacific Transportation Authority. Westerners need to form friendships and strategic alliances with Quebecers to achieve an understanding of each other's concerns, and to pursue common interests, in particular, a re-balancing of the powers within Confederation. Strategic alliances are required between the Western and East Coast petroleum sectors, to advance mutual interests and protect provincial jurisdictions. And strategic alliances need to be built between the New West and Ontario on every important front, from health and education reform to securing the fiscal and economic climate required to sustain the New Economy.

For these alliances to be lasting and truly beneficial, they need to be more than brokerage arrangements built on mutual self-interest. They need ultimately to be – as that Nova Scotian participant in the Confederation debates observed long ago – "unions of the heart," relationships based on understanding, mutual respect, and friendship that enable people to work together enthusiastically and successfully towards common goals. This was the essence of the pioneer spirit of the Old West that needs to be rekindled and expressed on our regional and national frontiers in the twenty-first century.

■

Canadians are becoming complacent, and even disillusioned, about democracy and democratic institutions. Voter turnout in our last federal election was 61 per cent, 15 per cent lower than in 1988. Politicians – the most prominent participants in our so-called democratic system – are held in low regard. The word most frequently used by voters to describe their feelings about the last federal election was "disappointment" – disappointment with the fact that their concerns, especially with respect to health care, were not responsibly addressed, and disappointment with the performance of all the leaders and parties. When the reaction to a national election, supposedly the ultimate expression of democracy, is profound disappointment, democracy itself is in trouble.

In the federal Parliament, our senior democratic institution, morale among the members, especially the backbenchers, is abysmally low, due to a lacklustre government agenda, counterproductive internal divisions on both sides of the House, and excessive party discipline. On December 3, 2001, I participated in one of my last votes in the House. A $6-billion supply bill went through in routine fashion, with most members not even knowing or caring what it was about. But there was a noticeable quickening of interest in the House when a private member's motion was put calling for the government to explain why it had reduced the strychnine level in gopher poison from 5 per cent to 3 per cent. Because this was a private member's motion, it was a free vote on which members could make up their own minds. Roars of approval went up from Prairie MPs as some government members from Ontario rose to support the gopher motion and members who were diametrically opposed to each other on everything else came together in the great gopher coalition. Separatists and federalists, French-speakers and English-speakers, government and opposition members, urban and rural members stood shoulder to shoulder on this groundbreaking issue. And when the measure passed by a vote of 134 in favour to 123 against, members cheered and crowded around its bewildered sponsor, Leon Benoit, to congratulate him on a job well done. I voted for the gopher motion myself, but when such a motion commands more interest in the House than a $6-billion supply bill, there is something wrong with the system.

One hundred and seventy years ago, ten years before Jerry Potts was born, one of the greatest political scouts who ever lived, the French nobleman Alexis de Tocqueville, rode across the United States to investigate the Democracy Frontier. In his scouting report he observed that the political parties of America, indeed of all free societies, could be split into the two great divisions – those animated by the "aristocratic passion," which seeks to limit the authority of the people, and those motivated by the "democratic passion," which seeks to extend it.

Those of us who are still animated by "the democratic passion" must scout both the heartland and the frontiers of democracy, this time for the purpose of discovering the root causes of its decline and the best measures to secure its revitalization. A plethora of proposals already exist for strengthening democracy in Canada – from electoral reform to direct democracy measures, from parliamentary reform to the absolute necessity of getting a democrat into the prime minister's chair. I support all of these, and wish to join with others similarly inclined, regardless of party, to increase dramatically public support for such measures and to secure their implementation. In my work with various public policy think-tanks and universities I also hope to explore the potential for establishing an Institute for Democratic Leadership – a gathering spot for scouts on the democratic frontier to assemble and promote their findings to the public and the commanders of various political troops. The programs of the institute would include: a School of Practical Politics, where participants in our political processes – from volunteers to candidates for public office and everything in between – could receive practical training in democratic ideology and practice; an Applied Research and Study Program that would bring democratic theorists and practitioners together to address the challenge of revitalizing democracy in Canada and elsewhere; and, in due course, perhaps the Democracy Export Program referred to earlier.

I would also like to work with others to advance the concept of electronic democracy and the use of the Internet to revitalize interest in democratic institutions and processes. I envision the creation and operation of a Virtual Parliament on the Internet. Imagine that you're a visitor to this site. You would arrive at a Virtual Building, with a Foyer, where you would register as either an observer or a participant. From there you might go to the Assembly Chamber, where you could join in discussions of major issues of the day and then vote on them; or to the Library, where you could find out everything you want to know about those issues; or to the Media Gallery, offering links to media commentary. You might also go to the Lobby, where you could hear and consider pitches from various interest groups, or to the Committee Rooms, where you could participate in the examination and drafting of bills. Then imagine that your input and your votes were passed directly to MPs and committees of the real Parliament.

There would be nothing to stop the organizers of such a Virtual

Parliament from experimenting with all of the many proposals for revitalizing our democratic institutions in Canada or making this Virtual Parliament more attractive than the stone-and-concrete version. The purpose would be to show Canadians an "ideal" democratic institution, to provide a practical demonstration of how it would work, to provide Canadians with opportunities to participate personally in order to whet their appetites for "the real thing," and ultimately to make the whole exercise so influential that federal parliamentarians would be obliged to listen and respond.

■

Since I first penned these words, the willingness and capacities of the Chrétien government to respond positively to scouting reports from the great frontiers of the twenty-first century have diminished even further than when I sat in Opposition. The challenge facing Canadians is not simply to replace Prime Minister Chrétien but to replace the government itself. My personal hope is that the Canadian Alliance, in co-operation with the Progressive Conservatives, will prove itself worthy to become that replacement, and more receptive to the reports of its scouts.

Over the next few years, I intend to scout these frontiers of the twenty-first century just as Jerry Potts scouted the last great frontier of the nineteenth century. It is not my intention to do this on my own – lone-wolf scouts too easily get lost – but in the company of others more familiar with the terrain.

I hope to do this scouting in the company of members of my family, many of whom are already active on these frontiers. I hope to do so in the company of old friends, including many of those whom I have met and come to value through my fifteen years of involvement in national politics. I hope to do so in the company of new friends, whose interests will make us fellow scouts and adventurers on these frontiers of the future.

Some of the trails we have ridden before. But this time I will do so free from the day-to-day pressures and constraints of partisan politics. No doubt I will see and hear some things I missed before. Other trails I have only read about or seen in the distance. But should I see or hear anything that strikes me as particularly relevant to the future well-being of the main company of Canadians, I will be reporting back to students on university campuses where I will be lecturing, through the forums and seminars of think-tanks with which I will be associating, and through the media and my personal Web site, *www.prestonmanning.ca.*

No doubt we will see and hear some things on the frontiers of the twenty-first century that require more than "discussion" around the campfire. In that case, it will be the duty of the scout to urge action – action to avoid the dangers and embrace the opportunities that lie ahead. Then, as always, decisions will have to be made – whether to continue huddling around the campfire of the status quo, endlessly discussing the future possibilities, or to break camp and move forward. I'm all for saddling up and moving forward! How about you?

LETTER TO THE PRIME MINISTER, JUNE 8, 1994

The Rt. Hon. Jean Chrétien
Prime Minister of Canada
House of Commons
Ottawa, Ontario K1A 0A6

Dear Prime Minister:

In recent weeks, members of the Reform caucus have asked your government to be more pro-active on the unity issue. Unfortunately, our questions have been dismissed as "hypothetical" or answered with the standard line that the best way to convince Quebecers to stay in Canada is to provide them with more of the same.

Such answers do not appear to be enough. There is a widespread concern that a vacuum has developed on the national unity front, and that the separatists are filling that vacuum by defining the terms and conditions of the debate on Quebec's potential separation from Canada.

Prime Minister, we cannot stand by passively and allow Quebec voters to make the decision – separation or Canada – without offering them a vigorous defense of Canada, including a positive federalist alternative to the status quo. And we cannot let them make their decision without disputing the separatist contention that separation will be a relatively uncomplicated and painless process.

The longer the federal government stays on the sidelines of this debate, the more momentum shifts to the separatist cause. The time has come for federalists to dispel the myths being propagated by Messrs. Bouchard and Parizeau.

The following are some of the hard questions being asked by rank and file Canadians regarding Quebec's potential separation from Canada. With millions of Quebecers indicating their desire to vote for the separatist Parti Québécois in the forthcoming provincial election, it is necessary to prepare for this challenge, and not bury our heads in the sand. It is my hope that the mere listing of these questions will help to dispel the myth that separation will be quick and easy, but I also ask that you give these questions some thought and provide Canadians with some specific answers.

A copy of this list will be given to the media and will be the focus of study by the Reform Party's Contingency Planning Group over the summer.

1. How would the Government of Canada respond to a formal request from the government of any province to secede from the Canadian federation?

2. What principles would the Government of Canada apply to ensure that the rights of those provinces and territories remaining in Confederation would not be prejudiced in any negotiations pertaining to the secession of a province from the federation?

3. What principles and procedures would the Government of Canada apply to securing ratification by the other provinces of the terms and conditions of any settlement between itself and a province that was seceding from the federation?

4. What principles and procedures would the Government of Canada apply in securing ratification by the people of all parts of Canada to those aspects of any agreements with a seceding

province that affect the interests of those living outside the
bounds of the seceding province?

5. What principles would the Government of Canada apply in
   establishing a mechanism by which any boundary disputes
   between a seceding province and the rest of the country, including those that might arise over maritime boundaries, might be
   resolved?

6. What principles would the Government of Canada apply in
   responding to petitions from regions within a seceding province
   that they be permitted to remain in Canada following the secession of the province of which they form a part?

7. What principles would guide the Government of Canada with
   respect to resolving the conflicting claims of the government of a
   seceding province and of identifiable groups within the province
   that might want to remain within Canada (for instance, aboriginal groups)?

8. What principles would the Government of Canada apply, in the
   event that a province were to secede, to requests for joint citizenship by residents of Canada and of the seceding province?

9. What provisions would the Government of Canada make, if
   any, to facilitate the voluntary movement of people from a
   seceding province, and to ensure that they would be guaranteed
   full portability of any contributory benefits programs into which
   they had paid while residing in that province?

10. What principles would guide the Government of Canada in
    determining any division of the federal debt with the govern-
    ment of a seceding province, and in seeking compensation for
    federal assets located on the territory of a seceding province?

11. What would the Government of Canada do in order to maxi-
    mize creditor confidence during the period in which the federal
    debt was being divided between the federal government and the
    government of a seceding province?

12. What principles would the Government of Canada apply in
    responding to a request from a seceding province that it con-
    tinue to use the Canadian dollar, or in responding to other
    requests affecting monetary policy?

13. What principles would guide the Government of Canada in its relations with foreign governments from whom a seceding province had requested formal recognition as a nation or other assistance?

14. What principles would guide the Government of Canada's response to requests from a seceding province to participate in international trade agreements, such as NAFTA and CUSTA, on terms similar to those obtained by Canada?

15. How would the Government of Canada respond to a formal request from a seceding province to enter into an economic union, free trade agreement, or any other "special association" with Canada?

16. What permanent guarantees would the federal government seek from a seceding province to ensure free and unhindered air, road, rail, and water transit between the remaining provinces and territories of Canada, through the territory of a former province?

17. What principles would guide the Government of Canada's negotiations with a seceding province relating to defence, including the disposition of military equipment, the right of passage for Canadian military forces across the territory or airspace of the seceding province, and the continuation of Canada's current military treaty obligations?

18. What principles and procedures would the Government of Canada apply in dealing with any public order emergency or threat to the security of Canada arising from a secession attempt by a province?

19. What principles would the Government of Canada apply to ensuring the environmental integrity and sustainability of ecosystems shared by Canada and a seceding province?

20. What principles would guide the Government of Canada in re-admitting a province which has seceded from Canada?

I have faith that the majority of Quebecers will reject the separatist option and reaffirm their commitment to Canada. However we cannot afford to be complacent or timid at this crucial point in our nation's history. It is our responsibility to advance a positive and unifying vision of Canada, and to honestly and openly consider the real consequences of separation, so as to dispel the myths being propagated by the separatists.

With a provincial election on the horizon in Quebec, your timely response to these questions would be most appreciated.

Yours sincerely,

E. Preston Manning, M.P.
Leader, Reform Party of Canada

ACKNOWLEDGEMENTS

THE STORY OF A DEMOCRATIC ADVENTURE IS BY DEFINITION A story of the many, not the few. The story of Reform and the Canadian Alliance is therefore not just my story but that of many other people without whose dedication, effort, and sacrifice there would be no story at all.

I am hopeful that many of those who have made unique and essential contributions to the formation and evolution of Reform and the Canadian Alliance will soon tell their own stories. In the meantime, I want to acknowledge as fully as I can the contributions of at least some of the people who made this story and this book possible.

In Chapter 10 you have already met my partner in life, Sandra, and the members of our immediate family, without whose love, support, and help neither this political story nor this book would have been possible. I also want to express to Sandra's parents, Mary and Gordon Beavis, and to other members of our extended family – the Stuffcos, the Harrisons, the Carters, Mike and Gee Fuller, Will and Henny Kroon, the Saskatchewan Mannings – my heartfelt thanks for their interest and support in all that we have undertaken.

With respect to our extended political family, let me start by expressing my gratitude to that first executive council of the

Reform Party, some of whom are now members of Parliament: Diane Ablonczy, Alan Beachell, Henry Carroll, Ron Gamble, Ian McClelland, Valerie Meredith, Bob Muir, Werner Schmidt, Gordon Shaw, Joan Tait, and Short Tompkins.

Special thanks to all the other "pioneers" who helped found the Reform Party in the first place and sustained it through the years, in particular, Francis and Harriet Winspear, the Fryers, the Piries, the Hillands, the Byfields, the Cavanaghs, the Todds, the Jack MacKenzies, the Barlows, the McCaigs, the Shaws, the Jim Grays, the Barry McDonalds, the "Ranchmen's Club gang," the Eltons, the Friths, the Virgil Andersons, the Gaytons, the Glens, the Copithornes, the Radlers, the Suitors, the Wes McLeods, the Cliff Breitkreuzes, Poul Hansen, Tam Deachman, Jimmy Howe, Harry Meyers, Marie Knowles, Ed McNally, John Poole, Carolyn Meraw, and Randy Lennon.

Space does not permit me to properly acknowledge the contributions and support of the various Reform and Alliance executive council members with whom I worked over the years. But in addition to those already mentioned, let me also thank Leonard Poetschke, Robert Beard, Ian Bourke, Brad Cather, Lorne Samson, and Gordon Arnell.

With respect to the Charlottetown Accord campaign – the first national campaign undertaken by the Reform Party – I wish to gratefully acknowledge the contributions of those campaign team members already mentioned, as well as those of fundraisers and executive councillors Don Leier, Mike Friese, and Myles Novak; Eowana Needham, one of our first organizers in Ontario; and Kara Tersen and all the "membership processing crew" at the national office in those days.

With respect to the 1993 federal election campaign, my profound thanks to the key members of our campaign team already mentioned. But let me add my special appreciation to all the courageous candidates who carried the Reform banner in that election and to other unsung heroes of our campaign team such as Maurice Carter, Delcy Walker, Faye van Wegen, Ken Greenfield, Erna MacDonald, John Franklin, and the Robarts family. Since that campaign was especially a "grassroots effort," let me also pay tribute to our first regional organizers – Paul Arnold and Darrell Frith on the West Coast; Betty Squair in Edmonton; Dennis Young on the Prairies; Betty Maxwell in Manitoba; Betty MacDonald in Ontario; Howard and Jane-Anne MacKinnon and Natalie Stirling on the East Coast; and to Diane Rodwell, the tireless organizer of our volunteers at the national office.

Upon our arrival in Ottawa after the 1993 election, our political family greatly expanded. In Chapter 5 I have mentioned many of our initial employees, but let me add my thanks to Linda Robar, Deborah Grey's first executive assistant; Stephen Greene, my first chief of staff; Dr. Darrel Reid, our first full-time director of research; Dr. Paul Wilson (later director of research for the Official Opposition); Lucille Hodgins, our first director of communications; Mitch Grey, my first legislative assistant; Louise Girouard, David Prest, Jim Armour, Larry Welsh, Phil von Finckenstein, and Morten Paulsen. Many of these people went on to occupy senior positions in our party and parliamentary offices, and my debt of appreciation to each increased with the years.

During my parliamentary years I was also blessed with the friendship and services of a number of gifted Question Period managers, researchers, and communicators like Jayne Sutherland, Laurie Throness, Denise Rudnicki, Ezra Levant, Sean McAdam, Devin Baines, Ken Boessenkool, Andrew Kosnaski, Dimitri Pantazopoulos, Scott Reid, Paul Hartzheim, Greg Yost, Renée Fairweather, and Michèle Austin. The smooth functioning of the Leader's Office itself would not have been possible without the expertise of staff like Chris Froggatt, Rossana Whissell, Dawn Ewonus, Lisa Samson, Kathryn Locke, Debra Porter, and my correspondence team including especially Salpie Stepanian and Debbie Campbell. My sincerest thanks to all of you.

My special thanks to each and every one of the "class of 93" – the fifty-two Reform MPs with whom it was my honour to first sit in the Parliament of Canada – and the "class of 97." I cannot say enough about the value of Deborah Grey's friendship and contributions as "the first lady of Reform." But, "Thank you, Deb – you are my ideal of a democrat and a reformer!" I also owe a special debt of gratitude to the other caucus officers who served me and the party so well, including Elwin Hermanson, Ray Speaker, Jim Silye, Diane Ablonczy, Jay Hill, Randy White, Chuck Strahl, Dave Chatters, Stephen Harper, Ken Epp, and Monte Solberg.

I have already mentioned my debt of obligation to the Stornoway crew – Evie Todd, Mary Beth Howitt, and my driver and security man, Sam Okoro. Special thanks also to David Kilgour for giving Sam another job when he needed it most.

I wish to again express my gratitude to the entire 1997 election campaign team – many of the members of which have been referred to already. In addition, I want to thank Randy Coupland, Howie May, Barry Firby, Christy Donaldson, John Armstrong, Gilles St-Laurent, Kevin Gaudet, and Line Maheux for their contributions.

With respect to the organization of the United Alternative conventions and the creation of the Canadian Alliance, I wish to thank each and every one of the many people who served on the convention and policy committees as well as those who undertook to serve on the first national council of the Canadian Alliance. I especially want to express my gratitude to former Ontario premier Mike Harris, Hal Jackman, Tony Clement, Tom Long, Bob Runciman, and Reuben Devlin. Special thanks also to Margret Kopala, Don and Sandra Morgan, Thompson MacDonald, Hugh Lynch, Clayton Manness, and Maurice Murphy, and to Mona Helcermanes-Benge and Ken Heit for their invaluable production support at our biggest and most important conventions.

A great debt of gratitude is owed by all of us to the five Reformers who served on the first United Alternative Steering Committee – Cliff Fryers, Rick Anderson (assisted by Lisa Samson), Jason Kenney, Ken Kalopsis, and Nancy Branscombe. The creation of the Canadian Alliance also involved a significant number of "large democratic exercises" – four big conventions and two party-wide referendums. Many of the people who played key roles in these events I have already mentioned, but I would like to add my thanks to David Salmon, Doug Kemp, Troy Tait, Jack Pike, and Terry Horkoff for the enormous amount of behind-the-scenes work that they did to make these exercises succeed.

With respect to the overall management of party affairs during my tenure as leader and afterwards, there are no words of gratitude adequate to say thanks to Glenn McMurray, executive director of both the Reform Party and later the Canadian Alliance, for his faithful and dedicated service to the party, democracy, and the country. Special thanks also to Cyril and Jackie McFate for their tireless work in the field, to Joni Kitchen, Marie Knowles, Brendan Robinson, and to Brad Farquhar for pioneering our political use of the Internet.

Space will not allow me to adequately express my appreciation to the hundreds of people who worked in the PM4PM campaign – many of whom have been mentioned already, but others who have not. In addition to my core campaign team I would like to add special thanks to Belinda Stronach for her unflagging support, as well as to Gerry Van Ieperen, Tory Robarts, Shuv Majumdar, Andrew Stec, Zubair Choudhry, Chris Warkentin, Scott McCord, Julie-Anne Miller, Lynette Corbett, Wally Butts, Kerry Boon, and Debby Sorochynski. Special thanks also to my son-in-law Howie Kroon and his friend Pat Carley for doing a yeoman's job in ensuring that the PM4PM campaign finished in the black.

I would also like to pay tribute to all of the candidates who contested the leadership of the Alliance, and especially to their long-suffering spouses and families. A special tribute is due to Leslie Pace, Tom Long's wife, who encouraged Tom to run even though she was expecting, and to little Veronica Long who was born in the midst of that tumultuous campaign, on June 10 (my birthday as well as hers).

This list of thank-you's and acknowledgements would not be complete if I did not express again my gratitude to all my key supporters and workers in Calgary and the federal constituency of Calgary Southwest who helped elect and re-elect me to Parliament, in particular, Harry Robinson, Jack Gallagher, Bruce and Rosa McDonald, Harold and Anne Davenport, Rod and Sara Peden, John Ellett, Clancy Patton, Stan Bengtsson, Audrey Cerkvenac, Ginny Cunning, John and Liz Traber, Megan Crossland, Lenora Southgate, Valerie Clark, Cheyanne Church, Barbara Waters, Jim Dennis, Ron Quigley, Gary Hennan, the Zyluks, and Laura Garrick.

On behalf not only of myself but also of my constituents in Calgary Southwest, I want to especially thank Dolores Potter for her nine years of service to me and the constituency as manager of my Calgary Southwest parliamentary office. Special thanks also to Bob van Wegen for all his help on party and constituency communications and to Cheryl Cain for her cheerful handling of thousands of phone calls.

There are also special supporters and friends across the country whose help and encouragement at specific times has meant a great deal to Sandra and me. This of course includes my core leadership support group of Cliff and Leslie Fryers, Rick Anderson and Michelle Williams, André Turcotte and Donna Kline, and the indefatigable Ian and Evie Todd. But in addition, I wish to mention with appreciation the help and encouragement of Darrell and Chris Frith, Kevin and Helen Jenkins, Paul and Lynne Arnold, John and Linda Berglund, Fraser and Judy Smith, Gordon Arnell, Gordon Wusyk, the Beyaks, Garfield Mitchell, Cindy and Ray Beland, Ken and Gail Stevenson, Ginny and Dale Assmus, Randy and Donna Murray, Ray and Vi Gideon, the Robarts family, Bob and Ruth Balisky, the Hursts, Andrew McCain, the Foxes, the Bells, Rick Rand and Sharon Barney, Fred and Niki Eaton, Reg and Carol Petersen, Innis and Mark McCready, Gilles and Mychelyne St-Laurent, Pierre St-Laurent, Larry O'Brien, Manny Montenegrino, and Denzil Doyle.

I would also like to acknowledge the support and prayers of many members of our home church, First Alliance in Calgary, for their love and support particularly during difficult times. The prayers and encouragement of Ray and Dee Matheson have helped us more than they will ever know.

Finally, I want to give special recognition to those who contributed directly to the completion of this book: to my agent, Michael Levine, for his help and advice; to Frank Dabbs, who assisted me in the preparation of chapters 1 and 2; to Reform-Alliance researcher Laurie Throness for his assistance in fact-checking; to Doug Gibson of McClelland & Stewart for his encouragement and support; to Laura Cameron on the marketing side, and above all to Jonathan Webb, my editor, for his great assistance in crafting my voluminous first draft into something readable.

I want to especially thank Jennifer Grover for cheerfully and enthusiastically helping me over the years to find the words and phrases that would express my vision of Canada, and particularly for her help in editing this volume.

And to Jean Marie Clemenger, who typed and re-typed every word of this manuscript – what can I say? Jean Marie has been my secretary and researcher for twenty-six years. During that time virtually every idea or concept I have formulated has also passed through her mind onto paper and to others. Thank you once again, Jean Marie.

Finally, I save my last thank-you and acknowledgement for those I will call "unnamed supporters and volunteers." Whatever I have been able to accomplish politically, as described in the preceding pages, could not have been accomplished had it not been for you – the unnamed but supremely important volunteers and supporters who did the bulk of the work and ultimately went to the polls and voted for Reform and Alliance candidates as an expression of your political will. Thank you from the bottom of my heart.

Preston Manning
Calgary, July 2002

INDEX